WEBMASTER SERIES

DATABASE
PUBLISHING

ON THE WEB & INTRANETS

WEBMASTER SERIES

DATABASE PUBLISHING

ON THE WEB & INTRANETS

Curt Lang
Jeff Chow

CORIOLIS GROUP BOOKS

Publisher	Keith Weiskamp
Project Editor	Jeff Duntemann
Copy Editor	Sarah Fraser
Cover Artist	Gary Smith
Cover Design	Anthony Stock
Interior Design	Bradley Grannis
Layout Production	Rob Mauhar
Proofreader	Kathy Dermer
Indexer	Caroline Parks

The Coriolis Group, Inc.
7339 E. Acoma Drive, Suite 7
Scottsdale, AZ 85260
Phone: (602) 483-0192
Fax: (602) 483-0193
Web address: www.coriolis.com

ISBN 1-883577-85-3 : $39.99

Printed in the United States of America

10 9 8 7 6 5 4 3 2 1

About the authors

Curt Lang
TextWorks, Inc.
clang@wimsey.com
http://www.wimsey.com/~jchow/webdb.html

Curt Lang started programming in 1974 as part of his job as a designer/builder of commercial fishboats. Using a line terminal connected to an IBM mainframe he wrote primitive BASIC programs for calculating the surface areas of curved steel shapes. When micros came along he quit his day job and has worked in the software industry ever since, first as a freelance consultant, then as product manager for a CBT authoring toolkit, then as manager of a consulting company that specialized in electronic publishing and databases, and then as president of a startup that developed 3D surface scanning instruments and software.

Jeff and Curt have teamed up several times to develop software products and in 1993 they began taking an interest in the Internet. Their first Internet product was a simple Windows email client called EasyMailer that sends and receives messages and files. They are now working on Web/database applications.

Jeff Chow
Advantage Online, Inc.
jchow@wimsey.com
http://www.wimsey.com/~jchow/webdb.html

Jeff Chow began programming in 1981 after two years as a hardware engineer at IBM in San Jose. He started with the Apple II, then worked with the first floppy-based IBM PCs, and participated in Microsoft's first developer seminar for Windows. He has been lead programmer on a series of successful software projects, including a large financial system, an authoring system for computer based training, and a teleconferencing system. He has also taught programming at BCIT and worked as a prototype developer in BCIT's ARCS Lab. Since 1994 he has been combining CGI scripts and Java with HTML documents to produce interactive Web sites. Jeff has a Masters degree in engineering from the University of Hawaii.

Acknowledgments

Special thanks to Iris Kobayakawa for her tireless research on the Web and newsgroups and for her helpful comments, and to Gordon Cornwall for his careful reading and thoughtful criticism of the manuscript. Thanks also to Jeff Duntemann and Ron Pronk of Coriolis for their patient editorial guidance. And finally, thanks to all the people that we interviewed for taking time to share their knowledge.

Contents

Chapter 8   DataRamp   187

Chapter 9   LiveWire and LiveWire Pro (Netscape)   223

Chapter 10   PowerBuilder 5.0   259

Chapter 11   Conversations with Some
Web Database Programmers   295

References   485

What's on the CD   495

Index   499

INTRODUCTION

The bleeding-edge Web crowd is out there chasing hypertext, animation, realtime video, stereo sound, morphing graphics, and long distance telephony, telling us endlessly how "cool" it all is. The rest of us look at the Web and think, *Wow, what a great medium for database publishing!* Hold the cool. Cool is fun, but some of us have work to do. Instead, give us a solution to a real business problem, something as simple as making significant databases available over the Web, through common Web browsers rather than custom database clients.

Happily, those solutions are out there, and while they don't get half the hype that mighty morphing power graphics do, they're here now, they work, and they're not rocket science in any sense of the term.

What This Book Is About

Publishing is the orderly presentation of information for some audience, through some persistent (that is, lasting—not simply spoken on a soapbox) medium. This medium has traditionally been printed paper, but anyone who hasn't lived in a refrigerator box for the last several years knows that this is changing. *Database publishing* is the presentation of database information—usually tabular lists of items like names, places, sales figures, statistical percentages, and so on, as opposed to simple text as you'd find in a novel or newspaper.

Our title says it all: *Database Publishing on the Web and Intranets* speaks to the challenge of presenting database information over the World Wide Web, used either globally (over the Internet) or within a delimited corporate environment (over an "Intranet").

Note that "presentation" here is a very key term. We're talking about putting database information where people can access it, using tools specific to database publishing. This is *not* the same thing as database *programming*, such that you'd have to do to implement an elaborate order-entry system with accounting feeds, calendrics, statistical analysis, and all the trimmings. That's a separate and important discipline with its own tools and its own books, at least one of which is also published by Coriolis Group Books. (See the book listings at the end of this book.)

Whom This Book Is For

The book was written for people who want to create Web/database publishing systems:

- Publishers—who initiate the publishing activity and determine the content;

- Web application developers—who want to create Web-enabled application software that involves database presentation;

- Database programmers—who want to use the Web to deliver information stored in legacy databases and are seeking alternatives to augment their traditional client/server programming tools;

- Webmasters—who create and maintain Web sites and want to know how to build Web database sites;

- ISPs (Internet Service Providers)—who maintain the host platforms for Web sites serving the Internet and who want to add Web database capability;

- Network Administrators—who maintain internal LANs and who want to install and maintain Intranets within their corporate boundaries;

- Product Developers—who want to create tools and applications for the Web database environment.

What This Book Tries to Achieve

Simply stated, our goals are to help you get oriented to the subject and save you some time getting started. The book also provides lots of introductory information about new tools so that you can select the ones that are right for your project.

What This Book Covers

The book focuses on the messy region where Web and database technology is in the process of converging. We have tried to give practical answers to basic questions like

- What is Web database technology?

- What is it used for?

- How do you use it?

- What tools are available?

Other than to provide context, we have avoided detailed discussions of the parent technologies (Web and database) since there are plenty of good books about HTML and SQL.

Chapter 1 is about the background technologies that led to the emergence of Web database technology. It gives brief questions and answers about the Internet, Intranets, the Web, and database software.

Chapter 2 is about the architecture of Web database applications. It identifies the kinds of software components used in Web database installations and describes how they fit together and how information flows between them.

Chapter 3 is about techniques. It gives a checklist of common user-requirements questions and shows how the answers to these questions influence the selection of platforms and tools. It closes by proposing a simple Web database design process.

Chapter 4 reviews the essential HTML knowledge needed for building Web database applications. Forms, tables, and JavaScript are covered and a simple "Hello Database" program is described.

Chapters 5-10 take close-up looks at six new Web database development tools. Each close-up includes a product description, a list of features, a "Hello Database" sample program, and an interview with the developer.

Chapter 11 takes a quick look at what some people with Web database experience have been doing. It contains four short interviews, three with developers and one with a content person.

Chapter 12 is a directory of Web database software tools with descriptions of more than 80 products (mostly very new). A wide range of product types is covered, including Web database middleware products, full-text retrieval software, and relational DBMS tools with new Web interfaces.

The CD at the back of the book is packed with code samples, evaluation versions of tools, source listings, and the products database.

The Technologies That Enable Web Database Publishing

To publish is to inform, in an orderly and persistent way. Yelling "the British are coming!" in the village square at midnight may inform, but the presentation isn't especially orderly—nor does it last more than a few seconds. Villagers who don't come home until 1:00 A.M. will miss the message. Write the message on a piece of paper and nail it to the church door, and you're publishing, because the message persists so that all who pass the church will see it until the paper is torn down. (Probably by the British.)

We've come a long way from the days of town criers yelling in the village square and nailing theses to the cathedral door. Paper has ruled publishing for over a thousand years, but it no longer rules alone. Electronic publishing provides a new medium through which information may be presented, with flexibility and power undreamt of by Benjamin Franklin and other paper publishers of yore.

Perhaps the most exciting of all electronic publishing mechanisms is the World Wide Web, which burst on the Internet scene in 1993, changing overnight the way Net people think about information, and plowing older mechanisms like Gopher into the soil of history.

This chapter is the start of our journey through the world of database publishing on the Web, and in keeping with the new medium, we're going to make heavy use of a publishing convention—the list of Frequently Asked Questions (FAQ)—that came to prominence with the Internet. We'll pose a question, and then provide an answer. This will help you get oriented, and help us organize the host of new technology concepts that bear on database publishing in this rich new medium.

In researching this chapter, we found a lot of helpful information in existing FAQs and white papers published on the Web. We have freely paraphrased portions of these documents, so we gratefully acknowledge the work done by members of the Web/Internet community. You will find source listings in the References section at the back of the book.

A Diverse Idea

Web database publishing software is based on several different enabling technologies, and the people who build Web database applications come from widely different backgrounds. In our two-year encounter with the subject we have met HTML programmers, DBMS programmers, C/C++ programmers, and an assortment of self-taught managers, entrepreneurs, and tinkerers from computing, business, government, education, public service, and the media. These people are getting their hands on the tools and building something—they are not just passive users. However, since a wide assortment of people with a wide assortment of skills are being turned loose on a wide assortment of tools, it is not surprising that people are finding gaps in their knowledge. For example, HTML programmers are often uncertain about database integrity and transaction control, and DBMS programmers are often unfamiliar with HTML and HTTP. Reading this book will help you fill in those gaps.

The Architecture of a Web Database Publishing System

A typical Web database publishing system (Figure 1.1) has a Web browser as its user interface, a database server as its information store, and a Web server connecting the two. The Web software elegantly simplifies and standardizes data presentation and the user interface, and the DBMS (database management system) organizes and standardizes data retrieval and storage. Some see this technology as a way of enhancing access to databases,

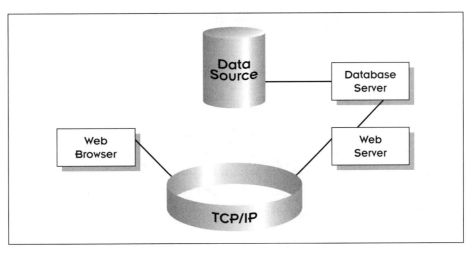

Figure 1.1 A simplified Web database installation.

and others see it as an improved way to manage the content of Web sites, but either way, the combination is stronger than its parts.

The only program the user needs to have installed on a machine is the Web browser, and—perhaps more importantly—the only program the user needs to *learn* is the Web browser. Users interact with the database through a form displayed on a Web page (Figure 1.2). Typical interactions include

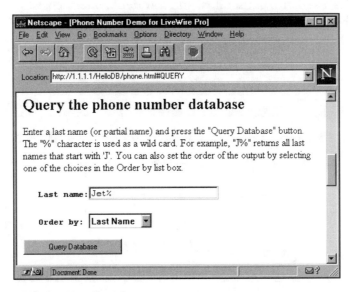

Figure 1.2 A Web database input form.

reading pages, clicking on links, selecting from listboxes, and keying queries and input into fields.

Information retrieved from the database can be displayed on the Web page as text, images, tables, graphs, or multimedia objects (Figure 1.3).

This typical model may look simple, but a great many Internet and Intranet publishing systems work this way and are considered a rousing success by their audiences and their publishers. For applications that require more complex user interfaces, there are standard ways to extend the Web browser and, for applications that require more powerful back-end processing, there are standard ways to extend the Web server and create programs in the middleware layer (Figure 1.4).

Web database publishing systems grew from well-defined parent technologies that developed separately and that had different design goals (Figure 1.5).

Each parent has important virtues:

- The Web has a crisply-simple definition of the user interface (pages and links), a well-thought-out declarative language for defining data (HTML, the HyperText Markup Language), a robust transfer protocol that permits a very high volume of traffic (HTTP, the HyperText Transport Protocol), outstanding support for delivering multimedia data, true cross-platform usability, and low deployment costs.

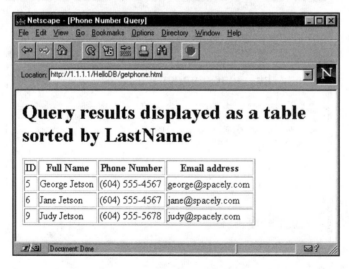

Figure 1.3   The results of a query displayed as a table.

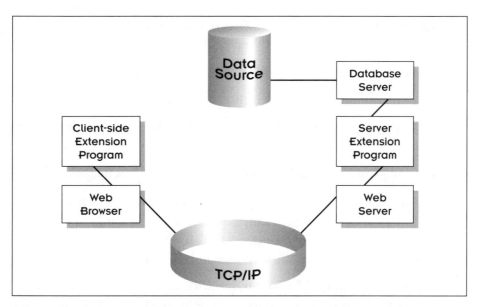

Figure 1.4   A Web database with client-side and server-side extensions.

- Database systems have clearly-defined data models (fielded/relational, full-text, object oriented), robust ways of storing and retrieving data (SQL, full-text retrieval, report generators), software tools for developing user interfaces and application logic (client/server tools), strong authentication and security methods, and reliable ways to control transactions and to maintain data-integrity.

It now appears that the market—publishers, programmers, and end users—has decided it wants a new generation of network publishing systems with

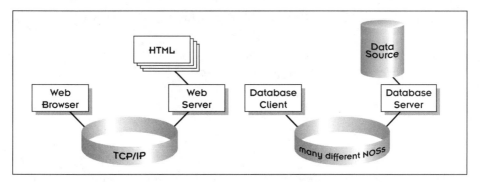

Figure 1.5   Web and DBMS tools grew up as distinct technologies.

the best features of both parents. This is a tall order, but the software industry is hard at work trying to fill it (Figure 1.6).

The software industry was jolted awake by three successive events:

- First came the rapid growth of the commercial Internet.

- Next came the even more rapid growth of the Web as the unifying Internet technology.

- And then came the explosive growth of the Intranet market.

The smoke hasn't cleared yet, but people are beginning to realize that yet another major change is happening to the software landscape, and, in response, a large amount of money and effort is being invested in developing new products. Some of the important players are:

- Sun, which dominates the Unix network server market and provides most of the hardware and software that runs the Internet and the World Wide Web

- Netscape, which emerged with a bang as the dominant developer of Web software

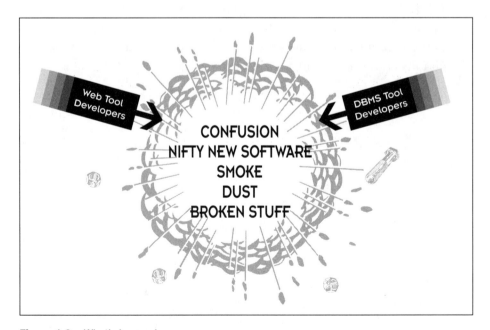

Figure 1.6 What's happening now.

- Microsoft, which entered late but is building a respectable base of network and Web servers based on NT

- Sybase, Oracle, and Informix, who are creating extensions to their DBMS products that integrate them with the Web, and an army of smaller software developers who see Web databases as a major opportunity and are hard at work finding niches and filling them

Frequently Asked Questions about Web Database Publishing

With that overview in mind, let's go through the foundation concepts in a little more detail, using the time-honored FAQ format.

What is Web database publishing?

As we stated earlier, Web database publishing is a new way to publish information electronically. A typical Web database publishing system has a Web browser as its user interface, a database server as its information store, and a Web server connecting the two.

What is Web database publishing technology based on?

The technologies that enable Web database publishing systems include the Web, databases, networks, and electronic document processing. Some related key concepts are cross-platform operability, user interface standardization, and multi-tiered client/server computing architecture.

What are the advantages of combining a Web browser with a database management system?

The Web offers: standardization of the user interface, high transaction volume (permitted by HTTP), and the ability to work across platforms and applications. It also offers the following: low-cost clients (browsers), simplicity of application development, easy maintenance, a highly standardized client/server relationship, a common way to display multimedia data, and the ability to use the Internet as a wide area network.

Databases offer: a powerful way to organize and maintain the information offered on a Web site, a way for users to search the information with SQL or a full-text retrieval engine, the ability to accept and store input from users, and a common way to store and retrieve multimedia data objects.

What are the limitations of combining a Web browser with a database management system?

Compared to a database client program, a Web browser has relatively weak input validation, and lacks built-in transaction controls. You can overcome both of these with Java or other tools, but database client programs have more ready-made features to carry out these tasks.

Compared to storing information on a Web site as HTML files, a database is more complex, needs more preparation before you can use it, has a steeper learning curve, and is more difficult to install.

Lastly, security can be a problem on public networks. For example, if you use an insecure Web server, or use a secure server with an insecure Web browser, the data passed between them will not be encrypted.

What does 'universal client' mean?

A *universal client* doesn't exist yet, but if it did, it would be a single user interface program that works across platforms. A universal client would be very valuable because it would free users from the burden of learning many different user interfaces and would open up computer use to a wider audience.

When GUIs were developed people imagined that they would work across applications. They do, but—partly because they are still very complex—GUIs have been adopted mostly by people who do a large part of their daily work on computers. The rest of the population (people who use computers infrequently) have reacted to GUIs with the same tepid response with which they greeted command line interfaces. Also, the existing generation of GUIs (e.g., Windows, Mac, X-Windows) were designed to work on specific platforms, so GUIs are not quite universal clients.

Will Web browsers become universal clients?

It seems to be a distinct possibility. In 1994 and 1995 the software industry was startled by explosive growth first of the Internet, then of the Web, and finally of Intranets using the Web. It soon became clear that at least part of the growth was fueled by the enthusiasm users had for the simplicity and usefulness of Web browsers. This sudden explosion of demand has suggested to software developers that the universal client may finally be here in the form of a Web browser. Note that Web browsers work across platforms, and can be made to work across applications, so they can cut down the number of idiomatic client interfaces that users have to learn.

Are some kinds of database applications more or less suitable for access with a Web browser?

Data warehousing is a natural application for Web database publishing. Data warehouses exist to bring business information from production databases to managers and business analysts, so the simplicity of the Web interface has high value in this context. The users of data warehouses query the database and do not update it, so database integrity is not at risk. The Web has great facilities for presenting graphics that enhance data.

Production databases reveal the weaknesses of the Web as a database client. The users of production databases perform frequent, complex input trans-actions that expose a working database to integrity violations, impure data entries, and de-synchronizations. The Web in its simple form (HTML and a Web server with a CGI program) is poorly equipped to deal with these demands. However, the Web in its more complex form (with client and server extensions) can be made to meet a large part of this requirement.

How long does it take to install a Web database site?

Not counting the time needed to create a database, a reasonably resource-ful programmer would need about a week to install a Web server and a DBMS, and to write a simple middleware application. A complex applica-tion could, of course, take longer.

Finding and choosing the right tools can also take time because you are dealing with two technologies that never came together before. For ex-ample, if you already have the database, you will need to find a middleware product that works with the database. You will also need a Web server that works with the middleware product and has the features you need. How-ever, there are no hard and fast rules for making these selections.

What are the implications of accessing a database with a stateless protocol?

In database client/server computing (i.e., non-Web) the client and the server maintain information about each other's state and dedicate an open communication session for the duration of a transaction. This dedicated session is one of the main ways database programmers maintain control of transactions.

The Web uses a stateless protocol (HTTP) that terminates after each request is satisfied. The Web browser sends a **GET** to the Web server, the Web server **PUTs** a response back to the browser, and then they both forget they ever met until the next exchange. This allows a lot of simple transactions (**GETs** and **PUTs**) to take place in any time period, but it does not permit a session in which a sequence of controlled input transactions can take place.

New techniques and tools (e.g., cookies, client extensions, server extensions) are being developed for the Web that deal with portions of this problem. However, no standard method exists for developers to have the best of both worlds (i.e., stateless protocols and session-oriented protocols).

Do any Web database standards exist?

A few Web database standards do exist. The CGI protocol standardizes the interface between a Web server and a server extension program. CGI will likely be around for some time, but it is being supplanted by several APIs (e.g., Netscape's NSAPI or Microsoft's ISAPI). ODBC standardizes the interface to some database servers, and Sun has proposed JDBC as a more general database interface. Many software developers have a stake in making their products work across the middle layer, so new standards will emerge.

What are some examples of Web database applications?

On the Internet:

- The American Red Cross has built a Web database site for organizing disaster-relief volunteers (**http://www.redcross.org/**)

- Thomas Register of Companies has published its entire directory (**http://www.thomasregister.com:8000/**)

- Federal Express has built a system that lets customers track their shipments (**http://www.fedex.com/**)

On Intranets:

- Law firms have built libraries of precedents and legal documents

- Drug companies track the documents associated with the approval process for new pharmaceuticals

- The contents of mainframe databases have been made available over the Web

Frequently Asked Questions about the Web

What is the Web?

On the Internet, the World Wide Web (WWW) is a vast collection of inter-connected documents, spanning the world. On an Intranet, a local copy of the same software that runs the WWW would connect documents stored inside a single organization on a private network. Web software uses TCP/IP to communicate on the network. It is based on a standard information exchange protocol (HTTP) and a standard method of structuring data (HTML) that simplifies presentation and user interaction. Its underlying metaphor is hypertext (pages and links).

What is HTML?

Hypertext Markup Language is the standard, declarative language people use to create Web pages. The current version of the HTML standard is 2.0, and 3.0 is expected to be adopted in 1996. HTML is modeled on SGML and uses tags to 'type' various parts of a document. This permits a wide variety of display devices to intelligently present the document. Here is a sample HTML document that displays some bold text:

```
<html>
<head><title>Sample</title>
<body>
<b>Bold text displayed here.</b>
</body>
</html>
```

What is HTTP?

Hypertext Transport Protocol is the language the Web server uses to talk to the Web browser. Its main functions are **GET** and **PUT**; the browser **PUT**s to and **GET**s from the server, and the server **PUT**s to and **GET**s from the browser. HTTP is stateless and asynchronous, so it is much faster than session-oriented protocols for processing large numbers of user-requests for information. It does this by opening a socket connection for only as long as it takes to deliver the page.

What is hypertext?

Hypertext is a method of presenting an electronic document so that portions of it appear as readable text and images and portions of it are links to other documents. You can identify links, which are embedded in a page of readable text, by their different color. When users click on a link, the document it is pointing to will appear. A Web browser is a hypertext browser that can link to documents stored anywhere on the Internet (or on an Intranet).

What is a URL?

Uniform Resource Locator (URL) is a standard for locating and accessing an object on the Internet. URLs can specify: servers, Web pages, email addresses, files, newsgroups, articles, or other items. Most often they refer to Web pages. Some examples of URLs are:

```
http://www.yahoo.com/headlines/index.html
http://www.thomasregister.com:8000/
ftp://ftp.microsoft.com
news:alt.Hypertext
mailto:SantaClaus@northpole.ca
```

The first part of the URL, before the colon, specifies the access method such as **http**, **ftp**, **news**, **mailto**, etc. What follows the colon varies depending on the access method you select. If the access method involves accessing an IP-based host, then a common format is used. It starts with two forward slashes (//) followed by the network host's fully qualified domain name or (less commonly) its IP address.

Since each host computer can house many servers, you can use a port number for further qualification. Normally, you can omit the port number since most servers are attached to their default port, such as port 80 for Web servers. Note that a colon separates the port number from the domain name and if you omit the port number the colon should be omitted as well.

A single forward slash (/) separates the host address from the remainder of the string, which is known as the 'URL-path'. The URL-path specifies the details of how to access the resource. For example, in the case of the **http** access method, this would be the directory path and file name of the Web page.

What is Java?

Java is a language developed by Sun Microsystems for use on the World Wide Web. Java provides Web pages with interactivity and works across platforms. Programs developed for the Web with Java are called 'applets'. Applets are stored on a Web server but executed on a Web browser, which is a new way of doing things that has wide implications for the computing community. Java is a general programming language that closely resembles C++ but has eliminated some of the confusing features of that language.

What is JavaScript?

JavaScript is a scripting language developed by Netscape for creating extensions to Netscape's browser and servers. It is similar to Java but simpler (i.e., Java is comparable to C++ in complexity, and JavaScript is comparable to Visual Basic). From a Web developer's point of view, the main difference between Java and JavaScript is that JavaScript integrates seamlessly with HTML but Java does not. People use JavaScript to enhance the Web browser, whereas they use Java more for developing applications that are distributed over the Web. A secondary but important difference is that for JavaScript the *source* code is downloaded along with the HTML document, whereas with Java only the bytecode compiled version is downloaded.

How difficult is it to install a Web page and Web browser?

People with no previous programming skills have learned to create Web pages in a few days. Installing a Web browser is also very easy and takes less than half an hour.

How easy is it to learn how to use a Web browser?

A Web browser has a strikingly understandable user interface that users can grasp in about half an hour. Usually, the more useful the software the more difficult it is to learn, but the Web has a very short learning curve followed by a fast and satisfying payback. If a few relevant pages are made available, most users will perceive the ratio of effort to results to be heavily in their favor. Also, the Web standardizes the key elements of presentation and interaction (text, links, forms) so once a user has had some browsing experience they will find it easy to interact with new pages.

What are NSAPI and ISAPI?

NSAPI and ISAPI are two APIs (Application Programming Interfaces) developed by Netscape and Microsoft respectively. These interfaces allow third-party software developers to write programs that interact with Web servers in a standard way. Before Web server APIs were available, developers had to use the CGI (Common Gateway Interface) protocol. This is still in use, but it takes up more of the server's resources and is relatively slow. By taking advantage of these APIs, developers can create third-party products for Web servers that will run faster, take less memory, and be more integrated with the Web server.

What are client-side extensions?

Client-side extensions are programs that extend the functionality of Web browsers. Examples are: Java applets, Netscape plug-ins, Microsoft ActiveX components, or helper applications. Browsers in their current form are excellent for viewing information, and also provide a good framework for interacting with programs. The best client-extensions are those that integrate so seamlessly with the Web browser that it is difficult to tell that they are there. The JavaScript language provides a way of achieving seamlessness because it is tightly integrated with the browser.

What are server-side extensions?

Server-side extensions are programs that extend the functionality of Web servers. These programs interface with the Web server by way of the CGI protocol or one of several APIs. If the extension program is implemented with CGI, then it will be a stand-alone, executable program. If the extension is implemented with one of the APIs, then it will be either a DLL (dynamic linked library) or a shared object. People use server-side extensions for a wide variety of purposes, such as connecting to databases, faxing out online orders, or performing online parametric modeling.

One example of a server-side extension product is LiveWire by Netscape, which we profile in Chapter 9. This product extends the Netscape Web server by allowing HTML documents to be processed by a JavaScript interpreter. This allows developers to customize a Web database site with JavaScript to meet their requirements.

What kind of data can the Web handle?

The first Web browsers only handled text, then graphics were added, and over a short time RealAudio, streaming video, and VRML (Virtual Reality Markup Language) were implemented. The Web uses the MIME standard, which is designed to handle all kinds of data, so the limiting factor for it is bandwidth, not data type. Bandwidth is quite limited on the Internet but much less so on Intranets. Thus, Intranets can comfortably transmit more multimedia information than the Internet.

Frequently Asked Questions about Databases

What are databases?

Database programmers distinguish between 'production' databases and 'query-only' databases. People use production databases to store business transactions (e.g., bank records, sales orders, customer accounts, payments), which they update continuously. Inserting data into these databases is complex, and insert/update errors can have serious consequences. Therefore, elaborate middleware and client programs are written to prevent integrity faults and the entry of incorrect data. Query-only databases (e.g., data warehouses, online procedure manuals, legal precedents, dictionaries on CDs) are maintained and updated infrequently and then only by people with special training. They are read by wide audiences with no special database skills, but since these databases are not updated by their users, data integrity is much less of a concern.

Originally, databases were only used to store fielded or tabular alphanumeric data, but today's databases hold text files, scanned images of pages, photographs, CAD drawings, video clips, audio, maps, VRML files, and more.

What are tabular databases?

A good example of tabular data is a phone book. It lists a vast number of names, addresses, and phone numbers. Systems for storing and retrieving tabular, alphanumeric data are among the oldest kinds of computing technology. In the '50s these systems were closely modeled on the hardware they used (e.g., punch cards, sorting machines) and were driven by primitive software. In the '60s the term 'database' first appeared in reference to complex data storage systems that held information about different kinds of entities in multiple tables and kept track of related transactions. Examples include customers, inventories, orders, invoices, accounts, shipments, and payments. Because money was often at stake and errors could result in serious inconvenience, the key issues for people working with tabular data became reliability, data integrity, and security. The sober atmosphere surrounding databases often startles programmers who come from different backgrounds, but there are good reasons for taking these issues seriously.

What are relational databases?

In the '60s software started to get a lot more abstract and increasingly became modeled on ideas about language and logic rather than on the underlying computing machinery. The term 'relational database' emerged from this movement to rethink the theory of databases. The relational model was conceived, and is still championed by, Edgar F. Codd, a mathematician from Oxford who was working then at IBM. Relational database management systems (RDBMS) have become the standard for tabular databases. The main problem they try to solve is: How can a database be updated without damaging the data? The second problem they try to resolve is: How can databases be queried so the answers will always make sense?

Greatly simplified, a relational database consists of tables containing columns and rows, rules defining the relationships between the tables, and a language (SQL) for manipulating the data and querying the database. Each table must contain information about only one kind of entity (e.g., employees, invoices, items in inventory) and the first column uniquely identifies each entity in the table. The data in every column must fit into a single category (e.g., phone number, hair color, zip code, part number) and must be a property of the entity. Think of the rows in a table as simple statements about the entity (e.g., employee #X has red hair, has this phone number, has that zip code, etc.). You can retrieve data both by category and by content. For example, you can select phone numbers (category) with a particular area code (content).

The challenge with databases is that it is very difficult to keep the contents of a database correct and up to date when data is added and modified. Hence, all the theory about structure and the rules about data manipulation. With a few tables and infrequent transactions it can look easy, but when the system is large (many tables, entities, relationships, transaction constraints, and integrity rules) and must support large numbers of transactions over long periods of time, then keeping the data clean, current, and connected becomes truly difficult. So, the stringent rules surrounding DBMS programming are necessary.

What is SQL?

Structured Query Language is a language for manipulating the data stored in relational databases. It was adopted as an industry standard in 1986. A typical SQL statement would be:

```
SELECT EmailAddress FROM PhoneNumber WHERE LastName='Flintstone' AND _
    AreaCode=604
```

This query requests all the email addresses from the PhoneNumber table where the last name is 'Flintstone' and the area code is 604.

What are BLOBs?

A *Binary Large OBject* is a data type that allows relational databases (which were originally designed to hold only alphanumeric data) to hold graphic images and other non-alphanumeric data objects. A database record would normally contain a pointer to the BLOB's location and some columns describing it, so you can handle BLOBs just like alphanumeric data.

What is client/server computing?

Client/server is a computing architecture in which client-processes request services and data from server-processes. Clients and servers can exist in the same memory space or can be on separate computers and exchange messages and data over a network. Client/server computing grew out of 'modular programming' in which programs were separated into small, functionally coherent modules that were easy to understand and therefore easier to develop and maintain. The most common partitioning of client/server functionality uses a client-process as a user interface and a server-process as a database server or file server. Today, the most common hardware implementation of client/server architecture would have multiple PCs running client processes and a multi-tasking host computer running server processes.

What is two-tiered client/server computing?

In two-tiered client/server computing a client talks directly to a server, with no other intervening processes (Figure 1.7). Two-tiered client/server is currently the most common architecture on microcomputer-based LANs, although this is likely to change in the near future. Two-tiered client/server architectures are characterized by 'fat clients' or 'fat servers' that perform all the necessary functions of an application between them. Hence, clients manage the user interface, validate data entered by the user, dispatch requests to server programs, and execute some business logic. Servers accept requests from clients, execute database retrievals and updates, manage data integrity, control transactions, execute business logic, and send data to clients.

A Web browser talking directly to a Web server is an example of two-tiered architecture. A PowerBuilder application directly connected to a Sybase database is also an example of two-tiered architecture.

What is three-tiered client/server computing?

A three-tiered client/server architecture introduces a third layer of processing between the client and the server (Figure 1.8). On PC-based LANs, three-tiered is the more recent architecture and what goes on in the middle tier is much less strictly defined than what goes on in the client and server tiers. An important advantage of three-tiered architecture over two-tiered is that it allows the client and the server to lose weight and become 'thin clients' and 'thin servers'. This means that the partitioning of function can be carried further, and greater modularity can be achieved. Advocates of three-tiered architecture usually agree that transaction control, business application logic, and computing resource allocation should be implemented in the middle layer. Other processes that could be implemented

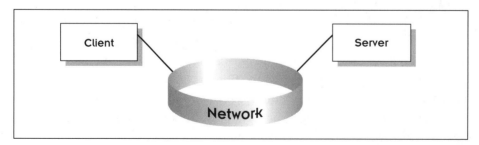

Figure 1.7   Two-tiered client/server architecture.

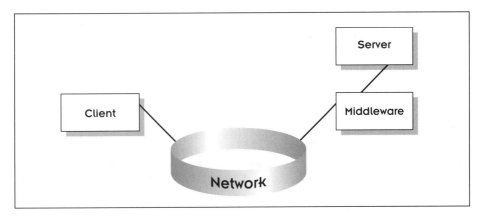

Figure 1.8   Three-tiered client/server architecture.

in that layer include translating data from legacy applications on mainframes, handling security and authentication, and generating reports.

What is multi-tier client/server computing?

The term 'multi-tier' refers to a variation on the three-tier architecture where multiple processes exist between the client and the server. The terms 'multi-tier' and 'three-tier' are sometimes used interchangeably and mean approximately the same thing. A Web database installation is an example of three-tiered or multi-tiered architecture where a Web server and a server extension program act as middleware between a Web browser and a database server.

What is middleware?

The term 'middleware' refers to processes that run between a client and a server in a three-tiered or multi-tiered client/server environment. Some people limit the definition of middleware to elements of the NOS (Network Operating System), and others use a broader definition that includes any kind of process that mediates between a client and a server. In this book we use the term 'middleware' in the broader sense.

What are stored procedures and triggers?

Stored procedures and triggers are used in two-tiered client/server architectures. They are built into the database server and are what make it a 'fat server'. Typically, they enforce transaction sequence and logic and implement business rules. Their purpose is generally to enforce data integrity.

What is ODBC?

ODBC (*Open DataBase Connectivity*) is an API developed by Microsoft. It provides a layer of abstraction so that a program can access data in a uniform, vendor-neutral way from many different databases. Each database requires an ODBC driver that converts ODBC SQL calls into a database's native calls and then performs the database interaction. ODBC also returns the result sets from queries in a uniform way to the calling program.

The advantage of not having to write multiple applications for multiple databases makes ODBC very attractive to both developers and users. A user can buy one program and use it across many databases. A developer can develop one program that will work on several databases.

ODBC is mainly used in the Windows environment but is also becoming available on UNIX.

What is JDBC?

JDBC (*Java DataBase Connectivity*) is an API developed by Sun/JavaSoft that was modeled after ODBC and is designed to provide a uniform, vendor-neutral way of accessing data from Java programs.

The JDBC specification has not been finalized but it should be completed by mid 1996. The current draft specification states that its main goal is to develop a 'call level' SQL for Java. As part of this, JDBC will provide Java methods that will pass any query string to the underlying DBMS driver, which will enable a Java application to make full use of the database's native calls. The interface will be consistent with the rest of the Java system with liberal use of strong typing wherever possible to catch errors at compile time.

What is a legacy system?

'Legacy system' is a term used to describe database applications that were built using software and programming practices that are no longer standard. Legacy systems often work very well but are difficult or impossible to modify, and it is hard to make their contents accessible to audiences who use modern computing systems. However, a great deal of useful information is stored in legacy systems (for example, in banks and government agencies) so the challenge is to construct bridges between them and more modern systems, rather than to rebuild them. The Web is seen as a good tool for building such bridges.

What is transaction control?

A transaction is a unit of interaction with a production database. A good example would be debiting or crediting your bank account at an Automated Teller Machine. You want to be sure that any funds you deposit go to your account. If the ATM runs out of cash after you have requested a withdrawal, you want to be sure that your account will not be debited. Several smaller database interactions are combined in each ATM transaction (e.g., entering your card, keying in your PIN number, selecting an action, keying in an amount, making a deposit, and receiving cash). In 'transaction control,' the rule is that the entire transaction must succeed or fail as a unit. Only successful transactions will be 'committed' and all unsuccessful or incomplete transactions will be 'rolled back' to a neutral state.

What is OLTP?

OnLine Transaction Processing actually means two different things. In its original narrow sense, OLTP refers to three-tiered client/server database applications that use a separate middleware program (a transaction server) to control transactions. This differs from two-tiered applications in which transactions are controlled by stored procedures and triggers in the database server. In its broader and more common usage, the term OLTP refers to any 'production' database, or any database application that is updated constantly and queried infrequently. OLTP applications are often contrasted with OLAP (OnLine Analytical Processing) database applications.

The Web in its simple form (HTML and a Web server with a CGI program) has no mechanisms for controlling transactions. However, in its more complex form (with client or server extensions) a Web database application can interact with the stored procedures in a two-tiered database server, or with a middleware transaction server.

What is OLAP?

Online Analytical Processing describes a kind of database application where the users simply query the database and do not update it. OLAP applications include 'data warehouses' and 'data marts'. The purpose of an OLAP application is to allow people to analyze data stored in production databases without interfering with the availability or integrity of the production system. While production databases must be current to the split second, OLAP databases contain historical records of transactions that have already been completed. OLTP databases are updated continuously, while OLAP databases are updated periodically by taking batch snapshots of a production database. Finally, OLAP databases are not structured according to the relational model but are often structured more like reports.

A major purpose of OLAP applications is to bring business information to people who are infrequent computer users, so the simplicity of the Web interface has high value in this context and makes OLAP an excellent candidate for Web database installations.

Frequently Asked Questions about Networks

What is the Internet?

Much has been written about the Internet elsewhere, and we assume that anyone reading this book knows something about it. Very briefly, the Internet is a huge network of computers that transmit data over the world's telephone systems using TCP/IP. It is based on robust technology and is becoming a de facto standard for networked communication. Most people use the Internet for email, file transfer, file searching, and browsing the Web. Originally, volunteer members of the Internet community developed the Web as public domain software.

What is TCP/IP?

Transmission Control Protocol/Internet Protocol is the standard set of communication protocols used in the UNIX environment. More recently, it has been adopted in Windows 95, Windows NT and Mac OS. TCP/IP is the most widely used network protocol.

IP is a protocol that delivers an IP packet from the source to the destination by making decisions at each router it encounters. An IP packet includes data, the IP address of the data's source, and the IP address of the data's destination. IP can break packets up and re-form them reliably at the receiving end, which is necessary as some hardware components can not handle large packets. IP does not guarantee error-free, in-sequence packets at the destination.

TCP is a protocol that makes sure that the IP packets are received in order and without corruption. A checksum, sent with each IP packet, is checked by the destination. Any mismatch in checksums causes the receiver to re-quest a re-transmission of the IP packet. Before data transmission begins, TCP establishes a valid connection between the sender and the receiver.

Together, the two protocols provide a reliable way of transmitting variable amounts of data over widely differing computers.

What is an Intranet?

Intranets are LANs running the same network protocols that run on the Internet (TCP/IP) and providing the same services that the Internet pro-vides (e.g., email, file transfer, file searching, and the Web). The term 'Intranet' first showed up in about mid 1995 to describe the home brew TCP/IP systems that companies were installing to publish internal corpo-rate information. Intranet publishing now appears to be growing faster than the Internet. In fact, Input, a market research firm in Mountain View, California, estimates that corporate spending on Internet/Intranet-related technologies and services will increase to more than $200 billion by the year 2000.

What do companies publish on the Internet or on an Intranet?

An InformationWeek survey of IS managers found that 76 percent of re-spondents intended to use Web software on Intranets to publish internal company information. Further, 72 percent intended to use Web software on the Internet to publish marketing information. To support this activity, every known category of database (relational, full-text, flat files, spread-sheets, and legacy) will be integrated with Web browsers. So, it looks as if Intranets will be hotbeds of Web database development activity.

What is a firewall?

A firewall is hardware and/or software that is placed at the entry point to a network. Its purpose is to prevent data from either entering or leaving a network unintentionally.

There are three basic kinds of firewalls: packet filter gateways, circuit-level gateways, and application gateways. Packet filter gateways monitor the source and destination IP addresses and ports of incoming and outgoing network traffic. Only authorized packets or sessions are allowed to pass in or out of the network. Typically this filter is part of the router.

Circuit-level gateways are like packet filter gateways, but they work at a different level of the OSI protocol stack. They make a remote machine think that the packets are coming from the firewall itself and therefore hide information about the actual network behind the firewall.

Application gateways are programs that accept connections but perform strong authentications, such as asking for passwords and requesting information about which server to connect to. They can perform other checks such as setting the time of day during which users can connect. Each software server (e.g., FTP or Telnet) that a user might want to connect to will require this gateway program. Some consider this the only true firewall because the other two do not authenticate the user and are subject to IP source address spoofing attacks.

Frequently Asked Questions About Electronic Document Processing

What is an electronic document?

An electronic document is the electronic form of what used to be represented on paper or film. This could include a letter, a report, a manual, an invoice, a patient record, a brochure, a contract, a transcript of spoken words, a scientific paper, a legal precedent, etc. Electronic documents also contain maps, photographs, engineering drawings, anatomical sketches, illustrations, diagrams, and paintings. More recently, electronic documents have come to include audio, video, and 3D geometrical models.

What is electronic document processing?

Any kind of computing technology or standard that permits the creation, maintenance, storage, retrieval, translation, or distribution of electronic documents qualifies as electronic document processing. Technologies include: file servers, online databases, the Internet, the Web, CAD and graphics software, full-text retrieval software, groupware, workflow software, OCR software, word processors, desktop publishing programs, and structured document editors. Standards include: SGML, HTML, VRML, TIFF, GIF, JPEG, MPEG, IGES, and PDES, to name a few.

What are full-text retrieval systems?

People use full-text retrieval systems to search documents and to retrieve the results of the search. The earliest versions of these programs only searched unstructured ASCII text files but newer full-text retrieval programs can also search files containing other kinds of data such as graphics and tables. Sophisticated full-text systems have Boolean or string handling operators for constraining the scope of a search. The grep utility from the UNIX shell is an early example of a text searching program.

What is a structured document?

A structured document has its contents separated into meaningful parts. The usual way of constructing a structured document is to classify the contents of the file into categories and apply tags to each categorized element. SGML, HTML, and CAD files are structured documents.

What is an unstructured document?

An unstructured document, such as an ASCII file, contains only one main type of data and no part of the data is differentiated from any other part. Documents with very simple structure such as a header and body (for example, email files and TIFF files) should probably be considered unstructured.

What is SGML?

Standardized Generalized Markup Language is the international standard (ISO 8879) for document interchange. SGML was designed to permit the sharing of information in documents across publishing systems (for example, word processors, document editors, and electronic displays). It works by separating content and structure from format. All the elements in a document are bracketed with tags that identify the element's type. For example, tags identifying the author's name, the author's affiliation, and the body of a work would look like:

```
<au>William Shakespeare</au>
<aff>Globe Theatre</aff>
<body>To be or not to be...etcetera</body>
```

After the document has been tagged, any program that displays the document can apply a consistent but different typographical treatment to the text between the tags (for example, author names to be centered, Times Roman, 10 pt; body to be left-aligned, Times Roman, 11 pt). Several standard sets of tags have been developed for different user groups (for example, authors, manufacturers, and mathematicians) and you can define custom tags for a particular document.

A good example of an SGML document is the Oxford English Dictionary on CD-ROM. The entire dictionary has been tagged so users can search the dictionary both by type and by content. Another good example is any Web page, since HTML is derived from SGML. SGML is an open standard that you can use to represent any kind of data, including graphics, CAD data, cartographic data, or source code.

What are document management systems?

Document management systems are a class of software for creating, storing, searching, and distributing electronic documents. They usually include full-text retrieval abilities and work with both structured and unstructured documents. They are primarily proprietary systems and are often designed to serve a particular industry or profession (e.g., litigation support systems for law firms or certification tracking systems for pharmaceutical companies). A Web database application could handle many of the tasks performed by earlier-generation, proprietary document management systems.

Components and Architecture

Web database applications make use of new kinds of software components arranged in novel patterns. Everything is still evolving, but a few reliable categories of software and architectures seem to be emerging. This chapter looks at some of the architectures and describes how they differ from each other, and how you can use them to solve different kinds of application problems.

From Two Tiers to Three

Web tools and databases are two distinct technologies that were developed separately, but both are based on a two-tiered client/server architecture. (See Figure 2.1.)

The partitioning of function between a Web browser and a Web server is very distinct. The Web server delivers HTML pages and the Web browser displays those pages by interpreting the HTML tags. Neither side can alter this division of labor. Because of this standardization, many different vendors can create Web browsers. This is one of the reasons why Web technology is being adopted so quickly.

The partitioning of function between database clients and database servers is much less distinct. Decisions about

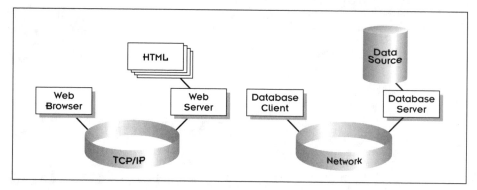

Figure 2.1   Web tools and DBMS tools are based on the two-tiered client/server architecture.

partitioning are often made by application programmers and are influenced by factors related to a project's requirements. This lack of standardization means that significant programming effort is usually needed to implement changes to a database client and/or a database server. Part of the effort will involve bringing both ends into sync.

Adding a Third Tier

Web database applications combine their two-tiered parent technologies into a new kind of system that is based on the three-tiered client/server architecture. The client tier is occupied by a Web browser, the server tier is occupied by a database server, and the middle tier holds a Web server and a server extension program (Figure 2.2). This architecture reduces network traffic, makes components interchangeable, and increases security. However, this architecture also makes database transaction processing more difficult because of the stateless nature of the HTTP protocol that is used to transfer data between the Web browser and the database server.

The Web browser sends Web page requests or data requests to the Web server. The Web server services the page requests and passes the data requests to the server extension program. The server extension program then accepts the requests that are passed to it, converts them to a form that the database server will accept (for example, ODBC SQL), and passes them to the database server. Next, the database server performs a database task, such as a query or an insert, and returns a result set to the server extension program. Finally, the server extension program converts the

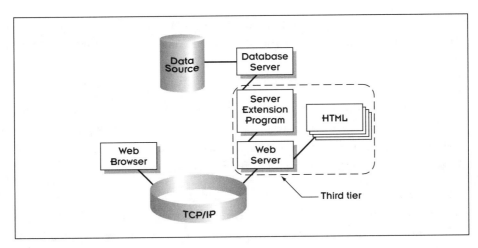

Figure 2.2   A typical three-tiered Web database application.

database results to a form that the Web browser will accept (for example, HTML), and passes them to the Web server, which in turn passes them to the Web browser.

Server Extension Programs

One of the main reasons for using a server extension program in the middle tier is to take advantage of the standards that already exist at the two outermost tiers by translating between them. Other uses for server extensions are handling database connections to reduce network traffic, and maintaining a pool of open database connections to reduce overhead associated with opening and closing the database. Server extensions also support interchangeability at their standard interfaces. Thus, Web servers and database servers can be replaced or upgraded with relative ease.

Server extension programs come in several varieties, each of which has its own advantages and disadvantages. Although there is no definitive classification for them, we found that they fall into three categories: straight CGI, hybrid CGI, and API.

Straight CGI Server Extension Programs

CGI was the first protocol that enabled developers to write programs to augment the functionality of a Web server. Most of the early Web database products were written using CGI, and the straight CGI architecture (Figure 2.3) is still the most portable across different Web servers. Straight CGI is also found in many custom-developed Web database applications, partly because lots of public domain CGI routines are available.

A Web server communicates with a CGI program through environment variables and through the operating system's standard input. Things like URL parameters and the user's IP address are passed via environment variables, and user-input from forms is passed via standard input.

You can develop CGI server extension programs in many languages but the most commonly used ones are PERL, C, and shell scripts. The choice of language can impact the overall performance of the Web database system. For example, every time a Web browser makes a database request, the Web server executes the CGI program to perform the request. If the CGI program uses an interpreted language such as PERL—in Windows NT the PERL interpreter is more than 500K in size—this large executable file will be loaded for every request. The PERL interpreter will then allocate its resources and start interpreting the CGI PERL script, which takes more time and resources and can quickly exhaust a small server when many users are requesting data.

A feature that is common to most commercial CGI server extension programs is the use of templates. Templates are HTML pages with additional

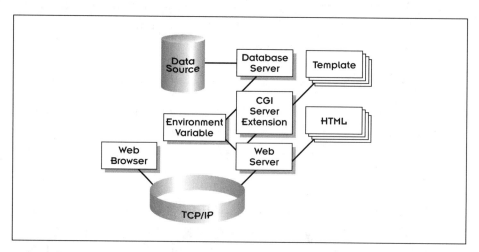

Figure 2.3   A Web database application using straight CGI.

non-HTML tags that are specific to the vendor's CGI program. When a Web browser initiates a database request, it sends the name of the template file. The CGI program then reads the template file and performs the database request specified in the template. For example, in Cold Fusion, the template file **getphone.dbm** contains this snippet:

```
<DBQUERY NAME="FindPerson" DATASOURCE="PhoneList"
      SQL="SELECT *
           FROM PhoneNumber
           WHERE LastName like '#LastName#'
           ORDER BY #OrderType#, FirstName  ">
```

As you can see, this looks partly like an HTML document and partly like an SQL statement. The tag **<DBQUERY>** is not an HTML tag, but is specific to Cold Fusion.

Another way that commercial CGI server extensions work is by embedding SQL statements in an HTML page. This means that when the Web browser transmits input data, the SQL statement is also sent to the Web server. In this case, the CGI program needs no template file since it just formats the SQL statements and passes them to the database server. However, template files are more secure than embedded SQL because a SQL statement on the client side could be modified by an unfriendly user. This could lead to the user obtaining unauthorized data or modifying or deleting data in the database.

Since most Web database products use templates, we show the templates attached to the server extension program (Figure 2.3) for many of the subsequent architectural drawings.

Hybrid CGI Server Extension Programs

The hybrid CGI architecture (Figure 2.4) retains the portability that comes with CGI but achieves better performance than straight CGI. Hybrid CGI is similar to straight CGI except that the server extension program has two components: a 'thin' CGI program and a much larger partner-process. (See Chapter 5, Cold Fusion and Chapter 6, dbWeb.)

For each request from a browser, the Web server calls the small CGI program and passes data to it. However, the CGI program simply passes the data to the partner-process and does little else.

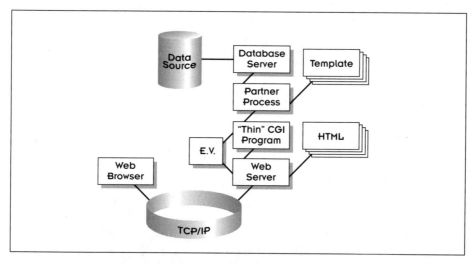

Figure 2.4   A Web database application using hybrid CGI.

The partner-process (a 'system service' in Windows NT or a 'daemon' in Unix) is loaded only once—usually when the operating system is started up—and remains available in the background. Inter-process communication methods (for example, 'named pipes') allow multiple CGI programs to communicate simultaneously with a single service or daemon. Most of the familiar servers (for example, Web servers, database servers, and FTP servers) are implemented as services or daemons.

Almost all of the real work is done by the partner-process. Thus, the CGI program can be very small, and will therefore load more quickly and will use less of the system's resources. This is an important point since every browser-request runs a separate instance of the CGI program.

The partner-process can also improve performance by keeping database connections open after a CGI program has terminated. This 'caching' of database connections reduces the time needed to respond to the next database request.

APIs

Some Web servers provide an API to server extension programs that can be used instead of CGI. In this architecture (Figure 2.5) the server extension program is implemented as a DLL (in NT) or as a shared object (in Unix). (See Chapter 9, LiveWire Pro.)

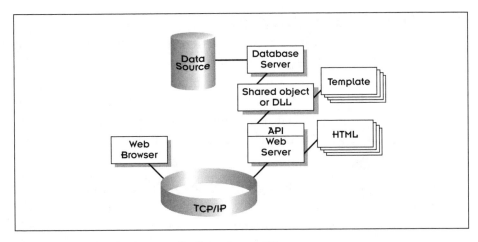

Figure 2.5   A Web database application using an API.

A server extension program implemented as a DLL or a shared object is essentially a group of compiled object code library routines that are called by the Web server as if they were part of its core program. This extends the functionality of the Web server in ways that would be impossible for a CGI program. A CGI program is only called once in the Web server's request-response cycle, but API calls to DLLs or shared objects can be called throughout the cycle, which provides more opportunities to control the situation.

APIs are specific to particular Web servers. The two most popular APIs are Netscape's NSAPI and Microsoft's ISAPI, and many commercial server extension programs implement both APIs.

The API approach is the fastest of the three architectures because there is no need to repeatedly load a CGI program, no need to use inter-process communications, and no need to close a database connection after a request.

There is a risk associated with using an API—it could bring down the Web server if either the Web server's API calls or the server extension program's API functions are not robust enough. Remember, DLLs or shared objects actually become a part of the Web server's core functionality. If a CGI program aborts, the Web server will keep on working and eventually the aborted CGI program will be removed from memory.

ODBC for Web Database Systems

Many server extension programs use an architecture that includes an ODBC layer (Figure 2.6). ODBC is an API that provides a uniform way of calling a relational database. Since it works with many different database products, it is a natural choice for developers of server extension programs. The presence of an ODBC layer also means that if you change the database, the templates and ODBC SQL statements will continue to work without modifications.

ODBC has a reputation for being slow, which in some cases is true, but it depends on how well the particular driver has been implemented. Some drivers work at the DBMS's proprietary interface, which means they add a layer and are slower. Other drivers bypass the proprietary interface and talk directly to the database, so no extra layer is added and they work as quickly as the native database drivers. With some non-SQL databases, ODBC is bound to be slower because it translates ODBC SQL calls into non-SQL calls. For example, dBase will perform faster when using its own direct non-SQL calls than when using ODBC SQL calls that have been mapped onto dBase calls.

ODBC SQL is also a well thought out data manipulation language. In fact, it is better than some of the native database languages, which lack important features and require more coding.

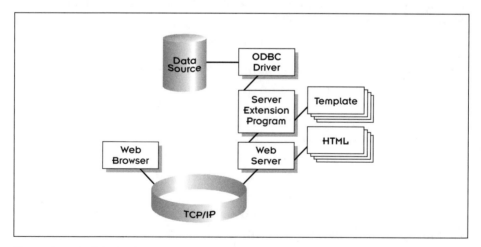

Figure 2.6   A Web database application with ODBC.

ODBC works by creating a layer between the calling program and the database. A basic ODBC system for a Web database consists of five parts:

- **Server extension program**—this program translates Web browser requests into ODBC SQL statements, submits them to the data source, by way of the ODBC driver, and retrieves the results. An example of an ODBC function call is **SQLConnect**, which connects to the data source when given a data source name, a user ID and password, and a few other parameters.

- **ODBC driver manager**—this is a DLL that is linked with a server extension program. One of its purposes is to load the ODBC driver for the requested data source. It also checks many of the ODBC function calls before passing them on to the ODBC driver. Further, it can trace function calls and save the results to a trace file for debugging purposes.

- **ODBC administrator**—this is a program that the system administrator uses to maintain a registry that associates a data source name with an ODBC database. The advantage of this indirection is that if the database moves to a different directory or server, only a quick change using the ODBC administrator is necessary for the server extension program to keep working. (See Figure 2.7.)

- **ODBC driver**—this is a driver, often developed by the vendor of the database, which performs database interactions. It translates ODBC SQL

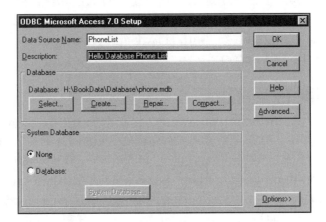

Figure 2.7   ODBC administrator.

statements into the database's native statements (SQL or non-SQL) and then makes the call. There are two types of drivers: single-tiered and multi-tiered. Single-tiered drivers connect directly to the database files and perform the entire database interaction. Multi-tiered drivers (two-tiered or three-tiered) connect to the database's proprietary interface layer, which performs the database interaction.

- **Data source**—this is a term used in ODBC programming to refer to a database, its associated operating system, and any network information needed to access it. This cluster of information is stored in the registry maintained by the ODBC administrator.

The sequence of events begins with the server extension program making an ODBC SQL function call to a data source. This causes the driver manager to find the particulars of the data source by looking in the registry. The registry holds the information that defines the data source and is configured by the ODBC administrator. The driver manager loads the driver, and once the driver is loaded, the manager checks the function arguments for validity and, if they are valid, passes them to the driver.

The ODBC driver translates an ODBC SQL function call into a native database call and performs the request. For simple database systems, the driver is single-tiered, which means that it directly accesses the database tables. For more complex database systems, the driver is multi-tiered, which means that it passes the converted ODBC SQL statements to the DBMS to perform. Both types of drivers receive database result sets and return them to the server extension program. The server extension program then combines the database result sets with HTML and passes them back to the Web browser via the Web server.

Client-side Extensions

A client-side extension is a program that adds to the capabilities of a Web browser (Figure 2.8). You can use client-side extensions for many purposes but one of their main functions is to perform input field validations. (Note: Input validation programmed on the server side increases network traffic and is cumbersome for users, since an entire HTML page must be returned to explain an error.)

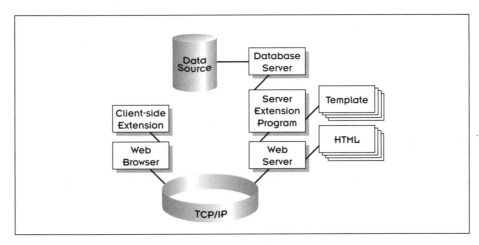

Figure 2.8   A Web database application with a client-side extension.

Although there are no formal classifications for client-side extensions, they currently fall into four categories: helper applications, pluggable applications, Java applets, and scripts.

Helper applications (Figure 2.9) were the first generation of client-side extensions. A helper application is a stand-alone program that runs on the

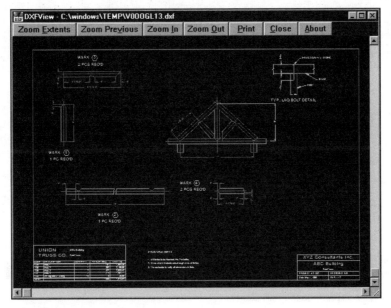

Figure 2.9   A helper application.

user's PC and is invoked by the Web browser. For this to work, you must pre-configure the browser to execute a particular helper application when the user clicks on a hypertext link that contains a particular file extension. For example, to use the ParaGrafix helper application a user would go to ParaGrafix Web page, click on a link that downloads the ParaGrafix viewer, and install it on his/her browser. From then on, that user could click on a link to download DXF files and look at them with the viewer. A characteristic of helper applications is that the Web browser downloads data into a temporary file before it executes the helper application. This can take a long time for big data files.

Pluggable applications (Figure 2.10) are like helper applications in that their purpose is to process and display data that the browser cannot handle directly. However, pluggables are more closely integrated with the browser. You can also program them to start displaying part of a file before it has been completely downloaded.

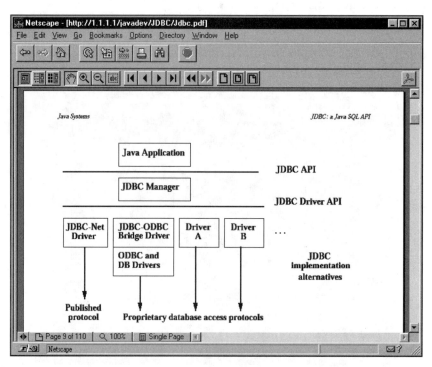

Figure 2.10   A pluggable application.

Pluggable applications currently come in two flavors: Netscape plug-ins or Microsoft's ActiveX controls. Both require the user to download the program ahead of time and install it. There is no compatibility between these two types of pluggable applications and internally they work quite differently. ActiveX controls use OLE as their standard mode of interaction with a browser, whereas plug-ins use normal API DLL methods.

Java applets (Figure 2.11) are compiled programs that are downloaded when an HTML page is requested and are then run by the browser. Applets run as bytecode interpreted programs, which reduces the likelihood that they will transmit a virus, since each instruction is validated before being run. Several browsers support Java applets (for example, Netscape, Sun, and Oracle) and many companies have licensed Java. Thus, more Java-enabled browsers are sure to appear. One of the strongest advantages of a Java applet over helper applications and pluggable applications is version control. This is because an applet will be downloaded every time it is used—so everyone will always be using the latest version.

Scripts (Figure 2.12) are programs embedded in an HTML page. Scripts integrate well with the Web browser because they add functionality without changing the look and feel of a standard Web page. JavaScript, from Netscape

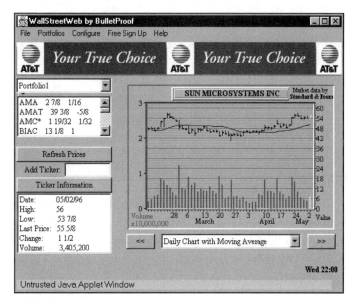

Figure 2.11   A Java applet.

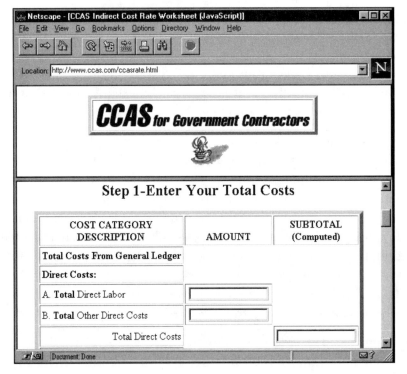

Figure 2.12 A JavaScript database entry form.

and Sun, is currently the predominant script, but Microsoft is vigorously promoting VBScript. In both cases, scripts fit well with Web database systems because of their ability to provide input validation in HTML input forms. Currently, only the Netscape 2.0 browser supports JavaScript, but vendors who license Java automatically get a royalty-free license to JavaScript. Hence, there is a good chance we will be seeing more JavaScript-enabled Web browsers in the near future.

Java Applets

Since Java is a full-strength programming language, it follows that Java applets are the most capable kind of client-side extension program. Applets are particularly well-suited for complex Web database applications (Figure 2.13) because they take advantage of Web standards and also provide full control of both input and output.

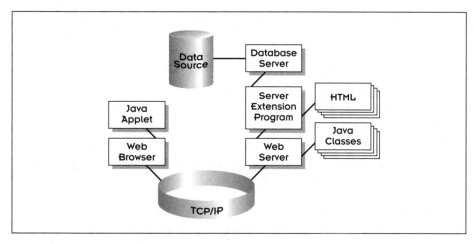

Figure 2.13 A Web database application using a Java applet.

With an applet, a programmer can control input validation to the level of each keystroke or mouse movement. You can display error messages with simple message boxes or custom helper windows. For data display, Java windowing classes are built with the Web's dynamic line wrapping in mind. Java applets have a somewhat different look and feel than standard Web pages, so applets and HTML may not appear to integrate seamlessly.

Applets transmitted over the WWW never write to the client's machine because the Java interpreter in a Web browser will not allow data to be written to the client's disk. This precaution was taken to prevent malicious applets from altering the client's files.

Although it may seem inefficient to download an applet every time it is used, it actually happens quite quickly. A Java-enabled browser (such as Netscape) incorporates many of the system and low-level Java classes with which applets work. The applet only contains the Java code specific to the application, and Java loads classes as they are needed. For example, the WallStreetWeb stock charting applet (Figure 2.11) only takes a minute or so to download even though it downloads all the charting routines and 100 days worth of data.

You can embed a Java applet in an HTML page using the **<applet>** tag. For example, for the stock charting program, the HTML page contains this snippet:

```
<applet code=WallStreetWeb.class width=10 height=10>
</applet>
```

Once the browser sees **<applet>** a **GET** request is sent to the Web server asking for the class **WallStreetWeb.class**. The Web server sends Java code to the browser as the MIME type **text/plain**. Technically, the Web server should return the code with the MIME type **application/octet-stream**, but most Webmasters have not configured their Web servers to associate files ending in **.class** with that MIME type, so the browser ignores the **text/plain** MIME type and assumes it is receiving code.

Once this Java class is downloaded, each bytecode instruction is verified and the initial method of the class is activated. Classes that are not implicitly needed by this downloaded class are not loaded (unless the developer purposely loads them). When a class that has not been loaded is needed the browser will retrieve it at that time.

Although Java classes are downloaded via HTTP, a Java applet can choose a different protocol for its communications. For example, an applet could contain a Telnet protocol class (a session protocol) to allow it to connect to a Telnet server hosting a legacy DBMS system. To the user, the applet would present a modern user interface, while behind the scenes it would be communicating with the legacy database via standard Telnet screens.

Mixed Web Database Systems

A mixed Web database system (Figure 2.14) uses a Web browser to download a database client application that has been implemented as a client-side extension (that is, a helper app, a plug-in, or an applet). Once the database client is running, it uses a session-oriented protocol to communicate with the database server. (See Chapter 8, DataRamp and Chapter 10, PowerBuilder 5.0.) In this architectural variation, the web components and the database components work together but not as a three-tiered application. Instead, they function as a pair of two-tiered applications working side-by-side.

This architecture combines the strengths of the Web with the strengths of traditional database client/server systems. A Web page provides a convenient and familiar starting place where users can find and launch database cli-

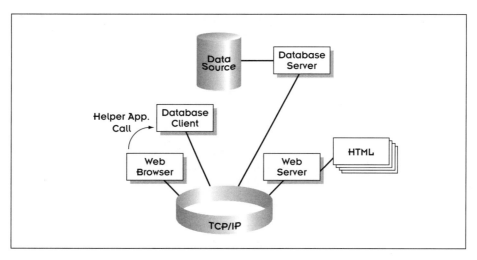

Figure 2.14 A mixed Web database application.

ent applications. Developers can also use the Web page to provide training and help for database client applications. A database client can contain all the input validations that it needs and, because it uses a session-oriented protocol, it can also have full transaction control. (Note: Input validation and transaction control are generally weak in the Web environment.) Perhaps the most useful feature of the mixed architecture is that it allows developers to take database applications that already exist and deploy them over the Web with very little modification.

Since applications based on the mixed architecture use a session-oriented protocol they will have much less capacity to service many users at once than is possible with HTTP.

Legacy Databases

A legacy Web database system (Figure 2.15) uses a Web browser to query and update legacy databases. The reasons for doing this include making the contents of the database available to a wider audience, avoiding the costs of adding terminals, and modernizing the user interfaces of older databases.

In the past, developers would often integrate a Web browser with a legacy database by having the Web browser bring up a Telnet client. For example,

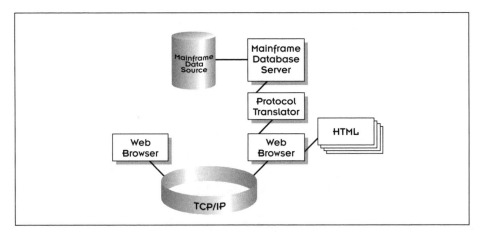

Figure 2.15   A Web database application with a legacy database.

if a URL contained **telnet:** instead of **http:** (as in **telnet://rs.internic.net**) a pre-configured Telnet client would be loaded and automatically connected to the domain **rs.internic.net**. Although the browser took care of some of the complications, the developer was still forced to struggle with the many varieties of user interfaces.

A more robust integration of a Web browser with a legacy database would use a 'translation server' or 'protocol translator'. A translation server is a server extension program that translates input data from a Web browser into a data stream that a terminal can accept and then translates the terminal data stream output into HTML. Translation servers are attractive because the legacy system doesn't need to be changed, which is a big advantage because legacy systems are difficult and costly to modify.

Combining Web front ends with legacy databases has the potential for greatly extending the usefulness of both technologies because a great deal of useful information is stored on mainframes. However, integration is not a simple matter because the Web uses a stateless protocol and legacy systems use session-oriented protocols.

One person investigating translation servers is Louis Perrochon at the Institut für Informationsysteme, Department of Computer Science in Zürich, Switzerland. He is working on 'The Translation Server Project' (**http://www.inf.ethz.ch/department/IS/ea/tsp/tsp.html** and **http://**

www.inf.ethz.ch/department/IS/ea/publications/nsc94.html), which is investigating the use of translation servers to interface Web browsers to legacy systems that use terminal connections such as VT100s. His approach is to create a schema template that holds the dialog between a user and the terminal. When a Web browser makes a request, the translation server parses the schema and generates an HTML input form to obtain additional information from the user. It then translates and sends the input data to the legacy DBMS. Finally, the result sets are translated to HTML and sent back to the browser.

CHAPTER

Design and Development

Web database publishing systems are a new kind of application working in a new software environment. That means no one is an expert in building them straight away and you cannot use the formal design methods developed for other kinds of software projects. Therefore, developers will have to rely on their experience and use common-sense methods such as incremental design and development, scope-reduction, and prototyping.

The open network environment—whether a LAN or the Internet—is a big place in which lots is happening and lots can go wrong. Simplicity is a strong defense against unforeseen problems, so it is a good plan to keep the scope of an application smaller than you might think you want. You can always add more functions later.

No matter what the project, software development loops iteratively through the same basic steps: research the requirements, draft a design, select tools, build and test a prototype, build and test a working system, and maintain the system. So, in the absence of a magical design formula, this chapter walks through the steps and offers a simple checklist of questions to raise and points to consider. If you start by asking these questions, then you should soon find yourself asking the questions that are pertinent to your own application.

Establishing the Requirements
The Big Picture
What is the purpose of the application?

Is it for electronic commerce? Customer support? Public relations? Customer education? Public education? Internal communication between members of a group? Dissemination of information within a company?

Knowing the broad purpose of your application helps to keep it on target. Answering this question first will help to establish a criterion for evaluating requests for features.

What is the immediate goal?

Sales? Save money by replacing paper publications? Make published information more current?

Who is the audience?

Is the audience a well-defined group? Do you have a demographic profile of them? How many people are in the audience? Are they members of your organization? Are they existing customers? Potential customers? Members of the public? How will they access the site?

There are many ways to implement a Web database system. Knowing the audience will tell you what kind of security you need, which Web browser features you can use, and so on.

Who is the competition?

Is there another Internet site doing something similar? What is it doing? Will yours be compared to it? What differentiates your application?

It is always difficult to spec out the hardware and software requirements for a commercial Web database site. Knowing something about competing sites might give you ideas about the level of traffic to expect or the kind of people accessing the site.

What is being published?

Is the site going to be an electronic magazine? A directory? An information provider that sells information? A free service that gives away information and runs ads? A business application?

Constraints

How much bandwidth will you need?

How many visitors per day do you anticipate? How many interactions per visit? Will the site display multimedia objects? Will people download files from the site? How long will it take to service each request?

A general rule of thumb for ISPs (Internet Service Providers) is to have one phone line for every 10-15 subscribers. Otherwise there will be too many busy signals when they dial up to use the service. This concept also applies to Web database sites. If your bandwidth is too low and you are sending lots of data and graphics, then your Web server will inevitably reach its connections limit and turn away new connections. Unfortunately we have not heard of a good rule of thumb for sizing Web sites, but consider this: an ISDN 1 "B" channel connection to the Internet gives you a 56 or 64 kilobits/second bandwidth. It will only take a handful of users (maybe 3 to 10) doing heavy downloading using 28.8 kilobits/second modems before you have used up your bandwidth. The Web server will keep making new connections, but things will slow down for everyone. Eventually, the Web server will reach its connection limit as more users come in.

Will the application run on the Internet?

The apparent bandwidth of an application on the Internet will be limited not only by the server's capacity but by the Internet itself and by the user's modem. Users dialing up to the Internet will perceive it as quite a slow device, so use graphics and other multimedia objects sparingly. Further, you should establish reasonable limits on the size of result sets returned by database queries.

Will the application run on an Intranet?

Will other applications share the server? Which application will have priority?

The bandwidth of applications on Intranets will be much higher than on the Internet since data is transmitted over a LAN. This means that large graphics and multimedia objects can be used more freely since they will be transmitted quickly.

Are you using a Web front-end to augment a database?

Does the database exist already? Does the database application already exist? Is the project to port an existing application or must you develop a new one? Will users only query the database or will they add information to it? When users add information, will transaction control be needed? How will the contents of the database be updated?

The Web is strongest for querying databases and weakest for adding data to them. HTTP was designed for downloading HTML pages, so performing database updates could require a mixed approach using both a Web browser and a database client. It depends on what kinds of transaction controls are needed.

Are you using a database server to augment a Web site?

What database features do you need: searchability? stored procedures? fine-grained access control?

Not all Web database applications require a database server. In cases when the content is changed infrequently, or the amount of data is small, you could create a macro to convert your database into static HTML pages.

How available does the application have to be?

Do you require 100 percent availability? Is there a time of day when the application can be shut down? How will you handle recovery from failures?

What exists already and what must be built?

The simplest case would be if someone else provided everything except the application. The most complex case would be if you had to provide not only the application, but the Web server, the database server, the middleware components, a box to run everything, network connections for the users, and a network connection for the server box. The reality will probably fall somewhere between the simplest case and the most complex case—third party ISPs usually don't have a database server installed, and internal LANs usually don't have a Web server installed.

What types of data will be handled?

Multimedia data? Tabular alphanumeric data? Full text? CAD files? Audio files? Video files?

You might need special data viewers (helper applications or pluggable applications) for CAD files or video clips. You can use a special server for RealAudio data that begins playing sound files immediately rather than waiting until they are completely downloaded.

Details

Who will be responsible for maintaining the content?

'Editors' are usually responsible for the content of a text database. 'Database administrators' are usually responsible for the content of a fielded database. Whatever they are called, someone has to do it.

Who will be responsible for maintaining the Web server?

Will there be an official Webmaster? Who will keep the site logs? Who will take care of problems?

It is a myth to think that Web servers run twenty-four hours a day, seven days a week without any problems. It is always a surprise when a Web server stops working, but it happens. Servers can be stopped by boundary conditions that only happen under a certain combination of TCP/IP stack, type of Web server, and memory. Also, if a server is connected to the Internet, the ISP might power down the host for a second and if your system isn't set up to automatically re-dial and re-establish a connection, then it will be down until you start it up again.

What kind of security will you need?

Will user authentication with IDs and passwords be enough? Do you need to control access to selected Web pages? Do you need to control access to database tables or fields? What liabilities will occur if the security measures fail?

For a Web database system, security can be controlled on the Web server, on the database server, or in the server extension program. Each has advantages and disadvantages.

Will the audience need training?

Do they have Web browsers? Do they know what to expect on the site? Will using the application become part of their job?

Error handling for Web database systems is still relatively simple compared to database clients. Some training may be needed if serious transaction processing via the Web is part of the requirement.

Basic design and development documents

There are no hard and fast rules, but a design document should probably include some combination of the following:

- a written statement of the requirements

- a list of features to be included, based on the requirements

- a list of features to be excluded from the current version

- a functional specification describing all input forms, reports, database tables, and functions

- a data flow diagram showing the elements and how they will connect

- a database specification including data definitions, database schema, and an entity relationship diagram

- an environment specification describing hardware, operating system, Web server, supported Web browsers, network, firewall, network connections, and development tools

- a plan for assembling the database contents

- user training and documentation

- a maintenance plan

- a testing plan

- a plan for logging and log-analysis

The project itself would ideally be completed in stages with some useful function delivered at each stage. A project document would probably include:

- a project schedule with deliverables and dates

- a list of personnel and a schedule of their availability

- a list of other necessary resources (i.e., computers, network connections, software)

- a budget showing the estimated costs of the people and resources used

Selecting Tools

How do you find out what tools are available?

The best information source is the WWW. Most vendors of Web database software have a home page and many offer downloadable trial versions of their products. Other information sources are newsgroups and mailing lists. (See Chapter 12 for a list of Web database tools and URLs.)

Is it the right kind of tool?

The available tools have been designed for specific purposes. A large number of them are for connecting Web servers to relational DBMS products and most of these use the ODBC interface. Others are for connecting Web servers to full-text databases.

Does it do what you need?

Some applications require complex input screens that are beyond the abilities of HTML, while others will work comfortably within HTML's constraints. Some applications require transaction control and others don't. Some tools are very easy to use but have limited function, while others are more like full programming languages. You can do more with the latter, but they demand more skill and effort from the people who use them.

Should you design and build your own middleware (i.e., with CGI and PERL) or should you buy a ready-made tool?

If you build your own CGI middleware some drawbacks are:

- a PERL interpreter and script needs to be loaded every time a user initiates a call, and a PERL interpreter can be quite large (500K)

- with CGI, a new connection to the database must be made for every call; some vendors of middleware software have thought this out and provided solutions (e.g., a pool of cached database connections so the database doesn't have to be opened and closed for every query)

On the positive side:

- if your database server or Web server is not supported by the middleware vendors and there is no possibility of changing to a more mainstream server, then a custom CGI program will let you build your own middleware layer

- you can build a custom security layer into a CGI program

Does it have good error messages?

It is very important that a Web database product gives you good error messages. In the Web database environment, standard debugging techniques, such as using a print statement to track the value of a variable, don't work, so without good error messages you are lost.

Building a Prototype

It is a good idea to start a project by first building a prototype. A prototype will let you obtain feedback from the people who are paying for the project and from the people who will be using the application. Web database publishing is still in the 'innovator' stage, and when technology is this new it is hard to get a new concept across without showing something to people.

You can build a minimal prototype by using static HTML files to simulate the database content. Forms can also be used by setting the value of the **action** attribute in the **<form>** tag to the URL of an HTML page that contains sample results. When the **submit** button is pressed it will look as if real data is being retrieved but in fact it will just be simulated.

A more capable prototype could include a live database with test data and the ability to query the database from the forms. All input validations could be left out of the forms, and all stored procedures and integrity enforcement could be left out of the database. This prototype would be able to test and demonstrate all the planned functions but would be easy to break with bad input.

Quality Assurance

What should you stress test?

Does the application break when usage is high? What happens when lots of users hit at once? Can the security be hacked? Do all the browsers you intend to support work? Do the validation functions on the input forms work?

You can break testing down into two parts. The first part should test that the input data is getting to the server extension program correctly. It should also test that the retrieved data is getting back and being displayed correctly under all kinds of conditions. The second part should test that the database is handling the database requests correctly for all kinds of input.

What should be beta tested?

The prototype and the finished application should be tested on real users to make sure that the interface is usable and the directions are easy to understand.

How should you test the content?

Have you spell-checked the pages? Have you looked at the graphics on a display that uses the worst case resolution and color? Have you properly acknowledged trademarks? Have you attributed quotations to their authors? Have you cleared copyrights? (See References, Miscellaneous for editorial style guides.) Have you applied all the editorial tests to both the database contents and the HTML pages?

Maintaining the System

Who will maintain the HTML and the server extension program?

When you add or remove pages, will all the links still point to the right places? When a new database field is added, has it also been added to the forms and tables on the Web pages?

There are several products coming to market that will make it easier to maintain links. However, we know of nothing that automates the synchronization of the Web and the database in a Web database application. Therefore, when database tables are changed, manual maintenance of the Web pages will be needed.

Who will maintain the content?

Are database updates done periodically? Does the site accumulate files or data? If so, how (and when) will old data be purged?

HTML pages also require updates as information changes. It is a good idea to put a date at the bottom of a page that states when the page was last updated.

Gotchas

Your application may need to do iteration and conditional testing on the Web page to carry out the required database operations.

Many of the Web database tools are weak on control structures and are limited to declarative programming (like HTML). If your application needs looping or conditional testing, then you should consider getting a Web database tool that includes a full programming language.

Large files abort in mid-transmission.

Sending big files over the net with HTTP can be difficult, and if a file transfer fails, then it must be started over again from the beginning. FTP is more robust for sending large files, so consider installing an FTP server for such cases.

HTTP's statelessness takes database programmers by surprise.

For example, an application requires that user-authentication be maintained over a series of database interactions, but there is no 'session'. Cookies are intended to help with this but only a few browsers currently support cookies. Hidden fields with forms can also be used but both methods take extra programming effort and this sort of thing can be done much more simply with database client/server tools.

There may be no ODBC driver available for your database.

If the middleware product you want to use only works with ODBC, then you need to be sure that a driver exists for the database you intend to use.

SQL statements on the browser can be hacked.

If the SQL statements are embedded in the HTML input form, then a person could easily save the HTML page locally and change the statement before re-submitting the form. This could cause serious damage to your database or result in data being retrieved by the wrong people.

CGI programs calling other programs can be hacked.

CGI programs that call other programs with the user's input data as arguments represent a serious security hole. Users can input data to do unintended things such as: obtain the password file, shut down the server, or destroy the hard disk. User-input should be checked before letting the CGI program submit it as arguments to the calling program. The Web site **http://www.cerf.net/~paulp/cgi-security/** has more information on CGI security issues.

HTML Essentials for Web Database Publishing

This chapter introduces the essential elements of HTML that you need to know to create Web pages that connect to databases and describes a simple 'Hello Database' program that illustrates how the elements can be used together. The elements are:

- accepting user input with forms, and using JavaScript for input validation,

- displaying database query results with tables, and

For readers who want more details after reading this introduction, Netscape's JavaScript documentation file is included on the CD-ROM (**\BookData\Docs\Chap4\jsdoc.zip**) or you can obtain it from their Web site (**http://home.netscape.com/eng/mozilla/2.0/handbook/javascript/index.html**). Also, the reference section of this book lists several books and URLs that offer in-depth treatment of HTML.

The Idea of HTML

HTML consists of tags that bracket every element in a document (i.e., sections of text, and images). The tags identify whatever they enclose as a member of one of the standard HTML categories. So, a Web browser can render them intelligently on many different devices. Every HTML document begins and ends with a pair of **<html>...</html>** tags and is divided into a head and a body with the tags **<head>...</head>** and **<body>...</body>**:

```
<html>
<head>
<title>A Simple HTML document</title>
</head>

<body>
This is text for the simple HTML document.
</body>
</html>
```

The title will usually show up in a browser's caption area but the rest of the head will not be displayed. The body will be visible, as shown in Figure 4.1.

'Static HTML' and 'Dynamic HTML'

Static HTML documents are written once and placed on the Web server. When a Web browser requests a static HTML page, the Web server always sends it in exactly the same form it was created in. (See Figure 4.1.)

Dynamic HTML documents are generated on-the-fly in response to a request from a Web browser. The program that generates them is called a 'server-side extension' (that is, a Web database middleware product, or a custom-made CGI script). The Web server itself takes no part in the dynamic generation process, and simply passes page requests to the server extension program and transmits the returned HTML to the Web browser.

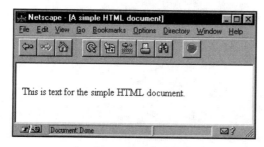

Figure 4.1   Web browser viewing a simple HTML page.

Both approaches are usually combined in a single Web database site, with static HTML used to create input forms and dynamic HTML used to display query results.

Creating Input Forms

To gather input, a Web page uses an input field (or a cluster of fields) associated with a **submit** button. Users key data into the fields and press the **submit** button, and the Web browser sends the input data to the Web server for processing. To build an input screen you need to know how to specify input forms and how to lay out the screen. We discuss screen layout in the section called 'Displaying database query results' because the techniques for laying out database results and input fields are identical.

Specify input fields with the HTML **<form>...</form>** tags. Anything between these tags must be an interactive input form element. The form could be as simple as a single field, or as complicated as a multi-field screen with radio buttons, checkboxes, and scrolling windows.

The two main attributes of an HTML form are **method** and **action**. The **method** attribute tells the Web server how to deliver the input data to the CGI program. There are two types of methods: **get** and **post**. Specify the method as:

```
<form method=POST action=/cgi-bin/query.exe>
```

If the **get** method is specified (**get** is the default method), then input data is passed from the Web browser to the Web server. Next, it travels from the Web server to the CGI program via an environment variable and the CGI program's command line arguments. Because operating systems place a limit on the amount of environment variable space and command line argument space available when shelling to a CGI program, the **get** method is seldom used.

With the **post** method, the Web server passes data to the CGI program via the operating system's standard input, which has no size limit, so most server extension products use the **post** method.

The **action** attribute tells the Web server what is to be done once the user presses the **submit** button. If the server extension program uses CGI, then specify the CGI program name on the action line:

```
<form method=POST action=/cgi-bin/query.exe>
```

If the server has an API (e.g., NSAPI or ISAPI), and the server extension program uses the API, then specify an HTML document name on the action line:

```
<form method=POST action=getphone.html>
```

For this **action** line, the Web server reads the HTML file **getphone.html**, but a DLL (in Windows NT) or a shared object (in Unix) intervenes and processes the file along with the input data from the form.

We wrote the code snippet below to use the Cold Fusion server extension program, which uses CGI:

```
<form method=POST action=/cgi-shl/dbml.exe?template=getphone.dbm>
```

The **action** tells the Web server to run the program **dbml.exe** in the **/cgi-shl/** directory. Note that **/cgi-shl/** is most likely an alias for the Web server, so the actual CGI program would be in another directory. The **method** to transmit the data is **post**, so an unlimited amount of data can be transmitted. The '**?**' after the CGI program name tells the Web server to save the string **template=getphone.dbm** to a standard environment variable is called **QUERY_STRING**. The Cold Fusion CGI program **dbml.exe** reads this environment variable to find out which HTML/DBML template to use. Not all server-side extension products make use of the '**?**' but many do, as it provides an easy way to transmit additional information.

Notice that Cold Fusion uses a 'name/value pair' to specify the template file (**template=getphone.dbm, name=value**). All data that passes from the Web browser to the Web server uses the name/value pair method. An HTML author does not actually code the HTML input form this way, but understanding this concept makes it easier to understand how to construct input fields and to know what to do when the input looks mangled.

When a user presses the **submit** button, the Web browser takes all the input field data and creates one string containing a series of name/value pairs separated by the '**&**' character. For example, here are two name/value pairs:

```
Name=Fred+Flintstone&Address=128+Granite+Drive
```

This string is sent to the Web server, which passes it on to a CGI program for database processing. The Web browser automatically translates certain characters to prevent confusion. In this case, it translates spaces into '+' signs. Some other characters that are automatically translated are '=' and '%'.

Again, the HTML author doesn't directly work with this format, but knowing how the Web server handles the input data helps to understand the next tag, **<input>**.

The Input Tag

Specify input fields with the **<input>...</input>** tags, which are used only between **<form>...</form>** tags. The input tag has many attributes, but the most important ones are **name**, **value** and **type**. Other attributes, such as **size**, **maxlength**, **min**, and **max** are useful to further qualify an input field. However, some of these attributes (such as **min** and **max**) are in the HTML 3.0 draft specification and have not been implemented in browsers. Most people use the Netscape Web browser, which supports the essential HTML 3.0 draft specifications and some extra HTML tags that have not yet made it into the specification. Microsoft's browser (Internet Explorer 2.0) mainly supports HTML 2.0 tags, but has some HTML 3.0 tags and also some of their own tags. We will focus on the tags supported by Netscape's 2.0 browser.

Name Attribute

The three main attributes of the input tag are **name**, **value** and **type**, which all browsers support to some extent.

As we mentioned earlier, all input data is transmitted as name/value pairs, and the **name** attribute is used to identify the name of the input field when it is submitted to the Web server. Here is an example where the HTML author specifies a single-line text field with the name **LastName**.

```
Enter your last name: <input type=text name=LastName>
```

If the user entered 'Flintstone', and pressed the **submit** button, the browser would take the name of this field, **LastName**, and the entered value, **Flintstone**, and form the name/value pair **Lastname=Flintstone**. The browser does this for all the input fields between the **<form>...</form>** tag and creates one long name/value pair string, which it then transmits to the Web server. The **name** attribute also provides a way for the browser to 'group' radio buttons and checkboxes, which are discussed below.

Value Attribute

Use the **value** attribute to assign an initial value to the input field. For instance, this text field:

```
Last name: <input type=text name=LastName value=Rubble>
```

assigns an initial value of **Rubble,** which is displayed when the input screen first appears. If the user pressed the **submit** button without making any changes to the field, then the name/value pair transmitted would be **LastName=Rubble**.

If no **value** attribute is specified for radio buttons or checkboxes, then the value defaults to the string '**on**'. However, for other types of input fields, the value defaults to a null string. So, if no value is specified, and the user enters nothing in the text field as in the following example:

```
Last name: <input type=text name=LastName>
```

the value would be a null string and the name/value pair transmitted would be **LastName=**.

Type Attribute

Use the **type** attribute to specify the kind of input a field will accept. Types include: single-line text field, multi-line text field, password field, checkbox, radio button, or numeric field with range checking. If no **type** attribute is specified, the browser defaults to a single-line text field. Let's take a look at each of these field types.

Single-line text fields (type=text)

Employ single-line text fields when you want the user to enter a short text string (Figure 4.2).

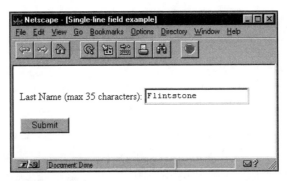

Figure 4.2 A single-line text field.

Specify the visible width of the field with the **size** attribute, and use **maxlength** to set the maximum number of characters that users can enter:

```
Last Name (max 35 characters): <input type=text name=LastName size=20
maxlength=35>
```

The text field is identified by **LastName** and displays a width of 20 fixed-width characters. If a user types more than 20 characters, then the field will scroll horizontally and allow users to enter a maximum of 35 characters.

Password fields (type=password)

Use a **password** field to control access to a database (Figure 4.3).

When a user enters a text string, the results will be displayed as asterisks. Note that passwords are not encrypted when they are transmitted to the Web server.

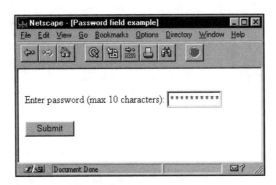

Figure 4.3 A password field.

```
Enter password (max 10 characters): <input type=password _
   name=DBPassword size=10 maxlength=10>
```

Radio button (type=radio)

Utilize radio buttons to let a user select one alternative out of a set of alternatives (Figure 4.4).

When one button is selected, the other radio buttons in the group will be unselected. To specify this in an HTML document, use the same **name** for the entire group of radio buttons, which makes them act as a group (if they aren't grouped, they won't act like normal radio buttons):

```
Select the credit card to place the order:<br>
Visa <input type=radio name=CreditCard value=Visa checked>
Master Card <input type=radio name=CreditCard value=MCard>
American Express <input type=radio name=CreditCard value=Amex>
```

When the user presses one of the radio buttons, the other ones will be turned off because they all use the name '**CreditCard**'.

Checkbox field (type=checkbox)

A checkbox is a two-state input field with programmable values. A single checkbox lets a user select between two alternatives. A group of checkboxes lets a user select multiple alternatives from a set of alternatives (Figure 4.5.)

If you do not specify any **value**, then the default value will be '**on**' when the checkbox is checked. However, the HTML 3.0 draft specification states that there is no default **value**, so it is probably better to always use the **value**

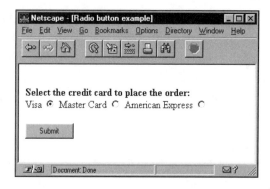

Figure 4.4 Radio buttons.

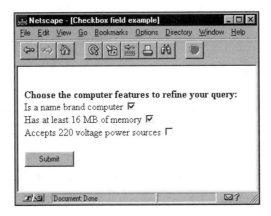

Figure 4.5   Checkboxes.

attribute. If a checkbox is not checked, then no name/value pair will be
sent to the Web server. So, if it is important that a value be sent to the Web
server whether an alternative has been checked or not, it is better to use
radio buttons.

Also if the **checked** attribute is included, then the checkbox will be initially set to the 'checked' state:

```
Choose the computer features to refine your query:<br>
Is a name brand computer <input type=checkbox name=IsNameBrand _
   value=yes checked><br>
Has at least 16 MB of memory <input type=checkbox name=16MBPlus _
   value=yes checked><br>
Accepts 220 voltage power sources <input type=checkbox _
   name=Handles220Volts value=yes>
```

In this example, the HTML author assumes that most people would be
looking for a name-brand computer with at least 16 MB of memory, so
both of these items have the attribute **checked** included with their **input**
tags, but not everyone requires 220 volts compatibility so no **checked** attribute was included for this checkbox field. The resulting name/value
pairs string would be:

```
IsNameBrand=yes&16MBPlus=yes
```

You can also group checkboxes. The critical difference between grouped checkboxes and grouped radio buttons is that for grouped checkboxes, the **name** will be transmitted to the Web server for every checked item.

```
Enter all of the credit cards that you have:<br>
Visa <input type=checkbox name=CreditCard value=Visa>
Master Card <input type=checkbox name=CreditCard value=MCard>
American Express <input type=checkbox name=CreditCard value=Amex>
```

When the user checks both the Visa and Amex checkboxes (Figure 4.6), the Web browser will form the name/value pairs:

```
CreditCard=Visa&CreditCard=Amex
```

It is up to the server extension program to store the various values to the same field name *cumulatively*. If the server extension program doesn't process the fields this way, then only the last value, **Amex**, will be saved.

Range fields (type=range)

A range field is a single-line text field where the values are limited to a numeric range. This type is specified in the HTML 3.0 draft specification, but at the time of writing neither Netscape Navigator 2.0 nor Microsoft Internet Explorer 2.0 had implemented this feature. We are showing it here to provide an example of an input validation field. **Range** is used in conjunction with **min**=*n* and **max**=*n* attributes. If either of the **min** or **max** values are real numbers, then real numbers will be allowed, otherwise only integer values will be allowed. The HTML 3.0 specification states that a

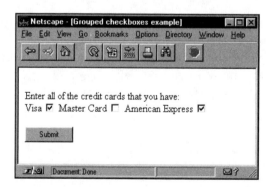

Figure 4.6 Grouped checkboxes.

default value will be calculated to be the average of the **min** and **max** values. In this snippet, we have specified a number between 1 and 100 and set the default value to 1:

```
Enter quantity: <input type=range name=Qty min=1 max=100 value=1>
```

Hidden fields (type=hidden)

Server extension programs use hidden fields to hold information. Users cannot see them or enter data into them. One use for hidden fields is to add validation rules to input fields (Figure 4.7).

As an example, Cold Fusion's CGI server extension program uses hidden fields to do server-side input validations, including range checking. To range-check this field, we defined a text field to accept input from the user and we then added a hidden field with the validation rule. Here is the code:

```
<form method=POST action=/cgi-shl/dbml.exe?template=question.dbm>
    How many hours a day do you spend on WWW?
    <input type=text name=WWWPoll size=5>
    <input type=hidden name=WWWPoll_range VALUE="MIN=0 MAX=24" >
    <input type=submit value="Submit answer">
</form>
```

When the user enters a value into the **WWWPoll** field and submits the form, the Cold Fusion server extension program scans the input form for validation rules. For Cold Fusion, a validation rule is identified as a hidden field in which the hidden field's name is an amalgamation of both the input field's name and the validation rule's name, separated by an '_'. In

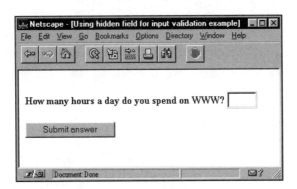

Figure 4.7   Using a hidden field for input validation.

this case, the validation rule's name is 'WWWPoll_range'. If Cold Fusion determines that this rule has been violated, then it returns an HTML page explaining the error and asking the user to return to the previous input form and try again.

Some developers of server extension programs use hidden fields to provide a way to add custom information to forms, including input field validation information. A completely different way to perform input validation would be to use the validation rules stored in the database server, but this would mean that the input field would be stored in the HTML document and the validation rule would be stored in the database. So, maintenance would be more difficult. Hidden fields keep the input field and the validation rule in the same HTML document.

Submit button (type=submit)

The **submit** button type allows the HTML author to specify a button that sends data that has been entered into an input field to the Web server.

The **value** attribute specifies the button's label. When the **name** attribute is used, a name/value pair string is submitted to the Web server, which is useful when multiple **submit** buttons are used on a form. For example, Figure 4.8 shows an input screen where the user could press the '**Purchase Now**' button or the '**Save Shopping Cart**' button. Without a **name** attribute, no name/value pair will be sent to the server, which means that the identity of which button was pressed would be lost. Here is how the **name** attribute is used:

```
<input type=submit name=UserAction value="Purchase Now">
<input type=submit name=UserAction value="Save Shopping Cart">
```

If no name attribute is specified, neither the name/value pair **UserRequest=Purchase+Now** nor **UserRequest=Save+Shopping+Cart** will be sent to the Web server.

Reset buttons (type=reset)

A reset button is used to reset all the input fields to their initial values (Figure 4.9).

Figure 4.8 Submit buttons.

Like the **submit** button, you can specify a label by using the **name** attribute:

```
<input type=submit value="Click here to sign in">
<input type=reset value="Reset screen">
```

The Textarea Tag

Use the **<textarea>...</textarea>** tags to create a multi-line window that users can edit and can contain an optional initial text value set by the HTML author (Figure 4.10).

Both tags are always required, even if no initial text is specified. The **name** attribute is used to identify this field. The **rows** and **cols** attributes define

Figure 4.9 Reset button.

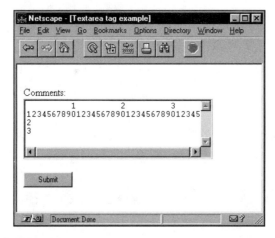

Figure 4.10   The **textarea** tag.

the visible height and width of the text area, but entered text can extend beyond these boundaries by using horizontal and vertical scroll bars. For example, the **textarea** field named **notes** is set to be 5 rows high and 35 characters wide as shown below:

```
<textarea name=notes rows=5 cols=35>
         1         2         3
123456789012345678901234567890012345
2
3
</textarea>
```

The text is displayed in a fixed-width font, so the characters of your initial text will be completely displayed if kept within these limits.

For Netscape 2.0 browsers, the text can word-wrap in various ways. The attribute **wrap** can be set to **off**, **virtual** or **physical**.

- **wrap=off** means that no word-wrapping occurs. Lines are sent to the Web server exactly as they are.

- **wrap=virtual** means that individual lines will word-wrap on the screen, and when they are sent to the Web server, each word-wrapped line will be sent as one continuous, long line.

- **wrap=physical** means that lines will word-wrap on the screen, but when they are sent to the Web server, each screen line will send as an individual line.

For example, this snippet turns word-wrapping on and only puts line breaks at the end of each paragraph:

```
<textarea name=notes rows=5 cols=35 wrap=virtual>
</textarea>
```

The Select Tag

You can use the **<select>...</select>** tags to show a set of input options in a compact way. This feature is particularly useful when there are several options (Figure 4.11).

To specify the options, use the **<option>** tag for each option item. This tag has a set of attributes, but can be used 'as is' with only the descriptive text following and without a closing tag. The code snippet shows a dropdown listbox with field name **product**:

```
<select name=Product>
<option>Kona coffee
<option>Blue Mountain
<option>Java
</select>
```

To designate a listbox, use the **size** attribute and specify the number of options to show at once. To specify that the user can choose more than one option, use the **multiple** attribute (Figure 4.12).

Figure 4.11 A dropdown listbox.

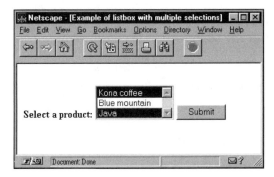

Figure 4.12 Regular listbox with multiple selections.

For example, to specify a listbox that shows three visible rows and allows multiple selections:

```
<select name=Product size=3 multiple>
<option>Kona coffee
<option>Blue mountain
<option>Java
</select>
```

When you select an **option**, its value will be the descriptive text following the **option** tag. For instance, choosing **Kona coffee** would cause the Web browser to form the name/value pair **Product=Kona+coffee**. It would be better if the browser used Kona Coffee's product code for its value instead. This would make database querying and maintaining the Web page easier. To do this, the **option** tag has a **value** attribute and when you use it, the name/value pair will contain the option's **value** rather than its descriptive text:

```
<select name=Product size=3 multiple>
<option value=CF101>Kona coffee
<option value=CF201>Blue mountain
<option value=CF301>Java
</select>
```

Now choosing **Kona coffee** results in the name/value pair **Product=CF101**.

Finally, if you want to set an initial **option**, use the attribute **selected**. For instance, to specify that the **Java** option is initially highlighted, use:

```
<select name=Product size=3 multiple>
<option value=CF101>Kona coffee
<option value=CF201>Blue mountain
<option value=CF301 selected>Java
</select>
```

For the Netscape 2.0 browser, you can designate more than one **selected** attribute when the **multiple** attribute in the **select** tag is used. The same warning that applies to grouped checkboxes applies here: For multiple selections, multiple name/value pairs are sent to the CGI program. Unless the CGI program is able to handle the values *cumulatively* for the same field, only the last value will be preserved.

Using JavaScript for Input Validation

When it comes to handling input validation, the HTML 3.0 draft specification is weak. For simple applications, input validation could be handled by a server extension program, but for applications with many fields, the multiple validation loops would be too slow and annoying to the user. A better way would be to provide the browser with input validation capability, and this is one of the things JavaScript is good for.

JavaScript is an interpreted, object-based scripting language that has predefined objects and functions. They include 'loose typing' (which means that when a variable is assigned a value, the variable takes on the type of the value that has been assigned to it), and a small number of data types (numeric, Boolean and string). These features make JavaScript easy to use and accessible to a wide audience of developers. At the time of writing, JavaScript was available only in the Netscape 2.0 browser, but has a good chance of becoming more widely used because the companies that license Java from Netscape and Sun also get a royalty-free license to JavaScript and may incorporate it in their browsers. (Oracle, IBM, and Microsoft are among the many Java/JavaScript licensees.)

Java could also be used to give the Netscape browser full control of each input field, so why use JavaScript? One problem with Java applets is that the input fields look different than standard HTML input fields do. This is not a problem when the entire application revolves around the Java applet, but in cases where HTML input forms will almost do the job, or when the developer wants to use HTML tables for displaying output, it is a shame to switch over to a full Java applet. Another 'problem' with Java is that because it is a full-strength programming language it requires considerable skill from its users. However, JavaScript is simple enough that someone whose programming experience only includes writing spreadsheet macros could use it.

The following section shows how to use JavaScript to create an input form containing two fields that do input validation: the first field will accept only integers between minimum and maximum values, and the second field will accept only email addresses.

Integer Range Input Field

An input type specified in the HTML 3.0 draft specification is **type=range**. We touched on this briefly in the **type** section and noted that it was not implemented in the Netscape 2.0 browser, so we will create this validation loop with JavaScript. The field should accept integers within a range specified by a minimum and a maximum value. If the number is not within the specified range, then an error message should be displayed to indicate the correct range. If the user enters any characters that are not digits, then an error message indicating that only digits are allowed should appear when the user tries to move to another field or presses the **submit** button. Finally, if the user leaves the field blank, an error message should be displayed stating that an integer is required.

The JavaScript function **isValidInt** in Listing 4.1 fulfills these requirements.

Listing 4.1   Integer input validation function isValidInt

```
// Function: isValidInt
// Purpose:  check for valid integer within a range.
function isValidInt(str, min, max) {

    // check for blank field
    if (str == "") {
        alert("Enter an integer in the field, please.")
        return false
    }

    // check for non-digits
    for (var i = 0; i < str.length; i++) {
```

```
        var ch = str.charAt(i)
        if (ch < "0" || ch > "9") {
           alert("Only digits are allowed.")
           return false
        }
    }

    // check if within range
    var val = parseInt(str, 10)
    if ((val < min) || (val > max)) {
      alert("Try an integer from " + min + " to " + max)
      return false
    }
    return true
}
```

The function **isValidInt**, like all JavaScript functions, begins with the key-word '**function**' followed by the function name and a list of arguments separated by commas. These arguments are dynamically typed. This means that when the **isValidInt** function is invoked the arguments take on the data type of the value that was passed to them. Numerics, Booleans, and string values can be passed to each argument. In this case, **isValidInt** is expecting a string followed by two numbers.

The benefit of not having to deal with variable types is that it simplifies coding and reduces the learning curve. However, type safety (statically typed data) is an important part of all major programming languages because bugs are brought to the surface by the compiler, where they can be caught rather than letting them become buried to cause havoc later. Neverthe-less, since a scripting language is meant for a wide audience and is only meant to supplement an application, 'loose typing' is a better choice than 'type safety'.

The first part of the **isValidInt** function checks for a blank field (text fol-lowing the '//' is a comment).

```
// check for blank field
if (str == "") {
   alert("Enter an integer in the field, please.")
   return false
}
```

If nothing is entered, a dialog message box will be displayed with an appropriate error message. When the user clicks the OK button in the message box, the function will return **false** to the calling routine.

As mentioned before, the syntax of JavaScript resembles Java, which in turn is similar to C++. For example, the equality operator in the first **if** statement is '=='. This should look familiar to those familiar with C or C++. Or take the **for** loop, which checks each character of the string:

```
// check for non-digits
for (var i = 0; i < str.length; i++) {
    var ch = str.charAt(i)
    if (ch < "0" || ch > "9") {
        alert("Only digits are allowed.")
        return false
    }
}
```

It looks exactly like a **for** loop in C++ with its ability to declare the auto variable **i** inside the **for** construct. The only difference is that the keyword **var** is used instead of a specific data type.

The **for** loop needs to know how many characters were entered. This can be obtained from the variable **str**. JavaScript is based on an object-oriented model, which means that variables are treated as objects. A JavaScript object has properties and methods associated with it. To access a property of an object, use the notation:

```
objectName.propertyName
```

In this example, the string property **length** contains the length of a string object. So, using the above notation, **str.length**, retrieves the number of characters entered. Note that property names are case sensitive.

In addition to properties, an object has methods. In JavaScript, methods are functions associated with an object. A method is called using this notation:

```
objectName.methodname(args)
```

For the function **isValidInt**, the variable **str** calls the method **charAt** with the position of the character to return. Note, that in JavaScript, **0** is the first position in a string and that object names are case sensitive.

The rest of the **for** loop checks each character to see if it is in a valid character range from '**0**' to '**9**'. If any are outside this range, then an appropriate message box is displayed and returns **false**.

Finally, if the string **str** passes these checks, then the next step is to turn **str** into an integer. The methods associated with a string object can only return variations on the string itself, so to convert **str** to an integer, you need to use one of the built-in JavaScript functions. The function we need is **parseInt,** which takes in a string and a radix and converts the string into an integer in a given number base (radix).

Once **str** has been converted, the integer range can be checked. If the integer is found to be outside the given range, an error message composed of the entered value and the range limits is displayed, as the code snippet below shows:

```
// check if within range
var val = parseInt(str, 10)
if ((val < min) || (val > max)) {
    alert("Error: You entered " + val + ".  Try an integer from " + _
      min + " to " + max)
    return false
}
```

Although **min** and **max** are integer types, JavaScript's loose typing permits the concatenation of literal strings with numerics using the '+' operator without a lot of fuss. If the range limits are set to 101 and 808 and an input string of 900 has been entered...

```
isValidInt("900", 101, 808)
```

then the composite error message would be as shown in Figure 4.13.

So far we've described the basics of creating a JavaScript function, working with objects and properties, and creating an error message. It is actually

Figure 4.13   Displaying an error message.

quite easy to integrate this with HTML input forms, but before we explain this, let's create another input validation field that accepts only email addresses.

Email Address Input Field

The requirements for this input validation field are to only accept email addresses and to display an appropriate error message if something different is entered. This implementation only checks if there is an '**@**' symbol somewhere in the input string, which falls short of doing a thorough job. That's because there is a rarely used alternate style of email address that does not use the **@** symbol, but it gives us an example to work with.

The function we defined is called **isValidEmailAddress** and is shown in Listing 4.2:

Listing 4.2   Input validation function for email addresses— isValidEmailAddress

```
// Function: isValidEmailAddress
// Purpose:  to check for a valid email address
function isValidEmailAddress(str) {
   // check for blank field
   if (str == "") {
      alert("Enter an email address in the field, please.")
      return false
   }
   // check for '@' sign
   else if (str.indexOf("@", 0) == -1) {
      alert("Error: You entered " + str + ". Email addresses should _
         have an '@' in it.");
      return false
   }
   return true
}
```

It is similar to the previous input validation function in that the first part of the code checks for a blank string. If the string is blank, then the function displays an error message and returns **false** to the calling routine.

The second part of the code scans the variable **str** for the '**@**' symbol, so we need a JavaScript method to search a string for a particular character. The string method **indexof** takes as input a string to search for and a starting position to search from. The second argument is optional and if no starting position is specified, then it defaults to **0**. The first argument is capable of searching for substrings in strings. If the '**@**' symbol is found, then this method returns the position, and if it is not found, then the method returns **-1**. In that case, we create a composite error message, which informs the user what was entered and what is required.

Although this is a simplified input field validation function, it is a definite improvement over having no validation at all. Also, doing input validation on the server side involves returning error messages via HTML pages, so it is much more interactive if the user sees a pop-up error message box instead.

Putting It Together

Now that we have created two different input validation functions, it is time to see how well they integrate with HTML input forms. One way to call a JavaScript function is to place the call between **<script>**...**</script>** tags in the **body** of the HTML document. For instance, placing the **alert** function as shown:

```
<body>
<script>
alert("Hello World!")
</script>
</body>
```

would display a '**Hello World!**' message box as soon as the HTML page was loaded. We will discuss the **<script>** tags later because they are used to declare our JavaScript functions in the HTML document.

Another way to call a JavaScript function is by defining it to be an event handler. An event handler is a function that gets called when an event occurs. (An event is an action such as a click of the mouse button.) The Netscape browser passes events to an event handler, which acts on them. By designating a particular function for a particular event, the Netscape browser invokes that function every time that event occurs. The events that the Netscape browser recognizes are shown in Table 4.1:

An event handler is specified in an HTML tag as an attribute. The general notation is:

```
<TAG eventHandler="JavaScript Code">
```

For instance, our integer input field validator function could be specified as:

```
<input type=text name=AreaCodeField value="" size=8 _
    onChange="isValidInt(this.value, 101, 808)">
```

The **isValidInt** function is designated as the **onChange** event handler for this field. This means that after the user enters a value and moves the focus out of that field, **isValidInt** is called to validate the entered value. Two things to note: First, because an event handler function is specified between double quotes, any literal strings between those double quotes must be delimited by single quotes to prevent conflict. For example:

```
<input type=text name=test onChange="isValidInt('900', 101, 808)">
```

Table 4.1   The conditions that trigger an event handler.

Event Handler	Trigger condition
onBlur	User removes focus from a form element
onClick	User clicks on a form element or link
onChange	A text, text area or select field loses focus and its value has changed
onFocus	User sets focus to a form element
onLoad	When an HTML page is loaded
onMouseOver	User moves the mouse pointer over a link or anchor
onSelect	User selects text within a text or text area
onSubmit	User presses the submit button
onUnload	When an HTML page is unloaded

Second, the keyword **this** refers to the current object. In this case, **this** refers to the input field and **this.value** refers to its data. You can also refer to the form that the input field is in as **this.form**.

The **onChange** event handler is invoked when the user exits the input field. What if the user decides to just press the **submit** button without even going into that field? Then the form would be submitted without the field being validated. To prevent this, you can use the **onSubmit** event handler, which is placed as an attribute in the **<form>** tag. For instance, we wrote a function **checkAll,** which validates all the input fields and only submits the data if they are *all* valid. This is specified in the form tag as:

```
<form name=MainForm method=POST action=inputjs.html onSubmit="return _
    checkAll()">
```

When the user presses the **submit** button, **checkAll** is invoked and returns a Boolean. This return value is passed on to the form by using the keyword **return**. If the function returns **true**, then the form is submitted to the Web server, but if it returns **false**, then the form will not be submitted. So as you can see, you can not only control the input fields, but you can control the form as well.

The other new attribute in the **form** tag is the **name** attribute, which is used to identify the form in the same way input fields are identified. By naming the form, a JavaScript function can access each of the form elements. For instance, to access the value of the **AreaCodeField** you could enter the statement:

```
document.MainForm.AreaCodeField.value
```

The **document** object is the current HTML document. One of the document's properties is the form we named **MailForm**. One of **MailForm's** properties is the input field **AreaCodeField**. And finally, one of **AreaCodeField's** properties is **value,** which gives us the value that we wanted.

Now let's take a closer look at the function **checkAll** that we designated as the **onSubmit** event handler. The requirements are that if any of the input fields are invalid, then this function should return **false**. If all the fields have been validated, then this function should display all the inputs and give the user a last chance to double-check them and press OK or Cancel. Listing 4.3 shows the function that accomplishes this:

Listing 4.3 Form level event handler function—checkAll

```
// Function: checkAll
// Purpose:  verify all fields and confirm before submitting
function checkAll() {
   if (!isValidInt(document.MainForm.AreaCodeField.value, 101, 808))
      return false
   else if _
      (!isValidEmailAddress(document.MainForm.EmailAddressField.value))
      return false
   else {
      if (confirm("Please double check? Area Code = " + _
         document.MainForm.AreaCodeField.value + " Email address = " + _
         document.MainForm.EmailAddressField.value))
           return true
      else
           return false
   }
}
```

This function calls both input field validation functions. Once each function returns true, a confirmation message box will pop up. This message box is similar to the alert message box, except it also has a Cancel button. If the user presses the OK button, **confirm** returns **true**. But if the user presses the Cancel button, **confirm** returns **false**, which in turns causes **checkAll** to return **false**. This in turn, returns **false** to the form and prevents submission of the form.

Okay, now we are about ready to put all of the pieces together to see how all this fits together. The only remaining piece is to explain where to place JavaScript functions in the HTML document. If you remember, earlier we said that the first way of calling JavaScript is to use the **<script>...</script>** tags. Placing JavaScript function definitions between these tags loads them into memory. The best place to put these function definitions is in the head part of the HTML document. Doing this allows the functions to be loaded into memory before the body of the document is loaded, which is important because any JavaScript functions that are called in the body need to be in memory already. The order of things is important in JavaScript and being aware of this can help when you are faced with JavaScript error messages.

The **script** tag has an optional attribute that identifies the language in use:

```
<script language="JavaScript">
```

This is not that important right now, but could be important in the future when more scripting languages become available.

Finally, browsers that are not JavaScript-enabled might think the JavaScript code is text and try to display it, so it is best to enclose all of the functions within one pair of comment tags <!-- ... -->, making it look like one big comment. Be sure to use '-->' to end the comment, as opposed to the older style of just '>', so it won't conflict with any '>' symbols that may be used in your function definitions. Here is an example:

```
<script language="JavaScript">
<!-- hide script from old browsers
function HelloDB() {
    alert("Hello Database")
}
// end hiding from old browsers -->
</script>
```

Now we are ready to put all the pieces together, as Listing 4.4:

Listing 4.4   Using JavaScript for input field validation— inputjs.html

```
<html>
<head>
<title>Input Validation using JavaScript</title>
<script language="JavaScript">
<!-- hide script from old browsers

// Function: isValidInt
// Purpose:  check for valid integer within a range.
function isValidInt(str, min, max) {
```

```
    // check for blank field
    if (str == "") {
       alert("Enter an integer in the field, please.")
       return false
    }

    // check for non-digits
    for (var i = 0; i < str.length; i++) {
       var ch = str.charAt(i)
       if (ch < "0" || ch > "9") {
         alert("Only digits are allowed.")
           return false
       }
    }

    // check if within range
    var val = parseInt(str, 10)
    if ((val < min) || (val > max)) {
       alert("Error: You entered " + val + ".  Try an integer from " + _
         min + " to " + max)
         return false
    }
    return true
}


// Function: isValidEmailAddress
// Purpose:  to check for a valid email address
function isValidEmailAddress(str) {
   // check for blank field
   if (str == "") {
      alert("Enter an email address in the field, please.")
      return false
   }
   // check for '@' sign
   else if (str.indexOf("@", 0) == -1) {
      alert("Error: You entered " + str + ". Email addresses should _
         have  an '@' in it.");
      return false
   }
   return true
}


// Function: checkAll
// Purpose:  verify all fields and confirm before submitting
function checkAll() {
   if (!isValidInt(document.MainForm.AreaCodeField.value, 101, 808))
```

```
            return false
        else if _
            (!isValidEmailAddress(document.MainForm.EmailAddressField.value))
            return false
        else {
            if (confirm("Please double check? Area Code = " + _
                document.MainForm.AreaCodeField.value + " Email address = " + _
                document.MainForm.EmailAddressField.value))
                return true
            else
                return false
        }
}


// end hiding from old browsers -->
</script>

</head>

<body>

<form name=MainForm method=POST action=inputjs.html onSubmit="return _
    checkAll()">

Enter your area code between 101 and 808:<br>
    <input type=text name=AreaCodeField value="" size=8 _
        onChange="isValidInt(this.value, 101, 808)">
<br>
Enter an email address:<br>
    <input type=text name=EmailAddressField value="" _
        onChange="isValidEmailAddress(this.value)">
<p>
    <input type=submit name=button value="Test">

</form>

</body>
</html>
```

Load this HTML document:

```
\BookData\Docs\Chap4\inputjs.html
```

into the Netscape 2.0 browser and try entering various values. Invalid values will result in error messages as soon as the user moves the focus out of the current field. If you press the **Submit** button with any of the fields set incorrectly or left blank, then an error message will appear and the form will not be submitted. If the results are valid, the user gets one last chance to decide whether to send the input form, or not, as shown in Figure 4.14.

In this example, you can tell when the form has been submitted because the HTML page will reload and reset all the fields. In a real Web database application, validated inputs would be sent to the Web server, where a CGI program would use the data for querying or updating the database.

As you test out this input form, imagine how difficult it would be for the user to have to deal with each error message by resubmitting the input form to the server for validation. Doing as much of the input validation on the client side as possible will result in much more responsive Web database applications.

Displaying Database Query Results

Web pages dynamically reformat the information that they display. So, to display database results, you need to understand how to lay out text in an environment where the font and viewing area are not completely controlled by the HTML author. The techniques for accomplishing this apply equally to designing input screens, so because the techniques are so similar, we will only focus on how to display database results.

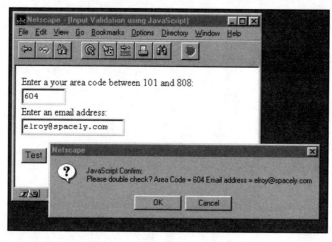

Figure 4.14   Valid input ready to be sent to the Web server.

There are two ways to display database results using HTML: preformatted text or tables. Using preformatted text means displaying text in a fixed-width font so that the alignment of data is correct in all browsers. Using tables means tagging the data as table elements. Tables have the advantage over preformatted text because they can use variable-width fonts and still maintain proper alignment. Tables are part of the HTML 3.0 draft specification.

Generally speaking, using HTML to display data is not as controllable as it is with database client development tools. This is because the data must be displayed on various browsers, in variably sized viewing areas, and with user-selected fonts. Nevertheless, the universality of the Web browser's interface is very appealing to users and provides consistency and predictability.

Displaying Results As Preformatted Text

Displaying text in a fixed-width font is done with the **<pre>**...**</pre>** tags. Text between these tags will be displayed exactly as laid out in the HTML document (Figure 4.15). This does not mean that the rendering will be the same for different users or Web browsers, since the user controls the type and size of fixed-width font. Nevertheless, columns of text will remain columnar, and if the user narrows the browser's viewable space, then the text will not wrap (Figure 4.16). This snippet uses the **<pre>**...**</pre>** tags:

```
<pre>
ID Name                   Phone Number    Email address
1  Fred Flintstone        (808) 987-6543  fred@bedrock.com
8  Pebbles Flintstone     (808) 987-6543  pebbles@bedrock.com
2  Wilma Flintstone       (808) 987-6543  wilma@bedrock.com
</pre>
```

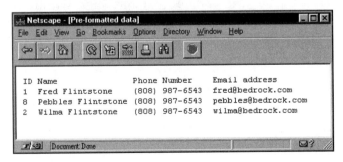

Figure 4.15 Preformatted data.

Figure 4.16   Preformatted text in a narrower view.

Use preformatted text for simple layouts or when the audience might have browsers that do not support tables. In general, tables should be used whenever possible (this applies to input screens as well).

Displaying Query Results in a Table

HTML tables are indispensable for displaying database query results and they are also essential for laying out input screens. What makes tables so powerful is that each cell dynamically optimizes itself for best viewing. This means that if the user narrows the browser, then the data in each table cell will try to accommodate to the change by wrapping.

The discussion of tables covers the features implemented in the Netscape 2.0 browser. The current HTML 3.0 draft specification discusses more table features than are implemented in any major browser.

HTML Table Essentials

Define an HTML table with **<table>...</table>** tags. Within these tags are additional tags that specify the table row **<tr>...</tr>**, data cell **<td>...</td>**, header cell **<th>...</th>**, and caption **<caption>...</caption>**. Each table tag also has a set of attributes that change its characteristics.

This illustration (Figure 4.17) shows a very simple table that would be sufficient for simple columnar reports, consisting of three columns, each labeled with a header, and a caption at the top. This code snippet shows how to do this:

```
<table>
   <caption align=top><b>Simple Table</b></caption>
   <tr>
      <th>Col1<th>Col2<th>Col3
   <tr>
      <td>Cell11<td>Cell12<td>Cell13
   <tr>
      <td>Cell21<td>Cell22<td>Cell23
   <tr>
      <td>Cell31<td>Cell32<td>Cell33
</table>
```

The **caption** tag requires both start and end tags. Any text between these tags becomes the caption of the table. The caption's placement relative to the table is determined by the **align** attribute. It can be **top** or **bottom**. Note that **left** or **right** is specified in the HTML 3.0 draft specification, but has not been implemented in Netscape browser 2.0. Another difference is that, in Netscape, it defaults to **top** whereas in the HTML 3.0 draft it is deliberately left unspecified.

Use the tags **<tr>**, **<th>**, and **<td>** to define the table itself. All of these tags have *optional* end tags. However, when we embedded a table within a table with the optional end tags left off, Microsoft Internet Explorer 2.0 displayed these tables correctly, but the Netscape 2.0 browser displayed them incorrectly.

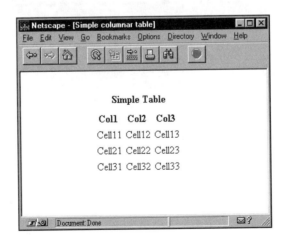

Figure 4.17   Simple columnar table.

The tag **<tr>** defines the start of a row. Following this tag are tags that identify the table cell type such as **<th>** for header cell, or **<td>** for data cell. The header cell is used mainly for labeling columns and rows. The data cell is used to display each database item.

You can change the look of the table by changing attributes. The attributes that work with most browsers are: **border** (Figure 4.18), **width** (Figure 4.19), **cellpadding** (Figure 4.20) and **cellspacing** (Figure 4.21).

- **border, border=**n—specifying this tag puts a visible border around the table and between cells. You can specify an optional border width. For example, **border=5**, sets the border thickness to 5 pixels.

- **width=**n —specifies the table width, where n is width in pixels. The width can be a percentage of the window width when '%' is used. For example, **width=50%** sets the table to half the width of the browser's window.

- **cellpadding=**n —specifies the amount of space to pad around inside the cell (both horizontally and vertically), where n is in pixels.

- **cellspacing=**n —specifies the amount of space between cells, where n is in pixels. This is done by 'thickening' up all the borders (both around the table and between cells).

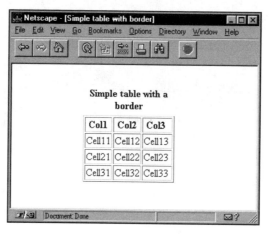

Figure 4.18   A simple table with a border.

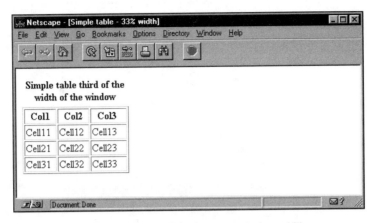

Figure 4.19   A simple table that is 33% of the browser window width.

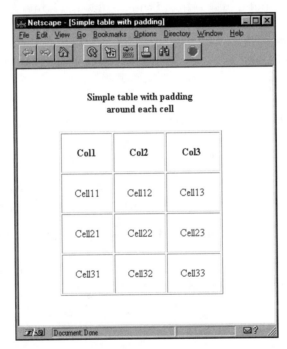

Figure 4.20   A simple table with padding around each cell.

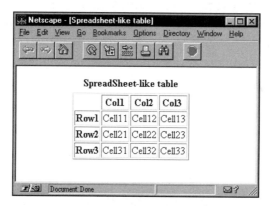

Figure 4.21   A simple table where the cells are kept apart.

The HTML snippet that produced the display in Figure 4.18 follows:

```
<table border>
    <caption align=top><b>Simple table with a border</b></caption>
    <tr>
        <th>Col1<th>Col2<th>Col3
    <tr>
        <td>Cell11<td>Cell12<td>Cell13
    <tr>
        <td>Cell21<td>Cell22<td>Cell23
    <tr>
        <td>Cell31<td>Cell32<td>Cell33
</table>
```

The HTML snippet that produced the display in Figure 4.19 follows:

```
<table border width=33%>
    <caption align=top><b>Simple table half the width of the _
        window<b></caption>
    <tr>
        <th>Col1<th>Col2<th>Col3
    <tr>
        <td>Cell11<td>Cell12<td>Cell13
    <tr>
        <td>Cell21<td>Cell22<td>Cell23
    <tr>
        <td>Cell31<td>Cell32<td>Cell33
</table>
```

The HTML snippet that produced the display in Figure 4.20 follows:

```
<table border cellpadding=20>
   <caption align=top><b>Simple table with padding around each _
      cell</b></caption>
   <tr>
      <th>Col1<th>Col2<th>Col3
   <tr>
      <td>Cell11<td>Cell12<td>Cell13
   <tr>
      <td>Cell21<td>Cell22<td>Cell23
   <tr>
      <td>Cell31<td>Cell32<td>Cell33
</table>
```

The HTML snippet that produced the display in Figure 4.21 follows:

```
<table border cellspacing=20>
   <caption align=top><b>Simple table where the cells are kept _
      apart</b></caption>
   <tr>
      <th>Col1<th>Col2<th>Col3
   <tr>
      <td>Cell11<td>Cell12<td>Cell13
   <tr>
      <td>Cell21<td>Cell22<td>Cell23
   <tr>
      <td>Cell31<td>Cell32<td>Cell33
</table>
```

As you can see, these simple **table** attributes can affect the overall look of the table quite a bit. The HTML 3.0 draft specification contains more table attributes, but these have not yet been implemented by Netscape or Microsoft.

Rows and Columns

The attributes of table rows and table cells can also change the look of a table. For instance, you can make a table look like a spreadsheet by using the tag **<th>** instead of **<td>** for the first element of each row (Figure 4.22).

Database Publishing on the Web and Intranets

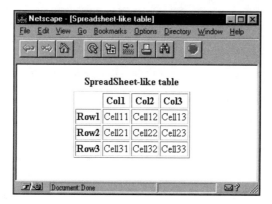

Figure 4.22 A spreadsheet-like table.

The HTML snippet that produced the display in Figure 4.22 follows:

```
<table border width=50%>
   <caption align=top><b>Spreadsheet-like table</b></caption>
   <tr>
      <th><th>Col1<th>Col2<th>Col3
   <tr>
      <th>Row1<td>Cell11<td>Cell12<td>Cell113
   <tr>
      <th>Row2<td>Cell121<td>Cell122<td>Cell123
   <tr>
      <th>Row3<td>Cell131<td>Cell132<td>Cell133
</table>
```

In a spreadsheet, you can resize individual column widths to make the cells easier to read. To accomplish this with tables, use the **width** attribute in the table data or header cell tags. To set the second column to a width of 100 pixels, use **width=100** in the table row tag as shown in Figure 4.23. The browser will only set this width if the browser's viewing window is wide enough to display the entire table. Otherwise, it will be less than the specified amount.

The HTML snippet that produced the display in Figure 4.23 follows:

```
<table border width=75%>
   <caption align=top><b>Varying column widths</b></caption>
   <tr>
      <th><th width=100>Col1<th>Col2<th>Col3
```

```
   <tr align=center>
      <th>Row1<td width=100>Cell11<td>Cell12<td>Cell13
   <tr align=center>
      <th>Row2<td width=100>Cell121<td>Cell22<td>Cell23
   <tr align=center>
      <th>Row3<td width=100>Cell131<td>Cell32<td>Cell33
</table>
```

You can also specify the width by using a value that is a percentage of the table width. For instance, **width=75%** would create a column that is approximately 75 percent of the table's width. This works in the Netscape 2.0 browser, but not in Microsoft's 2.0 browser.

Note that the table cell attribute **width** is specific to certain browsers such as Netscape's browser or Microsoft's Internet Explorer. The HTML 3.0 draft specification uses a different approach to setting column attributes. It specifies column widths with two other tags, **<colgroup>** and **<col>**. The latter tag works within the former tag to characterize one or more columns, but these tags have not yet been implemented in either of the major browsers.

A simple way to improve the spreadsheet-like table is to add the attribute **rowspan=**n to the table cell tag. Use this attribute to specify the number of rows a cell can span across. This is quite a powerful feature because it allows tables to break out of the rigid row and column mold. For instance, adding **rowspan=3** to the previous spreadsheet table changes the look of the last column (Figure 4.24).

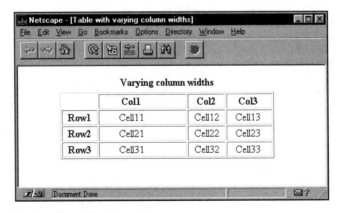

Figure 4.23   Varying the width of a column.

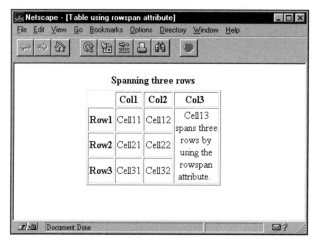

Figure 4.24 Using the **rowspan** attribute.

The HTML snippet that produced the display in Figure 4.24 follows:

```
<table border width=50%>
   <caption align=top><b>Spanning three rows</b></caption>
   <tr>
      <th><th>Col1<th>Col2<th>Col3
   <tr align=center>
      <th>Row1<td>Cell11<td>Cell12<td rowspan=3>Cell13 spans three rows _
         by using the rowspan attribute.
   <tr align=center>
      <th>Row2<td>Cell21<td>Cell22
   <tr align=center>
      <th>Row3<td>Cell31<td>Cell32
</table>
```

We placed the **rowspan** attribute on the last column, but we could have easily placed it on any column.

The complement of the attribute **rowspan** is the attribute **colspan=**n, which allows a table cell to span across columns. For example, adding **colspan=3** to the spreadsheet-like table changes the look of the last row (Figure 4.25).

The HTML snippet that produced the display in Figure 4.25 follows:

```
<table border width=50%>
   <caption align=top><b>Spanning three columns</b></caption>
   <tr>
```

```
        <th><th>Col1<th>Col2<th>Col3
    <tr align=center>
        <th>Row1<td>Cell11<td>Cell12<td>Cell13
    <tr align=center>
        <th>Row2<td>Cell21<td>Cell22<td>Cell23
    <tr align=center>
        <th>Row3<td colspan=3>Cell31 spans 3 cols
</table>
```

We could have placed the **colspan** attribute on any row.

You can use both attributes together to provide a nice way of presenting individual records from a database. For example, a simple employee record (Figure 4.26).

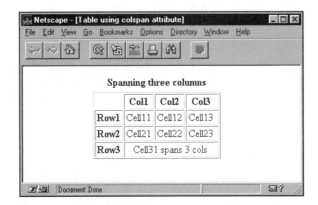

Figure 4.25   Using the **colspan** attribute.

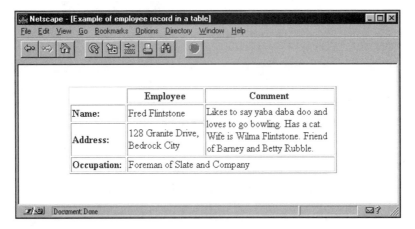

Figure 4.26   A sample employee record in a table.

The HTML snippet that produced the display in Figure 4.26 follows:

```
<table border width=75%>
    <tr><th><th>Employee<th>Comment
    <tr>
        <th align=left>Name:
        <td width=300>Fred Flintstone
        <td rowspan=2 valign=top> Likes to say yaba daba doo and loves to _
            go bowling.  Has a cat.  Wife is Wilma Flintstone.  Friend of _
            Barney and Betty Rubble.
    <tr>
        <th align=left>Address:
        <td>128 Granite Drive, Bedrock City
    <tr>
        <th align=left>Occupation:
        <td colspan=2>Foreman of Slate and Company
</table>
```

In this example, we introduced two new attributes: **align** and **valign**. These attributes apply to individual cells or to all the cells in a row. The first attribute, **align**, is used for aligning cells horizontally. Its attribute values are: **left**, **right**, and **center** which align the text to the left side, right side, or centered within the cell respectively. If all the cells of the row are to be horizontally aligned, then the **align** attribute should be placed in the **<tr>** tag. For example, all the cells of the row could be aligned at once (Figure 4.27):

The HTML snippet that produced the display in Figure 4.27 follows:

```
<table border width=75%>
<tr align=left>  <td>first<td>second<td>third
<tr align=right> <td>first<td>second<td>third
<tr align=center><td>first<td>second<td>third
</table>
```

Note that a single cell can override the row's cell alignment by simply including the **align** attribute in the cell's **<td>** tag.

The attribute values of **valign** are: **top**, **middle**, **bottom**, and **baseline**. The first three attribute values align the text to the top, vertical center, or bottom within the cell. Like **align**, vertical alignment can be done for an entire row by placing the attribute in the **<tr>** tag.

Figure 4.27 Using the align attribute.

The last attribute value, **baseline**, is used to align the first text line to a common baseline. This is mainly used when the table has both text and images and the images vary in size. For example, Figure 4.28 shows three cells with images of different sizes, but the first text line of each is aligned across the whole row.

The HTML snippet that produced the display in Figure 4.28 follows:

```
<table border width=100%>
   <tr valign=baseline>
      <td width=33%><img src=star.gif>first column of text
      <td width=33%><img src=news.gif>second column of text
      <td width=33%><img src=cart.gif>third column of text showing that _
         the first line is in each column is aligned to a common baseline.
</table>
```

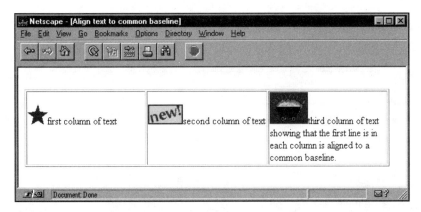

Figure 4.28 Aligning text to a common baseline.

Tables within a table

There are times when using combinations of the attributes **colspan** and **rowspan** won't give you the style of reporting you are looking for. It could be as simple as displaying a list of people's addresses with greater control of the border. For these and other situations, creating a table within a table might be the answer.

For example, let's say we want to display a series of employee records without row and column headings. We also want the employee information on the left and the comment on the right, and borders to separate records, but not the fields within records. The first step is to create a table for a single record (Figure 4.29):

The HTML snippet that produced the display in Figure 4.29 follows:

```
<table border=0 width=80%>
   <tr>
      <td width=50%>Fred Flintstone</td><td rowspan=3 valign=top>Likes _
         to say yaba daba doo and loves to go bowling. Has a cat. Wife _
         is Wilma Flintstone.  Friend of Barney and Betty Rubble.</td>
   </tr>
   <tr>
      <td>128 Granite Drive, Bedrock City</td>
   </tr>
   <tr>
      <td>Crane operator</td>
   </tr>
</table>
```

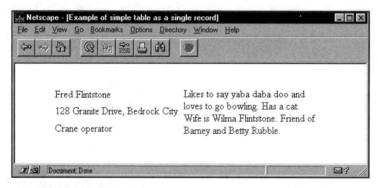

Figure 4.29   Simple table as a single record.

Notice that we used the optional end tags, **</td>** and, **</tr>**. This is not normally required, but Netscape 2.0 does not display this nested table correctly if the end tags are left out.

Now let's take that single record table and make it into a row in another table. When we add more 'table' records we get the table shown in Figure 4.30.

The HTML snippet that produced the display in Figure 4.30 follows:

```
<table border=1 width=80%>
   <caption align=top><b>Three tables within a table</b></caption>
   <tr>
      <td>
         <table border=0> <!-- first record table -->
            <tr>
               <td width=50%>Fred Flintstone</td><td rowspan=3 _
                  valign=top>Likes to say yaba daba doo and loves to _
                  go bowling.  Has a cat.  Wife is Wilma Flintstone. _
                  Friend of Barney and Betty Rubble.</td>
            </tr>
            <tr>
               <td>128 Granite Drive, Bedrock City</td>
            </tr>
            <tr>
               <td>Crane operator</td>
            </tr>
         </table>
      </td>
   </tr>
   <tr>
      <td>
         <table border=0> <!-- second record table -->
            <tr>
               <td width=50%>Barney Rubble</td><td rowspan=3 _
                  valign=top>Friend of Fred and Wilma Flintstone. _
                  Loves to go bowling. Wife is Betty Rubble.</td>
            </tr>
            <tr>
               <td>130 Granite Drive, Bedrock City</td>
            </tr>
            <tr>
               <td>Conveyor operator</td>
            </tr>
         </table>
      </td>
   </tr>
```

```
<tr>
   <td>
      <table border=0> <!-- third record table -->
         <tr>
            <td width=50%>Wilma Flintstone</td><td rowspan=3 _
               valign=top>Likes to cook and loves to go bowling. _
               Has a cat.  Husband is Fred Flintstone. Friend of _
               Barney and Betty Rubble.</td>
         </tr>
         <tr>
            <td>128 Granite Drive, Bedrock City</td>
         </tr>
         <tr>
            <td>Cafeteria worker</td>
         </tr>
      </table>
   </td>
</tr>
</table>
```

Putting tables in tables pretty much achieves the look we wanted. You could come close by using a single table, but it would still have a dividing border between the employee information and the comment on the right (Figure 4.31), which does not group the information as nicely.

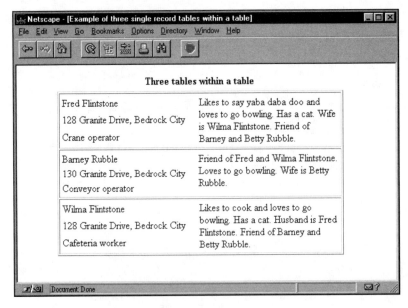

Figure 4.30   Three single record tables within a table.

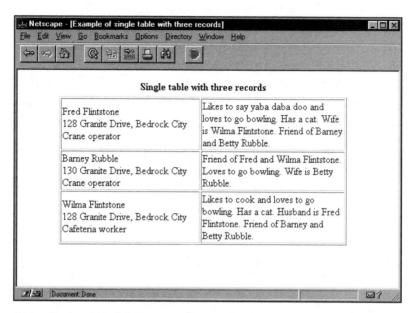

Figure 4.31 Single table with three records.

The HTML snippet that produced the display in Figure 4.31 follows:

```
<table border=1 width=80%>
    <caption align=top><b>Single table with three records</b></caption>
    <tr>
        <td width=50%>Fred Flintstone<br>128 Granite Drive, Bedrock _
        City<br>Crane operator</td>
        <td valign=top>Likes to say yaba daba doo and loves to go bowling. _
        Has a cat.  Wife is Wilma Flintstone.  Friend of Barney and _
        Betty Rubble.</td>
    <tr>
        <td width=50%>Barney Rubble<br>130 Granite Drive, Bedrock _
        City<br>Crane operator</td>
        <td valign=top>Friend of Fred and Wilma Flintstone.  Loves to go _
        bowling. Wife is Betty Rubble.</td>
    <tr>
        <td width=50%>Wilma Flintstone<br>128 Granite Drive, Bedrock _
        City<br>Cafeteria worker</td>
        <td valign=top>Likes to cook and loves to go bowling.  Has a cat. _
        Husband is Fred Flintstone. Friend of Barney and Betty _
        Rubble.</td>
</table>
```

One final note: As mentioned earlier, tables are not limited to just displaying output text. You can also use them to create good-looking input screens. For example, if you take the employee record table in Figure 4.26, and replace the text with input fields, then you have an input screen (Figure 4.32). We left the border visible to show how this works. However, to make it look more like a traditional input screen, the table border should be turned off.

The HTML snippet that produced the display in Figure 4.32 follows:

```
<table border>
 <caption align=bottom>
  <input type=submit value="Insert into database">
  <input type=reset  value="      Clear       ">
 </caption>
   <tr><th><th>Employee<th>Comment
   <tr>
      <th align=left>Name:
      <td><input type=text name=Name>
      <td rowspan=2><textarea name=comment rows=3 cols=25 _
        wrap=virtual>enter you comment here</textarea>
   <tr>
      <th align=left>Address:
      <td><input type=text name=Address>
   <tr>
      <th align=left>Occupation:
      <td colspan=2><input type=text name=Occupation size=50>
</table>
```

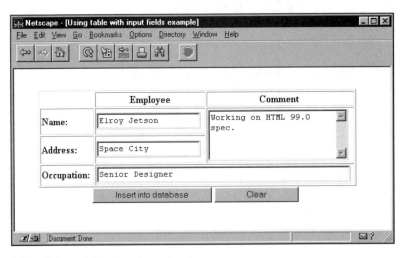

Figure 4.32   Using a table to make an input screen.

The 'Hello Database' Example

We created the Hello Database program to demonstrate the Web database products that are profiled in Chapters 5 to 10. It uses some of the HTML essentials discussed above and we stripped out as many nonessentials as possible to keep it simple and clear. The code for each product's Hello Database program is included on the CD-ROM so that readers can get their hands on it and experiment.

The basic Hello Database program performs a query and inserts a record into the database. The database is a simple flat-file phone list containing these fields:

- UserID (primary key)

- FirstName (text)

- LastName (text)

- AreaCode (text)

- Phone (text)

- EmailAddress (text)

Most of the server extension products profiled start with the HTML document, **phone.html,** which contains both the query and insert forms. In this chapter, we use HTML source code (Listing 4.5) written for Cold Fusion. (See also the file **\BookData\Demo\Cfusion\phone.html**.)

Listing 4.5   The main Hello Database HTML document—phone.html

```
<!-- Phone Number Demo for Cold Fusion -->

<html>

<head>
<title>Phone Number Demo for Cold Fusion</title>
</head>

<body>

<h1>Phone Number Demo for Cold Fusion</h1>
```

```
<hr>

<p>This demo shows how Cold Fusion can be used to do the two basic _
   database operations: query and insert.  The design of the demo and _
   its  <a href=#DATABASE>database</a> is kept extremely simple on _
   purpose so we won't confuse you with a lot of extraneous detail.</p>

<h2>Demo</h2>

Try out these operations to see how Cold Fusion implements these operations.

<ul>
<li><a href=#QUERY>Query</a> the phone number database
<li><a href=#INSERT>Insert</a> a phone number record
</ul>

<hr size=5>

<! -------------------- Q U E R Y ---------------------->

<a name=QUERY>
<h2>Query the phone number database</h2>
</a>

<p>Enter a last name (or partial name) and press the "Query Database" _
   button.  The "%" character is used as a wild card.  For example, _
   "J%" returns all last names that start with 'J'.  You can also set _
   the order of the output by selecting one of the choices in the Order _
   by list box.</p>

<form action=/cgi-shl/dbml.exe?template=getphone.dbm method=POST >

<pre>
   <b>Last name:</b><input type=TEXT name=LastName value= "%" _
     maxlength=25 size=25>

   <b>Order by:</b> <select name=OrderType>
     <option value=LastName selected> Last Name
     <option value=AreaCode> Area Code
     </select>
</pre>

<p><input type=submit value="Query Database" size=20></p>

</form>
```

```
<hr size=5>

<! -------------------- I N S E R T ---------------------->

<a name=INSERT>
<h2>Insert a phone number record</h2>
</a>

<p>Enter all the information for the new phone number record and press _
   the "Insert Record" button.  Then use the <a href=#QUERY>query</a> _
   operation above to confirm that it was inserted.</p>

<form action=/cgi-shl/dbml.exe?template=insphone.dbm method=POST>

<pre>
   <b>First Name:</b>    <input type=text name=FirstName value= "" _
      maxlength=20 size=10><b>    Last Name:</b><input type=text _
      name=LastName value= "" maxlength=20 size=13>
   <b>Area Code:</b>     <input type=text name=AreaCode value= "" _
      maxlength=5 size=5>        <b>Phone number:</b><input type=text _
      name=Phone value= "" maxlength=20 size=13>
   <b>Email Address:</b> <input type=text name=EmailAddress value= "" _
      maxlength=35 size=35>
</pre>   <input type=submit value="Insert Record" size=20>
</form>

<hr size=5>

<a name=DATABASE>
<h2>Database Fields</h2>
</a>

<p>The database for this demo is simply a flat file.  Here is a list of _
   the fields.</p>

<ul>
<li>UserID   (primary key)
<li>FirstName
<li>LastName
<li>AreaCode
<li>Phone
<li>EmailAddress
</ul>

</body>
</html>
```

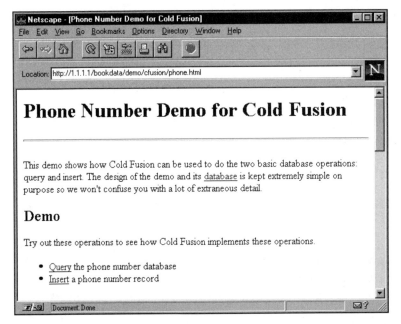

Figure 4.33 Hello Database screen.

The first screen from the Hello Database demo, Figure 4.33, shows the two hypertext links **Query** and **Insert**. Clicking on either of them takes you to an input screen, which tries the database operation on the Web database product. To see Cold Fusion perform a query, enter a last name or partial last name, and the order in which to display the results into the query input screen (Figure 4.34). Press the **Query Database** button and it will display an ordered result set (Figure 4.35).

Similarly, to see how Cold Fusion performs an insert, enter data into all of the input fields (Figure 4.36), and press the **Insert Record** button. To provide feedback to the user, the entered data will be displayed in an HTML page following the insert operation (Figure 4.37). To confirm the insertion, perform the query again to list the newly inserted record (Figure 4.38).

The Hello Database program is just a starting point in understanding the workings of a Web database product. Each product also comes with examples that are useful when you want to concentrate on the finer details. The Hello Database examples that go with each product profiled in Chapters 5 to 10 do not all implement the query and insert in exactly the same way, but they all follow the basic scenario.

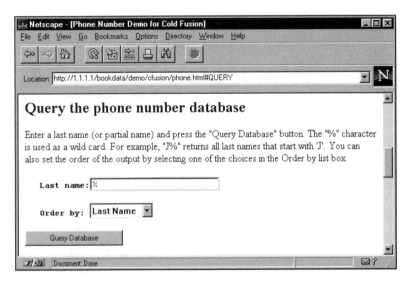

Figure 4.34   Query input screen.

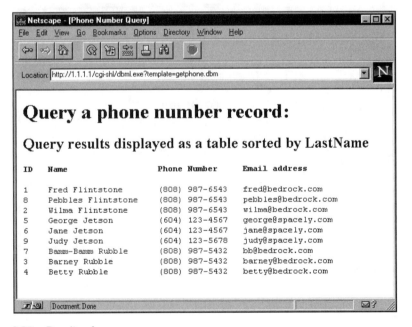

Figure 4.35   Results of a query.

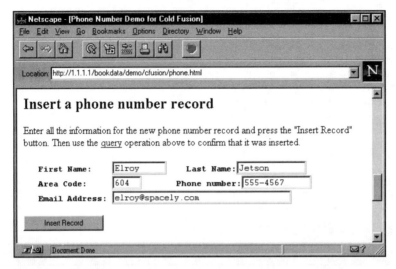

Figure 4.36   Insert input screen.

Figure 4.37   Insert feedback screen.

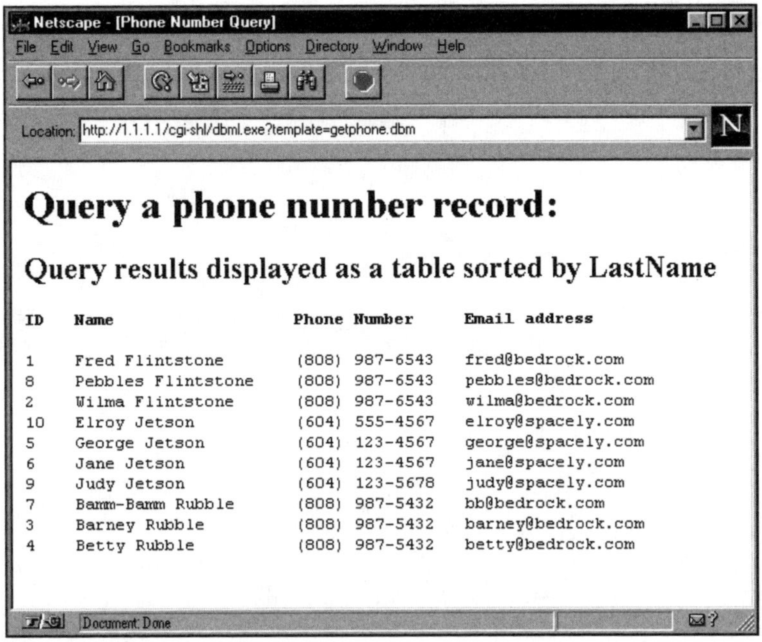

Figure 4.38   Query results after insertion.

Cold Fusion

Cold Fusion
Allaire Corporation
7600 France Avenue South, Suite 552
Minneapolis, MN 55435
Phone   (612) 831-1808
Fax   (612) 830-1090
Email   info@allaire.com
URL   http://www.allaire.com

Overview

Cold Fusion, from Allaire Corporation, is a middleware product that lets you connect Web pages to ODBC databases without writing any CGI scripts. You make it work by freely mixing DBML (DataBase Markup Language) tags with HTML (HyperText Markup Language) in a standard Web template. If you know HTML, DBML will be easy to understand.

Cold Fusion consists of two programs that run on the server. One is a small CGI executable, and the other is a Windows NT system service that loads in the HTML/DBML template file, interacts with the database, and returns a formatted result. Figure 5.2 shows how things fit together.

115

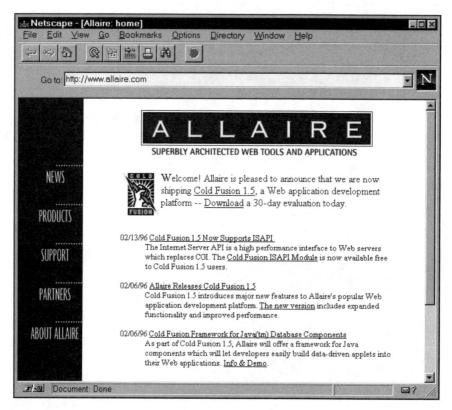

Figure 5.1   The Cold Fusion home page.

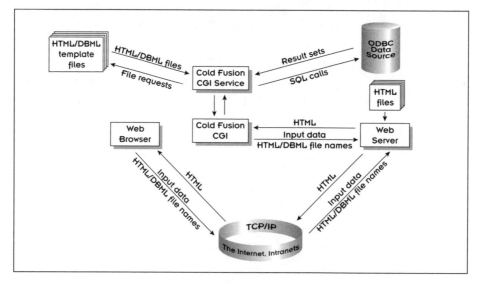

Figure 5.2   How the components of Cold Fusion fit together.

To create a Web page that interacts with a database, you create an HTML template file that mixes HTML tags and Cold Fusion's DBML tags. The HTML tags will be processed by the Web browser and the DBML tags will be processed by the Cold Fusion programs on the server. The HTML tags create the page and set the scene, and the DBML tags handle the data. To manipulate the data you can use the DBML tag **<DBQUERY>** followed by an ODBC SQL statement. Other tags are available for data manipulation, but this is all you really need. There is a way of doing input validation, and you can create your own customized error messages that will come up whenever a user enters the wrong input.

The following code snippet uses the DBML query tag:

```
<DBQUERY NAME="FindPerson" DATASOURCE="PhoneList"
      SQL="SELECT *
           FROM PhoneNumber
           WHERE LastName like '#LastName#'
           ORDER BY #OrderType#, FirstName  ">
```

The above code would be placed in an HTML/DBML template file, and there also needs to be an HTML input form on the Web page that will request this template. When the user presses the **Submit** button on the form, its contents are sent to Cold Fusion's CGI executable (**dbml.exe**),

Table 5.1   Some of Cold Fusion's Basic DBML Tags

Tag	Purpose
DBQUERY	Submits a SQL statement to the database (e.g. **select ***, **delete ***, **insert into** etc.)
DBOUTPUT	Displays a query's result set. HTML tags can be freely intermixed
DBTABLE & DBCOL	Displays a query's result set as a pre-formatted table
DBSET	Assigns a value to a variable
DBIF, DBELSE	If..then logic
DBTRANSACTION	Provides a way of rolling back a series of SQL transactions on an error condition

which then hands the data to their Windows NT system service, which in turn loads in the HTML/DBML template, runs the query, and returns the result set.

To call one HTML/DBML template file from another, input forms and URLs can both be used. The query parameters may also be URL parameters, part of the result set of previous queries, or independent DBML variables. The ability to use the result set of one query to drive another is very powerful. For one thing, it makes it easy to create a report containing hyperlinks, which can be used to drill down to the next level of detail.

The main job of the CGI executable, **dbml.exe**, is to pass the query string on to Cold Fusion's Windows NT system service. You might ask why the CGI program doesn't just process the HTML/DBML template file itself. It's done this way for efficiency: Each time the Web server is requested to run a CGI program, it first has to load up the program, set up the appropriate environment, and start the program running. This not only takes memory, it takes a significant amount of time, and if the database is being queried heavily, the overall performance of the Web server will be poor. So Allaire put most of Cold Fusion's functionality into their Windows NT system service rather than into their CGI executable. Only one copy of the service is loaded into memory, and it is only executed once. Since it is over 600 KB in size, it's easy to see that you would not want to load it up every time a query is requested.

Features

Environment

On the server side, Cold Fusion works on Windows NT 3.5 and Windows 95. The recommended memory capacity is 24 MB RAM for Windows NT or 16 MB RAM for Windows 95. On the client side, all that is required is a Web browser capable of interpreting standard HTML.

Trial Version

A trial version is available from the Cold Fusion Web site at **http://www.allaire.com.** (See Figure 5.1.)

Web Server Compatibility

Cold Fusion works with any Web server that conforms to the CGI standard.

ODBC Compatibility

Cold Fusion has been tested with a number of Microsoft and Intersolv ODBC drivers, and several 32-bit ODBC drivers for different databases are provided with the package. Allaire says that as long as an ODBC 32-bit driver conforms to Level 1 of the ODBC API, supports the Core SQL Grammar, and handles certain date and/or time functions, the driver should work.

Learnability

There is a tutorial written as a Web page. It's light and easy and it got us going quickly. There is one well-chosen way of doing everything so the confusion factor is kept low. Cold Fusion's approach looks simple, but it lets you do a lot of what you need to do. The approach is well suited for those who have some experience with SQL and HTML. If you have a few hours to put together a prototype with their 30-day trial product, you will get a good idea as to whether Cold Fusion will work for your project.

Programmability

There is a simple **IF/ELSE** statement implemented by the DBML tags: **<DBIF>**... **<DBELSE>**...**</DBIF>** that lets you specify which part of the HTML/DBML template is invoked. For example, you could display a record only if data was present in it. However, there is no way to program a loop, which would be very useful when updating records.

Efficiency

You can specify how long to keep a database open between calls. Opening an ODBC database can be notoriously slow and to keep things moving along Cold Fusion provides a way of keeping the database open for a specified length of time between calls to the database.

Security

Access to the HTML/DBML templates can be restricted by IP address and permission can be granted for specific SQL operations (such as read-only).

Error Handling

Cold Fusion returns detailed error messages when it cannot find a variable that was specified in the HTML/DBML template file and offers hints as to what might be the problem.

Debugging

There are a number of options that can be set to make debugging easier:

- Show CGI variables

- Show debug information for queries (time, records, SQL)

- Show SQL and data source names in error messages

- Email error reports to the administrator

Input Validation

Input field validation is specified using a hidden field in the input form. Some standard validations are integer, float, range, and date. In some cases Cold Fusion can edit an input instead of returning it if it's invalid. For instance, if you have used the **<DBINSERT>** tag, and the user tries to insert a number containing commas, they will be stripped out before being inserted.

Support for Transaction Control

The **<DBTRANSACTION>** tag supports transaction consistency across queries. All queries contained between a pair of **<DBTRANSACTION> </DBTRANSACTION>** tags are treated as a transactional unit, which means that changes made to the database will not be permanently committed until all queries in the transaction block have executed successfully. If an error occurs in one of the queries then all changes made by previous queries in the transaction block will be rolled back.

Cookies

Cookies provide a way for the Web database author to store information on the client side so it can be retrieved later. This can provide information that is necessary when doing 'shopping cart' or commerce type of Web database sites. Once the cookie has been written on the client side (saved in **cookies.txt**) then every time the user accesses the Web pages, the user's browser will send back the cookie information.

At the time of writing, only Netscape Navigator and Microsoft Internet Explorer handle cookies but it seems likely that this technique will be implemented on other browsers.

Email

You can send database output to email rather than to a Web browser. Because the email tag works like **<DBOUTPUT>**, all the features available in Cold Fusion can be used this way.

Hello Database with Cold Fusion

Notes on setting up the Hello Database program and Cold Fusion:

- From the CD-ROM, copy the file **\BookData\Products\CFusion\ cf15eval.zip** to a temporary directory on your hard drive then unzip it with a program like winzip or pkunzip. The setup program will walk you through the installation process. We recommend that you use the default directories suggested by the Cold Fusion setup program.

- From the CD-ROM, copy the file **\BookData\Demo\CFusion\phone.html** to the directory **\BookData\Demo\CFusion** on your hard drive.

- From the CD-ROM, copy the files **\BookData\Demo\CFusion\Template\ *.dbm** to Cold Fusion's template directory (most likely **\CFusion\Template**) on your hard drive.

- Make your Web server's root document directory the same as the root directory of your hard drive.

- Run the Hello Database demo by starting your Web browser and pointing it to the URL **http://1.1.1.1/BookData/Demo/CFusion/ phone.html**. Substitute your own IP address or domain name for **1.1.1.1** if necessary.

Query

Querying a database using Cold Fusion is done in two steps. The first step is to create an HTML input form which accepts the query information, and the second step is to create an HTML/DBML template on the server side which describes the query and specifies how to display the results.

The Hello Database program's query input form (Figure 5.3) asks a user for a last name and an ordering sequence for the output. After the form is submitted, the database returns a list of all people in the phone number table who share that name. The **Last Name** field contains an initial default value '**%**', which is the ODBC wild card that signifies that any characters in the **Last name** field will match. To return only last names that start with 's' you would enter '**s%**'.

To change the displayed order of the result set, select the **Ordered by** listbox and change the current selection to **Area Code** then press the **Query Database** button to run the query.

The HTML input form to create this query screen uses the **<form>** line (Listing 5.1) to specify which HTML/DBML template file to use when the user presses the **Query Database** button (Figure 5.3).

Listing 5.1   Partial listing to show the query input form

```
<! -------------------- Q U E R Y --------------------->

<a name=QUERY>
<h2>Query the phone number database</h2>
</a>
<p>Enter a last name (or partial name) and press the "Query Database" _
    button.  The "%" character is used as a wild card.  For example s% _
    returns all last names that start with 's'.  You can also set the _
    order of the output by selecting one of the choices in the Order by _
    list box.</p>

<form action="/cgi-shl/dbml.exe?template=getphone.dbm" method="POST" >

<pre>
    <b>Last name:</b><input type="TEXT" name="LastName" value= "%" _
      max_length=25 size=25>

    <b>Order by:</b> <select name="OrderType">
      <option value="LastName" selected>Last Name
      <option value="AreaCode">Area Code
      </select>
</pre>
<p>
```

```
<input type="SUBMIT" value="Query Database" size=20></p>
</form>
```

The text following the **action** attribute specifies what happens when the user presses that button on the input form. This is similar to running a command line program with arguments. The first part of the action line specifies the CGI program. Here the program is **dbml.exe** which is located in the **/cgi-shl** directory. The text following the question mark after the call to the CGI program is called the CGI 'query string' (note that this name has nothing to do with querying a database). For Cold Fusion, the query string specifies the filename of the HTML/DBML template file that the CGI program loads up, which in this case is **getphone.dbm**.

As soon as the user hits the **Query Database** button, the input information will be sent to the Web server and then to Cold Fusion's system service which will load the **getphone.dbm** HTML/DBML template file (Listing 5.2).

The **getphone.dbm** template file follows the structure of a regular HTML document, but with the addition of Cold Fusion's DBML tags. The SQL query is specified between the DBML tags **<DBQUERY>...</DBQUERY>.** It is placed at the start of the file as it does not integrate with the HTML tags for displaying the results as do the **<DBOUTPUT>...</DBOUTPUT>** tags.

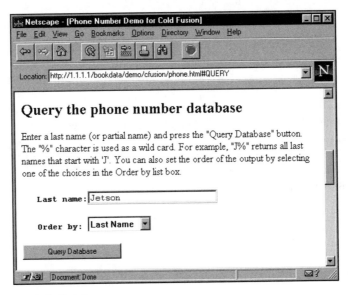

Figure 5.3 The Hello Database query screen.

Listing 5.2 The complete listing of the HTML/DBML template file (getphone.dbm) that queries the phone number database

```
<!-- Query -->

<!-- Select all fields from the PhoneNumber table for all
     records where the LastName is like the one requested and
     order the results by the ordering method requested and
     secondarily by the first name. -->
<DBQUERY NAME="FindPerson" DATASOURCE="PhoneList"
     SQL="SELECT *
          FROM PhoneNumber
          WHERE LastName like '#LastName#'
          ORDER BY #OrderType#, FirstName  ">

<!-- Page header -->

<html>
<head>
<title>Phone Number Query</title>
</head>

<body>
<h1>Query a phone number record:</h1>

<!-- Display with the header the sort order.  Note that the variable
     must be enclosed in DBOUTPUT tag to display -->

<!-- List the phone numbers in a table  -->

<DBOUTPUT>
<h2>Query results displayed as a table sorted by #OrderType#</h2>
</DBOUTPUT>

<DBTABLE QUERY="FindPerson" COLHEADERS><DBCOL HEADER="<b>ID</b>"
WIDTH=3 TEXT="#UserID#">
     <DBCOL HEADER="<b>Name</b>"            WIDTH=20 TEXT="#FirstName# _
          #LastName#">
     <DBCOL HEADER="<b>Phone Number</b>" WIDTH=15 TEXT="(#AreaCode#) _
          #Phone#">
     <DBCOL HEADER="<b>Email address</b>" WIDTH=25 TEXT="#EmailAddress#">
</DBTABLE>

</body>
</html>
```

The **<DBQUERY>** tag specifies the name of the query, the ODBC database, and the ODBC SQL statement. The name of the query '**FindPerson**' is used later in the HTML/DBML template file.

```
<DBQUERY NAME="FindPerson" DATASOURCE="PhoneList"
     SQL="SELECT *
         FROM PhoneNumber
         WHERE LastName like '#LastName#'
         ORDER BY #OrderType#, FirstName  ">
```

Note that Cold Fusion requires '#' around each variable name. The results will be ordered by the field specified by the **#OrderType#** input variable and secondarily ordered by the **FirstName** database table field.

Cold Fusion takes this **<DBQUERY>** tag and executes the ODBC SQL command on the specified ODBC datasource. With some data sources, notably SQL Server, it seems necessary to specify the actual database name in the query as an explicit table name qualifier, e.g: 'dbname.PhoneNumber'. The result set retrieved from the database (Figure 5.4) is further processed by Cold Fusion in the rest of the lines that follow in the HTML/DBML template file.

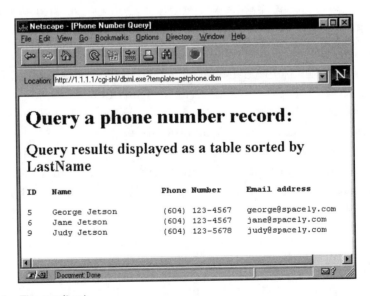

Figure 5.4   The result set.

One of the first DBML tags to be processed is the **<DBTABLE>** tag. This tag is used to display the query in tabular format. The first parameter after this tag is the query name which defines the result set to use (**FindPerson** in this example). Having the ability to specify multiple query names allows multiple queries to be defined in one HTML/DBML template file, which is important in developing full reports.

```
<DBTABLE QUERY="FindPerson" COLHEADERS>
     <DBCOL HEADER="<b>ID</b>"            WIDTH=3 TEXT="#UserID#">
     <DBCOL HEADER="<b>Name</b>"          WIDTH=20 TEXT="#FirstName# _
        #LastName#">
     <DBCOL HEADER="<b>Phone Number</b>"  WIDTH=15 TEXT="(#AreaCode#) _
        #Phone#">
     <DBCOL HEADER="<b>Email address</b>" WIDTH=25 TEXT="#EmailAddress#">
</DBTABLE>
```

We wanted to show column headers above each column so we used the optional attribute **COLHEADERS** after the DBML tag **<DBTABLE>**. Cold Fusion has a number of other attributes of **<DBTABLE>** that do things like setting the maximum number of rows to display or rendering the table as an HTML 3.0 table instead of defaulting to the **<PRE>** format.

The other DBML tag, **<DBCOL>**, works in conjunction with **<DBTABLE>**. This tag specifies the column header, the column width, and the field name.

You may be wondering how Cold Fusion differentiates between an HTML input form variable and a database table field name. If the names are unique, Cold Fusion can keep track of which came from where. However, if a database field name is identical to an HTML input form variable name, then you need a qualifier in front of the variable name to distinguish the two. For example, in the demonstration code both the HTML input form variable and the database table field names were labeled '**LastName**'. If we had wanted to use both variables between the DBML tags **<DBOUTPUT>**…**</DBOUTPUT>** then we would have had to qualify the HTML input form variable by prefixing it with the word '**Form**' as in **#Form.LastName#**.

Insert

Inserting a record into the database is also done in two steps. The first step is to create the insert input form and the second step is to create the HTML/DBML template file.

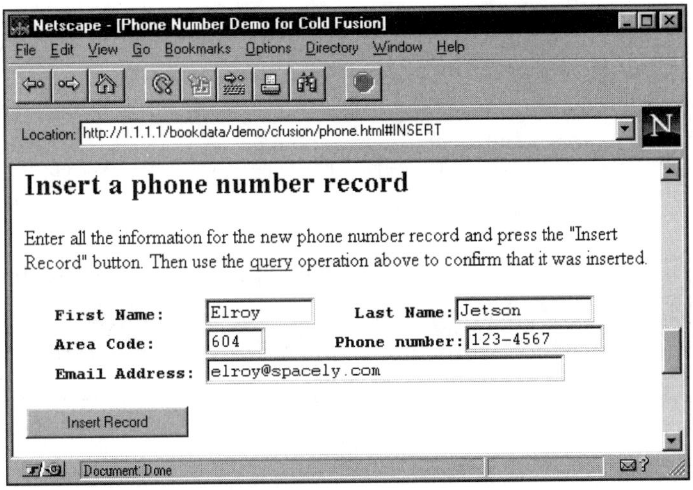

Figure 5.5 The Hello Database insert screen.

In the insert input form (Figure 5.5) users will enter a person's name, phone number, and email address, then press the **Insert Record** button. None of these input fields have client-side validation logic attached to them. Server-side input validation is possible with Cold Fusion.

The HTML input form that creates the insert form uses the **<form>** tag **action** attribute (Listing 5.3) in much the same way as was explained in the query example.

Listing 5.3   Partial listing of the insert input form

```
<! -------------------- I N S E R T --------------------->

<a name=INSERT>
<h2>Insert a phone number record</h2>
</a>

<p>Enter all the information for the new phone number record and press _
    the "Insert Record" button.  Then use the <a href=#QUERY>query</a> _
    operation above to confirm that it was inserted.</p>

<form action="/cgi-shl/dbml.exe?template=insphone.dbm" method="POST">

<pre>
    <b>First Name:</b>     <input type="TEXT" name="FirstName" value= "" _
    max_length=20 size=10><b>    Last Name:</b><input type="text" _
    name="LastName" value= "" max_length=20 size=13>
```

```
    <b>Area Code:</b>       <input type="TEXT" name="AreaCode" value= "" _
       max_length=5 size=5>          <b>Phone number:</b><input type="text" _
       name="Phone" value= "" max_length=20 size=13>
    <b>Email Address:</b> <input type="TEXT" name="EmailAddress" _
       value= "" max_length=35 size=35>
</pre>    <input type="SUBMIT" Value="Insert Record" size=20>
</form>
```

It consists of two parts: the CGI program **dbml.exe** which is the same one used in the query (Cold Fusion has only one CGI program), and the template parameter which is **insphone.dbm**. The four input fields are of type **TEXT**. The important thing to note here is that the names of the input variables are identical to the names of the database table fields. By following this approach, the actual DBML tag to insert the record is extremely simple. The HTML/DBML template file **\BookData\Demo\CFusion\ Template\insphone.dbm** in Listing 5.4, defines where to insert the phone record and shows how to create a typical HTML reply message.

Although we didn't show it here, the other way of inserting a record is to use the straightforward **<DBQUERY>** tag with an appropriate ODBC SQL insert statement. This provides a more flexible and useful approach to data inserts and updates. However, the way we showed it here does not require any knowledge about SQL for inserts and updates.

Listing 5.4   The complete listing of the HTML/DBML template file (insphone.dbm) to insert a phone number record

```
<!-- Insert -->

<DBINSERT DATASOURCE="PhoneList" TABLENAME="PhoneNumber">

<!-- Status message of the inserted record -->

<html>
<head>
<title>Insert a phone number record</title>
</head>

<body>
<h1>Insert a phone number record:</h1>

<h2>This record has been inserted</h2>
<DBOUTPUT>
```

```
<pre>
   <b>Person:</b>        #FirstName# #LastName#
   <b>Phone number:</b>  (#AreaCode#) #Phone#
   <b>Email address:</b> #EmailAddress#
</DBOUTPUT>
</pre>

</body>
</html>
```

In the example, the **<DBINSERT>** tag has two attributes: **DATASOURCE** and **TABLENAME**. All that is required is to specify the ODBC data source **PhoneList** and the database table name **PhoneNumber** to access the proper database. All the data that comes from the HTML input form is then automatically inserted into the database as a new record. Once again, note that these variable names must match the database table field names for this operation to work. Other options that can be specified are the owner of the table and which HTML input form fields can be inserted.

As a way of providing feedback to the user, the **<DBOUTPUT>** tag is used to display the HTML input form field variables (Figure 5.6).

Note that the results displayed in Figure 5.6 are not the actual retrieved results of the newly-inserted data. To achieve this, another query would be required.

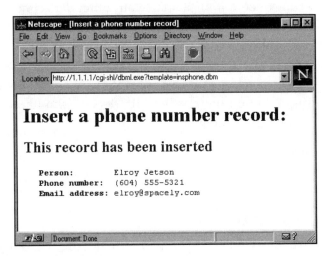

Figure 5.6   The inserted data record.

Interview with J.J. Allaire of Allaire Corporation

J.J. Allaire and a group of fellow programmers started their company in the fall of '94. We talked to J.J. about his company, the Web, other Web/database software, and how he sees Cold Fusion developing.

How many people are in the company?

Twelve altogether. Four developers and three customer support. The rest are sales and management folks.

How are you marketing Cold Fusion?

We are doing it all on the Internet. The Internet is an amazing marketing channel. We have not placed one ad and we have had virtually no press. We shipped the product in July '95 and people started downloading it and orders started coming in. It was overwhelming to think that all these people were finding us, that just by posting on Usenet we could generate all this interest.

Who is using Cold Fusion?

Two major groups. One group is consultants and entrepreneurs, small companies who are getting started providing Web presence or developing client/server applications; the same people who picked up Visual Basic and are typically on the leading edge of technology adoption. Then within corporations there are a few different types of customers: one is the user who is in marketing or communications or any other department that might want to do some Intranet stuff—this is a technical user, maybe manages a LAN or knows a lot about PCs but isn't a programmer—and wants to build stuff for his department; this is the same kind of person you saw driving a lot of the early PC development in corporations: knowledgeable, highly technical end users. Then there is the MIS person who likes to push the envelope and try out new things.

What were you doing before you started Cold Fusion?

Mostly client/server software development. I had a consulting firm for about four years.

Were you doing applications or tools?

Applications. We used C++, Powerbuilder, Visual Basic and Delphi and did custom software development for people on LANs.

Did you work with any particular OS and database?

Windows NT and ODBC with Access and SQL Server.

When did you discover the Web?

Around the time of the first release of Mosaic. When we saw what a Web browser with forms and CGI could do, and the fact that it was completely open so anyone could publish, we began to think that the Web would replace proprietary online services.

Like CompuServe and AOL?

Yes. So we said okay, if the Web can replace the online services then it needs development tools for producing interactive sites, and those tools ought to be based on relational databases because that's a perfect technology for managing data. But we were still sort of on the sidelines at that point so we started doing Web development using CGI and C++, and through that experience we acquired an understanding of what was needed in a Web/database development tool and how to do it.

Do you think a Web browser can be a universal client?

Yes. It will get there. We didn't see this possibility at first but now we think that Web software could also replace proprietary DBMS clients in the LAN and mainframe and mini database environment.

The Intranet market?

Yes. I think even Netscape didn't realize that at first. Even as late as summer '95 they were focusing on document publishing, multimedia publishing, the big vertical applications they were planning on building. The merchant server and the commerce server were all oriented to public online services. Then all of a sudden everybody started realizing there's a lot of advantages to using the Web on internal networks. That took a lot of people by surprise.

The Web's definition of how you interact with a computer is so clear.

Yes! Pages and links!

What is Cold Fusion's most striking feature?

I would say its simplicity, where you just intermix HTML tags with DBML tags.

What else?

A lot of people like the setup program. It auto-detects everything and launches you into a Web browser that says: here's how you get started, here's examples, here's a tutorial, everything. In this market, a lot of people who are exploring aren't extremely familiar with the technical landscape of Web servers. People in communications departments or marketing departments are out there looking to see what they can do for themselves and to presume that they know how to configure a CGI program with the Web server is probably wrong, so we feel that having a great setup program that does everything for the user is really critical.

I've noticed on newsgroup discussions that people find it difficult keeping database field names in sync with the names in the HTML pages when changes are made. Have people mentioned this to you?

This is a general problem in any database development context. If you rename database fields you are going to have client software breaking.

So this problem won't go away?

It's going to happen. When I did client/server work with Visual Basic and we renamed a database field we had to go out and replace 200 binaries on 200 workstations. With the Web, everybody has got the page in their page cache and that's about the worst of it.

The Web already does pretty well when you just want to query a database, but it's not there yet for online transaction processing. Will we be able to do full-scale OLTP via the Web?

There's no reason why not. Client/server systems are evolving to having a piece of middleware that does the business rule logic and the transaction logic. People want to have a separate transaction server, and if you think about the Web server it's perfectly positioned to broker transaction logic and business rule logic and presentation logic. It's right in the sweet spot. I think there's a lot of opportunity for vendors to build transaction processing enhancements or take transaction processing engines and couple them with Web servers.

How does Cold Fusion fit in with this?

We want to let people use Visual Basic to do transaction logic and use HTML and DBML to do presentation.

Can the current version of Cold Fusion use Visual Basic this way now?

Not yet.

So how will it work in the future?

Two ways: a VBA (Visual Basic for Applications) interpreter would be embedded into Cold Fusion and the interpreter would execute scripts which had been saved in a script repository of some kind. The other way would be for Cold Fusion to call an OLE automation server written in Visual Basic, and in this case no program launch would be required.

Simple input validation is supported in HTML 3.0 and client-side input validation can be done with Java applets or plug-ins. What if you have to query a table to do an input validation?

A huge table, more than 1K, would be unpleasant to download. I think there needs to be a standard protocol for Web clients to make requests from servers that don't return HTML pages so Cold Fusion could return an untagged data stream for validation or for display in a Java applet.

How would someone choose between Visual Basic and Java?

Visual Basic is ideal for application programming and Java is a component building language the same way C++ is. Personally I love Java, it's very well designed and fixes every problem that I can identify with C++, but for everyday application and client/server programming Visual Basic would be more productive.

How about JavaScript?

Netscape could have taken Java from Sun and said "that's our server development language", but they didn't. They recognized that Java is too complex for most application development so they made up JavaScript. If you look at JavaScript it's a lot more like Visual Basic than it is like Java. It's also a typeless language like Hypertalk was so the user doesn't even have to understand the concept of a type.

What would you use?

I'm used to Visual Basic. Also, most of the developers on the NT platform know Visual Basic already. Visual Basic is very robust and the tools that come with it or are licensable are a lot farther along.

How do you see the future of NT as a platform for the Web?

We believed all along that Windows NT was going to be the platform for Web serving, even when there were no Web servers for NT. So we worked with 16 bit Windows because we knew we would migrate to 32 bit Windows. Even when we shipped the product in July of '95 you probably couldn't get an industry analyst to say Windows NT was going to be it, but now if you ask them, they are going to say yes, and in a year it's going to be overwhelming.

What do you think about the database connectivity that comes with Microsoft's Internet Information Server?

Their database stuff is pretty weak. It's pretty stripped down. It's going to meet the needs of people who are experimenting or haven't thought about using databases with the Web and want to get their first thing up. I think it'll help us because it will educate the market about what is possible. Suddenly, this database connector thing is going to be in their lap and they are going to try something and at a certain point they will start looking around for more power, and we have it.

Cold Fusion 1.5 is still CGI but it also uses a service that only loads once so it's quite fast. Are you still going to go to the API?

Yes. We are going to deliver the API stuff pretty soon. The API will ride right on top of that same service. That's why we did the architecture that way, so we could deliver the performance benefits of an API interface within the confines of CGI. If the server doesn't support a native API, or if the API is poorly documented or buggy, you are still going to get robust high performance.

Will Cold Fusion work with all the major APIs?

Yes. NSAPI, ISAPI, and WSAPI.

Do you have any comments on the various APIs?

O'Reilly's WSAPI is more extensive than Netscape's or Microsoft's in that it exposes more of the server's operation, you can do more with it. Whether that's good or bad I don't know. And Netscape's API also lets you do a lot with the Netscape server. A reason why Microsoft's API may succeed is because it is simple and there's only two functions that you have to implement and it's very clear how to use it. It's not flexible or deep but it's usable. One thing to remember about the API that's really important, and a reason why we did an NT service rather than doing the whole thing in the API, is when you are running as an API extension to a server you can crash the server. Any time you load up an API extension to the server you are exposing the server. Not only does the guy who wrote the server have to write bullet-proof code, but that extension writer also has to write completely bullet-proof code so there is a lot of risk associated with API extensions, and they may get a negative stigma associated with them, like DOS TSRs. So it's important to know that CGI is slow and it's not state-of-the-art but it is pretty robust; if a process is created and does something naughty or crashes, who cares? One client request didn't get serviced.

Do you have any performance benchmarks comparing CGI to DLL?

I think a DLL is a lot faster. The process creation time on NT is 100 to 150 milliseconds so you are going to save that every time. When you are talking about request times with Cold Fusion 1.5 coming down to 200 or 300 milliseconds on a fast machine, saving that 100 to 150 milliseconds could be significant.

dbWeb

dbWeb
Aspect Software Engineering, Inc.
Manoa Innovation Center
2800 Woodlawn Drive, #250
Honolulu, HI 96822-1865
Phone   (808) 539-3781
Fax   (808) 539-3785
Email   sales@aspectse.com
URL   http://www.aspectse.com

Overview

dbWeb lets you create Web database applications by filling
in forms. The process is simple enough that someone with
just a little knowledge of Web conventions and no knowledge of HTML or SQL can use it. The Web database applications created can have all the basic database features such
as query, insert, update, and delete. dbWeb consists of:

- An Administrator program that you use to create
  applications,

- A Repository that stores the applications,

- A small CGI program that is called by the Web browser,
  and

- A multi-threaded Windows NT service that is called by
  the CGI program and does most of the work.

Figure 6.1   The Aspect Software Engineering home page.

Figure 6.2 shows how the components of the dbWeb development environment fit together. To create an application, use the Administrator program to specify: which data sources will be used, which columns will be accessed, which fields will be hypertext links, and how the Web browser will display everything.

dbWeb uses a simple Query By Example (QBE) form for building up an application (Figure 6.3.) Called the 'Schema Wizard', it is very similar to the one used in Microsoft Access for setting up databases.

The information entered via the Schema Wizard is stored in a Repository and defines the application. A Repository is just a database that describes the tables and columns used and the properties of the columns (for example, sorting priority, column width, format, etc.).

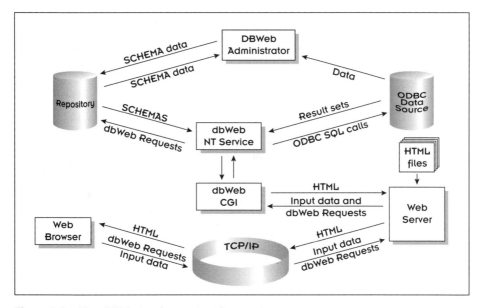

Figure 6.2 The dbWeb development environment.

A user runs a dbWeb application (Figure 6.4) from a Web browser by key-ing in a URL or by clicking on a link.This initiates a call to the CGI pro-gram, which in turn calls dbWeb's NT service. The NT service queries the Repository to find out what database instruction to carry out, then carries out the instruction and returns the results to the user's browser. In the browser, users will see standard Web input forms, tables, and hypertext links. However, the HTML code that puts these objects on display is all

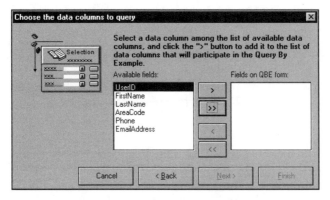

Figure 6.3 Selecting columns to query using dbWeb's Schema Wizard.

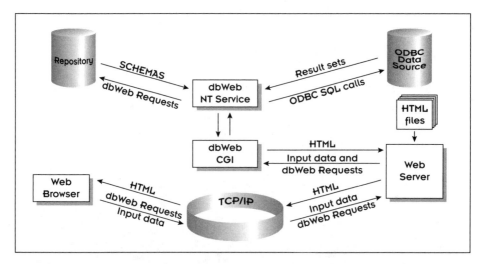

Figure 6.4   The dbWeb run-time environment.

generated by the NT service. Internally, the NT service uses ODBC SQL statements to interact with the database and generates on-the-fly HTML tags to format the results for display. Yet, the developer doesn't need to know anything about SQL or HTML.

Features
Environment

The dbWeb Administrator runs on Microsoft Windows 3.x, Windows 95, and a Windows NT 3.51 server or workstation.

The CGI program and the NT service run on a Windows NT 3.51 server or workstation.

The ODBC data sources can reside on Windows NT, Unix, VMS, or OS/2.

A minimum of 16 MB of memory and 10 MB of hard disk space is required on the server for either Intel or RISC-based systems.

Trial Version

A downloadable trial version is available from the Aspect Web site, **http://www.aspectse.com**. (See Figure 6.1.)

Web Server Compatibility

dbWeb will work with most Web servers that are CGI 1.1 compliant. Among these servers are: Alibaba, EMWAC, Netscape Communication Server, Purveyor, and WebSite.

Web Browser Compatibility

You can use any Web browser that supports HTML input forms, including: Netscape, NCSA Mosaic, Spry's Air Mosaic, Microsoft Internet Explorer, IBM's Web browser, and Netcom Netcruiser.

ODBC Compatibility

dbWeb works with databases that support 32-bit ODBC.

Learnability

dbWeb is very easy to learn since no programming is involved. The tutorial gives many examples of what you can do with the Schema Wizard.

How Programmable Is It?

dbWeb 1.0 uses an HTML template file called a DBX file. DBX files contain standard HTML tags and special delimiters that let you call dbWeb methods. There is also a DBX editor that lets you specify customized output displays, but since a DBX file is just ASCII text, you can use any text editor to create these files.

At the time of writing, Aspect Software Engineering had just released a server-side scripting language called iBASIC, which is an extended form of VBA (Visual Basic for Applications). iBASIC statements, between delimiter tags, are combined with HTML to dynamically control the content of the HTML file that is passed to the Web browser. Because iBASIC is a full language, loops, conditionals, and other program constructs can be specified. This would be cumbersome or impossible with extended HTML declarative tags.

Efficiency

dbWeb uses a very small CGI program that communicates with a much larger NT service that does the bulk of the work. This reduces the overhead associated with loading CGI programs and maintains high portability across

Web servers. Information is passed between the CGI programs and the NT service via named pipes, which achieves high throughput by allowing multiple instances of the CGI program to simultaneously communicate with a single NT service. (The "small CGI, large partner process" model seems to be emerging as the architecture of choice for Web database products.)

ODBC connections are dynamically pooled to reduce the number of times that a data source will be opened. This speeds up ODBC connection requests. The dbWeb Administrator lets you specify how long connections will stay open before they time out.

Security

The dbWeb Administrator allows the developer to specify the user ID and password of the data source when the secure connection flag is checked. When a user tries to gain access to the Web page, a standard Web browser user-authentication dialog box pops up to allow the user to be authenticated. The Web server saves the authentication information as environment variables that dbWeb uses when it connects to the database.

Note that neither the Netscape Web server nor the Microsoft Web server store passwords in environment variables, so this security feature is not useable with these Web servers. Aspect Software Engineering says that Alibaba WWW Server v2.0, WebSite 1.0, and Purveyor 1.2 support this feature. Note also that some Web servers use different environment names for the authentication variables. dbWeb will attempt to detect this during installation.

Error Handling

If an error occurs when accessing an ODBC data source then a formatted error message is returned to the Web browser (Figure 6.5). Error messages are combinations of dbWeb's explanation of the error, the exact SQL statement that dbWeb was executing, and a standard ODBC error message from the ODBC driver.

Debugging

Other than good error messages, dbWeb has no tools specifically for debugging.

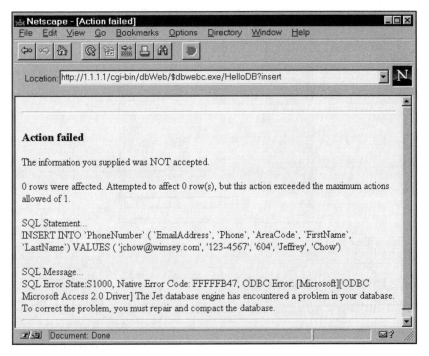

Figure 6.5   A sample error message.

Input Validation

With dbWeb 1.0, input fields will automatically be validated based on the data types specified in the database tables. For example, if the data type is an integer, then a dbWeb application will accept only numeric input. Any other type of input will cause dbWeb to send a user-defined message to the Web browser (Figure 6.6).

With iBASIC, it is possible to validate many more data types (such as zip codes or social security numbers) than are defined in the data tables.

Support for Transaction Control

The dbWeb Administrator program does not provide a way of handling commit and roll-back directly. However, it is possible to call the ODBC API functions to handle this.

Cookies

Cookies are not implemented in dbWeb 1.0.

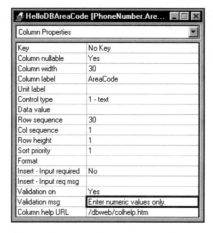

Figure 6.6　Specifying an error message.

Hello Database with dbWeb

We used dbWeb's Administrator program to create the Hello Database program, and since we only needed to point and click in the Schema Wizard, we developed the whole application in less than fifteen minutes. Since there is no code to show, we have written this section more like a walkthrough of the screen forms that we used.

Setup and Operation

From the CD-ROM, copy the file **\BookData\Products\dbWeb\ dbWeb100.exe** into a temporary directory on your hard drive.

- Run **dbWeb100.exe** to extract the files it contains.

- Run **setup.exe** and follow the instructions it gives, using the defaults where possible.

- From the CD-ROM, copy the files **\BookData\Demo\dbWeb\dbWeb.*** onto your hard drive into the directory **\dbWeb\Admin**; this will replace the existing **dbWeb.*** example files supplied by Aspect with ones that add the HelloDB schemas.

- Ensure that the **PhoneList** database is installed as an ODBC Access system data source.

- From the Windows NT control panel, double click on the service icon and start the dbWeb service running.

- Start the Web server running.

At this point, bring up your Netscape browser and enter the URL:

```
http://1.1.1.1/cgi-bin/dbWeb/$dbWebc.exe/HelloDBLastName?getqbe
```

(Don't forget to change **1.1.1.1** to your own domain name or IP address!) This should bring up dbWeb's dynamically created Web page to query the phone list.

Query

The first step is to run the dbWeb Administrator program, **DBWEBADM.EXE**. The window that shows up (Figure 6.7) displays all the current ODBC data sources that dbWeb is aware of.

To create the data source **PhoneList**, highlight the list box item **Data Sources and Schemas** and then click on the **New data source** button. The panel window that appears (Figure 6.8) is how the data source name is specified.

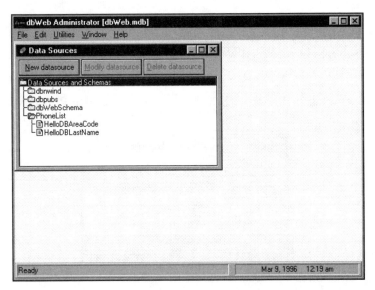

Figure 6.7 Current ODBC data sources in the dbWeb Administrator program.

Figure 6.8 Specifying a new data source.

Since the data source name must be on the list of ODBC data sources, the best way to get this name is to click on the button that looks like "…". Then, highlight the data source that shows up in the ODBC data source list box. Note that for a data source to work with dbWeb, it must have a 32-bit ODBC driver. The list box that dbWeb presents (Figure 6.9) shows which ODBC drivers are 32 bit and which are not.

If your data source doesn't show up in this list, then bring up the ODBC Administrator, click on the **Manage…** button in the ODBC group box, and follow the instructions. That's all that is needed to make dbWeb aware of a data source.

To specify a schema, highlight the data source named **PhoneList** and press the **New schema** button. A dialog box will appear with two buttons, **Schema Wizard** and **New Schema**, we selected **Schema Wizard**.

Next, select a table (Figure 6.10,. In our case, we chose **PhoneNumber**.

Figure 6.9 The dbWeb ODBC data source list.

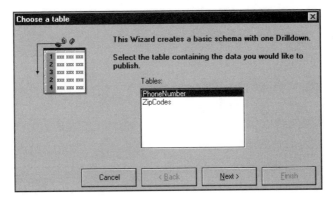

Figure 6.10   Specifying the database table.

The next dialog box (Figure 6.11) asks for the fields to be queried. Since the Hello Database program queries the **PhoneList** based on last name, we only listed the **LastName** field in the field's form list box.

Use the **Choose tabular form data columns** dialog box to specify which fields are to show up in a tabular format (Figure 6.12). This is where you specify the fields you want displayed after running the query. In this case, we select all the fields for display.

The **Specify a Drilldown Smartlink** dialog box asks which field is to become the **Drilldown SmartLink** (Figure 6.13). A **Drilldown SmartLink** is just another way of saying that when the results are displayed, the fields designated as SmartLinks will be tagged as hypertext links. Clicking on

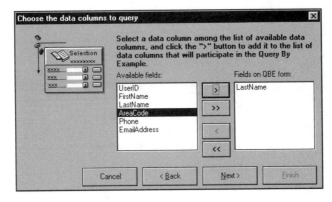

Figure 6.11   Specifying the field to query on.

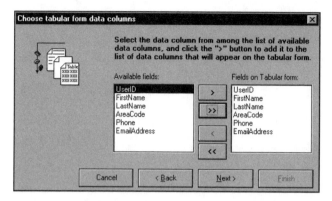

Figure 6.12   Specifying which fields to display in a table.

one of them will perform another query. For example, we choose to make the **AreaCode** field the Drilldown SmartLink field, so when the area codes are presented they will all be hypertext links. Clicking on one of the area code hypertext links runs another query listing only those records with the same area code. (The SmartLink query was not part of the Hello Database program specification, but you must specify one to complete the wizard session.)

The **Enter schema name** dialog box requests the name of the schema that was just created (Figure 6.14). We named the schema **HelloDBLastName**. At this point, the wizard offers us the opportunity to further modify this schema if we want to, but we want to try it out and see what the results look like, so we press the Finish button.

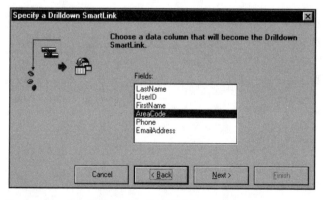

Figure 6.13   Designating AreaCode as the SmartLink.

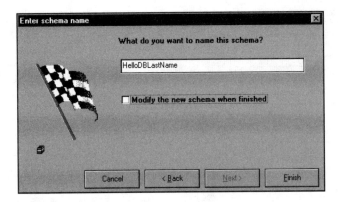

Figure 6.14 Specifying the schema name in the wizard.

As you can see, it was quick and simple to develop the initial schema. Now, we are going to browse this database Web site and see what appears in the Web browser. Since dbWeb creates all of its HTML pages dynamically, no HTML files will have been created as a result of specifying the schema. This means that to look at the Web site, you point your Web browser to a URL where dbWeb's CGI program resides. Further qualify the URL with the name of the schema and the type of query, which in this case is **getqbe**. So in this example, the URL is:

```
http://1.1.1.1/cgi-bin/dbWeb/$dbWebc.exe/HelloDBLastName?getqbe.
```

The query screen that appears in the Web browser (Figure 6.15) has just one field, **LastName**, to query on. In the other Hello Database programs we used the "%" character to help specify a finer control on which names to query. In dbWeb this level of control is contained in a drop down list box that gives several options for the type of last name to retrieve. If you don't specify any last name and press the **Submit Query** button, then dbWeb returns the entire list of last names up to the maximum number of rows specified.

As you can see from the tabular display of the query results (Figure 6.16), the width of each column is not optimal for presentation purposes. Most of the values in the columns are much shorter than the maximum column width defined in the database table. However, except for column width, the query input screen and the resulting data displayed look similar to the other Hello Database examples, yet no HTML or SQL knowledge was required.

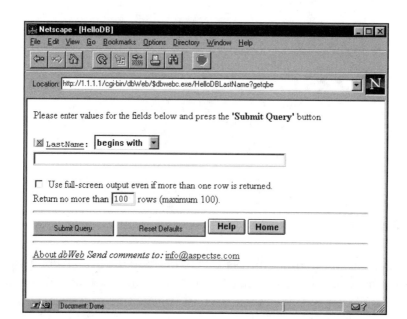

Figure 6.15   The query input screen.

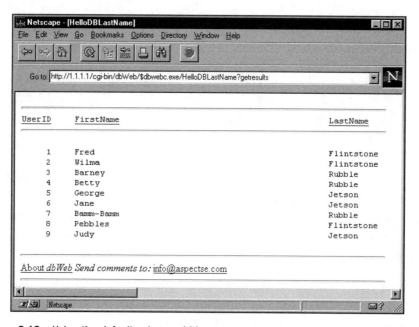

Figure 6.16   Using the default column widths.

Now let's take a look at modifying the schema to make the presentation look more like the other Hello Database examples. Specifically, there are two items we want to change in the schema. The first is the column widths of the tabular displayed fields, and the second is to display the last names in alphabetical order. If the last names are the same, then we want the first names to be sorted alphabetically as well. Recall from the other HelloDB programs that this is equivalent to the SQL statement:

```
SELECT from PhoneList WHERE LastName LIKE InputLastNameValue ORDER BY _
    LastName, FirstName.
```

To modify the schema, we highlight the schema HelloDBLastName and click the **Modify schema** button. What appears is a dialog box with many tabbed panels. Some of the fields in the tabbed panels will be familiar because we first saw them in the Schema Wizard.

We use the tabbed panel **Tabular** to get to the section of the schema, which specifies the column width for table-formatted displays (Figure 6.17). Each field has an associated set of properties. For example, we highlight the

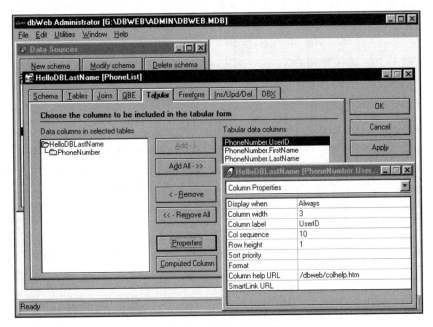

Figure 6.17   Setting the column width for the UserID field.

field **PhoneNumber.UserID** and click on the **Properties** button to bring up the associated properties of the **PhoneNumber.UserID** field. There are a number of different properties that you can adjust. Here, we modify the **Column width** field to 3 since the database is small and contains less than one thousand different user IDs.

Whatever value is assigned to the column property **Column label** will also appear as the header of a column. We change the value from **UserID** to **ID** since the column width is now only 3 characters wide. Additionally, the **Column width** property is shortened for each of the fields so that the results can be displayed without having to scroll horizontally.

The other feature we want to implement is to have the names sort alphabetically (primarily by last name and secondarily by first name). This is easily accomplished by setting the **Sort priority** property for both **LastName** and **FirstName**. In the **LastName** field, the sort priority is set to 1, giving it the highest priority. The **FirstName** sort priority is set to 2, giving it the next highest priority.

That's all that is necessary to meet the design requirements for the Hello Database program. So, let's take a look at how the results now appear in the Web browser. We use the same URL as before and click on the **Submit Query** button to show all the names in the phone list. Figure 6.18 shows the results of the modifications. All of the columns fit on one screen and when the last names are the same, those rows are sorted alphabetically according to the first name.

Although it was not part of the design for the Hello Database program, dbWeb hypertexted the area code data, and if a user clicks on an area code, then dbWeb performs another query. In the example, the query displays all of the names in the phone list with the same area code (Figure 6.19). You can configure the details of this query by modifying the schema SmartLink property.

So there it is. By using dbWeb's fill-in-the-forms approach, it is possible to create a Web page that queries a database without writing any HTML or SQL code. And, by using the Schema Wizard and then modifying the tabular presentation properties, we achieve the same functionality as in the other Hello Database programs.

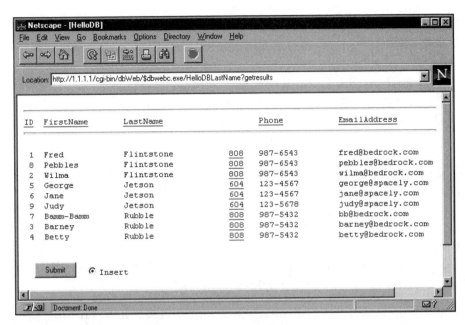

Figure 6.18   Customized column widths for better display.

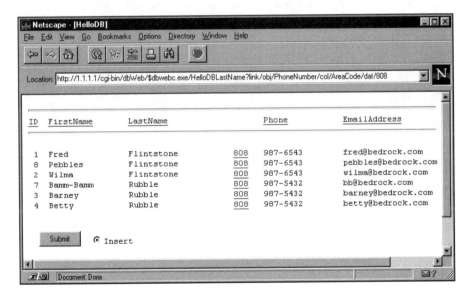

Figure 6.19   Results of clicking on the AreaCode SmartLink.

dbWeb's Special Use of URLs

With dbWeb, a Web database application can exist without a Web page so the URL is used to initiate a dynamic Web page. Since the URL also specifies the CGI program and the dbWeb command, URLs can become long and unwieldy. Thus, creating a static HTML page with a hypertext link to the URL would be a more elegant way to launch an application. This would require a small amount of HTML programming, but it is purely optional.

You may have noticed the one feature in the other Hello Database programs we were not able to directly implement. It is a way for the user to specify whether the results are to be displayed according to the **LastName** field or the **AreaCode** field. As we saw, setting the sort priority of any field is easy to do by just modifying the schema. Therefore, one way of allowing the user to specify which of the two fields to sort on is to create another schema similar to **HelloDBLastName schema**.

The schema called **HelloDBAreaCode** sets the **AreaCode** sort priority property to 1 and the **LastName** and **FirstName** sort priority properties to 2 and 3 respectively then, all the user has to do is use the URL:

```
http://1.1.1.1/cgi-bin/dbWeb/$dbWebc.exe/HelloDBAreaCode?getqbe
```

which runs the **HelloDBAreaCode** schema and displays the results ordered by area code.

What's more, both of these URLs could be on a static HTML page and the user could select either one of the hypertext links. This achieves the same functionality as in the other Hello Database examples as shown in Figure 6.20.

The HTML code that generates a display like this is straightforward:

```
<html>
<head>
<!----------------------->
<!- Hello Database Program              ->
<!- dbWeb                               ->
<!----------------------->
<title>Hello Database Program  </title>
</head>
```

```
<h1>Hello Database </h1>
<hr>

<h2>Query the phone number database</h2>
<ul>
<li><a href="http://1.1.1.1/cgi-bin/dbWeb/$dbWebc.exe/
   HelloDBAreaCode?getqbe">Click here to query by Area Code  </a>

<li><a href="http://1.1.1.1/cgi-bin/dbWeb/$dbWebc.exe/
   HelloDBLastName?getqbe">Click here to query by LastName  </a>
<p>
</ul>

<hr>

</body>
</html>
```

Insert

You can add an Insert form to the HelloDB application by modifying the schema. In the dbWeb Administrator program, we select the Schema Wizard, press the **Modify schema** button, and select the **Schema** tab panel (Figure 6.21). In the group of check boxes called **Allow actions on data**, we check the **Insert** check box.

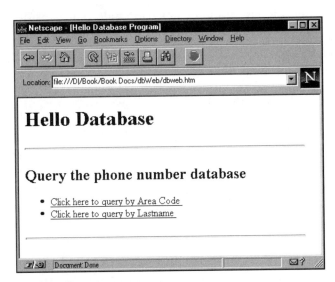

Figure 6.20 A simple HTML page linking both schemas.

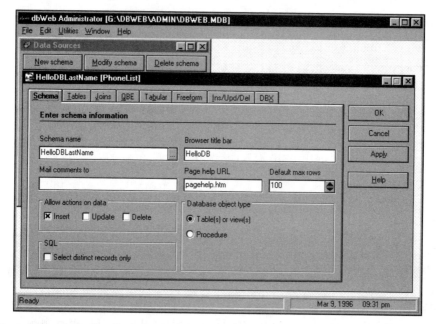

Figure 6.21   Activating the Insert feature.

When the **Insert** check box has been checked, the tabbed panel **Ins/Upd/ Del** panel becomes accessible (Figure 6.22). This panel lists the tables in the database. We double click on the PhoneNumber table to bring up all of its field names, then we double click each field name to add them to the **Insert data column** list box. Note that we do not add the **UserID** field as it is a counter in the Access database, and is updated automatically every time a new record is inserted.

To bring up the HTML input form that allows the user to insert a record, point the Web browser to (in this case) the URL:

```
http://1.1.1.1/cgi-bin/dbWeb/$dbWebc.exe/HelloDBLastName?getinsert
```

The '**getinsert**' parameter tells dbWeb's CGI program to return a dynamically created HTML input form to the Web browser, as specified in the **HelloDBLastName** schema.

The input form (Figure 6.23) displays each input field on a separate line. The length of the input text box for each field matches the column width

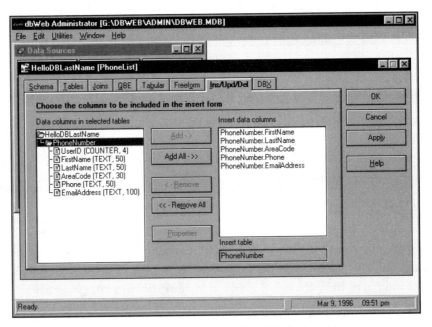

Figure 6.22 Specifying the fields that are to be included in the insert form.

as defined in the table PhoneNumber. You can modify the properties of the fields to provide tighter control of the insert transaction by, for example, doing input validations and returning custom-designed validation error messages.

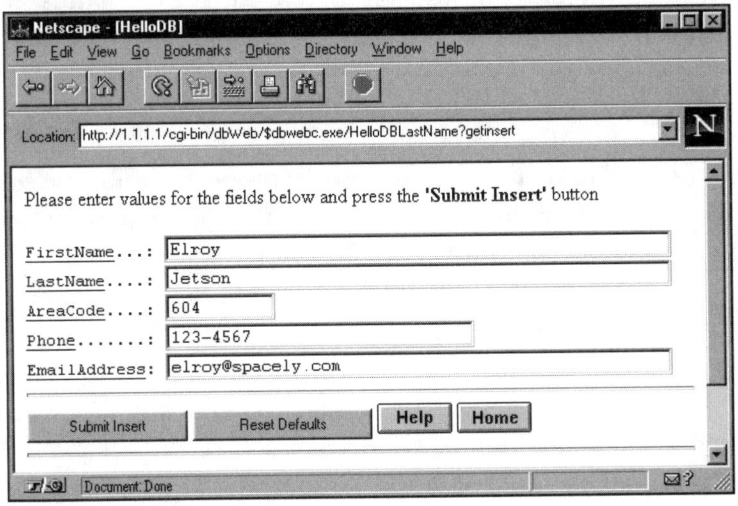

Figure 6.23 The HelloDB insert form.

So, we created an Insert form by using the Schema Wizard to modify the schema, and the same approach could be used to create Update and Delete forms.

Interview with Jim Laurel of Aspect Software Engineering

Aspect is a small company based in Honolulu, and dbWeb and iBASIC are their main products. Jim Laurel is a founder of Aspect and one of the developers of dbWeb. We talked to Jim about dbWeb, iBASIC, and the future of Web database development tools.

What was the design goal behind dbWeb and iBASIC?

With dbWeb we wanted to do a product for people who just wanted to publish a database on the Web and didn't want to deal with a lot of complexity. However, once people got going they asked for more power, so we developed iBASIC. dbWeb 2.0 will combine both tools, so it should be useful to both programmers and non-programmers.

Could you describe the different parts of dbWeb 1.0?

Sure. dbWeb 1.0 has four components: there's the NT service, the CGI program, the Repository, and the Administration tool. When the CGI program gets a request from the Web server it wakes up and establishes communication with the NT service through a named pipe. Then it hands off the request to the service, which deals with the request, and sends the results back up the pipe to the Web server, which then hands the results back to the browser.

How do you create an application with dbWeb?

You'd go into the Administration tool and select the columns that you want to have displayed on your form, and set properties for those columns—things like how wide should it be, and what the format should look like—and once you've defined all that, the Administration tool writes that information out to the Repository. Then, when a request comes down the pipe from the browser, the NT service goes and looks at the Repository and says, "I have this request to execute method x against this data source. How do I satisfy it?" and it finds the information it needs in the Repository. Then it goes off and queries the ODBC data source. Now, when it does that query it also does a couple of other things. If it's a query for a non-secure database, then the service looks in the connection pool and finds an ODBC connection that is open but currently not in use. Then it uses that connection to query the data source.

Does the developer have any control over the connection pool?

When you set up a schema with the Administrator you can decide how long the connections will live before they time out. Say you set the time-out at three minutes, then if you have a site that gets hit once every minute, that's great because the connection stays around all the time. So because the connections in the pool are recycled, the user that's making the query doesn't have to suffer the overhead for ODBC connect time.

When the NT service contacts the data source does it generate an SQL string?

Yes. Based on what's stored in the Repository, dbWeb generates the appropriate SQL string and sends it to the ODBC data source.

Could you tell us something about iBASIC?

We wanted to make the applications more customizable on the server side. Also, we didn't want to invent yet another proprietary language, so we asked ourselves, "What's the most popular scripting language right now that people with NT Web servers are familiar with?" And the answer was Visual BASIC. So, we are bundling a VBA interpreter (Visual BASIC for Applications) into dbWeb 2.0.

What's the relation between iBASIC and HTML?

You type in an HTML page and do callouts to VBA. An iBASIC script looks like an HTML page with little references to iBASIC functions right in line.

And what's the relationship between iBASIC and VBA?

iBASIC is 100 percent compatible with Microsoft VBA. The only difference is that it offers new methods to send output to the browser and new methods for retrieving information from CGI collections. All the environment variables and things that you work with in CGI are all implemented in iBASIC as collections.

Are collections a normal thing with Visual BASIC?

Yes, they are. For example, a simple Visual BASIC form that has some text boxes and buttons and things like that on it, also has something that you can access called a controls collection. You can loop through it and interrogate each element of the collection for things such as, "What kind of control are you? What is your maximum length?" and that kind of thing.

Could you say more about your extensions to VBA?

VBA doesn't understand Web servers and security and all that other Web stuff, but iBASIC does. We built a whole bunch of extensions to the VBA language that allow you to build Web applications really easily.

What do you think people will develop with iBASIC?

We've been coming to see that databases are just one kind of information that you can deploy over the Web, and there are lots of other things out there—there's audio, there are maps, there are instruments—that people want to publish. We saw databases as the first thing you'd want to attack, but we realized that once people got past databases they'd want to incorporate other kinds of information into their applications. That is something that iBASIC will make easy. For example, let's say you could be shown a graphical image of a map with pin points that described a national park. Wouldn't you like to click on one of those national parks and have a database query be fired that gives you information about that region? Or wouldn't it be really neat to execute a database query—let's say that you are looking for bookstores that carry a new book—and you could type your zip code in and you would get back not just a listing of the bookstores near where you live, but a map too.

What's the value of being able to program on the server side?

You name it. Federal Express could easily have done their package tracking with something like iBASIC. You can do traditional database applications, you can do equipment control applications, and the list goes on and on. Once you start thinking about something like iBASIC, which has access to the operating system APIs, and APIs presented by other pieces of software, and has access to OLE automation servers, you can begin thinking about publishing any kind of data you want on the Web. For example, through OLE automation over the Web, we've been able to take a browser and make a query that causes a copy of Excel to instantiate on the server, open a spreadsheet, retrieve information out of it, format it, and send it back out to the browser. So you think, gee, any application that can function as an OLE automation server can be a source of information that can be published on the Web.

You mentioned earlier that you could hook up a Web browser to some equipment?

Exactly! For example, say you had a medical device that monitored heart rate, and it's hooked up to a patient or an animal that you are experimenting on. Now, say you have a whole bunch of people that need current information on the information coming from the monitoring device in real time. Well, the monitoring device is going to have some kind of DLL that can be called to poll the device and get some information. So, with iBASIC, you could have all that hooked up to the server and the server could then respond to requests, make the connection to the hardware device, and send it back to the browser. And all you would have to do is declare a function and make a function call just like in Visual BASIC.

Would that program be able to handle multiple queries at the same time?

You bet. We have two versions right now. There's a CGI version that runs standard CGI 1.1, and there's a new version that is written for ISAPI. Under ISAPI there is higher concurrency because the ISAPI DLL is multi-threaded.

It sounds like OLE is important in this whole scenario.

The key thing that lets you do all this is OLE. iBASIC supports OLE automation servers. So, if you build an OLE automation server as an interface to your mapping or engineering software, or some equipment you had hooked up to an NT server, then you could have a Web server running on the computer along with iBASIC. And iBASIC could make function calls to the APIs for all those hardware devices.

That sounds pretty neat.

And when you start thinking about OLE, don't forget that more and more people are storing OLE objects inside BLOBs in databases. Thus, Web database stuff is going to become increasingly important, in my opinion, but it's not correct to think of databases only as rows and columns. OLE opens so many doors that I think that a lot of the energy being spent building OCXs on the client side will be directed back onto the server side as people start turning their sights back that way.

Do you see the OLE way of getting at databases—OLE DB—replacing the ODBC method?

I think so. OLE DB can use ODBC. It really wraps ODBC.

Do you think OLE DB is more general than ODBC?

Yes. There's also the possibility that it will run over a network that is really cool. You could have an OLE automation server that happened to be doing OLE DB, running on a computer elsewhere on your network, and the iBASIC machine comes along and wants to instantiate a copy of that OLE automation server and do something with it. There are a lot of different things you can do once you get into OLE.

That's great! It's tough writing about client/server because you define the client, you define the server, you define their functions, and then suddenly they switch roles!

You wouldn't believe the confusion that there is just between client-side and server-side scripting. A lot of people have trouble with that. Some people are calling the Web the next evolution of client/server and in one sense it is, but in another sense you could say it's the next generation host terminal!

Because the Web has a rather fixed definition of client and server?

It really does. I always laugh when we talk about the Web to people who are in corporate MIS and they say, "Oh, I'm an old COBOL guy and I don't really understand this new Web stuff", and I want to say, "Guess what? Your time is here again! The Web is the vt100 of the '90s!"

CHAPTER

7

JAGG

JAGG

BulletProof Corporation

15732 Los Gatos Blvd., Suite 525

Los Gatos, California 95032

Phone   (800) 505-0105 or (408) 374-2323

Fax   (408) 395-6026

Email   support@bulletproof.com

URL   http://www.bulletproof.com

Overview

JAGG lets developers use Java to create full-function database client applications that access the database through a Web server. Because it uses the stateless HTTP convention, many more database interactions can take place over a given time period than would be possible with a continuous database connection.

JAGG consists of a CGI gateway program called **Jagg.exe** that resides on the server side, and a Java class called **Jagg.class** that is compiled into a client applet that you write in Java. **Jagg.exe** accepts strings passed to it by the client applet—the strings must be ODBC SQL statements—then passes the strings to an ODBC data source. When the data source responds to a SQL statement, **Jagg.exe** passes the

163

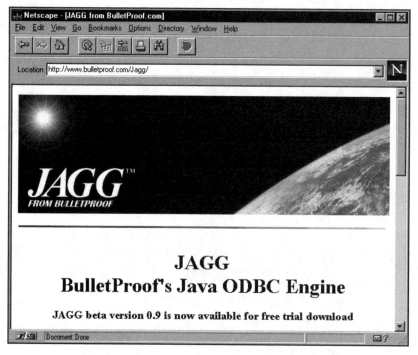

Figure 7.1 The JAGG home page.

result set back to the Web server, which in turn passes it back to the client applet. HTTP is used in both directions. Figure 7.2 shows how it all fits together.

Using Java on the client side means you can build very interactive client programs with rich features. Using stateless HTTP to communicate with the database—rather than maintaining an open TCP/IP link—means that database connections will be held by each client for a very short time, allowing for a large traffic load. However, using HTTP also means that defining and controlling multi-step transactions will be more difficult.

Features
Environment

Jagg.exe runs on Windows NT as a CGI program. **Jagg.class** can be compiled into any Java client applet developed on any platform that supports Java. Once it has been compiled, it will run on any Java-capable browser running on any platform.

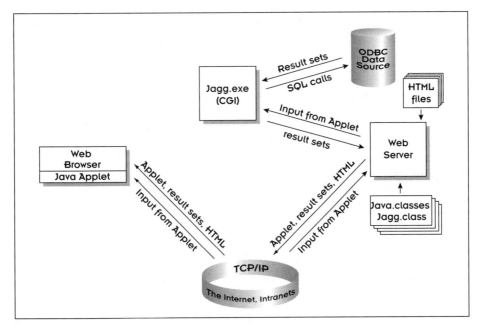

Figure 7.2   The components of JAGG.

Trial version

A trial version is available from the JAGG Web site **http://www.bulletproof.com/ Jagg/** (Figure 7.1.)

Web Server Compatibility

Jagg.exe works with any NT Web server that supports standard CGI.

Web Browser Compatibility

Java works with Netscape Navigator 2.0.

ODBC Compatibility

JAGG complies with ODBC Level 1.

Learnability

Most of your effort will be needed to learn Java (if you don't already know it). **Jagg.class** defines several methods but only four of them are necessary for data manipulation; the others do simple things such as get error messages, send passwords, and set data source names. JAGG also achieves simplicity by masking much of the detail of the ODBC layer. The documentation is skimpy, but it covers enough to get you going. There is no tutorial.

Programmability

On the client side, JAGG is very programmable since Java is a full-strength computer language. On the server side, **Jagg.exe** can not be programmed.

Efficiency

Java applets run as interpreted bytecode, which means that they are much slower than compiled C or C++ applications. However, the benefit of running interpreted code is that the applet works without modification on any Web browser that has a Java interpreter. You can program Java applets to do input edits and validations on the client side, which will reduce the amount of code transferred across the net.

On the server, **Jagg.exe** is a compiled CGI program written in C++ so it runs quickly. Note that CGI programs must be loaded every time they are called (in this case for every SQL statement). Thus, they incur some system overhead, but since **Jagg.exe** is relatively small (only 118K) the overhead is not great.

Security

Jagg.class provides methods for handling database level user-authentication with UserID, Password, and workstation ID. A Java applet can be programmed to enforce authentication. No encryption/decryption is provided for data transmitted across the network.

Error Handling

After making each SQL call, **Jagg.exe** sends back a success or failure flag. If a call fails, then your code can handle it by calling the class method **Jagg.getError**, which retrieves standard ODBC SQL error strings.

Debugging

JAGG provides no debugging tools and Java applets can't write to a file, so they have no way to record program faults. Except for the ODBC error messages, you're on your own!

Input Validation

Because JAGG uses Java on the client side, you can do very complete input edits and validations. Any input that can be handled with logic (for example, type checking, range checking, date checking, etc.) can be programmed, and input validations that require database table lookups can be handled by making SQL calls.

Support for Transaction Control

JAGG does not currently support transaction control.

Cookies

No cookies. Java applets cannot write to the hard disk.

Hello Database with JAGG

This program differs from the other Hello Database programs in two ways:

*   The output displays on the same HTML page as the input form. This is possible because the database results are returned as data instead of HTML text. So, the Java applet can display it in a screen area allocated by the Web browser.

*   The input form is specified using the Java language rather than using HTML input form tags.

Setup and Operation

*   From the CD-ROM, copy all the files from the directory **\BookData\ Demo\JAGG** onto the hard drive. Use the same directory structure and names.

*   From the CD-ROM, copy the file **\BookData\Products\JAGG\ jaggi0.zip** into any directory on your hard drive and unzip the file. This file contains documentation for JAGG. It's in HTML, so you can view it with a Web browser.

*   From the CD-ROM, copy the CGI program file **\BookData\Demo\JAGG\ JAGG.exe** to the directory where your Web server expects all CGI programs to run from. We placed ours in **d:\cgi-bin**, because our EMWAC Web server's data directory is set to **d:**.

- Set up your **CLASSPATH** environment variable **CLASSPATH=.;c\java\ lib\classes.zip**. This will ensure that the compiler will search the default directory when locating **Jagg.class**.

To run the demo, point Netscape 2.0 (or any other Java-capable browser) to the following URL:

```
http://1.1.1.1/BookData/Demo/Jagg/phone.html
```

(Don't forget to substitute your own IP address or domain name for **1.1.1.1**!) The Web page may take longer to load than a regular HTML page because it is downloading the Java applets. Make sure that all the applet classes are in the same directory as the HTML file **phone.html**. The applet tag in **phone.html** doesn't specify the attribute **codebase**, so the browser assumes that the classes reside in the same directory as **phone.html**.

Getting the Web browser to Recognize the Java Applet

The HTML tags **<APPLET>...</APPLET>** specify what Java applet the Web browser is to download. When a Java-capable browser sees these tags, it will make a request to the Web server to download the Java applet code. For example:

```
<applet code=GetPhone.class width=600 height=200></applet>
```

in the file **phone.html** tells the Web browser to run the class **GetPhone**, and to look for the code in the current directory where the **phone.html** file is located. It also says that the width and height of the applet are set to **600 × 200** pixels.

Note that this differs from how a JavaScript program would run. JavaScript code is located as text in the head part of an HTML file and is not compiled. In contrast, the downloaded class **GetPhone.class** is compiled bytecode, which reduces the amount of code that is downloaded.

Query

The Java applet program that queries the ODBC database (Figure 7.3) is called **GetPhone.java**. This simple program consists of two classes,

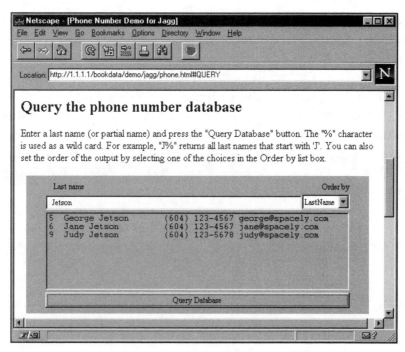

Figure 7.3   The Hello Database query input screen.

GetPhone and **QueryPanel**. **GetPhone** (Listing 7.1) is the applet class that
starts the whole thing going. In **GetPhone**, the only method used is **init**,
which is the standard way to start a Java applet.

Listing 7.1   The **GetPhone** class, which defines the applet

```
/**
 * GetPhone -- This class initiates the applet.
 */
public class GetPhone extends Applet {

   QueryPanel m_qp;

   public void init() {
      setBackground(Color.lightGray);
      setFont(new Font("TimesRoman", Font.PLAIN, 12));
      m_qp = new QueryPanel();
      add(m_qp);
      show();
   }

} // GetPhone Class
```

GetPhone sets some background colors and fonts and instantiates the **QueryPanel** class. Once instantiated, the **QueryPanel** object is added to the applet and displayed. The **QueryPanel** class does most of the work. It displays the panel that requests the query input, sends the query to the server when the **Query Database**1 button is pressed, and then shows the result set. **QueryPanel** has three member variables. The first, **m_lstResults**, is a listbox that displays query results and error messages. The other two, **m_lastnameField** and **m_lstOrderBy**, hold the input parameters for the query. Here is a snippet showing just these variables and the definition of the **QueryPanel** class:

```
/**
 * QueryPanel -- This class displays a panel to
 *               query the database "PhoneList"
 *               and show the results.
 */
class QueryPanel extends Panel {

    List m_lstResults;
    TextField m_lastnameField = new TextField("%", 65);
    Choice m_lstOrderBy       = new Choice();
```

QueryPanel's constructor method gets input from a user. To maintain the look of the screen we used the **Layout Manager GridBagLayout** from the Abstract Window Toolkit package that comes with Sun's Java Development Kit. Here it is:

```
/**
 * QueryPanel -- Constructor to build and display the panel to query
 *               the database.
 */
public QueryPanel() {

    // intialize
    super();

    // Set up layout for QueryPanel
    GridBagLayout gridbag = new GridBagLayout();
    GridBagConstraints c = new GridBagConstraints();
    setLayout(gridbag);
```

```java
// Set up default constraints
c.fill = GridBagConstraints.NONE;

// Add last name label
Label label = new Label( "Last name", Label.LEFT);
c.weightx = 0.0;
c.anchor = GridBagConstraints.WEST;
gridbag.setConstraints(label, c);
add(label);

// Add order by label
Label orderbyLabel = new Label( "Order by", Label.RIGHT);
c.weightx = 0.0;
c.gridwidth = GridBagConstraints.REMAINDER;
c.anchor = GridBagConstraints.EAST;
gridbag.setConstraints( orderbyLabel, c);
add(orderbyLabel);

// Add text field
c.gridwidth = 1;
c.weightx = 0.0;
gridbag.setConstraints(m_lastnameField, c);
add(m_lastnameField);

// Add order by drop down list box
m_lstOrderBy.addItem("LastName");
m_lstOrderBy.addItem("AreaCode");
c.weightx = 0.0;
c.gridwidth = GridBagConstraints.REMAINDER;
c.anchor = GridBagConstraints.EAST;
gridbag.setConstraints(m_lstOrderBy, c);
add(m_lstOrderBy);

// Add list box used to display the results
m_lstResults = new List(7,false);
c.weightx = 0.0;
c.gridwidth = GridBagConstraints.REMAINDER;
c.gridheight = 7;
c.fill = GridBagConstraints.HORIZONTAL;
gridbag.setConstraints(m_lstResults, c);
add(m_lstResults);

// Add start button
Button btnQuery = new Button("Query Database");
c.weightx = 0.0;
c.weighty = 1.0;      // makes button show under output display
```

```
    c.gridwidth = GridBagConstraints.REMAINDER;
    gridbag.setConstraints(btnQuery, c);
    add(btnQuery);

}
```

The next method, **handleEvent**, is called whenever a mouse click, a key-board press, or other event takes place. The code shows the series of steps that take place to verify that the **Query Database** button has been pressed.

```
/**
 * handleEvent -- Acts on the button press
 */
public boolean handleEvent( Event evt) {

if ( (evt.id == Event.ACTION_EVENT)
        && (evt.target instanceof Button)) {
        String sButtonName = (String)evt.arg;
        if ( sButtonName.compareTo("Query Database") == 0) {
            queryRecord( "PhoneList");
            return true;
        }
    }
        return false;
}
```

First, **handleEvent** determines that it was an action event and that the event was a button, and then it checks that the button was labeled **Query Database**. Once these conditions are met, **handleEvent** invokes the method **queryRecord** and passes it the value **PhoneList**, which identifies the data source to query.

The next method, **queryRecord**, is where **Jagg.class** does its real work:

```
/**
 * queryRecord -- Sends the query to the Web server which runs the
 *                database gateway to query the ODBC database.
 */
void queryRecord(String sDataSourceName) {

    Vector vecResults = new Vector();
    int iRecords = -1;
```

```
String sQuery = "SELECT * FROM PhoneNumber WHERE LastName LIKE '" +
   m_lastnameField.getText() + "' ORDER BY " +
   (String)m_lstOrderBy.getSelectedItem() + ", FirstName";

   // *** I M P O R T A N T ***
   // This URL starts up the CGI program ( ie Jagg.exe which is the
   // database gateway program).  You must change this URL to your
   // domain and the directory or alias to where the program resides.

   // Instantiate the access to the Jagg database gateway
   Jagg dbGateway = new Jagg("http://1.1.1.1/cgi-bin/Jagg.exe");
   Jagg.setDSN( sDataSourceName);

   // Do the query
   iRecords = dbGateway.execSQL(sQuery, vecResults);
   if (iRecords == -1)
       m_lstResults.addItem("Error: " + Jagg.getError());
   else
       showResults( vecResults, iRecords);

}
```

The **queryRecord** method constructs a query string by concatenating strings of literals and member variables together to form a SQL statement. Then, the class **Jagg** is instantiated to create a database gateway object. The input parameter to the **Jagg** class constructor is the URL that specifies which CGI program to run on the Web server. You also need to set the data source name, by using the class method **Jagg.setDSN**.

At this point, the SQL statement is sent to the Web server. This is accomplished with the method **execSQL**, which sends the SQL statement and accepts the returned result set, which it stores in a vector object called **vecResults**. The number of records returned is stored in the variable **iRecords** or, if an error occurs, **iRecords** will be set to −1. The class method **Jagg.getError** is used to return a string containing a standard ODBC SQL error message. The documentation suggests that, to avoid overloading the server, it is good practice to set the maximum number of rows that the query will return (the default is 100). We didn't bother to do this because of the small number of records in the sample database.

The last method, **showResults**, displays the results that have been saved in **vecResults**.

```
/**
 * showResults -- Separate out the retrieved information and displays
 *                it in a list box.
 */
void showResults( Vector vecResults, int iNumRecords) {

    String BLANKS = "                                    ";

    // initialize
    m_lstResults.delItems(0, m_lstResults.countItems()-1);
    m_lstResults.clear();
    m_lstResults.setFont( new Font("Courier", Font.PLAIN, 8));

    int i=0;
    String sRecord;

    // Get the separator string used to delimit each field
    String sSeparator = new String(Jagg.getSEP());

    String sDisplayRecords[] = new String[iNumRecords];

    // Set the display widths of the fixed font fields
    int iWidths[] = new int[4];
    iWidths[0] = 3;     // User ID
    iWidths[1] = 20;    // Full Name
    iWidths[2] = 15;    // Phone number (with area code)
    iWidths[3] = 20;    // Email address

    String sUserID, sFirstName, sLastName, sAreaCode, sPhone,
      sEmailAddress;
    String sTemp;

    // Loop through each vector element( ie one record) and add it to
    // the list box.
    for (Enumeration e = vecResults.elements(); e.hasMoreElements();
       i++) {
        sRecord = (String)e.nextElement();
        StringTokenizer fields = new StringTokenizer( sRecord);

        // Separate out fields
        sUserID       = (String)fields.nextToken( sSeparator);
        sFirstName    = (String)fields.nextToken( sSeparator);
        sLastName     = (String)fields.nextToken( sSeparator);
        sAreaCode     = (String)fields.nextToken( sSeparator);
        sPhone        = (String)fields.nextToken( sSeparator);
        sEmailAddress = (String)fields.nextToken( sSeparator);
```

```
        sDisplayRecords[i] = "";

        // Add User ID
        sUserID += BLANKS;
        sDisplayRecords[i] = sUserID.substring(0, iWidths[0]-1) + " ";

        // Add Full name. Put first and last name together
        sTemp = sFirstName + " " + sLastName + BLANKS;
        sDisplayRecords[i] += sTemp.substring(0, iWidths[1]-1) + " ";

        // Add phone number (with area code)
        sTemp = "(" + sAreaCode + ") "+ sPhone + BLANKS;
        sDisplayRecords[i] += sTemp.substring(0, iWidths[2]-1) + " ";

        // Add email address
        sEmailAddress += BLANKS;
        sDisplayRecords[i] += sEmailAddress.substring(0, iWidths[3]-1);

        m_lstResults.addItem( sDisplayRecords[i]);

        fields = null;
    }
}
```

Each element of the vector **vecResults** contains one row of the result set. The code loops through the vector and extracts rows, and then it extracts individual fields from each row. These fields are then formatted into a displayable string and added to the listbox **m_lstResults**. The fields in each row are separated by delimiters and the delimiter character is configurable when you execute a query. We used the **StringTokenizer** class to parse out each field. Finally, the parsed fields are strung together to form a display string and added to the listbox. At this point, the process loops again for the next record. This repeats until there are no more records in the vector.

Insert

The Java applet program that inserts a record into the ODBC database (Figure 7.4) is called **InsPhone.java**. Inserting a record is straightforward. First, place a second **<APPLET> ...</APPLET>** tag in the **phone.html file**, which will tell the Web browser to run the applet **InsPhone.class**.

```
<applet code=InsPhone.class width=600 height=200></applet>
```

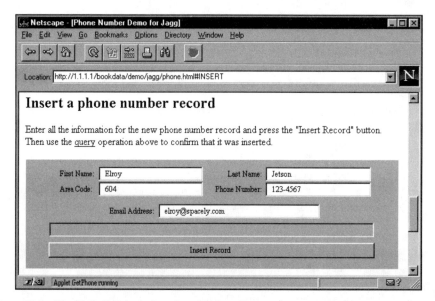

Figure 7.4   The Hello Database insert record input screen.

As always, a Java applet starts by running the standard **init** method of the applet class **InsPhone** (Listing 7.2). In this case, **init** simply instantiates the **InsertPanel** class and makes it visible.

Listing 7.2   InsPhone class, which defines the applet

```
/**
 * InsPhone -- Simple hello program to demonstrate inserting a record
 *             into a database using the Jagg ODBC gateway.
 */

import java.applet.Applet;
import java.awt.*;
import java.util.Vector;

/**
 * InsPhone -- This class initiates the class InsertPanel which does most
 *             of the work.
 */
public class InsPhone extends Applet {

    public void init() {
        InsertPanel ip = new InsertPanel();
        add(ip);
```

```
        show();
    }

} // end class InsPhone
```

InsertPanel is the class that does most of the work. This code snippet shows the member variables of **InsertPanel**:

```
/**
 * InsertPanel -- Class to get data and runs
 *                the SQL insert command.
 */
class InsertPanel extends Panel {

    // Member variables that hold the data to input
    TextField m_txtFirstName, m_txtAreaCode,
            m_txtLastName, m_txtPhone, m_txtEmailAddress;
    TextField m_txtStatus;
```

The **InsertPanel** constructor method displays input fields where the user can enter data that will be inserted into the **PhoneNumber** table.

```
/**
 * InsertPanel -- Constructor to build the input screen.
 */
public InsertPanel() {

    super();

    setLayout( new BorderLayout());

    // Get name and phone number (North panel)
    Panel nPanel = new Panel();
    nPanel.setLayout(new FlowLayout());

    Panel nwPanel = new Panel();
    nwPanel.setLayout( new GridLayout(0,1));
    Label firstName = new Label( "First Name:", Label.LEFT);
    Label areaCode = new Label( "Area Code:", Label.LEFT);
    nwPanel.add(firstName);
    nwPanel.add(areaCode);
    Panel nccPanel = new Panel();
    nccPanel.setLayout( new GridLayout(0,1));
```

```
Label lastName = new Label( "Last Name:", Label.RIGHT);
Label phoneNumber = new Label( "Phone Number:", Label.RIGHT);
nccPanel.add(lastName);
nccPanel.add(phoneNumber);
Panel ncPanel = new Panel();
ncPanel.setLayout( new GridLayout(0,1));
m_txtFirstName = new TextField( "", 25);
m_txtAreaCode = new TextField( "", 5);
ncPanel.add( m_txtFirstName);
ncPanel.add( m_txtAreaCode);

Panel nePanel = new Panel();
nePanel.setLayout( new GridLayout(0,1));
m_txtLastName = new TextField( "", 25);
m_txtPhone = new TextField( "", 15);
nePanel.add( m_txtLastName);
nePanel.add( m_txtPhone);

nPanel.add( nwPanel);
nPanel.add( ncPanel);
nPanel.add( nccPanel);
nPanel.add( nePanel);
add("North", nPanel);

// Get email address (Center panel)
Panel cPanel = new Panel();
cPanel.setLayout( new FlowLayout());
Label emailaddress = new Label("Email Address:", Label.LEFT);
cPanel.add( emailaddress);
m_txtEmailAddress = new TextField( "", 40);
cPanel.add( m_txtEmailAddress);
add("Center", cPanel);

// Status message area and submit button
Panel sPanel = new Panel();
sPanel.setLayout( new GridLayout(2,1, 0, 8));
m_txtStatus = new TextField( "", 50);
m_txtStatus.setEditable(false);
sPanel.add( m_txtStatus);

Button btnInsert = new Button( "Insert Record");
sPanel.add( btnInsert);

add("South", sPanel);

}
```

The method **InsertPanel** used to lay out the fields is a combination of **FlowLayout** and **GridLayout** from the AWT package in the Sun JDK.

The method **handleEvent** waits for the **Insert Record** button to be pressed, and then calls the method **insertRecord** and passes it the data source name **PhoneList**.

```
/**
 * handleEvent -- Check for action and initiate it.
 */
public boolean handleEvent( Event evt) {

    if ( evt.id == Event.ACTION_EVENT &&
        ( evt.target instanceof Button)) {
        String sButtonName = (String)evt.arg;
        if ( sButtonName.compareTo("Insert Record") == 0) {
            insertRecord( "PhoneList");
            return true;
        }
    }
    return false;

}
```

The method **insertRecord** first puts up a status message indicating that it is working. Then it forms the SQL string to insert a record. Java makes this part easy with its effortless string concatenation:

```
/**
 * insertRecord -- Creates and executes the SQL insert.
 */
void insertRecord( String sDataSourceName) {

    int iRecords = 0;

    statusMsg( "Working...");

    // Create the SQL insert statement by concatenating string together.
    String sql = "INSERT INTO PhoneNumber " +
            " (FirstName, LastName, AreaCode, Phone, EmailAddress) " +
            "VALUES('" + m_txtFirstName.getText() +
            "', '" + m_txtLastName.getText() +
            "', '" + m_txtAreaCode.getText() +
```

```
                 "', '" + m_txtPhone.getText() +
                 "', '" + m_txtEmailAddress.getText() + "')";

   // *** I M P O R T A N T ***
   // This URL starts up the CGI program ( ie Jagg.exe which is the
   // database gateway program). You must change this URL to your
   // domain and the directory or alias to where the program resides.

   Jagg dbGateway = new Jagg( "http://1.1.1.1/cgi-bin/Jagg.exe");

   // Set the data source name. Note that this is a class method
   // call (i.e.,you use the Class Jagg, rather than the instantiated
   // object dbGateway.)
   Jagg.setDSN( sDataSourceName);

   Vector vecResults = new Vector();
   iRecords = dbGateway.execSQL( sql, vecResults);

   if ( iRecords == -1)
       statusMsg( "Error: " + Jagg.getError());
   else
       statusMsg( "Record has been inserted.");
}
```

Now the SQL statement is ready to be executed. Only three steps are required:

1. The CGI program **Jagg.exe** on the server side is invoked by instantiating the object **dbGateway**.

2. The data source name is set using the class method **Jagg.setDNS**. (Note that the data source name is set using a class method rather than an instantiated method. This is done so you can set the data source name once at the beginning of the program and do many SQL calls without having to reset the data source).

3. The SQL statement is sent by using the **execSQL** method, as was done in the Query example.

If the insert is successful, then the variable **iRecords** will be set to 0. If there is an error, then it will be set to –1. Again, you can use the method **Jagg.getError** to retrieve the full ODBC error messages.

Note that when we tested this applet, using Sun's Java appletviewer, everything worked well. However, when we tested it with the Netscape Web browser, the error message **Document contains no data** was returned. BulletProof's support person thought this might be caused by the extra tight security measures found in Netscape's Java implementation, when the browser is used with a Web server that doesn't have access to a domain name server. In spite of this error message, the record was still successfully inserted.

Interview with Scott Milener of BulletProof

BulletProof Corporation is a six-person company in Los Gatos, California. Their first products integrated distributed databases with Motorola pagers over CompuServe. They then developed a Web site that uses a Java applet to gather stock prices. JAGG emerged from this development. We talked to Scott about JAGG, the Web, Java, and "Webtop" software.

How long has BulletProof been around?

About two years now.

What was the company's original mission?

To produce advanced tools and services for individual investors. Our first product was a service that tracks stock data for your portfolio on CompuServe and calls you on your wireless pager.

Did you have the Web in mind back then?

At the time, we only thought of the Web as a promotion medium. Java didn't exist and we didn't realize the Web's potential.

Tell us about WallStreetWeb.

WallStreetWeb (Figure 7.5) is a service for investors. People pay a small monthly fee and they enter the names of stocks that they want to track. Then, when they browse their account on WallStreetWeb, they can get up-to-date prices on those stocks and look at the stock information in a variety of graphs.

How does it work?

It's a Java applet that runs on your Netscape browser and talks to a CGI program on the server side. The applet downloads the price history of the stocks from a database and then generates the analytical charts on the user's PC.

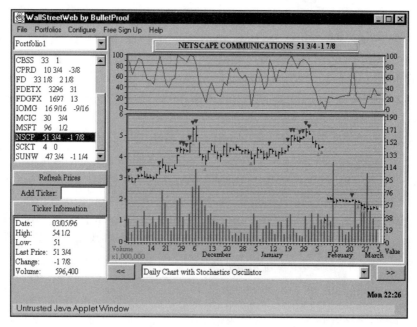

Figure 7.5   WallStreetWeb Java applet.

Did JAGG come out of that development?

Yes. JAGG is a development tool for producing similar Web sites with Java applets.

What is the market for JAGG?

Java developers and businesses worldwide. We've had requests from financial institutions, brokerages, online services, and companies that want to sell other stuff on the Web. Anyone who wants to develop a Webtop application that needs to get to a database.

Are these people giving you reasons for their interest?

How great the Web and Java are together! Everyone sees it. It's just a great way to disseminate and sell information!

How do you market JAGG?

On the Internet. We have been letting newsgroups know that it will be out soon, and we have a home page and some other people's links point to it.

How do you find the Web for reaching your market?

For reaching the Java market it's phenomenal! It's the only way to go! I can't imagine needing to put a Java tool on a shelf in a store. Anyone who is into Java is going to have a Netscape browser and be interested enough to browse Netscape's home page and find Java sites, and therefore find JAGG. So the Web has been phenomenal for that.

You said that JAGG gathers data. Can you explain how that works?

One part of JAGG is a Java class and the other part is a server engine that is a precompiled executable. The Java class can accept SQL statements written into your applet and knows how to translate those SQL statements across the Web to the server engine, which in turn talks to ODBC and says, "Here's a SQL statement, give me the data."

How does the applet do that? Through the Web server?

It works through the socket that the browser currently has open. It sends commands through the HTTP protocol with the SQL encrypted in there, and the server engine knows how to handle the SQL and how to grab the data from the ODBC compatible database. It can also work with a DBF file, so you don't even need to have a database.

How did your thinking change as you worked on WallStreetWeb and JAGG?

We realized there is a revolution happening here. With the power of Java we can build what I call a Webtop application and have it be as powerful as a desktop application. So, once you have that ability, why distribute a desktop application when you can do it over the Web and have the same power?

By "desktop application" you mean a program installed on your local computer and using all the resources, right?

Right. Like anything that you use today. But when we go Webtop you just pay a small monthly fee to use our service and our applet, and every time we fix a bug or do an update, everyone instantly has it. That's unbeatable. So we've gone Webtop and it makes no sense to go back.

So is your company reforming itself around this technology?

Right. The movement and energy in our company is all toward Internet services and Java and the Webtop idea.

What is JAGG written in?

The client-side applet is written in Java and the server-side engine is a CGI program written in C++.

What OS does the server engine run in?

It runs on Windows NT. By using translators you can get to Unix databases, but it's currently optimized for NT.

Are you concentrating on the NT platform?

Yes. Everything we are doing is on NT and it's clear that the growth is in NT. Our prediction is that Unix will be dead in five years.

Dead altogether? Or just dead as a Web platform?

As a Web platform. People are moving to NT.

I noticed that you are running the Microsoft Internet Information Server. Is that working out well?

Yes. We also use SQL Server, and the combination of NT and SQL Server has been excellent. It's clean and fast and has low overhead.

Could you do the same things you are doing with Java by just using the Netscape browser with extended HTML and input forms and sending back GIFs or graphs?

HTML doesn't even compare. You've seen WallStreetWeb, how fast it is and how it all comes up in one separate window. With HTML there is no way to terminate on actions, so you have to type something in and hit submit and then rewrite the whole form. And generating GIFs on the fly works, but it's so cumbersome. With Java it's like having a real local application running.

So most of the actual computing is done on the client side?

That's right. When you see a graph redraw, the algorithms are in the applet and we have validation code on fields. It's like a real Windows application.

A Web browser could replace a lot of the dedicated DBMS clients out there and become the universal client. Do you think that a Web browser combined with a Java applet could replicate all the functions of a database client?

I think it will for a lot of applications. It can't today, partly because of speed and because Java needs to get better, but bandwidth is increasing and I think within a few years bandwidth won't be a question anymore. By then Java will be solid and there will be more Web languages competing with Java. Also, the distribution model is so clean and that will drive acceptance.

How do you handle input validations with JAGG?
Basic field validation is all done in the applet with Java code. We can check types, formats, lengths, and we can also query the database.

What if a person typed in IDM instead of IBM into your WallStreetWeb Java applet?
Once they hit Enter we would go to the database and see if it existed.

Does JAGG use industry-standard security protocols or have you done your own?
Currently, Java is not secure. We have figured out ways of forcing some of it through the secure socket, but not consistently. We are going to let Netscape and/or Sun handle that issue.

Are you looking at Visual Basic scripting as an alternative language?
No.

Could someone rewrite a Visual Basic client program in Java using Jagg.class?
Yes, absolutely.

CHAPTER

8

DataRamp

DataRamp
Working Set, Inc.
8 Dover Lane
Lexington, MA 02173
Phone   (617) 674-2669
Email   sales@dataramp.com
URL   http://dataramp.com

Overview

DataRamp enables desktop client applications to access ODBC databases over TCP/IP networks. It's not *exactly* a Web database tool since it doesn't rely on HTTP and HTML, but it complements Web database tools very well and can be closely integrated with Web pages, so we included it.

The product consists of the DataRamp Server and the DataRamp Client. When they are installed, client programs—written in Visual BASIC, PowerBuilder and other languages—can be used to access ODBC databases—like SQL Server and Sybase—over the Internet and various Intranets. The DataRamp Server is a Windows NT service that listens for incoming requests from DataRamp-enabled applications. The DataRamp Client is a DLL that is linked

187

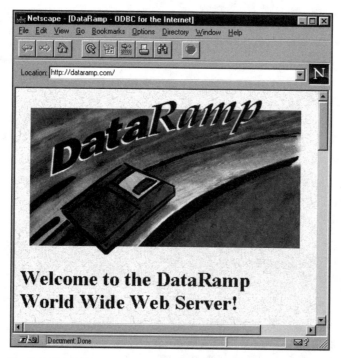

Figure 8.1   The DataRamp home page.

into an application program. Figure 8.2 shows how DataRamp can be used on a stand-alone basis. Figure 8.3 shows DataRamp integrated with a Web browser and server.

DataRamp is useful in any of the following scenarios:

- Your Web database application needs large screen forms with complex, built-in logic

- You want advanced transaction control

- You want to do cross-database SQL operations

- You have existing client/server applications that you want to use over the Internet

- You want to get tabular datasets onto the client side rather than hypertext

- You want to eliminate the cost of a privately maintained wide area network

- You want to perform remote database maintenance and administration

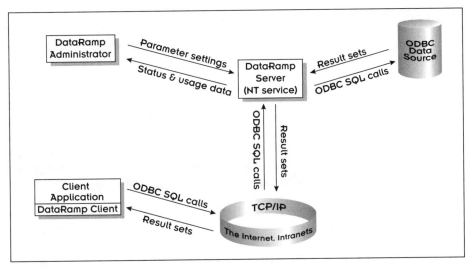

Figure 8.2 The components of DataRamp, used without a Web browser.

Features

Environment

The DataRamp Server runs on Windows NT 3.50 or later, Workstation, or Advanced Server. The DataRamp Client runs on Windows 3.1, Windows 95, and Windows NT.

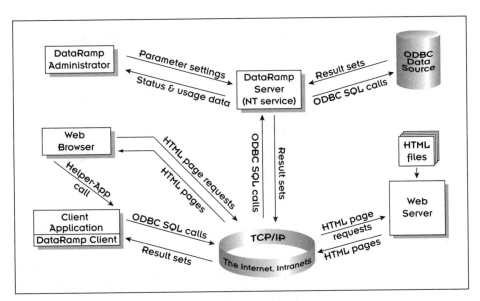

Figure 8.3 The components of DataRamp, used with a Web browser.

To install, configure, and use the DataRamp Server, you need:

- Administrator privileges, so you can use the Services applet in the Windows NT Control Panel

- A 32-bit TCP/IP stack

- An IP address, on which the DataRamp Server will listen for incoming connections

- Network access (if you are behind a firewall, you must establish outgoing and incoming TCP access on port 461 for DataRamp to work)

- 32-bit ODBC drivers (you must have at least one 32-bit driver on your system; the DataRamp Server does not work with 16-bit ODBC drivers)

- ODBC data source names (use the ODBC Administrator to create the data source names that will be accessible to DataRamp users)

Trial Version

- A trial version of the client-side module is available from the DataRamp Web site, **http://dataramp.com** (Figure 8.1).

- A trial version of the server-side program is available on request. Either email to **sales@dataramp.com** or phone them at 1-617-863-2339 and request a free 30-day evaluation copy. They will email you back instructions on downloading the server-side program.

Network Compatibility

The DataRamp Client can use any Winsock-compatible TCP/IP stack.

Web Server Compatibility

DataRamp can run by itself, without a Web browser, however it can be integrated with a Web browser by:

- Running it from a link on a Web page

- Using a Web page to introduce, document, and download a DataRamp-enabled client program

If a DataRamp-enabled client is called from a Web browser it will happily share the TCP/IP stack with the browser.

ODBC Compatibility

DataRamp supports ODBC Version 2.0. The DataRamp Client ODBC driver is Level 1 compliant and supports all Core and Level 1 API calls. Additionally, the following Level 2 calls are supported: **SQLForeignKeys**, **SQLMoreResults**, **SQLNativeSQL**, **SQLNumParams**, **SQLPrimaryKeys**, **SQLProcedureColumns**, **SQLProcedures**, and **SQLSetScrollOptions**.

Until DataRamp came along, ODBC gateways were provided by database vendors and each gateway worked only with its vendor's database. A DataRamp Server can talk to any vendor-provided ODBC gateway and interact with the database behind it.

Asynchronous ODBC calls

The DataRamp Server supports asynchronous ODBC calls even when the data source ODBC driver does not. With asynchronous ODBC calls, the user of a DataRamp Client program could make a query, and then go and do something else. A signal would let the user know when the query is complete and the results available. Some calls can take a long time, so this is a useful feature.

Learnability

DataRamp itself is quite simple and can be learned quickly. Most of your learning effort would be needed to master ODBC SQL and Visual Basic or PowerBuilder (if you don't already have these skills). It would also help to have a grasp of client/server architecture and TCP/IP networks.

Programmability

This is very complete. The development tools used to produce DataRamp-enabled client applications are full-strength languages with special extensions for database programming.

Efficiency

The speed of database operations done with DataRamp is affected by several factors. The ODBC layer adds overhead. The DataRamp Server layer imposes an additional speed penalty. However, the most significant influence on speed is the data rate of a typical 14.4 KBPS modem and the bandwidth of the Internet. Applications that make frequent requests for metadata (data that describes data) will run more slowly than applications that request metadata once and keep it on the client side for future reference. On a LAN with a high data transfer rate, ODBC calls for metadata might go unnoticed, but on the Internet they could be too expensive. Also, some ODBC calls are slower than others, so a careful choice of calls can make a difference. The DataRamp Server Administrator (Figure 8.4) records the number and size of messages sent and received. You can use this information to analyze message traffic and fine-tune an application.

Security

The DataRamp Server comes in a clear version and a secure version. The secure server uses RSA public-key encryption technology to protect data traveling over the Internet. When a DataRamp Client connects to a DataRamp Secure Server, the key exchange occurs automatically and transparently. You can also install DataRamp inside a firewall as long as the firewall administrator allows incoming and outgoing TCP activity on port 461.

Error Handling

The server returns ODBC SQL error messages to the client application.

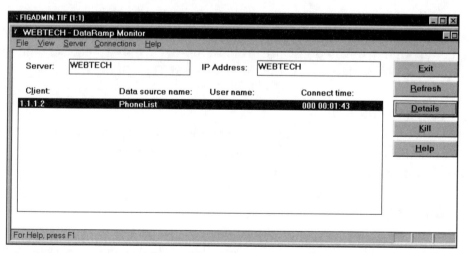

Figure 8.4 The DataRamp Server Administrator.

Input Validation

This is very complete. Client programs are programmed with full-strength languages and database access goes through whatever integrity constraints have been implemented in the ODBC database.

Support for Transaction Control

This is also very complete. The ODBC SQL standard permits good transaction definition and control, including rollback and commit.

Hello Database with DataRamp and Visual Basic

This version of the Hello Database program is a client application written in Visual Basic 3.0. We selected Visual Basic because it is the language of choice for many programmers. We could have used a higher-level tool, such as PowerBuilder, to write the application, but we thought that using a general-purpose programming language would better illustrate the steps involved in creating an ODBC client application.

Setup and Operation

Installing the DataRamp Server (Version 1.0)

- The DataRamp Server program is *not* on the CD-ROM. You can request a free 30-day evaluation copy and download it from their server. Once you get it down, put the self-extracting archive file **Serv01.exe** into a temp directory and run it.

- Run the Setup.exe program that has been extracted.

- Use the default directory suggested by the setup program, **\WINAPP\OSV3210**, in our case.

- The setup program will run you through the rest of the steps. The most important part is to ensure that the listening address is correct; it should be the name or IP address of the server, which in our case is **1.1.1.1**. Upon successful completion, the setup program will have installed an NT service called DataRamp Server. This will start up automatically the next time the administrator restarts the NT server.

- If ODBC 2.5 is installed, then not much needs to be done other than to make sure that your ODBC data sources are declared with the ODBC administrator. If ODBC 2.1 is installed, then make sure that the NT service is set to manual startup and that the Log On As Account (in the same screen as the NT Service startup screen) is set to This Account.

Installing the DataRamp Client

- You must install the DataRamp Client on every client computer that will call the DataRamp Server.

- On the client computer, put the self-extracting archive CD-ROM file **\BookData\Products\DataRamp\Cli3201.exe** (32 bit version) or **\BookData\Products\DataRamp\Cli1601.exe** (16 bit version) into a temporary directory and run it.

- Run the **setup.exe** program that will be extracted.

- If the DataRamp Client is being installed on the NT server host machine—which would happen when the server administrator wanted to test out the DataRamp Client without having to go to a separate computer—make sure that the DataRamp Server NT service is not running.

Establishing an ODBC data source with the Microsoft ODBC Administrator

Everyone who uses an ODBC database client application will need to tell the database client where to find the ODBC data source. You can do this with the Windows ODBC Administrator (Figure 8.5), which is found in the control panel of all standard Windows systems.

DataRamp provides a tutorial help file that does a good job of walking you through this process. To specify an ODBC data source, open File Manager and double-click on **\windows\system\osv10.hlp**, which will bring up the DataRamp help file. When the help file appears, click on the link **How to Use the DataRamp Client**, and then click on the link **Configuring the Client**. If you are using Windows NT, then the help file will be in **\winnt35\system32\osv10.hlp**. Use the ODBC data source name **PhoneList** where the tutorial asks for a data source name. It should be the same name as was specified on the server-side data source (that is, **PhoneList**). If no data source has been set up on the server-side yet, then you must do this first. Install the server-side ODBC data source as a System Data Source, specifying the ODBC Access driver. Name the data source **PhoneList** and have it point to our Microsoft Access database, **PHONE.MDB** (Figure 8.6).

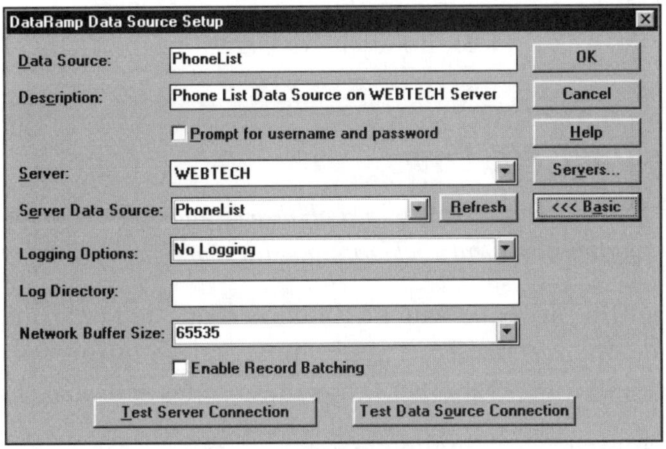

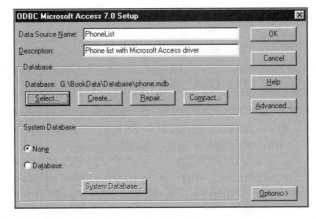

Figure 8.5   The ODBC Administrator showing the data source on the client side.

Figure 8.6   The ODBC Administrator showing the data source on the server side.

Visual Basic communicates with the installed ODBC drivers through a Microsoft-provided DLL named ODBC.DLL. This program is referred to as the Driver Manager, and it handles the communication between an application and the ODBC drivers. You can call functions in the Driver Manager from Visual Basic by using the **DECLARE FUNCTION** statement:

```
Declare Function SQLFetch Lib "odbc.dll" (ByVal hstmt&) As Integer
```

This declaration links a Visual Basic application to the ODBC.DLL. The declaration is found in the Microsoft ODBC SDK and is from the file **ODBCOR_M.BI**, which contains the ODBC core-level declarations. Another file, **ODBEXT_M.BI**, holds the declarations for ODBC Level 1 and Level 2 calls.

Handling ODBC SQL Errors

Note: The Hello Database program only demonstrates basic error handling. A working database client would require much more rigorous error handling.

When the ODBC driver executes a function requested by an application, a predefined code is returned. These return codes indicate success or failure, or give a warning. Table 8.1 shows these codes and what they indicate.

The basic approach to handling errors is:

1. Perform the ODBC function call.

2. Check the return code for **SQL_SUCCESS** or **SQL_SUCCESS_WITH_INFO**.

3. If an error code is returned, then the application should call the ODBC function, **SQLError**, to obtain more information about the error. If the return code is **SQL_SUCCESS_WITH_INFO**, then **SQLError** should be called because there is additional information that qualifies the success. It could be a general warning, or status information to be aware of for future calls, or other information.

ODBC provides a unified approach to working with databases and middleware from many different vendors. To identify the component in

Table 8.1   ODBC error messages.

Return Code	Description
SQL_SUCCESS	Function completed successfully. No additional information is available.
SQL_SUCCESS_WITH_INFO	Function completed successfully, possibly with a nonfatal error. The application can call SQLError to retrieve additional information.
SQL_NO_DATA_FOUND	All rows from the result set have been fetched.
SQL_ERROR	Function failed. The application can call SQLError to retrieve error information.
SQL_INVALID_HANDLE	Function failed due to an invalid environment handle, connection handle, or statement handle. This indicates a programming error. No additional information is available from SQLError.
Return Code	Description
SQL_STILL_EXECUTING	A function that was started asynchronously is still executing.
SQL_NEED_DATA	While processing a statement, the driver determined that the application needs to send parameter data values.

which an error occurred, errors are formatted in a way that tracks their origin. When an error originates in a data source the format looks like this:

```
[vendor-identifier][ODBC-component-identifier][data-source-
identifier]data-source-supplied-text
```

When an error originates in a component in a ODBC connection, it looks like this:

```
[vendor-identifier][ODBC-component-identifier]component-supplied-text
```

Table 8.2 describes each element in an error message.

Table 8.2   The elements of ODBC error messages.

Element	Meaning
vendor-identifier	Identifies the vendor of the component in which the error occurred or that received the error directly from the data source.
ODBC-component-identifier	Identifies the component in which the error occurred or that received the error directly from the data source.
data-source-identifier	Identifies the data source. For single-tiered drivers, this is typically a file format, such as Xbase1. For multi-tiered drivers, this is the DBMS product.
component-supplied-text	Generated by the ODBC component.
data-source-supplied-text	Generated by the data source.

If you see a message like this:

```
[Microsoft][ODBC dBASE Driver]Unable to allocate sufficient memory.
```

you will know the error occurred in the ODBC driver. From the message, you can identify the vendor of the component (Microsoft in this case), the name of the component (ODBC dBASE driver in this case), and lastly the actual error message.

If the error occurred in the data source itself, then you would see a message similar to:

```
[Microsoft][ODBC dBASE Driver][dBASE]Invalid file name;file _
   EMPLOYEE.DBF not found.
```

In addition to the vendor and component identification, it also includes the file format of the data source, in this case, dBASE.

For the Hello Database program we wrote two subroutines, **Attempt** and **DescribeError,** to make it easier to deal with ODBC SQL errors.

The **Attempt** subroutine checks for **SQL_SUCCESS**. When an error occurs it displays an error message in a dialog box and stops the program:

```
' Checks for success, stops if not
Sub Attempt (ResultCode As Integer, ErrorMessage As String)

  If (ResultCode <> SQL_SUCCESS) Then
    screen.MousePointer = Normal
    MsgBox ErrorMessage, StopIcon, "Unexpected ODBC Driver Function _
      failure"
    Stop
  End If

End Sub
```

The **DescribeError** subroutine retrieves the SQL error using the ODBC function call, **SQLError** and just displays it in a dialog box, as shown in Listing 8.1:

Listing 8.1   The DescribeError subroutine

```
' Displays all error if found
Sub DescribeError (ByVal hdbc As Long, ByVal hstmt As Long)
  ' Print an error message for the given connection handle
  ' and statement handle
  Dim rgbValue1 As String * 16
  Dim rgbValue3 As String * SBufferLen
  Dim Outlen As Integer
  Dim Native As Long

  rgbValue1 = String$(16, 0)
  rgbValue3 = String$(SBufferLen, 0)

  Do
    rc = SQLError(henv, hdbc, hstmt, rgbValue1, Native, rgbValue3, _
      SBufferLen, Outlen)
    screen.MousePointer = Normal

    ' See if error message was retrieved successfully
    If rc = SQL_SUCCESS Or rc = SQL_SUCCESS_WITH_INFO Then
        If Outlen = 0 Then
            MsgBox "Error -- No error information available", AttIcon, _
              AppName
        Else
            MsgBox Left$(rgbValue3, Outlen), AttIcon, AppName
        End If
    End If
  Loop Until rc <> SQL_SUCCESS

End Sub
```

Query

The query input form looks very much like the ones in the other Hello Database implementations but has some underlying differences. The main difference is that a user must first connect to the data source **PhoneList** through the menu selection: Connection | Connect to Phone List (Figure 8.7).

Behind the scenes

There doesn't appear to be that much difference between this interface and an HTML input form, but much more needs to be done to query the data source behind the scenes. Here are the basic steps for making ODBC calls to a data source:

1. Allocate memory for the environment.

2. Allocate memory for the connection and make the connection.

3. Allocate space for the SQL statement and make the SQL statement.

4. Receive and handle any return code results.

5. Free the statement.

6. Disconnect and free the connection space.

7. Free the environment space.

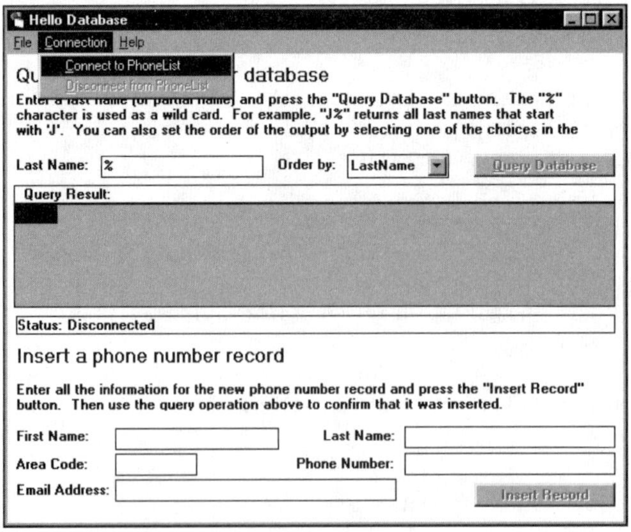

Figure 8.7 The Connect menu.

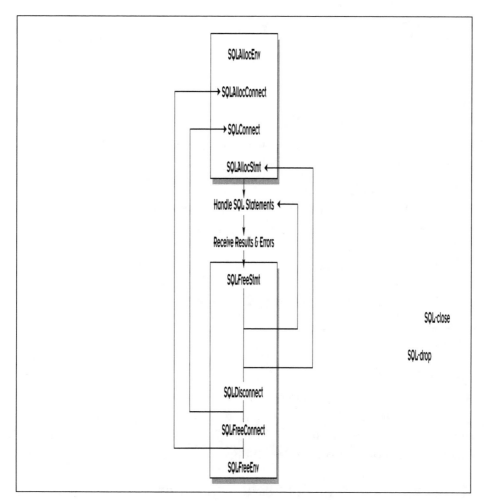

Figure 8.8   ODBC function-calling sequence and possible loops.

Figure 8.8 shows the sequence of events and the various points where these events can loop back.

Step 1 begins with the subroutine **Form_Load**:

```
' Initialize form
Sub Form_Load ()
  ' Set the caption
  Caption = AppName
  lstOrderBy.AddItem "LastName" ; order by These are the table field
names to _
```

```
    order by
  lstOrderBy.AddItem "AreaCode"
  Attempt SQLAllocEnv(henv), "Cannot allocate environment handle"
End Sub
```

SQLAllocEnv allocates memory space for the environment. This only has to be done once, and it causes the ODBC driver to initialize its environment, allocates memory to store information about the environment, and then returns a handle to that environment.

Before exiting the program, the allocated memory space in the ODBC driver needs to be freed up. You can do this with the ODBC function called **SQLFreeEnv**, which was used in the subroutine **Form_Unload**:

```
' Clean up before exiting
Sub Form_Unload (Cancel As Integer)
  ' Close any open connections and quit
  EndConnection
  Cancel = SQLFreeEnv(henv)
End Sub
```

Connecting to the data source

After preparing the environment, the next step is to establish the connection, which you do by allocating memory and then connecting. Perform these tasks in the functions called **BeginConnection** and **EndConnection**. BeginConnection is shown in Listing 8.2.

Listing 8.2   The BeginConnection subroutine

```
' Attempt to make connection.  If successful, allocate statement
' handle and place connection tag in the list box
Function BeginConnection (sDataSource As String)

  screen.MousePointer = HourGlass

  ' Allocate a connection handle
  Attempt SQLAllocConnect(henv, hdbc), "Cannot allocate connection _
    handle"

  ' Make the connection to the data source
  rc% = SQLConnect(hdbc, sDataSource, Len(sDataSource), "", 0, "", 0)
  If (rc% = SQL_ERROR) Or (rc% = SQL_INVALID_HANDLE) Then
    DescribeError hdbc, 0
```

```
      screen.MousePointer = Normal
      Exit Function
   ElseIf rc% = SQL_NO_DATA_FOUND Then
      screen.MousePointer = Normal
      Exit Function
   End If

   ' Allocate a statement handle
   Attempt SQLAllocStmt(hdbc, hstmt), "Cannot allocate statement handle"

   ' Houston, all systems go!
   frmQueryIns.mnuConnect.Enabled = False
   frmQueryIns.mnuDisconnect.Enabled = True
   frmQueryIns.mnuQueryDatabase.Enabled = True
   frmQueryIns.mnuInsertRecord.Enabled = True
   frmQueryIns.btnQueryDatabase.Enabled = True
   frmQueryIns.btnInsertRecord.Enabled = True

   BeginConnection = SQL_SUCCESS
   screen.MousePointer = Normal

   frmQueryIns.lblStatus = "Status: Connected"

   bConnected = True

End Function
```

The first thing the **BeginConnection** routine does is allocate memory for the connection. Then a handle to the environment and a pointer to the database connection handle, hdbc, is passed to the ODBC function **SQLAllocConnect**.

```
Attempt SQLAllocConnect(henv, hdbc), "Cannot allocate connection handle"
```

When the ODBC driver successfully allocates memory space, it assigns a value to **hdbc**. Use this to make the actual connection.

To make the connection to the data source, you use the ODBC function **SQLConnect**. The parameters are:

• The handle to the database connection

• The name of the data source

• The length of the data source name

- The userID and its length

- The password and its length

For our example, the data source did not require a user ID or password.

```
rc% = SQLConnect(hdbc, sDataSource, Len(sDataSource), "", 0, "", 0)
```

You can make simultaneous connections to other databases. Just allocate a new connection handle and use this handle when you make the **SQLConnect** function call.

The last item to allocate is memory space for the SQL statement. The ODBC function call **SQLAllocStmt** is passed down the connection handle and retrieves a statement handle.

```
Attempt SQLAllocStmt(hdbc, hstmt), "Cannot allocate statement handle"
```

Besides setting up memory, this also sets up the cursor. The cursor points to the next record to be retrieved. (This is a SQL concept that has nothing to do with the screen cursor.) Each statement handle has its own cursor, so you could allocate two statement handles and point to two different locations in the same data source.

Querying the data source

The subroutine **btnQueryDatabase_Click** is where the query happens. The **SQLQuery** statement is constructed by concatenating strings and variables together to form a query string that is assigned to the variable **sqlQuery**, as shown in Listing 8.3.

Listing 8.3   The btnQueryDatabase_Click subroutine

```
' Create and run the query when button is pressed
Sub btnQueryDatabase_Click ()

    Dim sqlQuery, sqlSelect, sqlWhere, sqlOrderBy As String

    screen.MousePointer = HourGlass
    lblStatus = "Status: Working..."

    ' Create the SQL statement
    sqlSelect = "SELECT * FROM PhoneNumber "
```

```
        sqlWhere = "WHERE LastName LIKE '" & txtNameLastQuery.Text & "'"
        sqlOrderBy = " ORDER BY " & lstOrderBy & ", FirstName"
        sqlQuery = sqlSelect & sqlWhere & sqlOrderBy

        ' Call the ODBC data source with the SQL statement
        rc% = SQLExecDirect(hstmt, sqlQuery, Len(sqlQuery))

        ' Show the result set or handle the error
        If rc% = SQL_SUCCESS Or rc% = SQL_SUCCESS_WITH_INFO Then
            lblStatus = "Status: Query done"
            FillForm hdbc, hstmt
          ' Using SQL_CLOSE, closes the cursor but does not
          ' free the statement resources so hstmt can still be used
          Attempt SQLFreeStmt(hstmt, SQL_CLOSE), "Unable to free statement _
            handle"
        Else
            lblStatus = "Status: Error        "
            DescribeError hdbc, hstmt
        End If

        screen.MousePointer = normal

End Sub
```

The variable **sqlQuery** is then passed to the ODBC function **SQLExecDirect** along with parameters for the statement handle and the length of the query string. The return code is then checked for success and, if successful, calls the subroutine **FillForm**, which displays the result set.

```
rc% = SQLExecDirect(hstmt, sqlQuery, Len(sqlQuery))
```

Once **SQLExecDirect** has finished, the ODBC function **SQLFreeStmt** is called with the flag, **SQL_CLOSE**. This closes the cursor associated with the statement handle but does not actually free the statement resources.

```
Attempt SQLFreeStmt(hstmt, SQL_CLOSE), "Unable to free statement handle"
```

Therefore, the statement handle can be used again without having to reallocate it. The next time a query is made, the cursor is opened and positioned at the top of the result set.

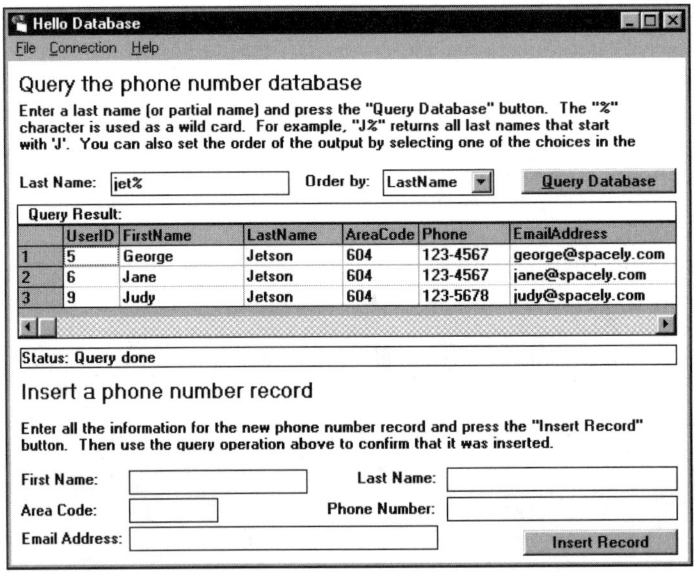

Figure 8.9   The results of the query.

Reporting the Results

The query results are displayed in a table (Figure 8.9). The subroutine that does this, **FillForm**, illustrates how to retrieve and show the data from the query result set. This subroutine is shown in Listing 8.4.

As each piece of data is retrieved, it is placed in a Visual Basic grid (**GRID.VBX**), which displays the results as a table. The Hello Database program requires the use of a later version of **GRID.VBX** than the one supplied with Visual Basic 3.0 (the updated VBX is included on this book's CD-ROM).

Listing 8.4   The FillForm subroutine

```
' Display the result set in a table
Sub FillForm (hdbc As Long, hstmt As Long)
   Dim maxColWidth As Long, ColTypeCode As Integer, ColNullable As Integer
   Dim Outlen As Integer, pcbValue As Long
   Dim ColScale As Integer, i As Integer
   Dim NumRows, NumCols As Integer

   Dim rgbValue As String * SBufferLen
   Dim ValidColumn() As Integer
   Dim rgbValueLen As Integer
```

```
' Get the number of columns in the result set
Retcode = SQLNumResultCols(hstmt, NumCols)
If Retcode <> SQL_SUCCESS Then
  DescribeError hdbc, hstmt
  Exit Sub
End If

If NumCols = 0 Then
  MsgBox "No results to show", InfoIcon, AppName
  Exit Sub
End If

ReDim ColWidth(NumCols + 1)
ReDim ValidColumn(NumCols + 1)

For i = 0 To NumCols + 1
  ValidColumn(i) = True
Next i

rgbValue = String$(rgbValueLen, 0)

' Retrieve the metadata for each column in the result set
' and initialize the column widths of the grid.
frmQueryIns.DataGrid.Rows = 1
frmQueryIns.DataGrid.Cols = NumCols + 1
ColWidth(0) = 5  'Column zero is the row number column.  It is 5
                 'characters wide.
For i = 1 To NumCols
  frmQueryIns.DataGrid.Col = i  'Move to current column

  ' Get column names, data type etc.
  Attempt SQLDescribeCol(hstmt, i, rgbValue, SBufferLen, Outlen,
  ColTypeCode, maxColWidth, ColScale, ColNullable), "DescribeCol Failed"

  frmQueryIns.DataGrid.Text = Left$(rgbValue, Outlen)
  If maxColWidth > MAX_WIDTH Then maxColWidth = MAX_WIDTH
  ColWidth(i) = maxColWidth  'Record the maximum text length for the
                             column

  ' Set column width based on the column width returned from
   'SQLDescribeCol
  frmQueryIns.DataGrid.ColWidth(i) = ColWidth(i) * 30
Next i

'Set up the grid for this result set
frmQueryIns.DataGrid.FixedRows = 0  'allow next step
```

```
frmQueryIns.DataGrid.Rows = 1          'clears the grid completely
frmQueryIns.DataGrid.Cols = NumCols + 1    'Set the new column count
rc = 1     'Set the row count to 1 (For Column Names)

Do    'Repeat this loop until all result rows are fetched

  ' Set the cursor to the next row in the result set
  Retcode = SQLFetch(hstmt)

  If Retcode <> SQL_SUCCESS Or Retcode = SQL_SUCCESS_WITH_INFO Then
    Exit Do
  End If

  frmQueryIns.DataGrid.Rows = rc + 1  'Increment the row counter
  frmQueryIns.DataGrid.Row = rc         'and move to the next row
  frmQueryIns.DataGrid.Col = 0
  frmQueryIns.DataGrid.Text = CStr(rc + start)

  For i = 1 To NumCols
    frmQueryIns.DataGrid.Col = i

    ' Get the next field at the current cursor.  This is an ODBC Call
    ' Level 1.  Used for unbounded data (ie SQLBindCol was not called).
    ' In this case it gets character type of fields.
    Retcode = SQLGetData(hstmt, i, SQL_C_CHAR, ByVal rgbValue,
      SBufferLen, pcbValue)

    If Retcode <> SQL_SUCCESS Then
      If ValidColumn(i) = True Then
        DescribeError hdbc, hstmt
        ValidColumn(i) = False
        If Retcode = SQL_ERROR Then
          MsgBox "Result Column " + Str$(i) + " will be ignored",
            AttIcon, AppName
        End If
      End If
    End If
    If Retcode <> SQL_ERROR Then
      If pcbValue = SQL_NULL_DATA Then
        frmQueryIns.DataGrid.Text = "NULL"
      Else
        frmQueryIns.DataGrid.Text = Trim$(rgbValue)
      End If
    End If
  Next i
```

```
   rc = rc + 1
Loop

If (frmQueryIns.DataGrid.Rows > 1) Then
   frmQueryIns.DataGrid.FixedRows = 1    'freeze the field names
   frmQueryIns.DataGrid.FixedCols = 1    'freeze the row numbers

   frmQueryIns.DataGrid.Row = 1          'set current position
End If

frmQueryIns.DataGrid.Col = 1

End Sub
```

We wanted a way to set the displayed column widths so that all of the data would appear on one screen. One way of doing this would be to hard-code the displayed column widths into the client application. However, this would cause maintenance problems later on if the column widths were changed (that is, we'd have to send everyone a newer version of the client application). So in the code above, we used a more flexible method that queries the data source for information about the column properties. Two ODBC SQL functions are used to obtain metadata—like column properties—at runtime: **SQLNumResultsCols** returns the number of columns in the result set and **SQLDescribeCol** returns other column-related attributes.

The statement handle is passed to the function **SQLNumResultCols**, which then returns the number of columns. If the number of columns equals 0, then no data was retrieved.

```
Retcode = SQLNumResultCols(hstmt, NumCols)
```

Several variables are passed to the function **SQLDescribeCol**:

```
Attempt SQLDescribeCol(hstmt, i, rgbValue, SBufferLen, Outlen,
ColTypeCode, maxColWidth, ColScale, ColNullable), "DescribeCol Failed"
```

It then returns the name of the column, the length of the column name, the SQL data type (**SQL_CHAR** in our example), the maximum width of the column, the scale of the column (which is not applicable here, so a 0 is returned), and finally a flag that indicates whether the column allows null values.

So, from the first ODBC function call, we can determine the number of columns and use this information to loop through the result set to retrieve specific information on each of the columns. In particular, we used the width of each column to determine the relative width for our grid.

The ODBC function calls **SQLNumResultCols** and **SQLDescribeCol** are only necessary to make **FillForm** a general-purpose routine. If you already know the number of columns and the other pertinent information of your result set then you do not need to use these functions.

The next two function calls, **SQLFetch** and **SQLGetData**, demonstrate one approach to retrieving data from the result set. The **SQLFetch** function takes a statement handle as input and returns a value.

```
Retcode = SQLFetch(hstmt)
```

If the returned value indicates success, then the cursor is moved to the next row of the result set. In our example, we did not use the function **SQLBindCol**, but if we had, the data would be moved to the allocated storage location. Instead, we used the ODBC function **SQLGetData**, which retrieves the values into a variable, one at a time, from each column of the fetched row.

```
Retcode = SQLGetData(hstmt, i, SQL_C_CHAR, ByVal rgbValue, SBufferLen, _
    pcbValue)
```

This function is the only Level 1 ODBC call that we used in this program. This function call is useful because you don't need to allocate memory space before performing the **SQLFetch** call. The input parameters to pass to this function are:

- A statement handle corresponding to the query statement

- The column number of the data field to be retrieved

- The type of data to retrieve. In our case, we knew it was **SQL_C_CHAR**, but we could have also used the information from **SQLDescribeCol** had we not known this data type in advance

- The buffer length where the retrieved data is stored

- The output parameters from **SQLGetData**

- The variable **rgbValue**, which holds the queried data

- The variable **pcbValue**, which qualifies the retrieved data (null, string length, etc.)

For display purposes, if the returned data is null, then we store the string **NULL** to the current grid cell. If it isn't, then we store the string value with any extraneous white spaces removed.

The **FOR** loop in this subroutine marches across each column of the row and adds it to the grid row.

The last subroutine to discuss is **EndConnection**. This is the complement to **BeginConnection**. **EndConnection** disconnects and frees up memory instead of connecting and allocating memory, as shown in Listing 8.5.

Listing 8.5   The En1dConnection subroutine

```
' Free up resources and disconnect if connected
Sub EndConnection ()
  ' Terminate the connection, deallocating statement and connection
    handles
  If bConnected Then
    Attempt SQLFreeStmt(hstmt, SQL_DROP), "Unable to free statement
      handle resources"
    Attempt SQLDisconnect(hdbc), "Unable to disconnect"
    Attempt SQLFreeConnect(hdbc), "Unable to free connection handle"

    frmQueryIns.mnuConnect.Enabled = True
    frmQueryIns.mnuDisconnect.Enabled = False
    frmQueryIns.mnuQueryDatabase.Enabled = False
    frmQueryIns.mnuInsertRecord.Enabled = False
    frmQueryIns.btnQueryDatabase.Enabled = False
    frmQueryIns.btnInsertRecord.Enabled = False

    frmQueryIns.lblStatus = "Status:  Disconnected"
    bConnected = False
  End If

End Sub
```

The first of the three ODBC function calls used in **EndConnection** is **SQLFreeStmt**. This function call was used before in **btnQueryDatase_Click** on the **QueryIns.frm** form. There, it was used to close the cursor by passing it the flag **SQL_CLOSE**. However, in this case, we are passing the flag **SQL_Drop**, which, in addition to closing the cursor, frees the resources allocated to the statement.

```
Attempt SQLFreeStmt(hstmt, SQL_DROP), "Unable to free statement handle
    resources"
```

This means that to perform another query, or any other data manipulation functions, the statement will have to be allocated again using **SQLAllocStmt**.

The second ODBC function call used is **SQLDisconnect**. This function takes the connection handle and disconnects from the data source.

```
Attempt SQLDisconnect(hdbc), "Unable to disconnect"
```

We follow this with the ODBC function **SQLFreeConnect**, which frees up the resources to the connection handle.

```
Attempt SQLFreeConnect(hdbc), "Unable to free connection handle"
```

This is just a basic approach to using ODBC calls. The difference between this sample application and a real application would be in the way the return codes are handled. Some of the ODBC functions have many possible return values, so much more complex error handling is required.

Insert

The input screen to insert a phone number record looks similar to the other Hello Database programs (Figure 8.10).

Other than requiring the user to make an initial connection to the database, there isn't much difference between this input screen and the other Hello Database programs.

The subroutine **btnInsertRecord_Click** inserts a record. It first forms the SQL statement and then executes it, which is what we did for the Query statement. It is shown in Listing 8.6.

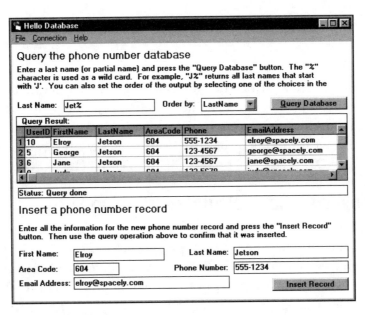

Figure 8.10   The insert screen.

Listing 8.6   The btnInsertRecord_Click subroutine

```
' Insert a record using ODBC function call
Sub btnInsertRecord_Click ()

    Dim sqlText, sqlInsert, sqlFields, sqlValues As String

    screen.MousePointer = HourGlass
    lblStatus = "Status: Working..."

    sqlInsert = "INSERT INTO PhoneNumber "
    sqlFields = "(FirstName, LastName, AreaCode, Phone, EmailAddress) "
    sqlValues = "VALUES('" & txtNameFirst.Text & "', '" & _
      txtNameLastIns.Text & "', '" & txtAreaCode.Text & "', '" & _
      txtPhoneNumber.Text & "', '" & txtEmailAddress.Text & "')"
    sqlText = sqlInsert & sqlFields & sqlValues

    rc% = SQLExecDirect(hstmt, sqlText, Len(sqlText))

    If rc% = SQL_SUCCESS Or rc% = SQL_SUCCESS_WITH_INFO Then
        lblStatus = "Status: Record inserted"
    Else
        lblStatus = "Status: Error                    "
        DescribeError hdbc, hstmt
    End If
```

```
screen.MousePointer = normal

End Sub
```

The SQL statement is formed by concatenating strings and variables to the variable **sqlText**, with the input values coming from the text boxes of the input form. The statement is then used by the ODBC function **SQLExecDirect** to perform the insertion. As always, the return code is checked for **SQL_SUCCESS** or **SQL_SUCCESS_WITH_INFO**.

Interview with Barry Rogoff of Working Set

Working Set, Inc. is a twelve-year-old company that develops specialized database tools for other software companies such as Powersoft, DEC, Computer Associates, and Microsoft. Barry is an engineer at Working Set who also takes care of user support and documentation. We talked about client/server technology, TCP/IP networks, and how DataRamp fits in.

What were you thinking when you started building DataRamp?

We saw an opportunity to develop a product that clearly needed to be built. Client/server database technology is extremely important. It often depends on local area networks or expensive, privately operated wide area networks, and since there are so many other protocols that work on the Internet, why not ODBC?

How would you sum up DataRamp?

The simplest way to describe our product is as an ODBC pipeline.

With one end on the client PC and the other end on the server?

The ends can be on the same machine or any two machines on any TCP/IP network, including LANs and the Internet.

How is DataRamp priced?

We are licensing by client seat, but our client cost is extremely low.

In your design, how important was it to work on both the Internet and Intranets?

When the project was initiated Intranets weren't really part of the picture. The original design was simply for an ODBC server that could augment or replace any number of vendor-specific ODBC drivers, but it quickly evolved into a product that combined TCP/IP technology with ODBC.

Since I could get to an ODBC database by using one of many client programs on a LAN, why would I use DataRamp?

It's true there are other protocols that work on Intranets. There are other ODBC drivers that support named pipes and TCP/IP, so we don't have as strong a differentiation there as we do on the Internet. One way that we do differentiate ourselves is that we are entirely vendor-independent.

How does that work?

Suppose you wanted to use SQL Server on an Intranet. You are going to be paying by the seat for your SQL Server clients. You could accomplish the same thing using a DataRamp client with TCP/IP and you would have a much lower per-seat cost.

Can multiple users come through the DataRamp Server?

It's multi-threaded. SQL Server is thread-safe, but some of them aren't, and then we create a separate process for each incoming connection.

What does "thread-safe" mean?

That a piece of software can handle multiple threads simultaneously, rather than just a single one.

Is being thread-safe a good thing?

Yes. In terms of system resources it's a lot less expensive on Windows NT to create a thread than it is to create a process.

So what happens when a database isn't thread-safe?

What actually happens is an OLE initialization error. Take for example Microsoft Access Version 2 driver. You can start that up in a thread and the first one works just fine but with the second one you get an OLE initialization error. If it's thread-safe, then you can start up as many of those as you want.

Who buys DataRamp?

We have 70 beta sites right now and they pretty much span the range of database users.

Users or developers?

Businesses that depend on a database.

For example?

Software developers, banks, credit card companies, and manufacturers.

Of those 70 beta sites, is there a predominant theme?

Probably 90 percent already have a client/server database application that they are deploying on a LAN or dialup network or some kind of wide area network and they want to make it accessible over the Internet.

Do they want to avoid the costs of maintaining dedicated networks?

Right. Essentially, they are looking to use the Internet as their wide area data network. They can deploy the client application on the Internet. It just involves a one-time download to some employee site or customer site and then they can do all the same database applications that they have been doing with dialup or local area over the Internet.

Were they already using ODBC or did they have to port their client applications over to ODBC?

Most of them were already doing ODBC.

What kind of background and experience are you finding among your customers?

They are primarily senior developers or development managers, and, depending on the size of the company, CEOs and VPs.

What kind of programming experience do they have?

A lot of PowerBuilder and Visual BASIC.

How long is it taking them to put your product to work and get some results with it?

It depends entirely on their expertise with ODBC. Some customers can install DataRamp and deploy an application within minutes. In other cases we have people who are writing Visual BASIC or PowerBuilder applications from scratch and have never done ODBC before.

So they are learning everything at once?

They have chosen to go the ODBC route because it's a complete database language and it only requires programming on the client end. Once the application is there, there's nothing to do on the server end but install the thing, whereas with hypertext database drivers there is a lot of CGI programming to do on the server side.

What is the predominant language for this kind of thing on the client side?

The data that I have puts it at about half Visual BASIC and half PowerBuilder. There is also a smattering of people using Microsoft Access as the front end and any number of other random things.

What kind of applications are people wanting to build?

A university wanted to know about using DataRamp to do admission applications and course registrations on the Internet.

What environment does your software work in?

Our server only runs on NT right now. Our client runs on Windows, Workgroups, and NT. We are planning to port our stuff onto Unix.

Can you access a Unix database through an ODBC driver?

Our server has to be on an NT box, but the database can be anywhere.

I am not clear on how ODBC extends to Unix. Does the vendor of the Unix database have to provide an ODBC interface?

As long as there exists an ODBC driver, we support it. It's a de facto standard.

So ODBC drivers exist in the Unix environment?

They exist across environments. In a similar client/server way the client part is on NT and the server part is on Unix.

So, for example, would Oracle and Sybase implement that interface across platforms?

Right. One of our beta sites is a DB2 shop running on NT.

You had a statement on your Web site about why dynamic Web pages aren't enough and why it's useful to get the real data down to the client side. I was wondering if you would speak to that. When you get the data down on the client side what do you envision people will be using it for?

There's really no limit to what you can do with data in the form of an ODBC application. You can make a local copy, graph it, analyze it, or run spreadsheet macros on it.

So it's in the after-processing that live data has an advantage over hypertext?

That's really only part of it. A problem with the hypertext approach is that hypertext is by definition stateless, and that conflicts with the idea that database operations are part of a transaction that either all succeeds or all fails.

And your approach is stateful?

ODBC is based on SQL, which has been around a long time and has gone through many iterations of standardization. The ODBC interface is complex and deals with a ton of vendor-specific SQL extensions and variations, but it pretty much does everything you need to perform database operations in a mission-critical way. If you are doing ODBC correctly you can depend on your application to do important business operations for you.

By calling stored procedures and triggers?

Stored procedures, triggers, assertions, and referential integrity. It's not to say that those things don't exist on the server side using HTML, but the difference is that when a constraint violation occurs in a database, with ODBC the client knows that the constraint violation occurred and can change something and try to commit it again or roll back the transaction. Whereas in a hypertext environment, the only way the client is ever going to know that something went wrong is if the hypertext application is programmed to tell the server somehow "you just got a constraint violation".

So there's a real distinction between dynamic Web pages and an ODBC connection?

Exactly right.

What about the point of view that says that stored procedures aren't the final answer and that you need a separate transaction server?

The X-open transaction architecture is based on a transaction manager that is separate from the resource managers or databases. That architecture has been adopted as part of the OSF DCE, and that's what Transarc's Encina is based on.

Right, but these tools don't seem to have been adopted yet in the micro environment.

It's only a matter of time.

You think so? So how will DataRamp fit into a world with transaction servers?

If somebody wanted to manage a distributed transaction from the client side, then DataRamp would support that to the extent that ODBC level 2 does. But I think it's much more likely that the distributed transaction would be managed on the server side, in which case it would be transparent.

So the client just makes the call and the server side says, "Oh, this happens to be on two different databases and I will handle all the complications"?

Right. The thing you are updating just happens to be a partitioned view, part of which is stored in Oracle in Poughkeepsie and part of which is stored in Sybase in Seattle.

So DataRamp enables a client application to get at control procedures that exist on the server-side if they are ODBC compliant?

Right. If somebody wanted to write a distributed database application and deploy it over the Internet where the client is doing cross-database joins, then they can certainly do that and could do two-phase commit because two-phase commit can be superimposed easily on ODBC.

A DataRamp-enabled client can establish its own TCP/IP connection, so it doesn't need a Web browser. How does DataRamp integrate with Web standards?

To start with, you'd be using HTTP to reach some Web site. Then a DataRamp-enabled client would come up as a Netscape helper application, and we are planning to have them work as official Netscape plug-ins.

Once the helper application or Netscape plug-in is running, does the connection switch from a stateless protocol like HTTP to a stateful one?

Yes. And in the same way that some hyperlinks will invoke FTP, you can have a hyperlink that will invoke our browser, or could invoke a PowerBuilder application, or a Visual BASIC application.

Why did you feel that it was important to integrate DataRamp with Netscape?

Well, we demoed our product at Internet World and it quickly became apparent that, to the people who attended that show, the Internet is the Web and the Web is the Internet, and if you are showing something that has no Web integration, nobody wants to see it!

Would DataRamp be useful in a data warehousing context?

Yes. In the data warehousing market you can view our product as a way of replacing a wide area network. Get rid of your frame relay connections or your ISDN connections, just throw them all out and use the Internet.

So if someone already had a data warehouse, DataRamp would be a good way to make it available?

Sure. Say you are McDonald's and you are test marketing whale burgers, and you want to find out how it's doing and you have to get data from 500 test market sites from Maine to Alaska. You can do it by implementing your own wide area network or you can provide those sites with just enough access to the Internet to be able to do a DataRamp operation.

Is your secure version getting a lot of attention for this kind of use?

A fair amount.

What happens when you put security in there? Do things slow down significantly?

Not much at all. The security algorithms are very fast. There is a small discussion of that in our help file under Performance. It's significant but not an impediment.

On the server side, is it listening on a particular port?

Yes. We listen on port 461.

Okay, and I noticed in your documentation that if you go through a firewall you have to get the firewall administrator to allow that through?

Yes. Our firewall support in version one is pretty primitive. To use DataRamp through a firewall you have to enable TCP/IP traffic on a specific port, and if you have a firewall that allows traffic to and from specific IP addresses, then you just use the IP address of the DataRamp Server.

Is that port number configurable? Could I change it to 361?

We don't support that right now.

So does that provide a security problem if that's a common port number?

Yes, just like any other published TCP/IP port, if somebody wants to hammer on it they can. We plan to support proxies in our next version.

Is there a limit to how many people can come in at once?

Yes, we have an administrator-settable limit. So in the case where someone managing a DataRamp Server finds that they are exceeding some system resource like sockets, they can set the number of DataRamp connections down to a reasonable limit.

Does having sockets give you the ability to have a stateful connection and control transactions?

To be even ODBC level 0 compliant, a database has to support simple transactions.

What language did you use to develop DataRamp?

Visual C++.

How about Java? It wasn't around when you started, but having a Java client would be another way of doing what you are doing.

Java is really interesting. We haven't looked at much of Java yet, but we are planning to.

Have you heard any strong reasons to integrate DataRamp more tightly with Web standards?

Well, we think there is a lot of data in the world in relational databases that are going to be very interesting to publish on the Web. The way we expect people to do that is to come to a Web site and click a button and get a data browser. If you decide that you want to use your own ODBC tool, then you can do that too.

I understand that you all work in different places.

We all work out of our homes.

Do you use the Internet to stay in touch?

Yes. We are doing distributed development.

How does that work?

For one thing, we have been using DataRamp from the beginning to manage our bug tracking.

What database are you using for that?

Our bug-tracking database is SQL Server and we use a PowerBuilder application.

Do you have a classification system for bugs?

Yes. It's a very simple app, you can pull up any existing bug or generate a report from the bug list, or enter a new bug.

Do you have a Notes kind of thing for sharing code or other information?

We were using Lotus Notes for a while and people in the company hated the interface so much that we've given it up. Even when Notes got to the point that you could use it on the Internet we used if for a week or two and then bagged it.

The Web cries out to be used for workgroups. It's the right interface. I hear that Tim Berners-Lee is working on that now but I haven't seen any results yet.

The interface that MOSAIC introduced to the world is great! People love browsing.

LiveWire and LiveWire Pro (Netscape)

LiveWire Pro

Netscape Communications Corporation

501 E. Middlefield Rd.

Mountain View, CA 94043

Phone	(415) 254-1900
Fax	(415) 528-4124
1-800-528-2285	(US & Canada)
Email	info@netscape.com
FTP	ftp.netscape.com
Corporate sales	(415) 528-2555
Individual sales	(415) 528-3777
URL	http://www.netscape.com

Overview

LiveWire uses a programming language to integrate a Web server with a database, and also comes with tools for developing and maintaining Web sites. The language, JavaScript, gives Web database developers a fluent way to build highly interactive Web database applications. LiveWire has four main components: the Site Manager, the Server Extension Engine, the Application Manager, and the Netscape Navigator 2.0 Gold Web browser/HTML editor.

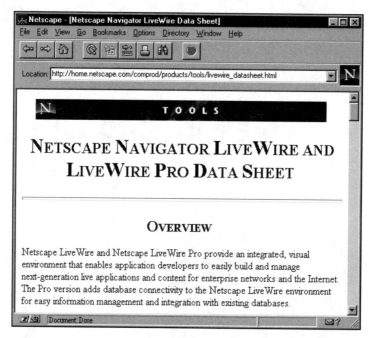

Figure 9.1   Netscape's LiveWire page.

Netscape describes LiveWire as being based on the three-tiered, client/server architecture (Figure 9.2). In this model, the three tiers are the client, the application layer, and the database server. With LiveWire, the Web browser functions as a client that can run on multiple platforms and can perform some client-side input validations. The Web server, with its associated server extensions and middleware, supports the application layer. The database server tier consists of one or more SQL database servers, typically running inside a firewall. This product profile concentrates on using LiveWire to create Web database applications that run in the middle tier.

You can develop LiveWire applications (Figure 9.3) by creating HTML documents that contain embedded JavaScript code. The JavaScript code is run by a JavaScript interpreter that is part of the Server Extension Engine. JavaScript is easy to learn and requires no detailed knowledge of Object-Oriented Programming, unlike its parent language, Java.

A LiveWire application can consist of three different types of source files: standard HTML files that build the static Web pages that make up the Web

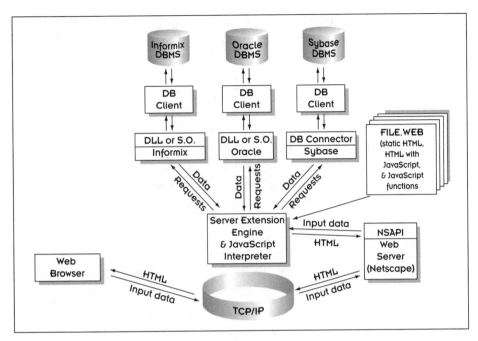

Figure 9.2   LiveWire's three-tiered architecture.

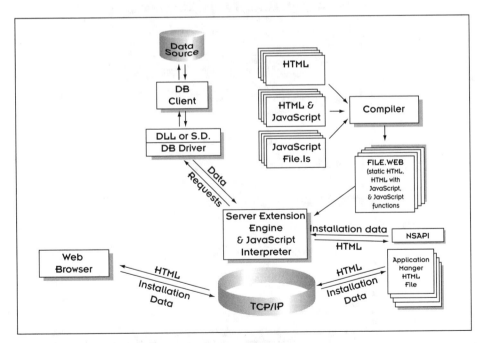

Figure 9.3   Components used to develop an application.

site; HTML files with embedded JavaScript code (Listing 9.1); and source files with the file extension **.ls** (Listing 9.2) that contain only JavaScript functions. In files containing both HTML and JavaScript, the JavaScript code is delimited by **<SERVER>...</SERVER>** tags. Source files hold JavaScript functions that are used more than once.

The LiveWire compiler compiles and links the source files into an executable called a Web file (file extension **.web**). The Application Manager installs the finished application on the Web server. The **.web** file contains the complete content of each of the individual source files. This is a good idea because it is easier to manage a single file than numerous separate files. Also, there is less chance of someone coming along and modifying just one of the files, which could result in a broken link.

As an example application, the Hangman game (Figure 9.4) is included with the LiveWire documentation and samples. The object of the game is to guess the letters of a secret word, in a given number of attempts, to prevent being "hanged."

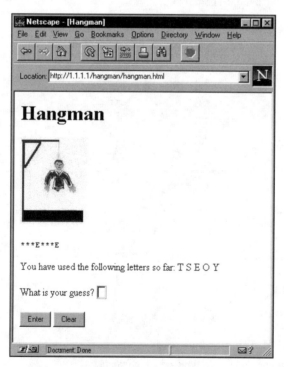

Figure 9.4   Hangman game in LiveWire.

Listing 9.1 and Figure 9.5 (**youwon.html**) show how you can make a Web page interactive by using server extensions.

Listing 9.1   An example of an HTML file with LiveWire server extensions

```
<html>
<head> <title> Hangman </title> </head>

<server>
if (request.again ==  "yes")
{
   client.gameno = 1 + client.gameno;
   client.newgame = "true";   // set flag to initialize new game
   redirect("hangman.html");  // redirect back to hangman page to
                              // play again.
}
else if (request.again == "no")
   redirect("thanks.html");  // redirect to thanks page.
</server>

<body>
<h1>CONGRATULATIONS, YOU WON!!!</h1>

<pre>
<server>print(client.answer);</server>
</pre>

<P>
<form method="post" action="youwon.html">
<P>
Do you want to play again?
<input type="radio" name="again" value="yes">YES
<input type="radio" name="again" value="no">NO
<p>
<input type="submit" value="Enter">
<input type="reset" value="Clear">

</body>
</html>
```

Notice how JavaScript code is embedded in standard HTML code using the **<SERVER>...</SERVER>** tags. If the user wins, then the HTML input form (Figure 9.5) asks whether the user wants to play the game again. When the user selects **yes** or **no** and presses the **Submit** button, the

Figure 9.5   Hangman Web page requesting a response.

youwon.html file is invoked again by the Web server. If the user selects yes, then the number of games is incremented and the Web server sends back the **hangman.html** file to start another game. If the user answers **no**, then the Web server is directed to return the **thanks.html file**.

An example of the third type of source file, which contains only JavaScript, is **hangman.ls** (Listing 9.2). The example shows the function **Substitute**, which looks through the secret word, character by character, forms a string, and keeps track of correct and incorrect guesses.

Listing 9.2   Example of an .ls file

```
// Helper function to look through word
// and make character substitutions.
// Word is the secret word.
// Answer is the answer so far.

function Substitute( guess, word, answer)
{
   var result = "";
   var len = word.length;
   var pos = 0;
   while( pos < len )
   {
```

```
      var word_char  = word.substring( pos, pos + 1 );
      var answer_char = answer.substring( pos, pos + 1 );
      if ( word_char == guess )
         result = result + guess;
      else
         result = result + answer_char;

      pos = pos + 1;
   }
   return result;
}
```

All of the files are compiled and linked with the LiveWire compiler to form the file **hangman.web**. The Application Manager (Figure 9.6), which is used to install the application, is itself a LiveWire Web site, which means you install the application using your Web browser. Once installed, you can access the Hangman Web site by pointing your Web browser to the URL **http://1.1.1.1/hangman/hangman.html**. (Be sure to swap out **1.1.1.1** for the IP address of your Web server.)

Figure 9.6 The LiveWire Application Manager.

Using the three types of files—HTML, HTML with JavaScript, and JavaScript function files—gives Web database developers great flexibility in creating a wide range of Web sites. Most other Web database tools either add new HTML tags or work solely with a language. However, LiveWire combines HTML with JavaScript functions to achieve greater power through synergy.

Features
Environment

LiveWire and LiveWire Pro work on Windows NT and Unix platforms.

For Windows NT, the version of NT should be 3.5 or higher, running on a minimum of a 486 processor with 10 MB of disk space. A minimum of 12 MB of RAM is required, but 16 MB is recommended.

For Unix, a minimum of 16 MB of memory and disk space of 10 MB is required. LiveWire has been compiled for the following versions of Unix:

- Digital Equipment Corp. Alpha (OSF/1 2.0)

- Hewlett-Packard 700-series (HP-UX 9.03)

- IBM RS/6000 AIX 3.2

- Silicon Graphics (IRIX 5.2)

- Sun SPARC (Solaris 2.3, SunOS 4.1.3)

Trial Version

A trial version of LiveWire will be available from the LiveWire Web site (Figure 9.1). There will be no evaluation version of LiveWire Pro.

Web Server Compatibility

LiveWire and LiveWire Pro work with the Netscape Communication Server and the Netscape Enterprise Server.

Web Browser Compatibility

Any Web browser that supports HTML input forms.

ODBC Compatibility

ODBC is supported for the Windows platform.

Learnability

You will need to learn the JavaScript language and the LiveWire Application Manager (Figure 9.6) reasonably well to create LiveWire applications. JavaScript is similar to Visual Basic in that both have simple constructs and type declarations are not required. No special tools, other than an editor, are required. Debugging is performed with the Web browser.

The LiveWire Application Manager is used to install newly created or updated LiveWire Web sites. The Application Manager runs from within a Web browser, so there isn't much of a learning curve. By following the examples provided with the sample applications, you will easily figure out how to add a new application.

How Programmable Is It?

LiveWire is extremely programmable because it uses JavaScript, which is a somewhat simplified but very useful programming language that can use objects. LiveWire makes good use of several predefined objects that are built specifically for Web and Web database related tasks. For example, the objects request, client, project, and server each have their own properties. A property of the request object is the client's IP address. (An IP address is a group of numbers identifying the Internet location that the user is making the request from.) You can obtain the client's IP address by referencing the request object's IP address property:

```
CustomerIPAddress = request.IP;
```

In addition to referencing predefined properties of objects, the developer can add properties to these objects to store additional information. For example, on the client object, one could create a customer ID property and could assign it the value 123:

```
client.cust.ID="123";
```

Efficiency

LiveWire eliminates the CGI layer and makes the Web server talk directly to the server extension engine via the NSAPI. This increases response speed by eliminating the overhead associated with CGI.

Security

LiveWire mainly leaves user authentication to the database or the Netscape Web server. However, since LiveWire supports objects that automatically maintain state information, it is simple to write a program that requires a user to sign in with a user name and password and authenticates the user before connecting to the database.

Error Handling and Debugging

Error handling is left up to the programmer, who will need to develop error handling routines in JavaScript for the server side of the application.

Debugging a LiveWire application is quite advanced. Netscape has provided a way of showing the application in one Web browser and the debug trace in another Web browser. The trace displays both the input form values and the current object values (Figure 9.7).

There is also a debug function, **debug**, that allows you to display a variable's value. For example, use the statement

```
debug("IP address = ", request.IP);
```

to display the IP address of the Web browser user making a request.

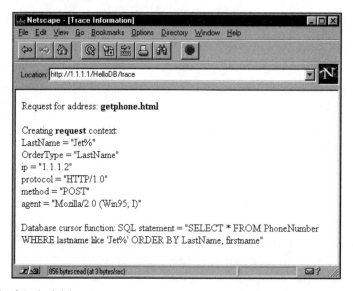

Figure 9.7 A typical debug trace.

Input Validation

LiveWire uses standard HTML input forms to request input from the user, so on the client side, input validation is limited to whatever HTML allows. For example, with browsers supporting HTML 3.0, you can limit an input field to a minimum and maximum numeric value. On the server side, it is possible to perform any kind of input validation because JavaScript gives you full control of the input data.

Support for Transaction Control

LiveWire uses three explicit JavaScript transaction control methods: **BeginTransaction**, **CommitTransaction**, and **RollbackTransaction**. A transaction is limited to the current HTML page. If the user exits the page before issuing either a **CommitTransaction** or a **RollbackTransaction**, then the transaction is automatically committed. Nested transactions and transaction-isolation levels are supported, but not necessarily across all of the databases.

Cookies

LiveWire uses five techniques for maintaining state information; two for the client side and three for the server side.

The client-side techniques are client cookies and client URL encoding. With client cookies, the server transfers all the state information to the client (as name/value pairs) using the Netscape cookie protocol. This is suitable for high volume applications, but will only work on browsers supporting the cookie protocol. The client URL-encoding technique works by appending the name/value pairs of all the state information to each URL in the HTML document. For this to work, all URLs must be dynamically generated.

The server-side techniques are short cookies, short URL-encoding, and IP address. The first two techniques are much like the two client-side techniques. However, instead of generating name/value pairs to save on the client side, an automatically generated name is saved on the client side. This reduces the amount of state information needed to be maintained on the client side. For example, with short cookies, an automatically generated name is saved on the client side in the cookie file. In subsequent transactions this name is sent to the server side, where the server uses the name to look up the actual name/value pair. Similarly, with the short URL encoding technique, the automatically generated name is embedded in each of the URLs on the HTML page. When the user clicks one of these URLs, the automatically generated name is sent to the server. There, the appropriate state information is retrieved based on this name. With the third technique, IP address, the client IP address is used as an index to the state information. This technique is best suited for Intranets where each user would have a separate, fixed IP address.

Hello Database with LiveWire Pro

The LiveWire version of the Hello Database program was created by writing HTML tags and JavaScript code. The HTML tags are identical to the ones used in the Cold Fusion Hello Database program. The difference mainly lies in how the Web pages are generated. In LiveWire, they are generated by weaving in JavaScript code with HTML tags.

Setup and Operation

Setting up LiveWire

We used an early beta version of LiveWire Pro with the Informix database, so the following installation instructions apply to that particular set of tools. For those readers who are using other database servers with LiveWire, we have included a comma-delimited text file version of the Hello Databasedata(**\BookData\Demo\LiveWire\phonenum.csv**).

The Informix DBMS component of LiveWire Pro was not available for distribution on the CD-ROM. Further, when Netscape releases LiveWire 1.0, there will be an evaluation version of LiveWire, but not of LiveWire Pro. The only difference between the two is that LiveWire Pro comes with the Informix database server. So, if you already have this database server, or any of the other LiveWire-supported database servers, you will be able to try out the Hello Database program once you obtain the LiveWire evaluation version. The following are the installation steps:

Note: LiveWire works with Netscape Communication Server Version 1.12 or higher.

1. Obtain a version of this Web server program and run the file name of the self-extracting archive file to extract it.

2. Run the **setup.exe** file.

3. As part of the setup, a Netscape Web browser will appear. When this happens, follow the instructions on the Web pages. Fill in each of the different sections to complete the installation of the Netscape server.

4. Obtain a copy of the self-extracting archive file for LiveWire. Extract the files and run the setup program.

5. LiveWire adds **/livewire/bin** to your user path. Add it to your system path, too.

6. Re-boot Windows NT and restart the Netscape Web server.

7. To check whether LiveWire has been properly installed, run the Application Manager. Do this using the URL **http://1.1.1.1/ appmgr/home.html** (substitute your domain for **1.1.1.1**). Note that although the Application Manager is under the LiveWire directory, you should not specify **LiveWire** in your URL path.

8. Install the Informix database by obtaining the self-extracting archive file **onlinent.exe**. Extract the files into a temporary directory and run the **setup.exe** file.

9. Follow the installation instructions. Be prepared to enter the serial number and password.

10. Extract the client archive file and run **setup.exe**.

11. This will set up the system path to the **\INFORMIX\bin** directory. If it doesn't, you should do this manually and re-boot the system.

12. To use the Informix database with the Netscape Web server, you must change the Web server to run as a user. Go into the startup of **Netscape Httpd-80 service** and choose **Logon As—This Account** and enter your account name.

13. On the client, run the Informix **setnet.exe** application and enter the required information as specified in the readme file.

Setting up the PhoneList database for the Hello Database program

1. From the CD-ROM, copy the **\BookData\Demo\LiveWire*.*** files onto your hard drive into the directory **\BookData\Demo\LiveWire**.

2. Run **setenv.cmd**, which comes with Informix. (It's labeled as the **Command Line Utilities** program in the INFORMIX **Online Dynamic Server** program group.) This sets up the environment variables.

3. From a DOS window, change the current directory to **\BookData\ Demo\LiveWire** on your hard drive.

4. Make sure the Informix NT services are started.

5. Run the Informix **dbaccess.exe** program from the DOS window. The program should be in the Path of executable files.

6. Select **Query-Language** menu pick.

7. Choose the **sysmaster@your_Informix_server_name**.

8. Select **Choose** menu pick and select the **MakeData** command file. If you don't see it, then you will have to enter the filename with the path, **\BookData\Database\MakeData**. This loads the script file.

9. Select **Run** from the menu to create and import the data into Informix. The data will be imported from the text file **phonenum.unl**.

There are two methods of embedding JavaScript in an HTML document. The first method uses **<SERVER>...</SERVER>** tags and the second uses the backquote `. The first way lets you embed multiple JavaScript statements between the **<SERVER> and </SERVER>**. Here is a snippet of code showing how these tags are used:

```
<p>Here is my <server>print("Hello Database");</server> program.</p>
```

Note that you cannot put any HTML tags or text between the tags because the compiler will try to interpret this as code.

The backquote "`", also called the back-tick, is used to delimit JavaScript code inside an HTML tag. This is needed because you cannot use another set of "<" and ">" inside an existing HTML tag. The following example uses the JavaScript string concatenation operator "+" inside an **<IMG>** tag to form the image filename **HelloWorld.gif**.

```
<img src='"Hello" + "World" + ".gif"'>
```

The backquote is only used inside HTML tags. Notice that the backquotes are used in pairs to delimit the entire JavaScript code.

Query

The Hello Database program starts off as usual with the phone.html home page (Figure 9.8).

The only item on this home page that is different from the Cold Fusion version of the Hello Database program is the **<FORM>** line for the **Query Database** button:

```
<form action="getphone.html" method="POST">
```

As you can see, no CGI executable is needed to process this query form. Simply specifying the HTML file is sufficient because when the Netscape Web server loads this file, it will process the embedded JavaScript code shown in Listing 9.3.

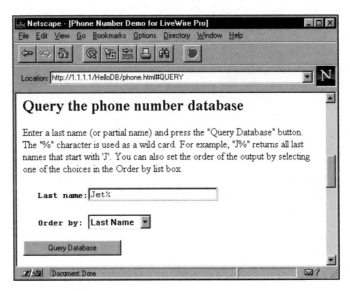

Figure 9.8   The query input screen.

Listing 9.3 HTML and JavaScript used to query the database

```
<!-- Query: Select all fields from the PhoneNumbers table for all
     records where the LastName is like the one requested and
     order the results by the ordering method requested and
     secondarily by the first name. -->

<html>
<head>
<title>Phone Number Query</title>
</head>

<body>

<!-- CONNECT TO THE DATABASE -->
<server>
if(!database.connected())
{
    database.connect("INFORMIX", "ol_Webtech",
                      "jchow", "", "PhoneList");
}

if (!database.connected())
{
    print("Error: Unable to connect to database.");
}
else
{
    results = database.cursor(
                "SELECT * FROM PhoneNumber WHERE lastname like '" +
                 request.LastName + "' ORDER BY " +
                 request.OrderType + ", firstname");
}
</server>

<h1>Query results displayed as a table sorted by
<server>print(request.OrderType);</server></h1>

<! -- DISPLAY ANSWER SET AS A TABLE -->
<table border>
<tr>
  <th>ID</th>
  <th>Full Name</th>
  <th>Phone Number</th>
  <th>Email address</th>
</tr>
```

```
<server>
while(results.next())
{
</server>
<tr>
  <td><server>print(results.userid);</server></td>
  <td><server>print(results.firstname + " " +
                    results.lastname);</server></td>
  <td><server>print("(" + results.areacode + ") " +
                    results.phone);</server></td>
  <td><server>print(results.emailaddress);</server></td>
</tr>
<server>
}
results.close();
</server>
</table>

</body>
</html>
```

When the user presses the **Query Database** button, the Netscape Web server will begin to process the HTML document called **getphone.html**. The first thing it will do is connect to the database. LiveWire works with objects, and in this case the object **database** is used to communicate and manipulate the database. As the snippet of code below (from Listing 9.3) shows, this object has a method called **connect**, which is how you request the connection:

```
database.connect("INFORMIX", "ol_Webtech",
                 "jchow", "", "PhoneList");
```

The first parameter specifies the type of database. In this case it is **Informix**, but it could have been a different one. The second parameter is the name of the database server. When we set up Informix, it suggested this as the database server name, which we accepted. The third parameter is the user name to log into the database. Note, that some DBMS systems will require the operating system login name instead. The fourth parameter is the password associated with the user name. None was required for this example. The last parameter is the name of the database.

If no connection is made, then an error message will be returned to the Web browser, to give the user some feedback, as this code snippet shows:

```
if (!database.connected())
{
    print("Error: Unable to connect to database.");
}
```

When a connection is made, the actual query will be performed by the JavaScript code below:

```
results = database.cursor(
             "SELECT * FROM PhoneNumber WHERE lastname like '" +
             request.LastName + "' ORDER BY " +
             request.OrderType + ", firstname");
```

The **request** object and the cursor object need some explanation. The **request** object is a predefined LiveWire object that holds the information the user requested in the HTML input form. This input form information is stored as properties of the **request** object. For example, **request.LastName** is the property of the request object that corresponds to the HTML input field name, **LastName**. Using properties to represent values for the HTML input form makes it very easy for the programmer to reference the information.

The object returned from the **database.cursor** method is a **cursor** object. In the example, we labelled the cursor object variable **results**. LiveWire returns a result set (Netscape calls it an "answer set") when the **database.cursor** method is called. This result set **cursor** object is like a virtual table with the columns and rows containing data specific to the query and the pointer pointing to a specific row. Furthermore, the properties of the **cursor** object are the columns of the result set. For example, **results.userid** holds the value of the user ID for the current row that the cursor is pointing to.

To get to the next row, the method **next** is used (for example, **results.next()**), as was done in the while loop to display a result set in an HTML table. Note that the cursor pointer cannot move backward to a previous row. To point to the previous row you would first close the existing **cursor** with the **close** method and perform the query again. (This is standard for ODBC and other database systems.)

The JavaScript **print** function displays results on the Web browser (Figure 9.9). Because this is being printed inside an HTML table, and HTML tags are not allowed between **<SERVER>...</SERVER>** tags, the **<SERVER>...</SERVER>** tags were used six times in the example. HTML and JavaScript code can become quite intertwined to the point where it can be difficult to read the document. An alternative would be to create JavaScript functions to display your own table, but this would take more work and probably not be as flexible as HTML tables.

Now we can build the Web site using the compiler **lwcomp.exe**. To make it easier, we created a bat file, **build.bat**, that included all the files related to this Web site.

```
lwcomp -v -o phone.Web phone.html getphone.html insphone.html
```

The first flag, **–v**, is for verbose output mode, so you can see the progress of the compilation. The second flag, **–o**, signals that the next parameter is the filename to which the binary compiled output will be saved (in this case, the file **phone.web**). The rest of the parameters are HTML files enhanced with JavaScript code. Every time you make a change, you will need to run the **build.bat** file to create and update the phone.web file (Figure 9.10). You will also have to choose Restart on the Application Manager (Figure 9.6) to reload **phone.web**.

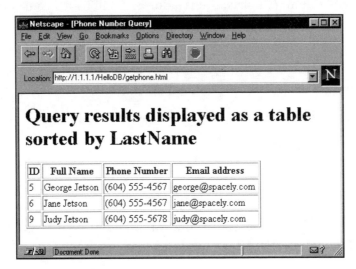

Figure 9.9 Results of the query.

```
MS-DOS Prompt                                              _ 8 X

D:\bookdata\demo\livewire>lwcomp -v -o phone.web phone.html getphone.html inspho
ne.html
Reading file phone.html
Compiling file phone.html
Reading file getphone.html
Compiling file getphone.html
Reading file insphone.html
Compiling file insphone.html
Writing .web file

D:\Book\Book Docs\LiveWire>
```

Figure 9.10   Compiling the application with the build.bat file.

Before you can run the Hello Database query demo, you must start the appropriate NT services and install the LiveWire application.

To start the NT service, double-click on the **Service** icon in the **Control Panel**, and then start the **INFORMIX-Online Dynamic Server**. This automatically starts up the **INFORMIX-Online Message Service**. Next, start **Netscape Httpd-80 service**.

To install the Hello database application, bring up the LiveWire Application Manager using a Web browser pointing to URL **http://1.1.1.1/appmgr/home.html**. (Replace the IP address **1.1.1.1** with your own IP address or domain name.) Click on the **Add New LiveWire Application** link to add the application. Then, fill in the parameters using the following values (Figure 9.11):

- URI Prefix: **/HelloDB**

- Object File Path: **/BookData/Demo/LiveWire/phone.web**

- Default URL: **phone.html**

- Initial URL: **phone.html**

- Client Mode: client-cookie (use the default)

To run the Hello Database query application, point your Web browser to **http://1.1.1.1/HelloDB/phone.html** and then select the **Query** hypertext

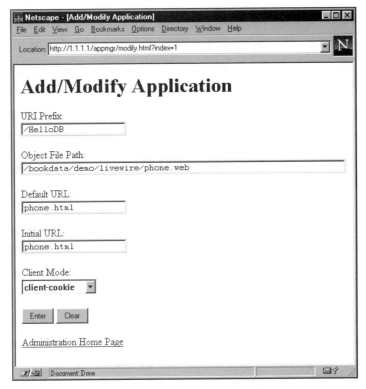

Figure 9.11   Installing the HelloDB application using the application manager.

link. This will bring up the query input screen (Figure 9.8) and you can then make a query (Figure 9.9).

Insert

Inserting a record using LiveWire requires four steps: get the input, connect to the database, determine the next available user ID, and insert the record using the execute database object method. Getting the input is straightforward by using the standard HTML input forms from the phone.html file (Figure 9.12).

Listing 9.4 shows the combined HTML and JavaScript code used to achieve the latter three steps listed above. You can connect to the database exactly the same way as was explained in the previous query example (that is, by using the database.connect method).

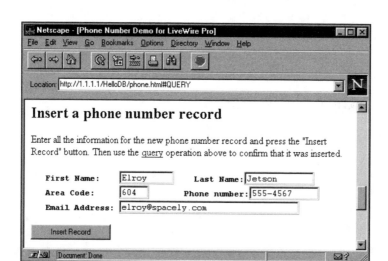

Figure 9.12 Input screen to insert a record.

Normally, the next available user ID would be determined by performing a straightforward query, such as **SELECT max(userid) from PhoneNumber**. This query worked from within the Informix program, **dbaccess.exe**, but it didn't work from within LiveWire Pro. So instead, we calculated the last user ID by iterating through the result set. We also noticed that in the **start.html** file of the video sample included with LiveWire Pro, they also determined **lastID** by iterating through the records as well. Perhaps this is a bug, but given the fact that we were using an early beta version, this is not alarming.

Listing 9.4   HTML and JavaScript used to insert a record

```
<!-- Insert -->

<html>
<head>
<title>Insert a phone number record</title>
</head>

<body>
<h1>Insert a phone number record.</h1>

<server>
if(!database.connected())
{
```

```
        database.connect("INFORMIX", "ol_Webtech", "jchow", "", "PhoneList");
}

if (!database.connected())
{
    print("Error: Unable to connect to database.");
}
else
{
    // Get highest current UserID
    lastID = 0;
    cursor = database.cursor("SELECT * from PhoneNumber ORDER BY userid");
    while(cursor.next())
    {
        lastID = cursor.userid;
    }
    cursor.close();

    // Insert new record with a unique ID
    if (lastID != null)
    {
        ++lastID;
        database.execute("INSERT INTO PhoneNumber values (" +
                        lastID               + ",'"  +
                        request.FirstName    + "','" +
                        request.LastName     + "','" +
                        request.AreaCode     + "','" +
                        request.Phone        + "','" +
                        request.EmailAddress + "')" );
    }
    else
    {
        print("Error: No userid defined");
    }
}
</server>

<h2>This record (UserID = <server>print(lastID);</server>)
    has been inserted.</h2>
<table>
<tr>
  <td><b>Person:</b></td>
  <td><server>print(request.FirstName + " " +
                    request.LastName);</server></td>
</tr>
```

```
<tr>
  <td><b>Phone number:</b></td>
  <td><server>print("(" + request.AreaCode + ") " +
                   request.Phone);</server></td>
</tr>

<tr>
   <td><b>Email address:</b></td>
   <td><server>print(request.EmailAddress);</server></td>
</tr>
</table>
</server>

</body>
</html>
```

To insert a record into the database, first create a SQL statement string specifying, in the proper order, the fields to be inserted. Then, use the database object method **execute** to perform the actual insertion:

```
database.execute("INSERT INTO PhoneNumber values (" +
              lastID                + ",'"  +
              request.FirstName     + "','" +
              request.LastName      + "','" +
              request.AreaCode      + "','" +
              request.Phone         + "','" +
              request.EmailAddress  + "')"  );
```

Notice once again the use of the **request** object's properties to reference the data that was entered into the HTML input form.

Once the insertion has been done, the inserted data will be displayed in the Web browser to give the user some feedback (Figure 9.13).

This result is displayed using JavaScript code and HTML table tags. Each data field was formatted as one row of the table. The combination of the JavaScript language and HTML tags not only reduces the development time significantly, but it also makes the look of the database report consistent with the rest of the Web pages.

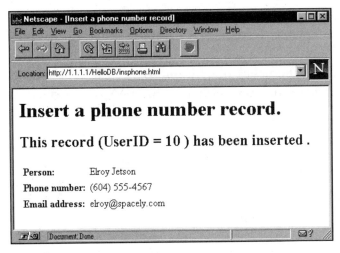

Figure 9.13   Results of inserting a record.

Interview with Len Feldman of Netscape

Len Feldman is product manager for LiveWire and LiveWire Pro. We talked about JavaScript, LiveWire, and Web database development.

Can you give us a description of LiveWire? What it's for? What it does?

LiveWire performs three basic functions. The first is that it enables you to create and manage Web content, second it allows you to create and manage Web sites, and third it allows you to create and manage Web applications. So in a nutshell, that's what LiveWire is about.

What is its single most important feature?

Boy, that's really hard to say because it has such a diverse range of capabilities. I think the most important ones are Web site management and Web application creation.

What are some of the things it does in Web site management?

Well, first it allows you to create Web sites from scratch without being an experienced Webmaster or HTML user. It allows you to view the organization of a Web site. It allows you to look at the structure of the Web site in terms of what pages are linked to what pages, and what content is physically located where, in the file system. It allows you to reorganize the Web site automatically without having to go in and fix lots of links yourself, so you can delete pages, add pages, and move pages around. And the site manager completely automates the process of fixing any links that break as you do that. It allows you to work on a Web site in an offline development area, and then click one button to publish the entire Web site to a Web server that you specify either on the LAN or anywhere on the Internet. And if you are using a Netscape 2.0 server, it does that with full access control.

How does access control work?

You can control a user's access, right down to the individual page. You can give an individual user access to read, or read and write, or do nothing, with any page in any subdirectory.

That sounds like it would be useful for a Webmaster.

Exactly. It's a very comprehensive tool for managing the content on a Web site. There are lots of other things that you need to do in terms of building that access control list, in terms of particular parameters that you need to set up for the server—the number of threads, all the addresses, and default pages and so on—and you still do that with the server administrator; but in terms of managing the content, the tool to do that with is the Site Manager portion of LiveWire.

From the point of view of database connectivity, is there a single most important feature?

The single most important feature there is the ability to have a high performance connection to virtually any database that you want to name, while being able to manage database connections and user-state information across hits.

And it does it in a common way, right?

Right. LiveWire keeps track of most of the overhead for you, so you don't need to figure out how to do that. You don't need to know how to maintain database connections in a connectionless environment, which is what the Web is. LiveWire does all that dirty work for you. You don't need to worry about, "...if I don't have a connection, how do I keep track from hit to hit as to who's using this and where they are in the transaction." LiveWire takes care of all of that through a very comprehensive user-state management system.

I noticed that.

And so, the whole architecture of application development and database connectivity is designed to allow people who are used to building today's legacy database applications to move to the Web. And, either interface those legacy applications to the Web or create new applications on the Web in very much the same way, with the same kind of tools that they've used in the past, without having to learn all the minutiae of how do you run applications on the WWW.

What's the difference between LiveWire and LiveWire Pro?

The only difference between LiveWire and LiveWire Pro is that Pro comes with the Informix database. All the database libraries are now in LiveWire so you don't need to buy LiveWire Pro to get the libraries.

What server-side interface method does LiveWire use?

JavaScript.

Does it use NSAPI internally?

Yes, but that's invisible to the user. Internally, it's wired through NSAPI, but the developer only sees JavaScript, not NSAPI.

What client side interface is used?

The client side is straight HTML input forms.

Does LiveWire handle full-text searching?

You can write applications that do. In the new Netscape 2.0 server, we have a standardized interface for full-text searches, and the new Enterprise Server comes with Verity built in. So it does enable you to access full-text databases.

When you say Enterprise Server, is that a new product?

That is the replacement for the Commerce Server. It's now called the Enterprise Server.

The Web environment reminds you that the term "database" covers both full-text and fielded databases.

LiveWire does direct SQL to Oracle, Sybase, Informix, and Illustra, and ODBC SQL to everything else, but SQL isn't used for continuous text search and retrieval databases. So when you want to do calls out to a continuous text search and retrieval database, you would use the server-side JavaScript hooks to get to the Verity engine or whatever backend full-text engine you are using.

So you use JavaScript for both kinds of databases?

It's still JavaScript. You are going to be calling C or C++ routines from JavaScript, or you may be calling NSAPI routines from JavaScript, but you will be doing it all in JavaScript.

Why did you choose the Verity engine?

Well, I'm not really the right person to talk to because that was handled by the server marketing team, not my group, but I can give you some insight into it. We have had a long relationship with Verity, starting with our publishing system—which is our high-end server database application that lets publishers put content on the Web; for example, the Dow Jones, the Discovery Channel, and the Wall Street Journal Web sites use it—and the publishing system uses the Verity search engine, so it was a natural choice for us. Also, as you pointed out a few minutes ago, we learned fairly early on that conventional relational or record-based databases are not the be-all and end-all for the Web. In fact, people needed continuous text search and retrieval capabilities well before they started attempting to do much relational database work on the Web, because companies have these huge databases of text documents that they need to make available to people. And, without some sort of a search and retrieval engine that can go out and find that content, then you have to index things and do keyword searches and put much more of the burden in the lap of the end user. So, we felt this was an essential capability to have, and Verity gave that to us.

Can other full-text engines be used?

Yes, the interface is designed so that other continuous text search engines can be plugged in, Basis for example.

That's the one from the Battelle Institute?

Yes, exactly. In fact, they are an OEM of ours and they package our Web servers with their Basis database, so the architecture is such that you can effectively snap out Verity and snap in other search engines. Other companies have also implemented their search engines on top of our server, so we made the architecture modular and flexible enough that if a customer wants to use another search engine or a search engine company wants to develop other search engines, then we can support them.

And the interface is still the JavaScript call?

That's right.

Have any interesting sites been built with LiveWire yet?

Since it's not officially shipped yet we don't have a list of sites that are up and running. I know of some sites that are using it internally, but I don't know of anybody that is in production publicly with it yet. Keep in mind the fact that we are really targeting the Intranet marketplace much more with this product than the public Internet marketplace. And so the real market for LiveWire—although lots of people on the public Internet I'm sure are going to use it—the primary target market is behind the firewall, so the vast majority of applications that people build with LiveWire will never be seen from the Internet.

That's interesting. Could you give us a couple of examples? Just describe them?

Well, yes, there are a couple of applications in development for maintaining inventory, for managing inventory records, and interfacing to legacy applications for inventory and accounts payable and accounts receivable. And there's a demo application that we are going to be releasing as part of LiveWire that will show a personnel locator application that will enable individuals who are looking for work to register information about themselves—you know: experience, background, areas of qualification—and then potential employers can search the database and pull out the records of people who fit their criteria.

Would that be done with a full-text or with a fielded database?

That will actually be implemented with a fielded database, but you could certainly implement it in a full-text environment as well.

A lot of client/server database developers are wondering if the transaction control they will have on the Web will be as good as what they are used to.

When you say transaction control, what are you talking about? Are you talking about commit and rollback and those kinds of things?

Those are the basic ones. There are other things like controlling the sequence of events.

Right. And the answer is yes. You won't find 100 percent of everything that is available on some client/server databases, but LiveWire provides all of the essentials that you need in order to do transaction processing and transaction management.

Was that a key design focus?

Yes.

It seemed like it was. We have reviewed a lot of other products and yours is the only one with five different ways of maintaining state, so I could see that that was pretty important for you.

Right. Keep in mind that most of the people on the team that designed and built LiveWire were system architects or key designers at Borland, on database products, or on Delphi. So, these were people who came into this with a very strong understanding of what was required for database applications and what was required for doing transactions with databases. So, it's not just a question of understanding SQL, and it's not just a question of how to connect things together with ODBC, but it's a question of understanding how all of that has to work in the connectionless, less-than-totally robust communications environment that is the Intranet or the Internet. And, those are issues that we jumped on very early on in the life of this product, and I think have really focused on.

Most people would acknowledge that there is a tradeoff between the stateless HTTP approach that handles transactions very quickly but sacrifices some control, and a dedicated session that has sure-fire transaction control but ties up the database longer.

Well, we've tried to deliver the best of both approaches. Depending on how fast the server is, the Web can handle a high volume of transactions, so we've done a number of architectural things to simplify transaction control and to get the performance up. One of them is what we just talked about, which is user-state management. We're doing all of the dirty work, and we're maintaining a separate client object for each client that's using the application. Each client object is uniquely identifiable and maintains all the information that the application developer wants to track about that client. So that's how you can tell one user from another, and from the application developer's point of view, you don't have to care at all that the connections are constantly being made and broken on the client side. All you know is that you've got a client and the client has these properties and this is what they want to do.

On the server side, we open up persistent connections to the database, so when we make a connection to the database, you can run multiple users through a single database connection. And again, the overhead for keeping track of that is all done by LiveWire, so you can transact a higher volume of business because you aren't constantly making and breaking database connections. You open up a connection when you run the application, and then you can keep that connection open as long as you want. It's completely programmable, you can open a connection and keep it going for the life of the program or you can put a ten-minute time-out on it that says, "If nothing goes through that pipe in ten minutes shut it down". So, you can run multiple clients through a single connection at reasonably good performance. And we've done some other things. The license that Informix provides for an online workgroup lets you have one developer and an unlimited number of users for the application, and up to 32 simultaneous connections, so that's a very high performance pipe. So, we've done everything that we can in LiveWire and with our partners like Informix to provide a high performance environment that enables you to handle a reasonably good amount of traffic without bogging down the server and without crashing the application.

I noticed when I installed the Informix server that I need to install the Informix client. Does LiveWire talk to the Informix client?

Yes, that's correct. Keep in mind that you have a beta copy and we're working on the integration, but the way it will work is that when you get LiveWire, you will get the client component for each supported database. So, you'll get a client component for Informix, for Oracle, for Sybase, for Illustra, and for ODBC. The Rogue Wave library—which is the library that we've licensed for database connectivity—uses whatever the native connectivity mechanism is for a specific database.

Are there any special reporting features that are part of LiveWire?

We have just signed a contract with Crystal that will let us bundle a copy of Crystal Reports with LiveWire.

Great. Crystal Reports is a nice product.

It's a brand new product for Crystal. It's a Web reporting engine that sits on top of the Web server, and will be bundled with LiveWire and all of our future servers. And that will run on Windows NT and all the Unixes that we support.

Speaking of platforms, what will LiveWire be running on?

Well, we will run on both Intel NT and Alpha NT and we also support Solaris, HPUX, IRIX, DEC Unix, and AIX.

That's pretty broad.

And pieces of it will run on Win 95 too, not the server parts because we don't have a Win 95 server yet, but later this year we will, and then all the LiveWire components will run on Win 95.

Could you label the different components that make up a LiveWire database connection?

You've got your client—your Web browser—and it's connected over the Intranet or the Internet to a Web server. Those two are talking through Web forms. They could also be talking through Java applets, but most people will do it through forms because that's the most standard HTML mechanism for variable data IO...forms and tables.

Okay, and on the server side you have some executable programs.

On the server side you have your Netscape server and your NSAPI interface, and on top of that interface, you have what we call the Server Extension Engine, which is the component of LiveWire that enables the server to run JavaScript. It's a runtime JavaScript interpreter, and it comes with the server, but it's developed by the LiveWire team. And riding on top of that you have the database connectivity library, which consists of multiple DLLs or multiple shared objects; and then there are the database clients, which connect to the databases; and then there are the databases themselves.

So your database client is a DLL?

In the Windows environment it's a DLL, and in the Unix environment it's a shared object.

So the other component is the database server itself?

Not quite. There's actually one more component, which is the database client library. In other words, the stuff that connects to Rogue Wave—and that can also be a DLL or a shared object, and those are supplied to us by the database vendors. And then on top of that is the database itself.

You were saying that you could have Java applets on the client side. Would they still talk through HTTP to the server side?

That's right.

How would you do queries, inserts, updates, and deletes with LiveWire?

First, you'd have to open a database and a table. Then there are a couple of ways to make the query. We have a standard JavaScript syntax for doing a query, which is just a JavaScript statement for querying the database. Or, if you want to create your own SQL statement in the SQL dialect that your database understands, you can go to SQL pass-through mode. And then reading from and writing to, there are JavaScript statements like record read, record write. So all the conventional reads and writes and joins are done through JavaScript.

What about security?

LiveWire uses whatever security the database has, so if you've got authentication on the database, then you can use that. In addition, it uses the access control list, which is part of the Netscape server, so you can control access to and from the application or any portion of the application through the access control list.

Does it go down to the field level?

No, not unless your database supports that. Our access control list gives you access control down to the page level, and then if you are also using the database's own functions it's whatever the database gives you. So, if the database goes down to the individual field level, then you can do that.

So an individual user, based on his ID, gets a tailored access using these two ways to specify access.

Right.

Are any programming languages other than JavaScript usable?

You can do everything in JavaScript.

Can you also use Java?

You can, but today there aren't a lot of linkages between Java and JavaScript on the server side. There will be in the future, but there aren't today. You can use Java and you can also use C or C++.

What documentation comes with LiveWire?

You get several docs. You get the LiveWire developer's guide, you get the JavaScript language reference, you also get the Navigator Gold documents as well.

Sounds pretty good. How is support handled?

There are different tiers of support available. Some free support when you first get the product, then you can buy additional support.

What other products compete with LiveWire?

The market right now is very broad and there's lots of stuff coming out. There is nothing as broad as LiveWire, but the products that probably come closest are Spider and Bluestone.

What differentiates LiveWire from Spider?

Well, let's see. Spider does nothing about content creation or site management. It's strictly a database connectivity and query tool. It currently doesn't support JavaScript as a programming language. And, in fact, I'm not sure it has a programming language other than C++. It's a visual design tool and LiveWire is somewhat less visual. LiveWire is quite a bit more flexible on the database side, but the main difference is not on the database side. It's all the other stuff LiveWire does, which is more general application development and content creation and site management.

What about Bluestone?

I'm less familiar with it, but I believe the situation is similar. Their focus is on database connectivity with some application development. Our focus is a major superset of that, as well as support of JavaScript and site management and content creation ability.

How would you describe the target market for LiveWire?

There are two markets for LiveWire. One market is the content creator and manager. These are people who want to create and manage Web sites.

They may be experienced Webmasters or they may be first-time users, but they are primarily interested in LiveWire for getting Navigator Gold and the site manager. The other audience is the application developer marketplace and it is a significantly different marketplace, although there is a good deal of overlap between Webmasters and Web application developers.

How do you define "Web application developer" to distinguish it from Webmaster?

Well, there's a pretty massive difference. A Webmaster, in my mind, is somebody who primarily focuses on creating Web sites, creating content and managing the content on Web sites, and is not really terribly involved in building programs or applications on top of the Web. In a similar way, in the Unix world the system administrator is mainly focused on making sure that the system gets up and is kept running, and that everything works and the connections work, and network works, and so on, and that's the equivalent of the Webmaster. And then the application developer is the person who says okay, all that stuff works, now what I want to do is write applications that run on top of that.

That's a good definition.

Now, there has been a lot of crossover because the tools have been so rudimentary for the Webmaster that in many cases they have had to write their own tools, so there are a lot of Webmasters who are also application developers. But, one of the goals we are trying to achieve is to make site creation and management simple enough that you don't need to know anything about programming in order to do that.

So if you want to develop an application, LiveWire is a good tool. Also if you want to manage the site you have developed, LiveWire is a good tool.

Exactly.

What kind of company is buying LiveWire?

It's not selling yet, but the companies that are evaluating it are everything from small 2- to 20-person Web site managers who are contract developers, all the way up to the IS operations in multi-billion dollar organizations that are looking to use this for inside and outside the firewall application development.

What kinds of individuals in the companies are buying it?

Typically a system administrator or a Webmaster or some sort of IS professional.

How long does it take someone to learn to use LiveWire?

It depends on the component and your level of experience. If you are focusing on the site creation and management part of it, you can probably learn all you need to do to get a simple site up and running in a few hours. On the other hand, if you are focusing on application development, then it's completely dependent on what your level of experience is. If you already have a reasonable amount of experience programming in C or C++, or almost any other language, then it will probably take you a few days to a few weeks to really fully understand all that you can do with LiveWire on the programming side. We provide a bunch of sample applications that come with the software, so you can start out with them and get productive very quickly, but in terms of really being able to master the software, it's going to take some time.

Would you like to add anything else to wrap up?

I would just like to call out the uniqueness of LiveWire in working with both Web site creation and management and Web application development. That's really unique right now in the marketplace. And the second thing is the true cross-platform nature of the tool. A lot of companies are talking about having cross-platform tools, but we are actually doing it.

CHAPTER 10

PowerBuilder 5.0

PowerBuilder 5.0

PowerSoft Division of Sybase Inc.

561 Virginia Road

Concord, MA 01742

Tel	(508) 287-1500 (switchboard),
	(508) 369-4695 (sales)
Fax	(508) 287-1600 (fax back)
FTP	ftp.powersoft.com
URL	http://www.powersoft.com

Overview

Web browsers and Web servers are at their weakest when handling database input and controlling transactions. PowerSoft's solution to this problem is to enhance PowerBuilder so that a PowerBuilder application window can work as a plug-in running in the Netscape Web browser. This means that you can use a Web page as a common starting point from which to access client applications. Further, the applications will have very complete data display, input handling, and transaction control capabilities.

As shown in Figure 10.2, a finished application has two components: the PowerBuilder 'plug-in', which is downloaded

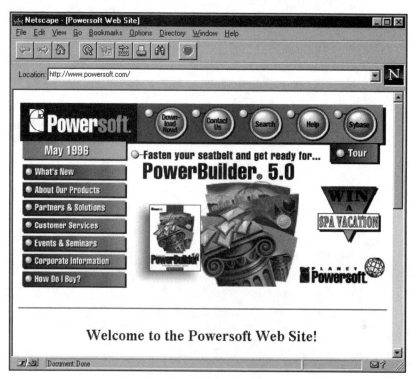

Figure 10.1   The PowerBuilder home page.

once and permanently installed on a user's PC in Netscape, and a client application, which is downloaded each time it is used. When the PowerBuilder plug-in has been installed, the user can click on a link containing an HTML tag that references a PowerBuilder client application. Then, the Netscape browser will download the client application and start it running.

PowerBuilder applications that were developed before PowerBuilder 5.0 was released can be converted to plug-ins. All of the functions that are normally found in the PowerBuilder DataWindow are available in the plug-in applications.

This approach has several benefits. The obvious benefit is that a Web database application can include full-strength OLTP database interactions. Another important benefit to this approach is version control: it is well

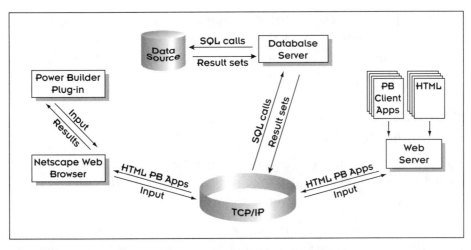

Figure 10.2   The components of a PowerBuilder plug-in application.

known that maintaining correct versions of client applications across a population of users can be difficult and can lead to errors. Distributing client applications as plug-ins will greatly simplify the process. Each time a user launches an application from a link on a Web page, only the latest copy of the client application will be downloaded and executed. Also, users will only need to learn one program (the Web browser) and use it to access many client applications. By doing this, you can reduce the cost and time of training. And finally, users won't have to download and install a new plug-in for every client application that they want to use. That's because once the PowerBuilder plug-in program is installed on the Web browser, it will be able to run any client application that has been created for it.

PowerBuilder 5.0 plug-in applications use a session protocol rather than HTTP. This makes it easier to program transactions but it also reduces the total number of clients that can connect to a database server during a given time. So, PowerBuilder 5.0 includes code that makes a database connection when a transaction is being submitted and disconnects when a transaction has been completed. This works automatically behind the scenes, which simplifies programming.

Plug-in applications built with PowerBuilder 5.0 will work over the Internet or on Intranets by using the session-oriented protocols provided by DBMS vendors or by third parties (for example, DataRamp for ODBC data sources [see Chapter 8], or SQL*Net for Oracle).

Features
Environment

At the time of writing this book, PowerBuilder 5.0 plug-in applications work on Windows 95, Windows 3.x., and Windows NT for Intel. Versions for Mac, Solaris, and NT/Alpha have been announced.

Minimum requirements for the Windows platform are a 386 SX, MS-DOS or PC-DOS operating system (version 3.3 or above), 12 MB RAM, Microsoft Windows 3.1, and 19 MB of hard disk space.

PowerBuilder supports a large number of databases (i.e., all ODBC, native drivers to Sybase System 11, Microsoft SQL Server 6.0 & 6.5, Informix, Oracle, and dBASE2). It also supports the Fulcrum and Verity full-text retrieval systems.

Trial Version

No trial version is available (Figure 10.1).

Web Server Compatibility

PowerBuilder 5.0 plug-in applications do not communicate with Web servers. The Web server is used only to download the PowerBuilder plug-in and the PowerBuilder client application to the Web browser. Once downloaded, PowerBuilder 5.0 plug-in applications interact directly with the database server.

Web Browser Compatibility

PowerBuilder 5.0 plug-in applications run on any Web browser that supports Netscape's plug-in technology. Currently this is only Netscape 2.0 or higher. PowerSoft intends to support the Microsoft Internet Explorer by using ActiveX controls.

ODBC Compatibility

ODBC version 2.5 or 3.0, Level 2.

Learnability

If you already know PowerBuilder, then it should only take a day or so to learn how to convert a PowerBuilder application to a plug-in. If you don't know PowerBuilder, then it can take some time to learn because it has many features. PowerSoft has provided a whole suite of code examples that you can easily browse. One way to make writing applications easier is with their 'Quick Application Generator', which will generate a series of template files that you can customize. In addition to the manuals, PowerBuilder 5.0 comes with online documents, some of which are multimedia.

How Programmable Is It?

PowerBuilder has an object-oriented scripting language that is similar to Visual Basic in that you specify actions based on events (such as a mouse click). There is an object browser to help you visualize the hierarchy of the system objects. They also provide a built-in editor with syntax highlighting to make viewing scripts easier. Plus, there are ways to insert predefined text into the scripts. There are hundreds of built-in functions that you can choose from to reduce the amount of programming that is necessary.

Furthermore, there are many ways of adding functionality to PowerBuilder applications such as using OLE 2.0, VBX, and DDE.

Efficiency

You can compile PowerBuilder client applications down to p-code (**.pbd** files) that will be interpreted at runtime, or compile them down to machine code (**.DLL** files) that will be executed by the native hardware. Machine code runs much faster than p-code but is non-portable.

Security

All the normal security features available to database client/server applications are available here. Once a PowerBuilder 5.0 plug-in application is connected to a database server there is no difference between a plug-in application and a regular database client application.

Error Handling and Debugging

During compilation, the compiler checks the code and displays messages for any compilation errors. At runtime, appropriate error messages are displayed for situations such as not being able to connect to a database. There is an interactive debugger that allows you to step through the script as you watch various kinds of variables (for example, local, parent, global, and shared).

Input Validation

Among the properties of PowerBuilder input fields are input validation specifications. Plenty of input validation expressions are possible using built-in functions, and you can also specify customized error messages. Another property of an input field is its edit mask, which filters out bad input as a user enters data.

Support for Transaction Control

Full transaction control is possible since a normal database client/server session connection is used.

Cookies

Cookies are not needed because the connection between the client and server is session-oriented rather than stateless.

The 'Hello Database' Program with PowerBuilder 5.0

The 'Hello Database' programs in this chapter show how to create a PowerBuilder 5.0 client application for the Netscape 2.0 Web browser. We will develop the database client in two stages as it is easier to test and debug this way. First, we will build and test the database client entirely in PowerBuilder 5.0, then we will modify it to work as a Netscape plug-in.

This Hello Database example uses a copy of the same Microsoft Access database **phone.mdb** (named **phone2.mdb**) that we used in the other chapters. This database will be served via ODBC from a local server.

Setup

1. Obtain a version of PowerBuilder 5.0 that contains the plug-in file **NPPBA050.DLL**.

2. Run the **setup.exe** file to install PowerBuilder.

3. Copy the plug-in file **NPPBA050.DLL** to Netscape's **plugin** directory.

4. Configure your Web server to associate the **pbd** file extension to the MIME type **application/powerbuilder**.

5. From the CD-ROM, copy the **\BookData\Demo\PBuilder*.*** files onto your hard drive into the directory **\BookData\Demo\ PBuilder**.

Developing in PowerBuilder

There are a few preliminary steps that need to be done before we can create the database client. The first thing is to make it easier for PowerBuilder novices to recognize the tools. PowerBuilder has many toolbars—each containing many icon choices. For novices it's best to check the **Show Text** checkbox (Figure 10.3 and Figure 10.4) to make navigation easier. This is done by choosing the **Toolbars** menu pick under the **File** menu when all applications are closed. Unfortunately, the icons are large and don't wrap across lines, so our figures show the toolbar icons with the text turned off to keep them a reasonable size.

PowerBuilder lets you work with live data while you are developing an application because it's easier to design a client application when you can see how the

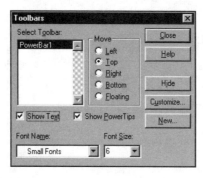

Figure 10.3 Toolbar dialog box.

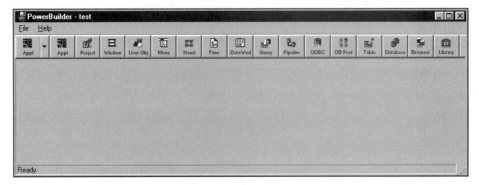

Figure 10.4 Toolbar icons with text.

actual data is going to fit the window. Before an application can be created, PowerBuilder needs to know the working database. This requires two steps: create the ODBC data source and define a PowerBuilder database profile.

The ODBC data source will be called **PhoneList2** and will point to the Microsoft Access database **phone2.mdb**. We didn't use our usual data source **PhoneList,** which pointed to **phone.mdb,** because PowerBuilder places some system tables in the database and we wanted to keep it separate.

The ODBC data source can be configured in the normal way by calling the ODBC administrator from the control panel. However, an easier way is to just click on the **ODBC** PowerBuilder toolbar icon, which brings up the dialog in Figure 10.5. First click on the ODBC driver that corresponds with the database type. Then press the **Create** button to create a new data source

Figure 10.5 Configure the ODBC data source.

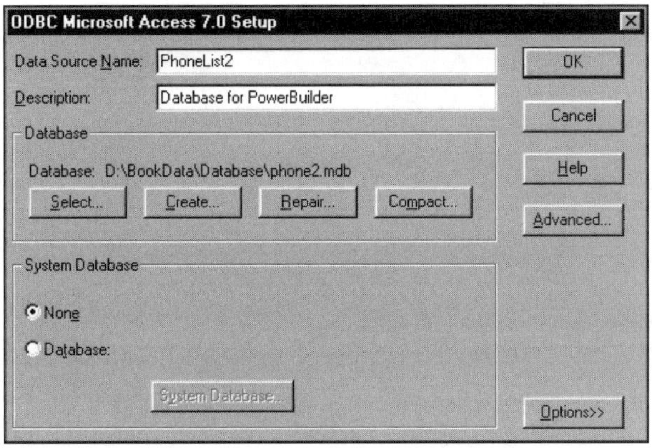

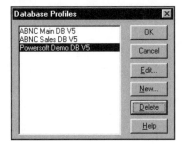

Figure 10.6   Selecting the database.

or press **Edit** to edit an existing one. As you can see in Figure 10.6, we've configured **PhoneList2** to point to the **phone2.mdb** database.

Now that the data source is established we can set up a PowerBuilder database profile that works with this data source. Do this by clicking on the **DBProfile** toolbar icon, which brings up all the database profiles that PowerBuilder is currently aware of (Figure 10.7).

By pressing the **New** button, we can create a new profile (Figure 10.8). It's not necessary to fill in all the fields because PowerBuilder will search the ODBC registry and fill in the required fields for you. All we filled in was the profile name and type of DBMS. When the **OK** button is pressed, a dialog box appears (Figure 10.9) with a list of available data sources. We selected **PhoneList2** and at that point PowerBuilder filled in the rest of the information (Figure 10.10). Now that PowerBuilder has this database profile, it knows where to go when it requires data for previewing a data form.

Figure 10.7   List of current database profiles.

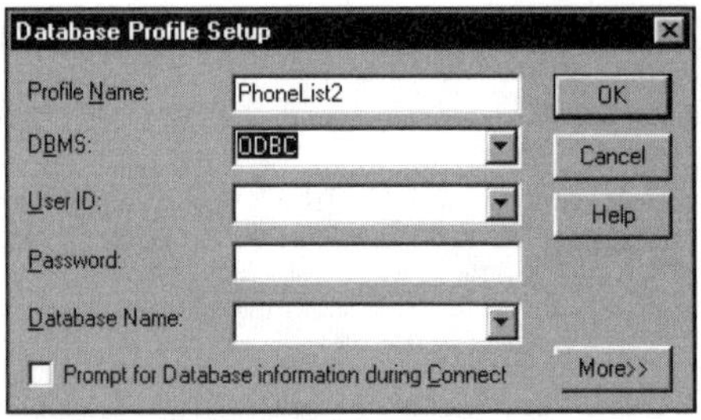

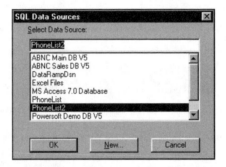

Figure 10.8 Setting up a database profile.

Figure 10.9 Selecting the ODBC data source for the current profile.

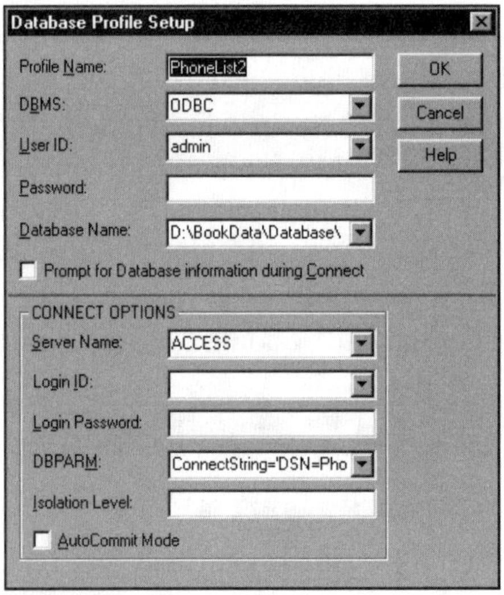

Figure 10.10 The new database profile.

The final thing that PowerBuilder does automatically is create several tables that it uses for internal housekeeping. These tables are placed in the Access database and start with the letters 'pb' (Figure 10.11).

Now with the preliminaries out of the way, we can begin to create the client application. This will consist of a PowerBuilder 'library', which will contain a PowerBuilder 'application', a DataWindow, a window, and some other components. Let's create the library and application first.

We begin by clicking on the **Library** toolbar icon. This brings up a hierarchical file list (Figure 10.12). Then, we create a new PowerBuilder library called **HelloDB.pbl** by clicking on the **Create** toolbar icon. All PowerBuilder libraries end in **.pbl**. Next, we click the Application toolbar icon **Appl** and click on its **New** toolbar icon to create a new application called **test**. At this point PowerBuilder asks if you want it to create an application template. We answer 'no' as we will be creating our own.

With the basic framework established, we can start building the windows and DataWindows for both the Query and Insert Hello Database programs.

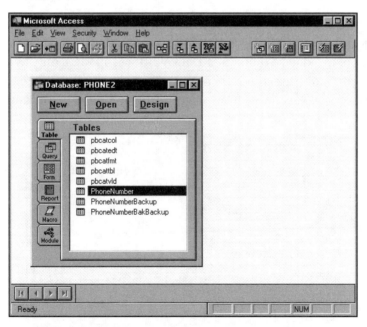

Figure 10.11   Tables added by PowerBuilder.

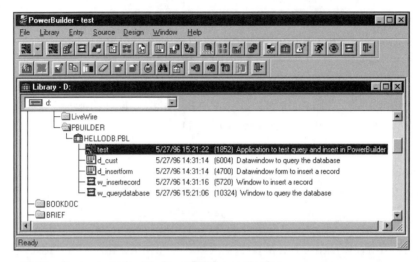

Figure 10.12   Components for this PowerBuilder application.

Query

A PowerBuilder application contains two primary components: a DataWindow that holds the data fields and a window that holds the DataWindow and other components such as buttons.

The DataWindow is like a window into the database where you can view and update the data. To create a DataWindow you click on the **DataWnd** toolbar icon and press the **New** button. You are given a choice of various presentation styles to choose from (Figure 10.13). We choose the tabular style.

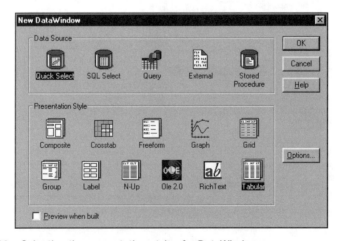

Figure 10.13   Selecting the presentation style of a DataWindow.

Next, PowerBuilder asks which table you want to create the DataWindow for, and when you have selected a table, it asks which fields you want to display. As you click on each desired field, they are displayed in the lower portion of the dialog box (Figure 10.14). When you press **OK,** PowerBuilder creates the DataWindow.

The next step is to customize each field to appear the way you want it. This is done by double clicking on the field and modifying its properties, such as border and alignment (Figure 10.15). The size of the field can be adjusted by dragging its edges. You can also use the cursor keys to move and size the field. Holding down the shift key while pressing the cursor key will size the field.

Once all of the fields have been edited and sized, the DataWindow is complete (Figure 10.16). If you want, you can select the **Preview** menu pick from the **Design** menu to see what the DataWindow will look like when it is filled with data.

When you exit this newly created DataWindow, PowerBuilder will ask for a name to save it to. We label it **d_cust** because it is a PowerBuilder convention that DataWindow names start with a 'd_' and window names start with a 'w_'.

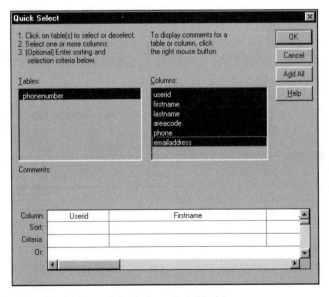

Figure 10.14   Choosing tables and fields for a DataWindow.

Figure 10.15 Properties of a DataWindow field.

The next step is to create the window that holds the DataWindow (Figure 10.17). Do this by clicking on the **Window** toolbar icon and pressing the **New** button. You will see a blank window that can be sized and filled with components such as buttons and DataWindows. For our program, we need to fill the window with a single-line edit box, a dropdown list box, two

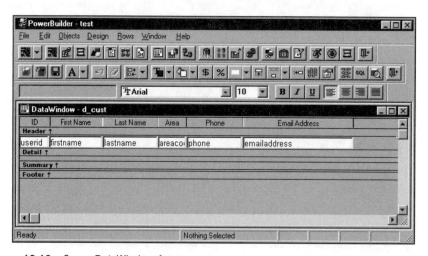

Figure 10.16 Query DataWindow form.

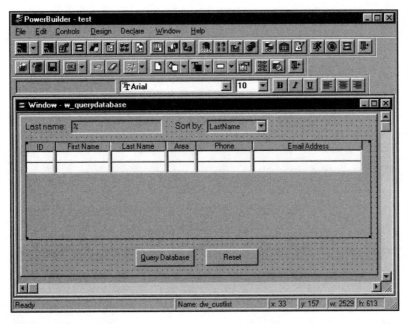

Figure 10.17   Query window.

buttons and the DataWindow that we have just created. To do this, click
the **Button** toolbar icon to display the components that can be placed in
the window. Then, pick a component, place it in the window, and then double
click on the component to bring up its properties. For the DataWindow component, set the DataWindow's property object name to **dw_custlist,** which is
the name the scripts will use to refer to this component. The PowerBuilder
convention is to preface DataWindow object names with 'dw_', single-line
edit boxes with 'sle_', and dropdown list boxes with 'ddlb_'.

At this point, we need to create the scripts that run the query. The first
thing we want to do is initialize the database system so that the database
client knows what data source to use. A script can be attached to each
component of a window, including the window itself. The best time for an
initialization routine to occur is when the window is first displayed. To get
to this event, click on the main body of the window and click on the **Script**
toolbar icon. You will see a blank window and several dropdown list boxes.
Choose the **Select Event** dropdown list box and select the **Open** event.
What you are doing is selecting the **open** event script, which the window
will run first when it is displayed (Listing 10.1).

Listing 10.1   Open event script for query window

```
//----------------------------------------
// Initialize for querying the database
//----------------------------------------

// Establish the ODBC datasource for the global
// transaction object sqlca
sqlca.dbms="ODBC"
sqlca.dbparm="ConnectString='DSN=PhoneList2'"

// Clear datawindow
dw_custlist.Reset( )

// Set up the datawindow to insert a record.
// SetTrans handles connecting, disconnecting
// and committing to the datasource automatically.
dw_custlist.SetTrans(sqlca)
```

The first thing to initialize is the data source with which the database client should connect. The default global transaction object **sqlca** needs to hold this information. For the Hello Database program, the properties of this object that require setting are the type of DBMS (ODBC) and any parameters associated with that DBMS (**PhoneList2**). Other programs might include things such as the login ID, login password, and the server name.

Next, clear the DataWindow fields of any data by using the **Reset** function.

Finally, the data source parameters assigned to the global object **sqlca** are used to set the internal transaction object of the database client. You can do this with either the **SetTrans** function or the **SetTransObject** function. We use **SetTrans** because it makes the connections only when necessary. **SetTrans** is mainly used when there are a limited number of connections to the database server or when the database server is installed at a remote location. It automatically handles connect, disconnect, commit, and rollback.

The alternate function, **SetTransObject**, lets you control when to connect, disconnect, commit, and rollback. **SetTransObject** would be used on a LAN, when there are lots of database connections available, or when you want the connection to remain open during the entire session.

The next script to write (Listing 10.2) is the actual query that is initiated when the **Query Database** button is pressed. We need a script that creates the ODBC SQL statement, runs it, and then retrieves the result set. The event that triggers this is the **clicked** event on the **Query Database** button. To get at this script, click on the **Query Database** button to make it the active component, get into script editing mode, and select the **clicked** event.

Listing 10.2 Query script

```
//----------------------------------------
// Query the database given the search fields
//----------------------------------------

string ls_sqlstmt

// Set the query
ls_sqlstmt = "SELECT * FROM PhoneNumber &
 WHERE PhoneNumber.LastName Like '" + sle_lastname.text &
 + "' ORDER BY PhoneNumber." + ddlb_sortby.text + ", _
  PhoneNumber.FirstName"
dw_custlist.SetSQLSelect(ls_sqlstmt)

// Retrieve the records
dw_custlist.Retrieve( )
```

The first part of the script creates the ODBC SQL statement by concatenating the literal strings with the user input from the single-line edit field **sle_lastname** and the user input from the dropdown list box **ddlb_sortby**. Next, the statement **sqlstmt** is assigned to the DataWindow object using the function **SetSQLSelect,** and then the function **Retrieve** is called to query the database.

The **Reset** button just resets the DataWindow and is programmed in the same manner as the **Query Database** button. Its script is just the one line:

```
dw_custlist.Reset( )
```

To make the application work in PowerBuilder, the window type is set to **Main** from its property dialog box (Figure 10.18). We will change this to **Child** later when we make the application work as a plug-in.

Upon exit, this window is saved to the name **w_querydatabase**.

PowerBuilder applications are initiated from a script that is defined in the event 'open event'. This event can be found by double clicking on the

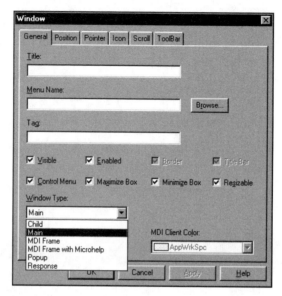

Figure 10.18 Property settings for a window.

application (**test** in this case) and then clicking on the **Script** toolbar icon. The only statement you will find there is:

```
Open(w_querydatabase)
```

which opens the window when the application is started.

Now the application can be run by clicking on the **run** toolbar icon that brings up the window **w_querydatabase** containing the DataWindow **d_cust** (Figure 10.19). When the **Last name** field is filled in and the **Query Database** button is pressed, the application connects to the data source **PhoneList2**, queries it, retrieves the data, and then disconnects (Figure 10.20).

If the application is not working correctly, you can bring up the debugger. Click on the **Debug** toolbar icon and select the window to debug (Figure 10.21), then double click on the line of script where you want the debugging to start from, and press the **Start** toolbar icon to start the debugging session (Figure 10.22).

Once the application has been debugged, only a minor change is needed to make it work as a Netscape plug-in. PowerBuilder applications are converted

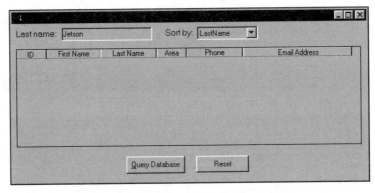

Figure 10.19 Querying the database as a PowerBuilder application.

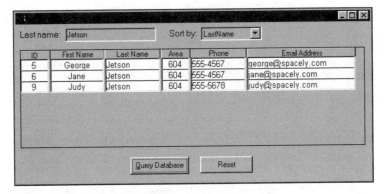

Figure 10.20 Results of the PowerBuilder query.

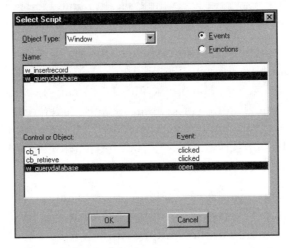

Figure 10.21 Choosing a window to debug.

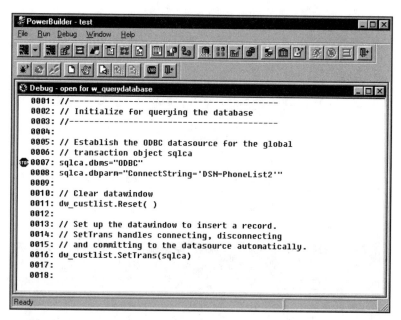

Figure 10.22 Script being debugged.

to plug-in applications by changing the window type from **Main** to **Child** using the same window property dialog box shown earlier in Figure 10.18.

Building the runtime library code is the final step. This code is downloaded by the Web browser when a Web page is requested. To create it, highlight the **HelloDB.pbl** library and select the **Build Runtime Library** from either the **Library** menu setting or by clicking on the right mouse button (Figure 10.23).

The window (Figure 10.24) shows the parameters that can be modified in creating this runtime library. The main question is whether to generate machine code or p-code. Machine code (DLL) runs faster, but is tied to a particular platform. P-code runs slower because it requires interpretation at runtime, but is platform-independent. We opted for p-code, which generated the file **HelloDB.pbd**. If we had chosen machine code, the file would have been called **HelloDB.dll.**

The final step is to create an HTML document that references the Query client application. This is done with the **<embed>** tag, which specifies the location of the runtime library and the window to invoke. You can specify the location with the attribute **src,** which is set to the URL where the

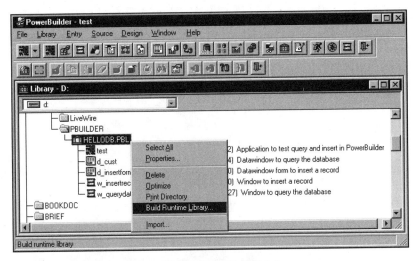

Figure 10.23   Building the runtime library file **HelloDB.pbd**.

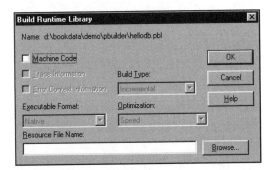

Figure 10.24   Setting the runtime library parameters.

HelloDB.pbd file is located. Specifying the window to invoke is done with the attribute **window** (Listing 10.3). The attributes **width** and **height** establish the window size within the Web browser. Two additional attributes that are available are **library,** which designates additional runtime libraries if needed, and **commandparm,** which passes any string to the PowerBuilder window when it calls the **CommandParm** function.

Listing 10.3   HTML to query the database using a plug-in application

```
<!-- Phone Number Demo for PowerBuilder -->

<html>
```

```
<head>
<title>Phone Number Demo for PowerBuilder</title>
</head>

<body>

<! ------------------- Q U E R Y --------------------->

<h2>Query the phone number database</h2>

Enter a last name (or partial name) and press the "Query Database"
   button. The "%" character is used as a wild card. For example, "J%"
   returns all last names that start with 'J'. You can also set the
   order of the output by selecting one of the choices in the Order by
   list box.<p>

<center>
<embed src=http://1.1.1.1/BookData/Demo/PBuilder/HelloDB.pbd width=750
   height=350 window=w_querydatabase>
</center>

</body>
</html>
```

If this is the first time a user is using a PowerBuilder plug-in application, then he/she will need to download the file **NPPBA050.DLL** and copy it to the Netscape **plugin** directory.

Now we can try out the Hello Database Query client application. Point your Web browser to **http://1.1.1.1/BookData/Demo/Pbuilder/ phone.html** and select the **query** hypertext link. (Be sure to change **1.1.1.1** to your own domain or IP address!) The runtime library file **HelloDB.pbd** will be downloaded and the window **w_querydatabase** will be displayed as part of the Web page (Figure 10.25). This plug-in application has exactly the same functionality as the PowerBuilder application that we used for testing and debugging. When you press the **Query Database** button it will bring up the same query results (Figure 10.26).

Insert

The steps needed to create a client application that inserts a record into the database are very similar to the steps used to create the Query client application:

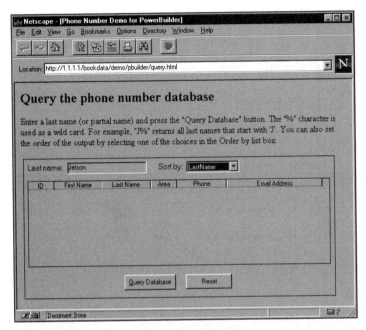

Figure 10.25 Querying the database from a plug-in application.

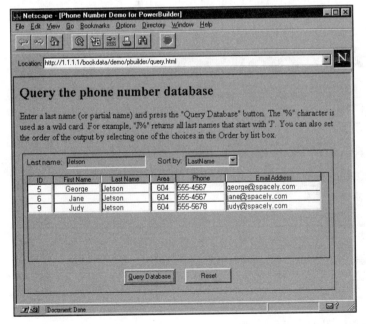

Figure 10.26 Results of the query.

1. Create a DataWindow input form.

2. Create a window to house the components.

3. Create a script to initialize the database client.

4. Create a button to initiate the transaction.

5. Create a script to insert a record.

6. Test and debug the application as a PowerBuilder application.

7. Convert the application to a client application.

8. Create an HTML document that references the client application.

The DataWindow **d_insertform** is created with the DataWindow painter as before, only this time we use the **Free Form** style instead of the **Tabular** style. The fields are sized and their properties are customized as needed. The DataWindow's property object name is set to **dw_cust** for referencing by the scripts.

For the fields to be editable, the field tab order must be non-zero. This is set by clicking on the **Tab** toolbar icon, which displays an editable number for each field. These numbers indicate the tabbing sequence (Figure 10.27).

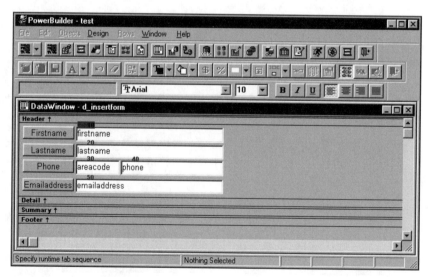

Figure 10.27   The Insert DataWindow form.

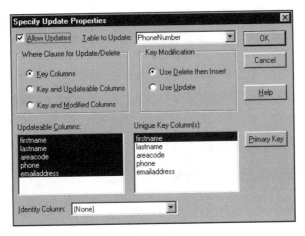

Figure 10.28 Update properties of a DataWindow.

For the database to be updatable, the update properties of the DataWindow must be set. The dialog box, **Specify Update Properties**, in Figure 10.28, is found on the **Update Properties** menu pick of the **Row** menu. The checkbox **Allow Updates** must be checked and all the fields that are updatable must be selected.

The window **w_insertrecord** contains the DataWindow and button that starts the transaction (Figure 10.29). As in the query application, the window's **open** event contains the script that initializes the database client (Listing 10.4).

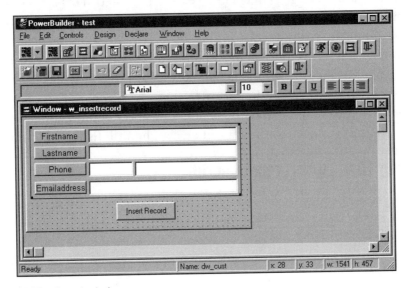

Figure 10.29 Insert window.

Listing 10.4   Open event script for the Insert window

```
//------------------------------------------------
// Initialize for inserting a record
//------------------------------------------------

int li_row

// Establish the ODBC datasource for the global
// transaction object sqlca
sqlca.dbms="ODBC"
sqlca.dbparm="ConnectString='DSN=PhoneList2'"

// Clear datawindow
dw_cust.Reset( )

// Set up the datawindow to insert a record.
// SetTrans handles connecting, disconnecting
// and committing to the datasource automatically.
dw_cust.SetTrans(sqlca)

// Prepare a new record for insertion
li_row = dw_cust.InsertRow (0) // insert at end
dw_cust.ScrollToRow (li_row)
dw_cust.SetColumn ('firstname')
```

This script is pretty much the same as the query **open** event script (Listing 10.4). The only change is that a new record is created. This is done so that when the window **w_insertrecord** is shown, the user will be looking at a new, modifiable, blank record in the database. The script associated with this button performs the update and prepares the next blank record (Listing 10.5). The first function **accepttext** ensures that the text in the data fields is set to the DataWindow's buffer, then the **Update** function is called to perform the database update (connecting and disconnecting automatically). If an error occurs, then it will be caught and displayed to the user.

Listing 10.5   Insert record script

```
//------------------------------------------------
// Insert the record
//------------------------------------------------

int li_rtn
int li_row
```

```
// Ensure that the datawindow contains
// text of the edited field
if dw_cust.accepttext() = -1 then
 return
end if

// Perform the actual update to the database
// Note: since we used SetTrans (during initialization),
// connect, commit and disconnect are executed automatically.
li_rtn = dw_cust.Update( )

// Handle error or prepare for next insert
If li_rtn = -1 Then
 MessageBox ('Could not insert the record', SQLCA.SQLErrText, _
  exclamation!)
 return
end if

// Prepare for a new record
dw_cust.Reset()
li_row = dw_cust.InsertRow (0) // Insert new row at end
if li_row = -1 then
 MessageBox ('Could not create a new record', SQLCA.SQLErrText, _
  exclamation!)
else
 dw_cust.ScrollToRow (li_row)
 dw_cust.SetColumn ('firstname')
end if
```

Upon a successful update, a new blank record will be created and displayed in the DataWindow.

This application can be tested and debugged by making the window **w_insertrecord** the **Main** window and getting the application **open** event to open this window. Once everything is working, you can change the window to a **Child** window and compile the runtime library as p-code to create the client application.

Listing 10.6. shows how the Insert client application is embedded in the HTML document. It is identical to the Query client application except that the **window** attribute is set to **w_insertrecord.**

Listing 10.6   HTML to insert a record

```
<!-- Phone Number Demo for PowerBuilder -->

<html>

<head>
<title>Phone Number Demo for PowerBuilder</title>
</head>

<body>

<! ------------------- I N S E R T --------------------->

<h2>Insert a phone number record</h2>

<p>Enter all the information for the new phone number record and press
   the "Insert Record" button. Then use the <a href=query.html>query</a>
   operation above to confirm that it was inserted.</p>

<center>
<embed src=http://1.1.1.1/BookData/Demo/PBuilder/HelloDB.pbd width=450
   height=250 window=w_insertrecord>
</center>


</body>
</html>
```

To test out the Insert client application, point your Web browser to **http:/
/1.1.1.1/BookData/Demo/Pbuilder/phone.html** and select the **insert**
hypertext link. (Be sure to change **1.1.1.1** to your own domain or IP address!) The Insert client application will be downloaded automatically and
will display itself in the Web browser (Figure 10.30). Note that it is not
necessary to download the PowerBuilder plug-in file **NPPBA050.DLL** again.
Once this DLL has been installed in Netscape it can interpret any **.pbd**
file, so that you can use any number of PowerBuilder client applications.

If you take your Web browser back to the Query client application Web
page and query the database again, then you can confirm that the record
was actually inserted into the database (Figure 10.31).

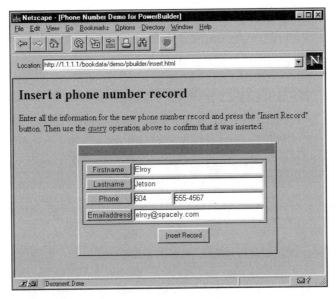

Figure 10.30 Input screen to insert a record.

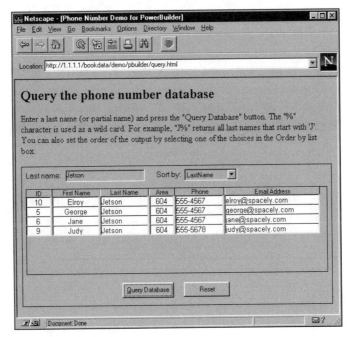

Figure 10.31 Results of inserting a record.

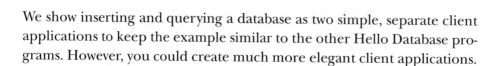

We show inserting and querying a database as two simple, separate client applications to keep the example similar to the other Hello Database programs. However, you could create much more elegant client applications.

Interview with Bob Zurek of PowerSoft

Bob Zurek is a member of the PowerBuilder development team at PowerSoft. We talked to him about the Web-related features that will be in PowerBuilder Enterprise 5.0 and about their new object server and other technology slated for release in the near future.

PowerBuilder has a lot of features, but we are specifically interested in how PowerBuilder 5.0 can make applications work over the Web.

PowerBuilder Enterprise 5.0 will allow a developer to transition his or her applications onto the Web for the Internet and Intranet. It will support plug-ins and ActiveX controls by use of a freely distributable virtual machine that works with a Web browser. It will also support an open development environment with OLE and CORBA.

Can you tell us more about the plug-ins?

The DataWindow object is being released as both a plug-in and an ActiveX control. And it's a full blown data-aware object, so when you hit the page, the DataWindow object could be embedded in the page under Netscape or under Internet Explorer. And, you would be able to browse and scroll through data and change data and update data and things like that.

So the PowerBuilder DataWindow will be visible over the Web?

Yes. Remember, presenting data from a database in HTML has a lot of restrictions. For example, scrolling. Say someone does a 500,000-row query. I can't imagine what the HTML is going to look like in table format. I believe that the browser would run out of memory before it could display it.

It wouldn't be able to download it. That's exactly a Web database problem we have found. One programmer we know creates a dynamic 70K HTML page, and he doesn't like it, but with the tools he had when he started his project that's all he could do.

Right. So having the DataWindow as a plug-in in a Netscape browser or an ActiveX control in Internet Explorer overcomes that problem and lets you scroll through data and manipulate the data. Plus the DataWindow uses native database drivers—it does support ODBC but our focus has been on direct interfaces to Oracle, Informix, SQL Server—so having that, you can exploit the best characteristics of the database.

Now, taking it one step further, we are trying to help people in the interim to give them an opportunity to take their existing client/server applications and transition them to the Web.

Can you give an example?

Yes. A customer of ours—the media company Showtime Network—has a beautiful inventory system. When they are shooting a Showtime special or whatever—they might need a certain stunt person, or a special kind of lighting—and they can go into this Windows application and put in all the parameters to a single document interface and find out if there is a stunt actor in that area or whatever. They were trying to transition that to a Web-based application and they found out about this plug-in application. In less than a day, they were able to move that window into the browser and make it available over the Web.

What would you say is PowerBuilder 5.0's single most important feature?

Bringing the PowerBuilder DataWindow technology onto the Web, because it will give programmers the ability to integrate Web browsers with robust interfaces to databases. It's also cross-platform and compiled, and it supports application partitioning.

By 'application partitioning' do you mean it uses the three-tiered architecture?

Yes.

Let's dwell on this three-tiered topic for a moment. What should be in the third tier seems to be an open question these days.

Client/server has been traditionally associated with a fat client and a thin database server. A problem I found when I was consulting before I came to Powersoft was that as you built these two-tiered models, your business rules would be embedded in the client. And, as you deployed these applications out to several hundred users, if you needed to change a single business rule, then you would have to go back to each one of the clients and re-install it. Also, the footprints got very big, so from a manageability perspective it sometimes got very difficult. So, people believed that there was a requirement to thin out the clients and bring the business rules out to a middle tier.

To a 'business rule server'?

Right. Then, if I changed the merit increase from 5 percent to 7 1percent because accounting found a chunk of money, I would only have to go to that middle layer piece, that object server, and change the business rule in that object and all clients would then be satisfied with that change.

Isn't PowerBuilder a prime example of the fat client?

That's exactly right.

So it sounds like PowerSoft is really going through a change here if you are now implementing middleware layers.

Yes. In PowerBuilder 5.0 you can now create an object-based server with less than ten lines of code. You can make the objects on that server available to the clients through a connection model that supports TCP/IP, named pipes, or Open Client/Open Server—because we get that for free now—and you can execute methods and set properties and stuff on that object server. It's a multi-threaded model and it also has hooks to the relational data store. So, people can actually move some of their stored procedure code out of the database and put it into more OO-based classes.

I've talked to people who were very keen on stored procedures and triggers when Sybase first came out with them, and now those same people say they hate writing stored procedures.

Right! How do you inherit and do functional overloading? You can take some of your business logic out of stored procedures and you can also build a layer of independence so you can unhook databases.

So your third tier contains your object server?

Yes. It's our own object request broker model and we will be moving it to CORBA over time.

When people say 'business logic', we always want to ask what they mean.

One classic example of dynamically changing rules is in automobile insurance rating systems where the rate tables and the actuarial rules change. So, you could have a rate object that would implement that set of business rules.

Referential integrity grows out of business logic, too, but I think it should stay in the database rather than be moved out to a middle tier.

Yes. I think so, too. Referential integrity supports the data model versus the integrity of the object model.

Does PowerBuilder's way of controlling transactions change because of the Web's stateless protocol?

The DataWindow plug-in uses a session-oriented protocol to communicate through the transaction object that uses native communication protocols. So, it would be using say, Sybase Open Client/Open Server via TCP/IP, or Oracle SQL*Net with TCP/IP, or what have you.

So, compared to HTTP, would this cut down on the number of transactions a PowerBuilder plug-in application could handle?

Yes, it would. Also, we are looking to see what kind of standards come out for doing transactions via HTTP, and whether session-oriented HTTP becomes a reality, and whether server vendors adopt it. We are looking at different flavors of attaching Web server front ends to the database, but it's all in the experimental stage.

So, right now PowerBuilder 5.0 does a classical session-based transaction without HTTP?

That's right.

Could you use HTML for a query but use a session when you do an insert?

When JavaScript can talk to plug-ins you will be able to communicate and get the information out and do a CGI post, for example. So, you can use the plug-in to do sophisticated client side validation and presentation. And then get the information out in a string format ready for posting and do a CGI or ISAPI or NSAPI call.

Can PowerBuilder 5.0 output HTML?

Yes. There's a file Save As command that lets you generate HTML. You create a new DataWindow—a grid or form would be best because we generate tables. You build your SQL and come back into the designer and you have a forms layout and you do a retrieve to bring the data into the report format, and then if you go to the file menu there is a Save As, and it has an

HTML option. But that's the visual side of processing. There's an object that gets generated called the DataWindow object, the object can be instantiated, and there's a method off it called Save As.

So I could be creating HTML pages from a program?

Right. And that object—the non-visual form of the DataWindow called the Data Store object that can be distributed onto a third tier—that object can be fired from a client with the HTML Save As. You can also build a batch-oriented system, you can put timers on the thing, so every five minutes you could execute the Data Store object, generate the HTML, and throw it off to a Web server.

So, in this case, PowerBuilder 5.0 would be used from the server side?

Yes, exactly. It's a server-based implementation of PowerBuilder. It's an object server that you can create.

Can PowerBuilder generate dynamic HTML pages?

It can. You don't have that piece in the beta. What we are working on now is from a hyperlink, you can execute a distributed object to CGI, NSAPI, and ISAPI. It'll hit the object and the object will generate the HTML and send it back to the Web page.

Okay, so I can build a traditional database client and it can actually talk to a Web server?

PowerBuilder's DataWindow objects can execute a query off the database and you can take that result set and generate standard HTML, because there is a method hung off that object that lets you do that, and there is also a visual mechanism in InfoMaker—which is a report writer—which lets the person generate a query and say, save the HTML to this location. Because the non-visual form of the data store object can be distributed, it is feasible for a remote client or a client sitting on a WAN to connect to a PowerBuilder object server and execute a data store object that would generate HTML. And that doesn't necessarily have to be done by a client. A developer can build an object server that—on a timed basis—executes the query, executes the method to save the data as HTML, and throws that back to a Web server.

That sounds like a data warehouse type of application.

Yes, exactly. Say for example, every morning at eight-thirty all my managers know they can get their variance report off my home page. So I would execute the query at six in the morning and generate the HTML so people could read it later.

So, would another example be, I've got a database client and I've just entered some data, and I push another button to generate the HTML and the next morning people get on their Web browsers and get the data from a home page?

Yes. The number of variations you can come up with is great. Just the fact that the object we have is very integrated with querying a database and can generate HTML gives you a lot of flexibility.

Does PowerBuilder 5.0 handle legacy data over the Web?

Think about the Web server connected to the legacy data, but, the legacy data is coming into the Web server converted to HTML and the Web viewer is looking at the data. This component is called Web.viewer and we're doing the productization now.

How about security?

PowerBuilder is security-neutral. We rely on the database or things like Open Client/Open Server to provide security.

Do you use any Web-related security features?

Could you elaborate?

Well, how about authentication from the Web server? It comes out as CGI environment variables that could be turned over to the object server and used if it wanted to.

When you connect to a database from within a PowerBuilder transaction object we support user and login IDs to the database server, specifically. It's an authentication-based model, and our object server also uses an authentication model.

But it's PowerBuilder's own method?

Right.

What programming languages are available?

PowerScript, C++, and OLE.

About how long does it take to learn PowerBuilder?

The average learning curve is three to six months to master it, but it only takes a day to get started doing something simple.

What kind of background do PowerBuilder programmers have?

They are application developers with Delphi, or Visual Basic, or COBOL experience.

What kind of applications will people build with the PowerBuilder 5.0 plug-in?

Mission-critical, distributed, client/server applications.

Proper OLTP applications on the Web?

Yes.

CHAPTER

11

Conversations with Some Web Database Programmers

We thought it would be interesting to interview some professionals who are working with Web database systems to get them to talk about their experiences. The first interview is with Gordon Cornwall, a seasoned programmer who talks about his experiences with Cold Fusion and the projects that he applied it to. The second interview is with Jeff Rowe, who runs a Web site focused on Web database technology and products. The third and fourth interviews are with a Web database developer, Tom Haedrich, and his client Dan Sullivan. They talk about the evolution of their product catalog Web site and what they learned while building and operating it.

Gordon Cornwall

gordon_cornwall@Softworks.com

Gordon Cornwall is a senior programmer at SoftWorks Consulting Ltd. in Vancouver, B.C. He has about twelve years of C and database programming behind him and has been developing Web database applications for about a year. We talked to Gordon about the applications he is working on and the tools he has used.

I understand the first Web database application you built was a time and billing system?

Yes. It's for our own software consulting company. We have several consultants in the field, and we had a manual time and billing system. People filled out paper time sheets and faxed them to the office. They got keyed into the database—with errors—and from that database information client invoices were manually generated, again, with more errors. And it was a time-consuming process. So the aim was to automate the whole process and we were interested in the Web because it was accessible to the people in the field.

We wanted a way for the consultants to enter their time and charge it to various projects, and, enter descriptive information about the time and a couple of other functions as well. Project managers in the field needed to be able to review the time entered by the consultants and accept it or not, as the case may be. Another aspect to this is the consultants billing the consulting company. One of the things we wanted was not to generate their invoices to the company, but to generate a report that would authorize them to invoice the company. Because again, that was an area where there were errors and a lot of back and forth. Plus, on the client invoice side we wanted the ability for the project managers and the product champions in the field to be able to review a client invoice and edit it before it was sent out. So what we ended up building was a system that's half Web-based in terms of front-end. The other half is a traditional client server application implemented in PowerBuilder that's used in the office.

Do the people working in the field come to the office?

They come infrequently.

So with all this shifting paper back and forth across town, was it difficult to correct errors?

Well, a lot was done via fax but it was time-consuming and required a lot of concentration, and still errors got through. The root problem was that the system was manual with all that that entails.

What kind of box is the database hosted on?

An NT box with SQL Server 6.

So you built a relational database application that stores time sheets and has an HTML interface that people use from remote sites, and, a PowerBuilder interface that people use in the office. What does the office application do?

It generates client invoices, maintains system tables, sets up projects, sets up clients. Also there is a function that allows data to be exported to the accounting packages. That makes sense to be done locally because all the accounting is done in the office.

So once you've generated invoices, do you hand something over to accounts receivable as well?

Accounts receivable and payable.

That sounds like a typical, old-fashioned database application, right?

That's right.

So how is it working out?

It's working well on the whole. Very minor glitches, but the system is in use and accepted.

Is that distributed Web interface on the Internet saving as much time and effort as you hoped?

Yes, it certainly is. Particularly in time saved. There's no administrative time to re-key time entries and to check them. The checking is done by the project manager on-site so it's as efficient as it could be.

When the project manager checks data on-site, is he using a Web browser or is he using the PowerBuilder client?

He uses a Web browser.

I assume he's authorized to look at the time records that are on his project, so how did you handle access control?

At various levels of user privilege. Each user is controlled by a database row, and one of its attributes is a privilege level. There's base level, project manager level, and administrator level.

How has the remote Web application worked out technically?

Well, it has been working fine. There haven't been any serious problems at all.

Are you using Microsoft's browser?

We use Microsoft or Netscape browsers, depending on what people prefer. The Microsoft browser works better with our time sheet screen, which is very large and complex. For some unknown reason, Internet Explorer handles it more efficiently.

Does the time sheet screen use tables?

Huge tables with many embedded selection controls, and it refreshes and scrolls more quickly with Internet Explorer.

What tools did you use to develop the application?

I chose Cold Fusion for this partly because it was the most mature product available at the time and was recommended. I haven't regretted the choice. It's very friendly from a developer's point of view—self-installing, no hassles—and it has good support on the Web. Cold Fusion has an excellent developer's forum. I've never seen a better one.

In terms of the quality of information?

Quality and quantity. And the way it works. I was able to post a question a couple of times and get an answer within 24 hours. And also just by browsing through other people's problems I was able to avoid a lot of hassles.

So support via the Web is effective?

Absolutely. You don't have to work your way through a lot of phone calls.

You said PowerBuilder was the other tool you used.

That's right, PowerBuilder, Enterprise 4.

Was this the Web-enabled version?

That version of PowerBuilder is not, but of course it's interesting now with PowerBuilder 5 coming out, which is Web enabled. I'm glad I chose PowerBuilder because I can now port various pieces of it to the Web.

Is there any reason to Web-enable the office application?

Not right now. But what I can see is re-implementing parts of the original Web application in PowerBuilder 5.0 because it has a more full-featured front-end.

Which parts?

The time sheet screens. It was implemented as a Web page and it has a couple of limitations. I can only update sixteen rows from the screen, so basically you're limited to sixteen rows of data. With a tool like PowerBuilder I can eliminate that restriction, and the code would be a lot cleaner.

Could you scroll up and down?

A PowerBuilder DataWindow is ideal for handling that type of thing. And the other pieces that are clunky and slow in the current HTML application are the client invoice review screen and update screen. Both of these involve transaction processing. I found that extended HTML application development tools are much better at reporting than at transaction processing.

When you say 'extended HTML' do you mean Cold Fusion?

Cold Fusion in this case. It's one of a genre of tools.

What is it about transaction control that you find inadequate with Cold Fusion?

Well, it wasn't so much transaction control as the inability to present variable numbers of rows for input. It was fine on the output side.

Did you find input validation a problem?

Input validation is somewhat weak in Cold Fusion, so it was a minor problem for me.

How did you solve it?

I didn't. I did what I could that was reasonable and let some things go.

Well, you've got a sophisticated group of users.

Yes.

Did you consider Java when you were thinking of handling multiple rows?

At that time I didn't know how to bridge the gap between Java and the database, and I didn't want to write all the low level code myself. I just didn't have a budget to do that. Now there are tools available for that.

When you were developing this application, what was the sequence of events? Did you start with the Web part and then build in the database or start with the database?

With the database. I designed the data and implemented the tables and stored procedures and triggers, then I built the Web front-end, and then I built the PowerBuilder front-end and some more pieces of both.

Are you happy with that process? Would you do it differently next time?

It worked fine from a functional point of view. Our mandate was a staged implementation, so after 30 days I had to provide something that could be used in the office. I chose to do the time sheet entry piece of it first, then in the second month I did the client invoicing side. In the third month I did some additional reporting and the export to the accounting system. So from a phase-in point of view, I think it was the right order.

What about training your users? Did it help that they already knew how to use a Web browser?

I think it did help. I didn't have any trouble training people to use the Web application at all. There was a little more trouble training on the PowerBuilder side, but just because the application had slightly more complex functions.

So it took a total of three work-months to build this whole thing?

Yes.

And it was just you?

Right. It's worth pointing out that using a tool like Cold Fusion, if you're going to do anything other than the bare bones, then you end up writing a lot of stored procedures and putting a lot of the smarts down in the database. You end up with a pretty fat server.

What would you do differently?

Well, time changes and technology advances, so I probably would seriously consider using different tools. But I was extremely pleased with Cold Fusion because it was so trouble-free. It had some shortcomings, but the developer's forum and the general level of support—the code examples, the documentation, the self-install—was great. I never got slowed down by that kind of stuff. Plus, I would say that the Cold Fusion language—the HTML extensions—is quite well-chosen for the purpose. You don't have to write a lot of code to get a lot of results.

You mentioned a limitation on the number of rows you can have on the screen. You also had to write a lot of code to submit the whole table full of rows at once.

Yes, I had to write some large stored procedures to save and also to retrieve the rows.

So that's a shortcoming in Cold Fusion. Could they come up with something to make that easier?

A loop construct would have helped a lot. Some of the things I did would have added complexity regardless of the tools, because the time sheet is laid out like a calendar. The weeks are across the top and every cell is a database row. But the fact that Cold Fusion lacked iteration made it a lot harder.

Could you comment on the design process?

I didn't know what the limitations of the Web tools were, so I started with a bare, functional description, and I developed a look and feel as I went along. I think if I had designed something and tried to reverse engineer it, then it would have been harder, not easier.

If PowerBuilder 5.0 was there at the time, would you have just done a database client and then a quick port to the Web?

I probably would have. It's a natural way to use PowerBuilder.

You mentioned you did another small Web database application. Can you describe it?

Well, this one is in progress. Its purpose is to centralize marketing information about data warehouse products and share the information within the company. Our major thrust right now is to develop a metadata repository product for data warehouse development, so we need to know what is out there. I found myself using the Web a lot—printing off all sorts of home pages, product pages, white papers—and putting them in binders and trying to distribute them. But I kept hearing, 'Well, Gordon, you've been doing all this market research, but I don't have access to it.'

People weren't reading the binders, so we needed a better way to publicize this information. So, we said, 'Okay, let's start a database.' But the problem with a database is, if you tried to put all the information into the database, then it wouldn't happen because it would be far too much work to maintain it. So, we played around with various ideas and thought maybe an Internet site with HTML and live links to the Web. But then again it seemed like quite a lot of work to build all those HTML pages for each vendor and product that we were interested in.

We finally settled on an intermediate idea where we'd have a minimal database with a table for vendors, a table for products, a table for URLs and a couple of other things. And, a small number of attributes in each table—name, description, and so—on in the case of product, we put price and installed base because these are numbers that are not very easy to come by and we're not going to find them on the Web page. So for each product, there's a product type—whether it's metadata, a repository, a front-end tool, or what have you so we can sort the products by function. There's price, installed base, and any number of URLs that can be live links to the Web or links to our own Intranet pages. We also scan in product literature and make Web pages out of that. So, the application centralizes all this information in a database, but everyone can get to it from a Web browser.

That's a really interesting application. When someone does research—competition research, market research, technical research—they need to share the results with other people in the company, and I know how hard that can be.

It's going to work a bit like SmartMarks, but all the links will be publicly accessible instead of just available to the owner of the browser. And, it's enriched with extra attributes and structure. Plus, everybody can add to it.

Did you use Cold Fusion for that project?

Yes. Because we had it, and for that it's fine.

Can you tell us about the new product that SoftWorks is developing?

We are calling it MetaVision. It's a metadata repository for data warehouses.

What does it do?

The initial release will be a technical users' tool. It's a place to store information about the data in a data warehouse—where the data comes from, the transformations that it goes through between the system of record and the warehouse, what happens to it in the warehouse, like summarizations. It contains business definitions of the data as well as technical information. So it's a guide for the business user or the business analyst, as well as for the IS guy.

Is it a kind of documentation or a program?

It's basically electronic documentation. But looking farther down the road, in a data warehouse you need to track versions of the data. Definitions of data elements change over time. With a data warehouse, you're extracting data from various operational systems, and those operational systems are changing, and the business practices around those operational systems are changing. So, if you have a data element—like sales region, and you have a northeast region—the definition of this element may change from one year to the next. It may include or exclude another state. So if you look at sales trends by region over a period of years, you may notice some anomalies that are explained not by differences in sales volumes but by changes to the definition of the data element. So, a metadata repository would track all that stuff.

Now, what's interesting is to interface the metadata with the query and analysis functions. There are a number of query and analysis tools used for querying data warehouses. Typically, they don't pay much attention to metadata. They all say they do, but it's usually limited to business definitions and maybe aliases and not much more, so changes in semantics are just lost. Part of the long-term strategy for MetaVision is to integrate the metadata with the query and analysis process. For that the Web is interesting because it is a good front-end for querying and analysis. Right now, we're seeing a trend toward Web front-ends for data warehouses.

So MetaVision will be a semantic filter with a Web front-end?

Yes. It will deliver an audit report with the results of a query. For example, 'Is there anything funny about the data that this query retrieves?,' or 'What are the sources of this data?,' or 'What are the transformations the data has been through?' This is all stuff that an analyst may want to know if someone challenges him or if he has any reason to doubt the validity of the results he's getting from the warehouse.

So MetaVision may not actually control the query, but it will provide parallel information that could be quite important to know. Why did you choose the Web as a front-end?

We see the Web becoming generally more important. I just think it's going to be in demand. You get the benefits of not having to distribute your client application and install it on all the PCs, and you get the benefits of platform independence.

What will you use to develop the interface?

I think I'll implement it in Web-enabled PowerBuilder. Why not?

You've been on a quest for Web database tools over the last six months. What have you looked at?

Well, Cold Fusion of course. We also looked at the combination of JAGG and Java. And Java with Optima ++.

What is Optima ++?

Optima ++ is a Sybase/PowerSoft product that hasn't been released yet, but it supports C++ and Java and databases. I saw that PowerBuilder 5.0 is Web-enabled, so you can take any PowerBuilder window and run it in a Web browser, I thought, 'Hey, this is great,' because I know that PowerBuilder is very full-featured, and I'm reasonably comfortable with it. I thought it would be better in terms of development efficiency than to go straight into Java at this time. Although Java is interesting, and I'm sure it'll mature.

What else will MetaVision do?

We're thinking of adding active metadata acquisition. Rather than just being a passive documentation system, it will go out and grab events as they are occurring to the warehouse. On a data warehouse, you have various kinds of tools operating—you have extraction processes, you have load operations, you have data mining tools, and you may have administrative functions like backup and restore—these are all things you want to know about and record in the metadata repository. 'When did the last load occur?', 'How fresh is my data?,' 'Was it a partial load?' Systems of record can be all over the place and you may do a weekly load from here, a monthly or bi-weekly load from there.

And those can all introduce semantic noise?

That's right. The data warehouse user ideally wants to intercept all these operations on the database and record them.

What advice can you give to someone who's just starting on a Web database project?

Try to match the tool with the need. If what you want to do is publish without input, then an extended HTML approach like Cold Fusion works extremely well. With very little effort you can generate all kinds of reports with live links and you can implement a drill-down capability and make it look pretty good just using HTML tables and HTML formatting. But if you want to do updates, particularly involving multiple rows or multiple tables, you should look for something else.

Any advice on the database side?

I guess if you were going with a simple Web database tool you might be tempted to denormalize the data design a bit to make things easier on yourself.

Did you find updating the database through SQL Server was adequate?

Very good. I encapsulated all the complexity in stored procedures, so it was actually better than I expected.

Are there any 'gotchas' that people should be aware of?

Well, there's iteration. And validation is another one if you're expecting it to be there, and you're using a tool that doesn't support it. The whole area of state information. User ID and password validation are kind of difficult to handle. You have to pay attention to it because a Web session is not really a session, it's more a series of encounters. You have to imagine somebody who signs on and bookmarks the Web page and then returns to it later from the bookmark and skips the sign-on screen. Or a different person using the bookmark. You definitely don't want to put your passwords into the HTML code that is generated at runtime because anybody can view the source and see the password.

Do you see more companies Web-enabling their products?

It is happening. Certainly on the query and analysis side, and there's quite a bit of buzz about it. For example, in the upcoming Data Warehouse Institute conference in July, there are four or five sessions on Web front-ends to a data warehouse.

Jeff Rowe

http://cscsun1.larc.nasa.gov/~beowulf/db/existing_products.html
j.p.rowe@larc.nasa.gov

Jeff Rowe works as a contract programmer at NASA in Langley, Virginia. He started out doing database work and then began putting together his department's first Web database installation. He also operates a friendly

Web site that focuses on Web database issues and has lots of links. We talked to Jeff about his experiences and the tools he uses.

What is your programming background, Jeff?

I'm kind of a nomad. I graduated in '92, and this is my fourth job. I've done development under PCs using DOS, Windows, and OS/2. I moved to Unix and did some system administration work for a while in San Antonio for Southwest Bell messaging, then moved here and worked for a Windows-based place. Then I moved over here to Langley NASA and found a home. I've been here about ten months.

What do you at NASA?

I worked on a large database called PRISM that was intended to be used by people with no computer training. I was doing a delete function in a complicated database that had all kinds of join conditions. It was very complicated.

Was this for the Web?

Not at first. I didn't get involved with the Web until June of last year. My team leader said it seemed to be a good idea to use a Web front-end to the database instead of the Motif GUI we were using with PRISM. And maybe we could even take some of the back-end code out of the database and apply it to the GUI front-end that's running on the Web. So he said, 'See if you can do this,' and I went out crawling all around the Web and found bits and pieces. But there wasn't anything that said, 'Here's how it works, this is an overview, this is how you do it', so I put up my Web site because I figured there were other people out there looking for the same information. I guess my pain could be their gain.

How did you approach this?

I used Mini-SQL, the freeware database—at least it's free for research institutes—and the only freeware product that I found that I thought was fairly robust was WDB, and I have kind of taken over development of it. The original author went back to Denmark to start up his own consulting company, so nobody was developing it.

Why were you looking for a freeware solution?

There was no funding to buy commercial stuff. And when I first started looking there may have been one or two commercial gateway products, and that's it. Most of the stuff out there were abstracts and white papers and proof of concept stuff. WAIS was around but there wasn't much for Web database. When I started out there were probably twenty Unix freeware products and maybe three or four products for Windows NT. I was just looking at that today, and it looks as if NT is about to catch up. Everything seems to be moving to NT.

So you liked Mini-SQL because it was free?

There wasn't a lot of commercial stuff out there, and we really don't have the funding to go out and grab something and play with it for money. Now a lot of the products have these thirty-day evaluation copies so you can grab one and see how it works, which is great for people who are curious. I've done that with Cold Fusion, and dbWeb, and WebDBC.

You have access to an NT server?

I've got an NT server and SQL Server at home.

What are the main questions people who come to your Web site are asking?

I get two camps. One is, 'I want to do the same thing you've done; tell me how.' The other camp is, 'I've tried to do this along similar lines, I'm using this product, I'm having a problem with this specific area; have you found a way to work around this?' When I first started out, a lot of people were working in Unix and using PERL and CGI, which is what I've used, and I had an idea what they were talking about. I've noticed recently the same questions have moved to Windows NT using ODBC and Microsoft Access, and I'm not up on that stuff. I bought a book on ODBC last night, as a matter of fact. And I figure I'm going to have to learn that on my own just in self defense. Because that seems to be the platform everything is moving to.

Among all the Web database products that you reviewed for your Web site, which ones stood out?

For Unix, Sapphire/Web and Spider both look good. For Windows NT, Cold Fusion seems to be the big one here, with WebDBC second. I've used dbWeb also, and it works well.

Macintosh?

No one uses a Mac for serious Web development because of the limited number of products available for it.

Are there any other classifications for the Web database products other than your current one that you might consider useful?

ODBC-compliant, GUI-based, PERL-based. I can't divide things into as many categories as I want, so the hardware platform seemed to be the best to go with.

Into what classification headings would you group the audience that is looking for these Web database products?

Unix people using PERL, and Windows NT people using ODBC. Those are practically the only two camps I see. The Unix camp is equally divided into SunOS, Linux, and 'Other.'

What are the pros and cons of having a database on the same server as the Web server?

Some pros are ease of use, central code repository, a single administration point. Some cons are that the user load on a busy Web site causes a performance hit on the database, or a hacker breaks in and has access to the database as well as the Web files.

Do you see PERL getting more or less popular for Web database solutions?

Taking into account the fact that the PERL interpreter must be run every time you do a database query, and also the fact that possible security holes exist that novice PERL programmers might not be aware of, PERL is firmly entrenched among Unix do-it-your-selfers who use a database and PERL extensions through CGI. All of that software is free, so it will never go out of style. Yes, there is a CGI/PERL performance hit for loading PERL, then loading the program, then compiling it, then running it, but it's free and you can't get around that. PERL is not the perfect tool for CGI because of the constant loading. But, until something else comes along that offers the same features and ease of use and is free, PERL will be the CGI programming language of choice.

As for security holes, I think that's a lot of smoke. Bad programs can be written in any language and give hackers a way into your system. PERL is no worse and is often better than shell scripts or C programs, especially if you use PERL's 'setuid' functions.

Do you think that there are additional security risks in using the Web as the gateway to the database, as opposed to a traditional database client/server solution? And if you say yes, then what do you think is the best way of dealing with security when you use the Web to access a database?

I have never addressed this issue and have heard little about it. I think the biggest security risk is by publishing the URL of your Web site, because it makes millions of people aware that your database exists. Anonymity is good security, but it sucks for distribution.

I think the HTTP server/client is equally as secure as a database client/server, more so if you use a secure server. In that case, using the Web *increases* your security in spite of the recently published breakdowns in the encryption. Most people don't realize, it took multiple supercomputers a week to break one key. The computers were programmed by people who had to be intimately familiar with encryption technology and the encryption method broken was the exportable 40-bit encryption that is *designed* to be broken. In my mind, this validated the encryption method.

Do you see CGI scripts being around six months from now for Web database solutions, or will the API solutions become more predominant?

CGI is a standard. That means anybody can use it. NSAPI and ISAPI are extensions, which means they work better, but only certain people can use them. Not every application will need the extensions because CGI will suit them fine. High-performance applications will move to the extensions because they need the better performance. Which way will they go? I think Unix will go Netscape, and PCs will go Microsoft.

CGI will be around forever, but will lose users as more people use the extensions. It's just two tools, and developers will choose what works for their applications.

What do you think are the key features that make a Web database product good?

A GUI-based front-end. Good manuals and/or online help. Plenty of examples. Good tech support. Good performance under load. Light use of computer resources.

What are some typical Web database solutions that you have come across?

Web database solutions are as varied as the databases they support. The only general types of solutions I've seen are the shopping cart for online stores and the text search engines like Yahoo.

Everything else is fairly customized depending on the data they publish to the Web. I know every database I put on the Web requires me to write more code and use very little of what I wrote before.

What do you think impedes OLTP on the Web right now?

I think it's the way you keep track of things that are going on currently. The stateless connections. I think that's the biggest part of the deal because once you log in, unless you've got some complicated method of keeping track, you don't have authentication that's easy to do. You have to authenticate them every single time they make a connection to the database. Or, you can't depend on the data you just got to update being the same data that you're sending back. Things like that. There's a lot involved with the front-ends of database applications that involve data safety, and I don't think you can do that with the Web, at least not yet. A lot of that's going to have to come either from the database or the gateway designers and I don't know how they are going to do it. But it's not my problem.

So is OLTP feasible on the Web at the moment?

I'm sure it's feasible, it's just not very usable for general applications. If the application is written correctly, and the database connection software behaves correctly, all of the connections should terminate correctly. This doesn't always happen in practice. I think that is one area in which the *database* vendors will have to address the problem, because they don't handle this situation well even outside of Web applications. I've seen defunct database processes running outside of the database server because someone logged off wrong, and I've seen ghost processes still running inside the database server for the same reason. The only way to kill the rogue processes is to restart the database or reboot the machine because the database connection software is stupid. That sucks.

How about using Telnet?

Yeah. HTTP does what it does very well, and I don't see any reason to take something that works well and make it do everything for everybody. That's not what it is intended to do. I just read they are coming up with a new HTTP protocol that's more efficient and will send things with smaller packets and use less network bandwidth, which is good. But if you are going to leave connections open, then it doesn't matter how efficient you are, you still have all that stuff floating around on the Internet going back and forth that you don't really need. HTTP is not set up to do that. It might come that for generic Web stuff HTTP will go one way. And then for OLTP and anything that needs that constant connection a different protocol will be designed that's got the same sort of thing that might co-exist with HTTP. And, the Web browsers could handle both of them. I don't know. But it just seems to me that if you want a constant connection, that's what Telnet is all about. You can Telnet somewhere and start up your GUI front-end and it runs on your machine and sends stuff across the network and that's what you got.

One of the really strong advantages to the Web for database management is the fact that it's on any computer that you want. You just find a Web browser that fits your machine, and you've got a front-end to your database. And if they had the two different protocols co-existing side by side, and you use the one that you need when you need it, instead of making one protocol work for everybody, that might work better. I don't see that you need to change something that works to make it do something it was never designed to do.

A lot of the current products seem to use some sort of template and custom tags in their Web database products to create HTML output reports. Instead of using these extra tags, do you think a better way to go is to have a full-blown language in these third-party Web database products?

That's a tough one. I hate non-standard extensions, but then the HTML committee is as slow as Congress when it comes to publishing a new version of the HTML standard. So, serious applications have to define their own extensions in order to provide the functionality missing from HTML. The best of a bad situation is to use the HTML that is available and add your own extensions when HTML won't handle it. That gives users a starting point for using your product because they are familiar with standard HTML, plus they can learn your extensions more easily because they are couched in a familiar format.

Do you think that a Web browser could become the universal database client?

Two things make the Web browser the front-end of choice—built-in networking support and cross-platform support. The rest is gravy. If no other

technology ever was added to the Web browser, those two items would draw application programmers.

Networking support eliminates the user license fiasco where database vendors require you to buy a license for every user. Since the Web server is the only user, you buy a handful of licenses and serve 100 people. Big cost savings.

Cross-platform support means you already have a GUI-based front-end for any computer you want to use for accessing your database. The database application programmers go out the window, the big consulting firm fees go out the window, and you rent a college kid for three months to build you an app. You just saved a million bucks. If you hire a full-time, bigshot programmer to build you a custom app, you still saved $920,000. It's hard to argue with real, tangible cost savings by using free products that are easy to program with.

The current solutions to retaining a session from one Web page to the next include inserting IDs into every link, user authentication, and cookies. Is this difficulty in controlling state information going to be a serious limitation to moving the Web browser toward being the universal database client?

Clever programmers have been getting around that kind of crap for years. I've been programming since the punch-card days, so maybe I have a better perspective on new technology, but the stateless connection is just a programming hurdle to get over with smart programs.

However, there is a 'keepalive' tag I've heard of in testing now that will keep a connection open. If its primary use is to keep a connection open long enough to load all the images and text on a single page, then it's a good thing. If it's used to dedicate a connection to a database app for three hours, then it's a bad thing.

The stateless connection does two things: it forces programmers not to be lazy and sloppy, and it decreases the time a network connection is exposed to the risk of tampering. It's harder to hit a moving target. Both of these are good things. The keepalive tag can help increase performance and decrease bandwidth consumption, so I'm all for it as long as it's used wisely. Long-term connections are better performed by Telnet. Don't break a good feature of HTTP.

Do you think one day that most Web servers are going to have a built-in database server, or do you think the gateway solution to databases will continue.

They already do. I've seen at least five full-blown Web database servers, not including Oracle's Webserver, which is a kludge. However, I'm not impressed with their capabilities because they are inherently limited by what HTML can do, but that's getting better and so will the products. They will be big in 18 months but are too limited to be truly useful today.

Many people already have databases they have no intention of giving up for new products, so gateway-based products will continue to appear in support of existing software.

What would you add to the current HTML spec or HTTP protocol to handle the problems with accessing databases from the Web?

Um, I don't think this is an HTTP or HTML problem. It's a database engine or gateway problem. HTML and HTTP have a life outside of databases, and it is unreasonable to expect the HT brothers to do everything for everyone. It's up to the database or, more reasonably, the gateway product to solve this problem.

In your opinion, is using the relational database model adequate for the Web, or will we need to go to more object-oriented databases to encompass more data types?

The relational database is adequate for an enormous number of applications now, so why would it change for the Web? The Web is a new medium, not a new application. Well, okay, it is, but not to a relational database. I think object-oriented databases will have a place in certain applications but not for everything, just like C++ has not replaced C for everything.

As I mentioned before about tools, application programmers will choose the tool that is appropriate for their task. OODBs solve some problems that aren't addressed by RDBs, but they aren't for everyone. I think OODBs will find a place on the Web as well.

Given this situation: A person has access to a Unix shell account where a Web server is running. He wants to put up a small database using a freeware SQL database server. However, he doesn't have authorization to start a database daemon on the Unix server. Can you think of a solution for him? I've seen this type of request several times. The main problem is not having superuser authorization. I think a small percentage of our readers who want a Web database solution without the cost of a dedicated Unix box and leased line will be interested in a solution to this problem.

I get this question a lot, too.

Well, I'm running a shareware database engine called Mini SQL under my own account and it has nothing to do with the root account. However, not many sysadmins would appreciate someone doing this. The only other option I know of is to find someone who has a database server and is willing to host your data for you for a small fee. There are a few around that will do this. I'm currently doing some consulting for a company that is doing exactly that. They are renting database space for $300 a month and I'm helping them design the front-end applications on the database server machine. Compared to the cost of a Unix box and database server, it's a great bargain.

Do you know of any Java examples that access databases?

I know of one product someone posted on my BBS called WebLogic dbKona. The URL is: HTTP://Weblogic.com/

I'm not currently involved with Java, as I think it's a good waste of bandwidth and nothing else, but it will take off, and I should know about it, so I'll start exploring it soon.

Where do you see the Web in the future?

I see it on Windows NT boxes. NT is cheap compared to Unix, and it's robust compared to DOS, so it appeals to the middle-of-the-road group, which is a large group of people looking for a Web presence.

The database of choice will be MS SQL Server because it's cheap compared to the Big 3, but it's robust enough to handle large applications. There is no clear winner in the NT Web server wars, but O'Reilly's WebSite looks very good. And Cold Fusion seems to be the gateway of choice.

Naturally, Unix boxes will continue to host the largest applications, and Linux boxes will host the do-it-your-selfers, but NT will get the rest.

Tom Haedrich

http://www.popco.com/

Tom Haedrich is a programmer at Popco (Point of Presence) in Seattle. Popco is an ISP and a Web presence provider to a variety of businesses and it also moderates a mailing list that discusses marketing on the Internet. Popco has a subsidiary called Buildcom that specializes in working with the building industry and one of Buildcom's Web database projects is an electronic commerce site called The Faucet Outlet. We talked to Tom about the tools he used in developing The Faucet Outlet and his experiences during the process.

What's Popco's main business?

We have a number of servers out in Seattle, and the clients often ask us to develop Web sites and run them for them.

And you focus on a vertical industry?

We've seen the Web development market go from a pretty unique thing to a commodity business in one year. If you have a database already built and get someone to build a template for you, then you can have a static Web site in a couple of hours (if you get someone who knows what they are doing). We decided to look at things that were a little more specialized, so we moved into the building industry.

Was The Faucet Outlet already in the retail mail order business?

Yes, they sell all the major faucet lines. They take orders, and if they can't ship, then they have other people who can ship as well, so they can handle quite a wide line.

Did they have a catalog?

Yes, and we worked with them to turn it into an online catalog. When we first started this it was a while ago, before people had even talked about integrating the Web with databases. So, the first version was homegrown, and we realized that later versions would be a nightmare to do that way.

Homegrown in what way?

A whole lot of looking at the catalog and building an HTML template for pages then a lot of cutting and pasting and scanning and re-keying. It was a real mess.

How many catalog items did you do by hand coding?

Initially we did about 250 to 300.

So you hand-wrote HTML and popped in the photos and text?

Right. A little bit of batch processing and lots of real late night stuff.

The idea for this book came partly out of thinking about the horrendous amount of work you'd need to do on a project like this.

Right. I've been there! Then we decided to get smart. We decided to build a static database, which is taking a simple database program such as FileMaker Pro and entering the information. So that's how we did the second stage of The Faucet Outlet. We loaded everything we'd done into the file program and took the HTML templates we did and coded them into calculation fields. Then we rolled all the data into the file and generated a static output file that had all the HTML tags around the data fields.

Were the graphics still separate GIF files?

Yeah. In fact what we did was set up a couple of main folders, and in the database itself it was all references.

How did that work out?

That actually works pretty well. And it didn't cost too much, and the client can manage it. The nice thing about FileMaker Pro is it only costs $100. And, they have a software developer's kit, a little stand-alone application, which you can send to a client and have them review it and then do updates to the database.

So what is the actual physical procedure of them updating the database and handing it over to you to make a snapshot?

They have a plain version of the database that they maintain and they export from it to another version of the database that we built—sort of a secondary prepping database—which serves as a filter to change the text information into an HTML template.

Did you use the report writer to do that? How did you generate the HTML tags that go around each field?

We design a template, and then that template is built into calculation fields in the report generator in the database. It looks at the fields and grabs the information and wraps it with tags, and then we export that as one long text file. Then we use a PERL processing script to cut the long file into individual HTML files. It works pretty well.

Did you look at products that create static HTML pages from databases?

We found that this was the easiest way and the most cost-effective in that our customers were either familiar with a database like FileMaker Pro or Access or FoxPro, which they had used to build their own little database on, so it was easy to get them to export information.

Would you use that now if you were going to start again?

Well, the third version of The Faucet Outlet is doing page building dynamically according to a query form. We talked to our customer about using FileMaker Pro, but they were running an Oracle database already, so they suggested we look at using that. When we first started, Spider and ORAPERL had just come out but we decided that sending some SQL queries through PERL was the easiest way to do it. A lot of the Web database packages work well, but when you want to do some complex things their products aren't as customizable as you want them to be.

Anything in particular? Like, harder-to-do reporting? Or input?

Well, when we first looked at Spider we found it was really quick and easy. But, we thought that in the long run, if you are looking at plugging into the inventory system or somehow getting more advanced, then you will have problems. We thought that the closer we get to being able to modify code and queries the better off we are.

Do you expect to continue to use PERL or some programming language and CGI?

Yeah, actually we are starting to take a look at the SQL side, the dreaded Microsoft NT side of things. I've been doing a lot of talking and reading and looking at NT and SQL Server, and I think they are slowly becoming fine products.

Do you see NT as an up-and-coming presence, maybe even overtaking Unix?

Hmm. I'd say, from the people I've talked to, that the need for databases and the need for managing information is on the rise. No one knew what data warehousing meant a year ago, and now people are throwing it around like, 'Yeah, that's what I did last week.' So, it seems like the easiest way to move into something like that without spending tens of thousands of dollars is that platform.

Cheaper than a Sun box?

When we first looked at The Faucet Outlet development we talked to an Oracle developer and they were talking about charging hundreds of thousands of dollars to get something built. For a company that does two to five million a year in retail sales, that was a really big investment for them. Maybe a Fortune 500 company wouldn't think twice about doing something like that, but for the middle and small business there's a real big question there.

Microsoft has always been strong in the middle to low end of the market.

You see Apple saying, 'Hey, you can run all this stuff on a Mac.' I was talking to a large furniture company that was going to make a Web server on a Mac. But, when it comes down to pure Web serving, a Unix box just makes the job a lot easier. And the nice thing, because of all the Internet hubbub, the prices of Unix boxes are also coming down, so it's becoming a more viable option. But then when you get a Unix box, you ask, 'What are we going to use as a Web server, and what are we going to use as a database?'

If you make NT your lower-end solution, will you still be going with CGI and PERL, or would you go with a Web database product?

That's sort of a quandary. I haven't taken the jump yet.

On PERL, because it's an interpreted language when you do a query, you have to run the CGI and then run the PERL interpreter, so it's fairly inefficient. Did you find that?

Yeah, it is CPU intensive. The Oracle stuff we did for The Faucet Outlet we ran on a pretty souped-up box. When you work with Oracle and ORAPERL you need a pretty high-end machine because that's the only machine that can handle it without slowing down.

We're working on a database for the home improvement industry that does lead generation. It handles a lot of text data and does auto indexing and auto archiving, and we looked at PERL, but we decided to build a subroutine library in C. We took all the special things that PERL could do that C had a tough time doing and wrote our own subroutines in C. Because C is compiled, it's much faster than PERL, and it's more flexible.

Does having your own library mean that you can put any database or Web server combination together?

Yes. We even wrote a server for ourselves with a lot of sockets that can keep channels of communication open, so if we wanted to plug in an Oracle solution we could do it easily.

The building industry isn't a particularly high-tech industry. Do their customers have terminals and Internet accounts? Are they comfortable with getting on the Web?

For the first six months we had to do a lot of education of our industry customers, but we've found that the consumers are driving the industry. Building products companies say, 'Do you have a lot of contractors online?' And we say, 'No, it's the consumers who are going on the net and educating themselves about what's available,' then going to the contractor and saying, 'Hey, can you do this for me?'

So you accidentally fell into this vertical niche?

We had first approached The Faucet Outlet, and then they introduced us to a couple of people and it just opened up.

What is their level of awareness of the Web?

Not that aware.

Since they had an Oracle database in-house they were obviously computer aware.

The building industry is very technology aware. There is a lot of product information, and there are price changes that happen quarterly. There is a huge outlet in New Orleans called LCR. All they do is buy faucets from the manufacturers and ship to supply companies, and when you walk in that place it's right out of Star Wars. A few years ago this industry was shaken into awareness by EDI, and that got them on the battle wagon. A lot of government departments pushed for EDI, and big retailers like Home Depot pushed for it and brought people in kicking and screaming, and then they said, 'Ahh! we can actually use this for something!'

How about online sales? When I looked at The Faucet Outlet I saw prices but I didn't see any way to purchase. Can you order online?

No, you can't. We have been thinking about it, but let me explain why we didn't do it. When we first did it the whole credit card scare was there. Then it turns out that the customers like to do a lot of online research and find out what they want, but finally they want to ask a human, 'Do you think this is the right faucet for me? Do you think this will work?' and that human voice saying, 'Yep, that's a good choice,' is important. It's working well for Faucet Outlet because they have reduced the time their sales people spend educating the customer, and it becomes much more, 'I saw this—will it work for me?'

Was that a design goal? Or did that just emerge?

We sort of rationalized that over time, and it proved to be right. When we first looked at it, we said, 'This could be a great educational tool,' and they said, 'That sounds like a good idea,' and we tried it, and it was! Then we found that a lot of people would just send in an order right away by email.

With a mail-to?

Yes. We found that people who want to order over the Internet will just go ahead and do it, and the people who are in doubt just pick up the phone and do a phone order. Also, there's a lot of other issues such as pricing and inventory availability; if you place the order online is it going to be in stock?

In other words, it's not quite as simple as it looks.

Right. Ordering sounds simple, but it's not.

Are you using the Netscape commerce server?

We've used Cybercash. Regarding the Netscape commerce server, their security is in the process of transmitting the communication, and Netscape lets you encrypt it. But we've found that the biggest security problems are related to storing the data and making sure that it's behind a firewall. Our thinking has been that it's a whole lot of work for someone to listen to all those telephone signals. But for someone to figure out, 'It looks like credit cards might be stored on that hard drive, let me break into that,' that looks a lot easier.

So you're less concerned about encryption than going behind a firewall?

Once we get a credit card number, what we do with it is a much bigger concern than how the card got from A to B.

What hardware and software platforms are you using?

It's all Unix. All our servers are Sun boxes. Most of the databases have been Oracle but we haven't been totally happy, so we are thinking about what the next step is going to be. We've just built our own server and are building some of our own database stuff as well. A lot of the code is our own C.

What makes Oracle a less-than-perfect database for you?

Well, it's a real heavy database that needs a lot of CPU power. We've talked a bit with Informix and Sybase. We'll probably just continue with Sun boxes and lots of power, but it's something I'm struggling with right now.

Are you thinking of Netscape's NSAPI or Microsoft's ISAPI?

We will probably continue with C and CGI for now.

Are you looking at using Java on the client side to make things more interactive?

That's a good question. Once again, I think it's a question of content. Java is an interpreted language and it has the same problems as PERL, so people will struggle with that. It will be a question of what we have to show off rather than to use Java. I don't know how exciting people will find it to see a toilet flushing on the home page. The problem right now is, is technology driving or are applications driving?

The Web is a great place to find out fast.

When someone slaps some content on my desk that needs it, then I'll use Java.

Are you collecting market information on your Web site on the person or the number of hits?

Totally! That's actually a whole issue. That's another database you need!

Do you offer questionnaires to browsers?

Yes. We see the Web as a two-way street. Some people treat it as a broadcast medium, but it's definitely two-way. As much as we shove down the pipe we try to get as much back by tracking user stats and doing surveys and analyzing responses.

Dan Sullivan

http://www.faucet.com/faucet/
faucet@faucet.com

Dan Sullivan is the president of RAL, the company that runs The Faucet Outlet Web site. He was the main person in his company who worked with

Popco to develop the site. We talked to Dan about his experiences as a businessman working with an outside developer to put a Web site together.

What gave you the idea to put The Faucet Outlet on the Web?

We saw the growth of the Web and the number of people who were accessing it each month and we felt that it was something we needed to check out. Also, we looked at the cost of developing an Internet site, as opposed to revising and printing future catalogs, and we felt that dollar-wise it was a winner. People in the plumbing industry are using EDI (Electronic Data Interchange) and putting catalogs on CD-ROMs. We felt that everyone would ultimately end up going the Internet route, so we figured our money would be invested better by going straight to the goal.

So people in your industry are becoming more computer and network aware because they are already using EDI?

Absolutely. And my market is primarily consumer, and we looked at the demographics of who was accessing the Web, and those were our customers.

What is your customer's demographic profile?

We looked at surveys and asked people and found that Web users had a higher median income, were homeowners, and were a fairly young segment. And most of them had PCs and were already checking in on the Web.

It's also said that Web users are heavily drawn from high-tech industries, and I was wondering if that applied to you?

It wasn't one of the main aspects, but in my mail order business there is an incredible amount of hand-holding that goes on. And we thought that people who could get involved with higher tech things online, they are the same people who will do the legwork necessary to research my type of product offering. So we wouldn't need to spend so much time on the phone with people who had accessed our online catalog.

Is that proving to be true?

Absolutely. That's one assumption that came through.

When you did your market survey did you get information from other Web sites or did you do your own polling?

We didn't do any polling. Between me and my boss we just spent a lot of time on the phone questioning site providers, and some people we know in other industries, who were looking into it. And we were getting real positive replies from those queries.

So it was informal research, but enough to give you a feeling of confidence that it was going to work out?

Precisely.

You mentioned CD-ROM. Did you look into that as well and compare the cost?

Yes, we did. CDs are definitely a great idea, but the problem is that my costs do not change on a uniform schedule. So, it didn't make sense to spend the money on something we could only update once a year. The initial investment was about the same, but for continual updating we felt that the Internet was the way to go.

Were you the person who initiated this project?

The owner of Faucet Outlet is David Berman. He is a very proactive type of guy. He turned me on to it, and between the two of us we did the research and checked it out on our own and decided that it was going to be a winner. When we developed the Web site we really thought it was going to be a marketing vehicle. We thought it would take two years before any real results came back, and we have been surprised that it has become an order-taking mechanism also.

In addition to being a publicity mechanism?

Right. We knew it would be a good PR vehicle because it could show product information to a consumer. We knew that's what the initial stress would involve, getting information out to the users to help them decide. We thought it would take about two years before we saw it generating direct sales, but luckily we've seen it a lot sooner.

Are sales made online, or do people phone your 800 number?

Right now I get two to five email messages a day where people are placing an order. Some of those people email me their credit card numbers, but most of them give me their phone number, and I call them back and take the order. So yes, it is via email and phone. Tom has been researching online order-taking software.

When you are talking with the customers, do you find a pattern?

Definitely. It's what I had mentioned earlier, when they have done all their research so I don't have to spend much time with them. They'll email me questions, and when they do call to place the order they will usually have one simple question, then they go ahead and give me the order.

Is that a big difference?

It frees up an incredible amount of my staff's time, and of course my phone bills have lessened.

Could you give us an example in terms of minutes per call?

Over the past twelve months my business has changed to people who are purchasing items for their whole house as opposed to a replacement order. So those people, when they call me on the phone, spend a total of twenty minutes or so, versus less than five minutes for leads from the Internet.

That's a big difference. These people who are doing their house, are they watching This Old House on PBS and buying do-it-your-self books?

A lot of professionals—doctors, lawyers—so I would say their leisure time is not as much as other segments of society, and I assume they go to the bookstore and buy five or six home improvement magazines.

We really thought business-to-business selling would catch on first on the Web. We thought that the argument for this was so strong, when you are selling engineered goods that take a lot of thinking to buy. So, it's interesting that you are seeing so much activity in retail.

Right, and you know what I've found—which is funny—my call reports at the end of each month show me that the majority of people surfing the Net are doing it during business hours. I thought it would be the opposite.

What sort of information do you get on your reports?

I get the number of hits, the time spent on each page, the most popular pages, popular states, countries, what online services visitors use, international users, corporate servers, and so forth.

Do you find many from out of the country?

A growing percentage from Canada, and I got an email from Israel this morning. We've had a lot from Japan. So it definitely has a nice international flavor.

About when did you conceive the project, and when did you go online?

Let's see...we've been on since January '95. It was probably four months earlier that we had done the research and knew we were going to go for it.

Do you consider it a success so far?

Definitely.

Some marketing people look for quantified statements of benefit. You have said that you spend less time on the phone. Are there any other benefits that you have been able to count?

Sales have increased a small amount. We didn't think we'd get any orders for some time, but probably about 3 percent of our monthly orders are now off the Web site.

And you haven't really been focusing on getting orders; you've been working on customer service.

Right. It's a nice little bonus. We didn't think it would be a commercial vehicle until we got some sort of ordering system online.

If you had it to do over, what would you do differently?

No regrets. We would have made it more interactive as we are doing now.

How do you get your link out to the public so they know to come in to your site?

We do some registrations to the various search organizations. Also, just with the PR that we've been receiving. People will email me, 'Gee, I just saw a great article on you in *Popular Mechanics.* I'm not shopping now, but I will be in three months and I'll keep up to date.'

So you are sending out press releases?

Yes, also people such as yourselves hear about us and call us, and that generates a lot of response. We devote the last page of the paper catalog to our Web site, and we've found a lot of consumers are just flabbergasted and hook online to us right away.

When you started did you have a database already, or did you start from your catalog and key in everything?

I operate internally off a product database, and we have a third edition of our paper catalog. We combined the text and numbers from the database with images we digitized from the catalog.

What is the database running on?

It's Q&A running on a PC.

Did you use that to generate information for your printed catalog?

No, for the Web site we thought that just text information wouldn't help the customers, so we digitized a lot of images and just used the text that went with those images.

So your database was to help the guy on the phone when a customer called?

Right. And the printer used it for part of the paper catalog.

So when you did the Web site, how did that work? Did you give Tom the database?

My artist and Tom put the artwork and text from the paper catalog online and then I downloaded my database for him, which he imported for the text part of the online catalog. A real problem was that when we tried to use images and data from the different manufacturers, they came in different formats, and we had to work on them before we could use them.

Did you have to re-scan their catalogs?

Some of the manufacturers are gaining speed technology-wise, so if they had digitized images they were kind enough to share those with us. But most of our initial work was handling and scanning images on paper.

It sounds like it was a fairly intensive effort to get all the pieces of data together from all the manufacturers.

I think I could have written the Bible with less pain.

Did that surprise you that getting the data and images together was so much work?

I thought that would be the easy part. I thought the manufacturers and their representatives would be able to help me along, but it wasn't the case.

We think the best approach is don't try to do everything all at once, just start small, and you can do it with small resources. There are people out there spending very big bucks on the Web, but the homegrown sites are often more effective.

It's just like government. The bigger the bureaucracy, the smaller the result.

Your audience is retail now. Are you planning to go for tradespeople, too?

When this company started out, the business was trade only, and I just wasn't making any headway, so that's when I opened it to everybody. But our next effort will be to reach builders and architects and designers. They've got the PC knowledge because of their CAD systems and the other software that they need for their businesses. And I see it as being a nice marriage because some of the building associations are developing their own sites.

So that's a place where you can post links?

Exactly.

Does your company use EDI?

Yes. With my major supplier.

How about tradespeople that could be ordering that way?

No. Most of the small contractors are too far back technology-wise. I know from my own experience I had to spend a lot of time learning about EDI and finding the right consultant to help me implement it in a PC environment because it's easiest with a mainframe.

So there is a PC interface to EDI?

Yes. That's what I use.

Did you have that before you started the Web project?

Yes.

Is that why you had a Windows system and a modem—to do EDI?

Correct.

Did that help when you got onto the Web? Did it seem more familiar because of that experience?

I wasn't quite as green. I had no qualms about just diving in and learning from my mistakes after my EDI experience.

You said your catalog price updates came at different times, so CD-ROM wasn't attractive for you. Do you do the updates directly onto your Web site yourself or how does that work?

Not yet. I fax them out to my provider. Tom is wary of training me on hypertext.

So they take care of you?

Yes.

If you had a system that would let you call up Web screens and type in your changes yourself, would you prefer that method?

Oh, definitely. The Web site gives people lots of information, but it's not helpful if I give them all that info, and then they find out that the price is wrong.

So it's got to be as up-to-date as possible?

Exactly.

What about inventory? Will that be part of it, too, later on?

Possibly. My EDI system is from GE, and they do a huge amount of research and programs on making EDI friendly for business. I've seen more and more articles in their journal about using EDI through the Internet.

Dan, if things progress and you get more orders, what would be the next thing you would do on your site?

I guess I'd ultimately like to turn the site into an online magazine of how-to and helpful hints. If people could learn a little bit and be entertained, then hopefully they will look at my product offerings. Then, secondly I'd like to make it the world's largest product catalog, or plumbing supply showroom.

In terms of stock covered?

In terms of images. When you go to a local supply house of whatever product line, they can only carry so much on display, and then you have to fall back to catalogs. I hope to have everything that you would find in a paper catalog online.

Not counting your consultant's time, how many work-months did it take to get this project going?

I'd say for about a three-month period, less than a quarter of my time was on the project. Doing the last revision of the catalog made it much easier to transfer that knowledge and data into the Web project.

CHAPTER

12

Web Database
Products

This chapter lists all the Web database software products that we could find information on. To collect this material we browsed the Web and exchanged email with the vendors. We also sent out 100 email questionnaires and received 29 detailed responses. Of course we couldn't review such a large number of products, so we have written brief summaries and then let the vendors speak for themselves by quoting what we thought were the clearest and most specific statements we found in their written material.

Our coverage is uneven because the available information is uneven, so just because we have a short entry for a product doesn't mean that we don't like it, and if the entry is long, it doesn't mean that we think it's wonderful. We also expect that we have overlooked many interesting products, so we encourage our readers—both users and developers—to tell us about products we have missed. (See 'About the Authors' for contact information.)

An abridged version of this chapter is on the CD-ROM in the form of an HTML file with the URLs as live links. If you load the file \BookData\ProdDir\products.html into your Web browser, you will be able to click on the URLs of the products listed here and browse the vendors' homepages.

We hope that by browsing through this chapter you will be able to find the tools that fit your needs. We recommend that you contact the vendors for the most current and detailed product information.

4W Publisher and 4W Publisher Pro

Summary:

4W Publisher is a development tool for generating static Web pages from databases. It works with Microsoft Access or ODBC databases. The standard version is a 16-bit Windows application. The Pro version is a 32-bit application that runs under Windows 95. It automatically builds main menus and keyword indexes. You can generate pages with separate headers and footers. It includes a selection of predefined Web templates. An automatic 'document modified' field can be included on a page. Product catalogs are cited as typical examples of what 4W Publisher is good at building.

Details:

URL	http://www.4w.com/4wpublisher/
Platforms	4WPub – Windows 3.1; 4WPub Pro – Windows 95, Windows NT
Web browsers	any
Web servers	any
Data sources	4WPub – MS Access 2.0; 4WPub Pro – MS Access 7, ODBC level 2
Memory required	4WPub – 8MB; 4WPub Pro – 64MB
Disk space required	2MB
Server side interface	CGI
Client side interface	HTML
FAQ	Yes, at Web site
Demo copy?	Yes, at Web site

Contact:

Information Analytics, Inc.
PO Box 80266
Lincoln, NE 68501

Tel	(402) 475-3150
Fax	(402) 475-6231
Email	4wpublisher@infoanalytic.com

They say:

About 4W Publisher:

"4W Publisher is a database-authoring package that you can use to design product catalogs. It uses an MS Access 2 database that contains several configuration tables used by 4W, and contains a table that holds user records or 'documents.' The user can define multiple indexes and page templates. When pages are generated (as separate .htm files) the page templates are used to combine header, body and footer. Changes to an entire Web site can easily be made by changing just the header and footer page components and then regenerating all pages."

About features:

"The ability to define style sheets and page templates to simplify site management."

"User-defined data fields may be inserted into documents. For example, a database field containing product price can be inserted into the page using a %%[price] reference. This allows the user to easily include information stored outside the body text of the page."

"You can generate indexes in virtually any HTML style, by defining style sheets that can contain tags for tables, bullet lists, etc."

A-XOrion Web Database Server

Summary:

A-XOrion is a CGI gateway program that connects a Web server to Microsoft Access and several other databases. It runs on Windows 3.1 or 95 and is written in Visual Basic. It can convert Access reports to Web pages.

Details:

URL	http://www.clark.net/infouser/endidc.htm
Platforms	Windows NT 3.5, Windows 95, Windows 3.1
Web servers	Netscape, Httpd for Windows 3.1, WebSite, FastTrack, ZBServer, FolkWeb
Data sources	MS Access, Paradox, Dbase, Foxpro, ODBC
Memory required	16 MB RAM
Disk space required	5 MB
Server side interface	CGI
Client side interface	HTML, optional Java
Demo copy?	Yes, at Web site

Contact:

Maarten C. Hoolboom

Email   mchm@msn.com

They say:

About A-XOrion:

"A-XOrion conforms to the CGI/1.1 standard. The A-XOrion server is built within the Microsoft Access environment. It will therefore be able to connect to tables from Microsoft Access, dbase, Foxpro, Paradox, and with SQL Server, Sybase, and Oracle through ODBC. A-XOrion requires Microsoft Access to be pre-installed. A-Xorion does not access data: MS Access does that and therefore: 'If MS Access can connect ('attach') to a (remote) database, A-Xorion can also!'....Database designers need to have or obtain good understanding of MS Access Report writing, as this is the powerful means by which A-XOrion creates output."

About database connectivity:

"The A-XOrion server and gateway technology uses the A-XWebFS message file system to transport queries, transaction requests and reports from Web server to database server and back. This means that you have the option to connect a PC database without using ODBC drivers. Or use both A-XWebFS and ODBC. A-XWebFS means also that you can design multi-server configurations—using one processor or using more than one processor in a multi-server, multi-processor networked environment! So long as the A-XOrion Servers and Web servers have access to a shared A-XOrion home directory, transaction requests and MS Access reports will be exchanged using the A-XWebFS Message File System."

About user authentication:

"The Logon Screen allows for a username/password check before the system presents a database form or a Web page. The name of the actual destination form-file or destination filename will be hidden to the enduser as you will be using an alias name for the destination. Usernames, passwords and destination Aliases can be entered and deleted at any time by the system management. Through the logon screen, you have a method of guiding authorized users toward their destinations as well as of monitoring access as every logon will be logged."

Amazon

Summary:

Amazon is a Web application server and development environment that allows access to corporate data from Web browsers for both Intranet and Internet applications. Applications use standard HTML Forms and can update or access data from virtually any Windows, Unix, or mainframe database, process the data and create dynamic Web pages of results. It comes with a programming language and makes use of the standard security methods used on the Web and on databases, and works with firewalls. Typical applications cited include automated subscription servers, online quote systems, online shopping, and product catalogs.

Details:

URL	http://www.ieinc.com/Webnews.htm
Platforms	Windows NT, Windows 95, OS/2
Web servers	Netscape, Mosaic, Microsoft IIS
Data sources	ODBC 32-bit level 2.1, Oracle, Sybase, SQL Server, DB2, Lotus Notes
Memory required	1 MB
Disk space required	10 MB
Server side interface	CGI, NSAPI, ISAPI
Client side interface	HTML 3.0
Demo copy?	Yes

Contact:

Intelligent Environments
67 South Bedford Street
Burlington, MA 01803-5132
Tel   (617) 272-9700, 1-800-669-2797 (USA)
Fax   (617) 272-9300
Email   amsales@ieinc.com

They say:

About database access:

"Amazon is database independent through its database access independent layer called SQLX. SQLX supports direct access to Oracle, Sybase, SQL Server, the DB2 family, ODBC, and Lotus Notes. ODBC (Windows only) provides access to a wide range of databases such as Access, Paradox, dBase, Excel, and text files. Lotus Notes is accessed using SQL to provide very high performance direct access to existing structured Notes databases."

About legacy databases:

"Amazon offers a high-performance secure way to connect your legacy systems directly into the World Wide Web. Amazon handles the complete range of corporate legacy systems including DB2, CICS, APPC, 3270/5250 terminal emulation, VSAM, Oracle, Sybase, SQL Server, and through ODBC, many more."

About business logic:

"The rapid growth of client/server has resulted in GUI applications developed in products such as Visual Basic and PowerBuilder. Unfortunately, such products completely tangle the business processes with obscure Windows handling code. All such applications will need to be rewritten to exploit the Web. Amazon separates the business logic from the GUI handling so you can build applications that have a Web interface or a Windows interface, without changing the business logic. This also means that Amazon preserves your valuable business logic through any future technology change."

About communications independence:

"Amazon is communications independent through its communication protocol called CPX. CPX supports WinSockets (TCP/IP), Named Pipes, APPC (LU6.2), IBM's CICS External Call Interface and direct calling of C, C++ and COBOL through a common verb set."

About terminal emulation independence:

"Amazon is terminal emulation independent as it uses the standard HLLAPI interface supported by Microsoft's SNA Server, IBM's Communications Manager, Attachmate's Extra, and WallData's RUMBA products."

About connecting to other applications:

"Amazon can call a C, C++, or COBOL application directly at the API level. Amazon can also call any existing applications written in a conventional language, such as Visual Basic or Borland's Delphi, using DDE (Dynamic Data Exchange), Named Pipes, or WinSockets (TCP/IP). Amazon can also use any OLE server or OLE control that supports OLE Automation (such as Microsoft Office)."

About security:

"Amazon supports standard Web security such as SSL (Secure Sockets Layer) and SHTTP. Amazon works behind security systems such as that provided by Netscape's Commerce Server and Microsoft's Internet Information Server. Amazon also works behind standard industry firewalls that block all unauthorized access to machines on the network. The link from the Web server to the application server can be TCP/IP or Named Pipes. Named Pipes provides a very high level of security as it runs rigidly under local program control and cannot be controlled or even accessed remotely."

"Amazon supports all the standard mainframe security features such as RACF. Amazon is unique in providing direct access to mainframe transactions through IBM's CICS. Using CICS in this way preserves the business logic, audit trails, security authorization, and data integrity inherent in your existing mainframe transactions. By using the External Call Interface (ECI) of the CICS common client mainframe, transactions can be initiated directly from any application server running Windows NT or OS/2 Warp."

About testing and debugging:

"The application server application can be stepped through a line at a time when the application is running. Breakpoints can be set on procedure calls, expressions, and changing variable values can be set up as watch points. A comprehensive SQL and communications trace system is also provided. It's tried and tested. Amazon's application engine is based on Intelligent Environments' AM product, which has been used to provide secure, robust, high-performance client/server applications for more than seven years. AM client/server applications scale to more than two thousand PCs running against mainframe MVS, VM, AS/400, OS/2, Windows, and Unix databases. It is a family of products. Amazon is supplied in three versions—Amazon Builder, Amazon Enterprise, and Amazon Unix. There are also add-in components available for specialized purposes such as Lotus Notes support, CICS access, and support for IBM's static SQL against DB2 databases."

About input validation:

"Full range of data validation, table lookup, cross-field validation, database lookup, date checking, range checking, and so on."

Autobahn

Summary:

Autobahn is a 4GL application development system that integrates with the Web via CGI. With Autobahn, developers can create interactive business applications that run on the Web and can access databases and return the results in an HTML document. It is a session-oriented server that can maintain user sessions between transactions.

Details:

URL	http://www.speedware.com/
Platforms	HP 3000, HP 9000, RS/6000, Windows NT, Solaris
Web servers	Netscape, NCSA, CERN
Data sources	Oracle, Sybase, TurboImage, Omnidex, Informix, SQL Server, DB/2 6000, Allbase, Image/SQL, NetBase, ISAM, flat files
Memory required	4 MB
Disk space required	4 MB
Server side interface	CGI
Client side interface	HTML
Mailing lists	speedware@cs.santarosa.edu (subscribe via: Maiser@cs.santarosa.edu)
Demo copy?	Yes, at Web site

Contact:

Speedware Corp.
150 John Street, 10th Floor
Toronto, Ontario
Canada M5V 3E3
Tel   (416) 408-2880, (800) 361-6782 (US & Canada)
Fax   (416) 408-2872
Email   boobp@speedware.com

They say:

About its 4GL programming language:

"Autobahn can use the full power of Speedware/4GL to run programs that handle forms, reports, jobs, batch updates, transactions, and calls to 3GL subroutines."

About distributed architecture:

"The Autobahn agent, the S/OAS, and databases can all be on different machines, so large organizations can use their resources as they prefer. For example, if you have a dedicated machine for the Web server, you can put the S/OAS on a production machine close to the data. In this way, you can build a firewall and spread the processing load."

About database access:

"Most data access is performed from 4GL calls with support in the language for embedded SQL."

BASIS & BASISplus WEBserver

Summary:

BASIS is a comprehensive document management system. The BASISplus WEBserver enables BASIS document databases to be accessed via Web pages.

Details:

URL	http://www.idi.oclc.org/
Platforms	Unix, Windows NT, OpenVMS, MVS
Web browsers	Netscape
Web servers	Netscape
Data sources	ODBC
Client side interface	HTML
Demo copy?	No

Contact:

Information Dimensions, Inc.
5080 Tuttle Crossing Blvd.
Dublin, OH 43016-3569
Tel   (614) 761-8083
Fax   (614) 761-7290
Email   Webmaster@idi.oclc.org

They say:

About applications for BASIS:

"Common applications include ISO9000 document control, regulatory compliance, litigation support, technical library automation, research information management systems, technical documentation, and content management for publishers. BASIS applications are usually characterized by small, medium and large document collections (five thousand documents would be considered small). The documents are usually intellectual property critical to a business operation (e.g., policies, procedures, regulatory filings, product specifications, and legal contracts). The documents often have a very long lifecycle within the organization (e.g., one to 20 years). Due to their criticality and sensitivity, the documents require robust protection and management controls."

About the difference between SQL databases and BASISplus:

"Relational database systems (RDBMSs) traditionally support highly structured data such as name, address, phone number, etc. BASISplus tables contain highly structured as well as unstructured data. The unstructured data is typically in the form of large fields containing words and other mixed objects. The highly structured data are usually attributes and relations about the unstructured data objects. BASISplus allows many different types of queries such as phrase searching, proximity searching, wildcard searching, and weighting, while traditional RDBMS character fields can be searched only with the more conventional relational operators such as Equals and Not Equals. So BASISplus allows querying at the word level, traditional RDBMSs allow it at only the cell or column level. BASISplus also provides the same level of search and display capabilities for very large columns in a table (like the body of text in a document), while many RDBMSs either store them as unsearchable BLOBs or do not store them in the database at all. BASISplus also allows the storing of arrays of structured data in columns, which can greatly reduce database complexity and the complexity of the applications manipulating it. Traditional RDBMSs do not support this feature. Arrays are an excellent structure for managing lists of authors, subject headings, revision histories, etc."

About the types of documents supported by BASIS:

"Documents can be popular word-processing documents, SGML documents, HTML documents, formatted text, tagged text, or bibliographic records."

About how documents get in the system:

"There are a variety of interfaces for building the applications that are used by workers who will be authoring and editing documents. The simplest is BASIS Desktop, an MS Windows interface that configures itself to the definition of your document collection. For more advanced customization, application development occurs in popular tools such as Visual Basic or PowerBuilder. The system is also equipped with utilities for power-loading large batches of documents."

About security:

"Users can be mapped to security access levels. Security is invoked at many different levels...access levels mapped to document security classes, such as Confidential, Internal Use Only, Secret, and Public...Users must be pre-registered and are authenticated when logging in to a BASIS application. Security locks can be enforced by application, user groups, user, record type (table), or views."

About document referencing and linking:

"The relational features of BASISplus support one-to-one, one-to-many, and many-to-many relationships between documents. You can use this to implement workflow, version control, and other complex data models. BASIS Desktop allows for references to be embedded within the text or bibliographic fields. A markup element, similar to an SGML markup element, is required to identify the object being referenced and the application that will be used to view the object. BASIS WEBserver exploits linking using the hypertext capabilities of the Web. BASIS 'Smart Query URLs' can be encoded in HTML 'navigation' documents or content documents. Traditionally, URLs are hardcoded from a source point to a destination. 'BASIS Smart Query URLs' are resolved dynamically using the searching mechanisms of BASIS. In this way, links need not be hardcoded and can vary dynamically according to user, application, context, security privileges, and other criteria."

About the BASIS Document Manager:

"Includes complete library services, full-text retrieval, document control, document delivery, security, and authentication. Documents, their attributes, and their structures are stored in BASISplus, an extended-relational database optimized specifically for document objects. Supported document types include SGML, HTML, tagged text, word-processing documents, and bibliographic records."

About using other development tools:

"Interfaces that populate and maintain document collections are provided ready-to-use or can be rapidly customized using popular development tools such as Visual Basic, PowerBuilder, Microsoft Word, or any other ODBC-compliant tool."

About their customers:

"Information Dimensions' customers work...in publishing, manufacturing, government, legal, pharmaceuticals, petrochemicals, utilities, aerospace, financial services, and other industries. Examples of organizations putting BASIS to work to exploit the full value of their critical business documents include: 3M, Shell, United Technologies, Musee d'Orsay, Saab Military, Electricite de France, News International, Axel-Springer, and the Taiwan Legislature."

Blackie/WWWEnterprise/15 (BWE/15)

Summary:

BWE/15 is an RDBMS gateway that allows the querying or updating of databases from a Netscape-like Web browser. Its features include user auditing, authentication, authorization, a text search engine, and support for binary data types.

Details:

URL	http://www.blackie.com/
Platforms	SUN OS 4.1.3, Solaris 2.3
Web browsers	All, Netscape
Web servers	All, Netscape
Data sources	Informix, Sybase, Oracle, IBM DB2, CA-OpenIngres
Memory required	16M
Disk space required	10M
Server side interface	CGI, NSAPI
Client side interface	HTML
Demo copy?	Yes, at Web site

Contact:

Blackie DBGateway Technologies Corp.
6167 Jarvis Avenue, #283
Newark, CA 94560

Tel	(510) 793-2552
Fax	(510) 794-9731
Email	market@blackie.com

They say:

About Blackie/WWWEnterprise/15:

"This package is an RDBMS gateway that allows transparent access from your Netscape-like browser to your RDBMS database. You can query or update your database via this product."

About features:

"...ease of installation...ease of use...dynamic and static form generation...instant access to your data...keyword search on your database via Blackie Search Engine...audit trail to track and analyze user activities...authorize user based on login name and password that you assign...."

About searching:

"The search engine returned hyperlinked titles ranked by number of hits. The hits in the document or text are highlighted and hyperlinked for ease of traversal. The search is nonintrusive and nondestructive. It does not change the way you have been using your data. It simply finds the information, and hyperlinks it for you. You may limit the number of matched titles to save you time from reading titles with low hits. You may search based on case-sensitive or non-case-sensitive keywords."

About SQL scripts:

"Make use of your SQL scripts for query and update. It gives you another way of accessing or updating the data. Your investment in those SQL scripts is not wasted. You don't need to reinvent the scripts to get to the information. You may print, mail, save, or search the returned data."

About auditing:

"You may choose to audit user login and database transactions. View the audit log for tracking purpose or analysis. Audit successful and failed login. Auditing may be turned on or off when needed. You may remove the audit log or save it without leaving your browser."

About authentication:

"Authenticate user based on password. Authorize user based on login identification. Along with your security policy, it can provide a secure environment for information sharing and privacy. Action of failed and successful login can be audited using BWE/15 Audit subsystem. Disallow root or superuser login to strengthen security."

Centura Web Data Publisher

Summary:

Centura Web Data Publisher enables client/server applications developed with the Centura database tools to be published as Web pages.

Details:

URL	http://www.centurasoft.com
Platforms	Windows NT, Windows 95
Web servers	All
Data sources	Oracle, Informix, Ingres, Sybase, SQL Server, dBASE, Paradox, Excel, ODBC level 2
Memory required	16Mb
Disk space required	20Mb
Server side interface	CGI, NSAPI, ISAPI
Client side interface	HTML
FAQ	Yes, at Web site
Newsgroups	comp.databases.gupta
Demo copy?	No

Contact:

Centura Software Corp. (formerly Gupta)
1060 Marsh Road
Menlo Park, CA 94025

Tel	(415) 321-9500, (800) 444-8782 (US & Canada)
Fax	(415) 321-5471
Email	info_usa@gupta.com
FTP	ftp://ftp1.gupta.com/gupta/

They say:

About using multiple databases:

"Centura Web Data Publisher will allow organizations to securely publish data from multiple databases on the Web. As Web browsers become more popular, users will want access to corporate data via the Internet. The Web Data Publisher, which can reside outside the corporate firewall, maintains an up-to-date repository of information from disparate databases such as Oracle and DB2 and securely delivers it to any Web browser."

About data replication:

"Centura Web Data Publisher incorporates built-in replication facilities. You can replicate data from heterogeneous corporate databases such as Oracle and DB2 onto the built-in SQLBase database that comes with the Web Data Publisher. You can then place this information outside the firewall, enabling users with Web browsers to view selected data without compromising the security of the corporate databases."

About input validations:

"Input validations are handled by the underlying SQLBase database with error messages returned via HTML."

About transaction control:

"The Web Data Publisher maintains state information between client and server, sequence, commit and rollback, and caches open database connections."

Cold Fusion

Summary:

Cold Fusion is a hybrid CGI product that lets you connect Web pages to ODBC databases without writing CGI scripts. You make it work by freely mixing DBML tags (DataBase Markup Language) with HTML in a standard Web template. Cold Fusion consists of two programs: a thin CGI executable and a Windows NT System Service that loads the HTML/DBML template and interacts with the database.
(See also Chapter 5.)

Details:

URL	http://www.allaire.com
Platforms	Windows NT 3.5, Windows 95, Windows NT DEC Alpha, Windows NT NEC MIPS
Web browsers	Netscape, Explorer
Web servers	All Windows NT and Windows 95
Data sources	ODBC level 2
Memory required	16MB min.–24+ recommended
Disk space required	11 MB
Server side interface	CGI, ISAPI, NSAPI, WSAPI
Client side interface	HTML
Mailing lists	www.allaire.com, support
Demo copy?	Yes, at Web site

Contact:

Allaire Corp.
7600 France Avenue South, Suite 552
Minneapolis, MN 55435
Tel   (612) 832-9030
Fax   (612) 830-1090
Email   info@allaire.com

They say:

About input validation:

"Input validations are available for integers, dates, and decimals. Also, by using ODBC it is possible to perform other validations."

About transaction control:

"The product keeps connections open across multiple sessions and users, allowing for high performance and scaleability. We also provide a simple and transparent user and session management system for those developers who want total security and state management for their applications. We support all ODBC standard transaction processing controls, including the ability to Read_Uncommitted, Read_Committed, Repeatable_Read, Serializable, and Versioning."

About security:

"Because our product is server independent, we support all encryption standards for secure transmission. Our product will work with clients through firewalls using standard HTTP proxy methods. Also, using Reverse-Proxy Lookup, it is possible to host an application inside a firewall and still make it available to end users outside the firewall. We have a standard user authentication and security framework, which allows for username and password authentication, transparent login via URL tokens or Magic Cookies, and a User Groups framework for creating application or object level security."

Crystal Web Report Engine

Summary:

The Crystal Web Report Engine enables the access of database reports generated with Crystal reporting tools from Web pages.

Details:

URL	http://www.seagate.com/software/crystal
Platforms	Windows NT, Windows 95, Windows for Workgroups
Web browsers	Netscape, Microsoft, HTML 3.0
Web servers	All, Netscape, Microsoft
Data sources	ODBC, Sybase, SQL server, Oracle, most PC
Memory required	8 MB
Disk space required	3 MB to 40 MB
Server side interface	CGI, NSAPI, ISAPI
Client side interface	HTML, Active-X
Demo copy?	Yes, at Web site

Contact:

Seagate Software Information Management Group
1095 West Pender Street, 4th floor
Vancouver, B.C.
Canada V6E 2M6

Tel	(604) 681-3435
Fax	(604) 681-2934
Email	sales@crystalinc.com
BBS	(604) 681-9516

They say:

About Web reporting:

"Predefined reports created with Crystal Reports or Crystal Info can be deployed across the World Wide Web. Users can publish reports in presentation quality, directly to HTML for viewing by common Web browsers. As a result, organizations can instantly distribute information-rich documents, complete with summarizing, grouping, and sub-totaling, to a broad audience via their internal or external Web servers."

About scheduled reporting:

"You can update the content of predefined reports automatically for distribution. A Web master can refresh report data to an organization's users according to any schedule, yet ensure that all report processing is done off-line. Reports can be scheduled to refresh based on a time (hourly, weekly, monthly, etc.) or an event such as an update to a data warehouse. Organizations that need regularly updated information can now easily schedule and distribute reports via the Web."

About reporting from Web logs:

"Webmasters can instantly turn Web server activity logs into meaningful, formatted information for better Web site management."

About the components of Crystal Web:

"The Crystal Web Report Engine is a combination of four components: the Crystal Web Publishing Interface, the Crystal Web Activity DLL, the Crystal Report Engine, and the Crystal Web Application Interface. Using the Crystal Web Publishing Interface, Crystal developers and end users can publish reports in presentation quality—directly to HTML format for viewing by common Web browsers. The Crystal Web Activity DLL enables the Crystal Report Engine to read all the fields in any Web server log as common database fields and then create in-depth reports. There is no limit to the level of detail and number of data views that Webmasters can access to analyze Web site activity. The Crystal Report Engine is the component of the Crystal Web Report Engine that retrieves selected data from the database, sorts, summarizes, and groups the data in any specified way, and then presents the final report in presentation-quality format. The Crystal Report Engine enables Web developers to add reporting capabilities to Web server applications with minimal coding. The Crystal Web Application Interface is the interface between Web server applications and the Crystal Report Engine. It allows parameters to be passed to the Crystal Report Engine for specifying report information."

DataRamp

Summary:

DataRamp is a middleware product that allows developers to use database client programs that access ODBC data sources over networks running TCP/IP, including the Internet. The DataRamp Server runs as a service under Windows NT. The DataRamp client module runs on all Windows platforms. (See also Chapter 8.)

Details:

URL	http://DataRamp.com
Platforms	server-Windows NT, client-all Windows platforms
Web browsers	Netscape
Web servers	Netscape
Data sources	ODBC level 2
Memory required	8 MB
Disk space required	client 2 MB, server 5 MB
Server side interface	TCP/IP, session oriented
Client side interface	Netscape plug-in
FAQ	Yes, at Web site
Demo copy?	Yes, at Web site

Contact:

Working Set, Inc.
8 Dover Lane
Lexington, MA 02173
Tel   (617) 863-2339
Fax   (617) 863-6220
Email   support@dataramp.com, sales@dataramp.com
FTP   dataramp.com

They say:

About using existing database clients:

"The software allows you to utilize an existing application. If you develop something locally, then you can deploy it without modification. Any PB, VB, C++, etc., application will work as it would locally."

About ODBC driver:

"The single client-side ODBC driver eliminates administration of multiple ODBC drivers across the enterprise and the Internet."

dbCGI Gateway Toolkit

Summary:

dbCGI is for integrating SQL databases with Web pages. It works by embedding SQL statements in HTML documents.

Details:

URL	http://www.corvu.com.au/dbcgi/doc/corvu/
Platforms	Unix
Data sources	Progress, Sybase, Oracle, Informix, Ingres, ODBC
Server side interface	CGI
Client side interface	HTML

Contact:

CorVu Pty Ltd.
Level 4, 1 James Place
North Sydney 2060
Australia

Tel	+61 2 9959 3522
Fax	+61 2 9959 3583
Email	enquiries@corvu.com.au.

They say:

About dbCGI:

"CorVu dbCGI is a CGI gateway between SQL databases and the World Wide Web. The major features are: Highly flexible HTML formatting of the output of SQL queries, which enables you to create both read-only and HTML form pages. Database independence, with the database specific modules each taking up around 250 lines of code. Ability to use HTTP query strings and form input in SQL. Security features allowing verification of input. Master/detail style output can easily be achieved. Support for BLOB data, such as images, sound and video. An easy-to-use syntax that is similar to the syntax of HTML itself."

About portability:

"...because the database-specific code takes around 250 lines of code, you can easily port CorVu dbCGI to any SQL database that supports access to dynamic SQL from the C language."

DBI

Summary:

DBI is an API for PERL scripts that allows programmers to access databases in a standard way.

Details:

URL	http://www.hermetica.com/technologia/DBI/
Data sources	ODBC, Oracle, mSQL, Ingres, Informix, Sybase, Empress, C-ISAM, DB2, Quickbase, Interbase
Mailing lists	perldb-interest@vix.com, perldb-interest-REQUEST@vix.com
Demo copy?	Yes, at Web site

Contact:

Email	descarte@hermetica.com
FTP	ftp.demon.co.uk, ftp.mcqueen.com

They say:

About DBperl:

"DBperl is a database-access Application Programming Interface (API) for the PERL Language. The DBperl API Specification defines a set of functions, variables and conventions that provide a consistent database interface independent of the actual database being used. The purpose of the DBI API (Application Programming Interface) is to define and implement a common interface to enable interaction between applications and various database engines. The DBI will allow the creation of database-manipulation scripts without regard for the engine being used to service the requests. It is important to remember that the DBI is just an interface, a thin layer of 'glue' between an application and one or more Database Drivers. It is the drivers that do the real work. The DBI provides a standard interface and framework for the drivers to operate within."

dbKona and htmlKona

Summary:

dbKona is a program written in Java (not an applet) that interfaces to many different databases. htmlKona generates Web pages from programs written in Java.

Details:

URL	http://www.Weblogic.com/
Platforms	Windows NT, Solaris
Web browsers	All
Web servers	All

Data sources	Oracle, Sybase, SQLServer, JDBC
Server side interface	CGI
Client side interface	HTML
Demo copy?	No

Contact:

WebLogic, Inc.
180 Montgomery Street, Suite 1240
San Francisco, CA 94104
Tel   (415) 394-8616
Fax   (415) 394-8619
Email   info@Weblogic.com

They say:

About dbKona:

"T3Server: A generic, multitiered application server that allows Java applications and applets network access to multiple, heterogeneous DBMSs and data sources. The T3Server is part of all of WebLogic's client-network (multitiered) environments...eventKona/T3: A set of Java objects for creating event-driven applications in a client-network (multitiered) environment...htmlKona: A Java program for generating complex HTML documents and constructing dynamic, sophisticated Common Gateway Interface (CGI) applications. htmlKona works seamlessly with Netscape's new Enterprise Server...dbKona: A high-level, general-purpose application programming interface (API) that provides database connectivity for Java applications in client/server (two-tiered) environments. dbKona is bundled with jdbcKona, a driver implementation of Sun's JDBC (Java Database Connectivity) interface... dbKona/T3: dbKona for the multitiered environment. This product includes all of the dbKona classes (shown above) plus the T3Server, for building data applications in the client-network environments."

About portability:

"A Java application compiled on one system platform will run on any other system that has a Java interpreter. This portability shortens application development time, since it reduces porting and maintenance issues."

About dbKona:

"The dbKona objects provide vendor-neutral connectivity to multiple databases in a two-tiered client/server environment. The dbKona architecture gives both database and non-database programmers easy access to database objects through a high-level Java abstraction. With dbKona, Java applications and their users can retrieve, view, add, update, and delete SQL data as vendor-independent data objects. dbKona uses native DBMS libraries, provides client-side caching, and supports concurrent heterogeneous database connections...Provides row/column accessors for getting and setting values...Minimizes SQL with the automatic generation of INSERT, UPDATE, and DELETE statements...Provides a programmatic interface to DDL that allows creating and dropping and tables, indexes, views, stored procedures, etc....Supports multiple, heterogeneous database connections."

About transaction control:

"In the two-tiered environment, the dbKona classes give Java applications DBMS session access to Oracle, Sybase, and SQLServer databases, along with the full range of program logic and program state supported by Java. In the multitiered configuration, dbKona/T3 supports server sessions maintained by WebLogic's T3Server on behalf of a Java dbKona/T3 client. The client can issue requests to the T3Server, disconnect, and reconnect at a later time to the same session. To maintain security, each session has a confidential ID that is known only to the client that initiated the session."

About dbKona/T3:

"The dbKona/T3 framework extends the power of multitiered architecture to the Java development environment. WebLogic's multithreaded T3Server acts as a high-performance application server managing database interaction between its clients and one or more heterogeneous databases. The T3Server eliminates the expense of purchasing, installing, and maintaining client-side licenses. And using the T3Server as a central repository of business logic makes it easier to manage and enforce these application rules...The T3Server supports Java-defined stored procedures and triggers, and cached data and cached logins for a single user or groups of users. dbKona/T3's request and reply protocol makes the T3Server optimal for wide-area network traffic. The T3Server also provides state for a stateless HTTP/CGI environment."

About netKona:

"The netKona objects provide network and systems management from your Java application(s) in both two-tiered and multitiered configurations.

netKona includes support for Simple Network Management Protocol (SNMP), Internet Control Message Protocol (ICMP, for traceroute and ping programs), and Microsoft's Desktop Management Interface (DMI) environment. With netKona, you can configure, control, and monitor all of your network objects—servers, applications, printers, routers, PCs, workstations, etc.—from any location within a single interface. Coupled with dbKona and eventKona, netKona provides a unique solution for managing system and network resources. In the multitiered configuration, netKona/T3 supports a full range of network management functionality including administrative history, event notification, remote configuration, network discovery, and detailed network knowledge. In the two-tiered configuration, netKona brings the power of network management functionality to small Java applets and embedded systems."

About htmlKona:

"htmlKona simplifies the task of programmatically generating complex HTML documents. htmlKona (formerly WebScript) is a convenient, easy-to-learn application useful both in an interactive CGI environment and for periodic generation of static HTML pages. htmlKona uses a canvas metaphor for HTML document composition and automatically manages CGI argument processing. Coupled with dbKona and dbKona/T3, htmlKona can automatically generate tables from queries and retrieve multimedia objects such as audio clips and GIF/JPEG images from heterogeneous databases for inCorp. in HTML pages."

dbWeb

Summary:

dbWeb lets you create Web database applications by filling in forms. The process is simple enough that someone with just a little knowledge of Web conventions and no knowledge of HTML or SQL can use it. The Web database applications created with dbWeb can do all the basic database functions such as query, insert, update, and delete. (See also Chapter 6.)

Details:

URL	http://www.microsoft.com/intdev/dbWeb/
Platforms	Windows NT 3.51
Web browsers	Netscape, Mosaic, Air Mosaic, Internet Explorer
Web servers	All CGI 1.1 compliant

Data sources	32-bit ODBC, SQL Server, Sybase, Oracle, Access, Visual FoxPro
Memory required	16 MB
Disk space required	10 MB
Server side interface	CGI
Client side interface	HTML
Demo copy?	No

Contact:

Since this book was written, dbWeb was acquired by Microsoft. Please contact: http://www.microsoft.com/intdev/dbWeb/

They say:

About dbWeb:

"Microsoft dbWeb is a gateway between Microsoft Open Database Connectivity (ODBC) data sources and Microsoft Internet Information Server (IIS). You can use Microsoft dbWeb to publish data from an ODBC data source on the World Wide Web (WWW) or on your internal network without specialized client software."

"With dbWeb, you create a schema that contains the specification for your data and the Web pages. Microsoft dbWeb then produces fully functional Web pages for retrieving and displaying your data. dbWeb supports real-time database queries based on a 'client-pull' model, formulating dynamic Web pages as users query your data source over the Internet. Visitors to your Web site can use familiar hypertext-style navigation via standard Web browsers to find information with little or no training."

"The dbWeb service is the component that handles the data processing between your ODBC data source and Microsoft Internet Information Server (IIS). This component processes the queries the user enters from a Web browser (for example, Microsoft Internet Explorer), and handles the communications between the browser, the ODBC data source, and IIS to display the results on a Web page. The dbWeb service is an ISAPI (Internet Server Application Programming Interface) application, thus providing better performance and easier setup than a CGI application."

About the development process:

"Microsoft dbWeb uses schemas to control how the database information is published on the Internet. Schemas define the query and resulting HTML pages that are displayed on the Web...No HTML or ISAPI programming knowledge is necessary to create the dbWeb schemas. The dbWeb administrator provides an interactive Schema Wizard, which uses questions and answers to create the schemas."

"You can use Microsoft dbWeb to publish information in HTML format without programming in HTML or the Internet Server Application Programming Interface (ISAPI). dbWeb supports dynamic data queries and basic row manipulation. You can also customize your Web pages using the DBX editor and the methods provided with the dbWeb administrator...Microsoft dbWeb administrator offers several levels of assistance in creating your Web pages...Schema Wizard, which prompts you with a series of questions, and then uses your answers to create a schema automatically. A schema defines the query and results Web pages...Schema window with tabs for creating and modifying a schema: You can choose data sources, set properties for fields on the Query-by-Example (QBE) Web page, and set properties such as Automatic Links to display a single record from the tabular Web page...Customizable templates for Web pages...DBX editor to fully customize your Web pages by entering HTML code directly into the specification for the Web page...Properties and methods for complete control of your Web pages...Links with properties you can set easily to jump to data displayed in other schemas or to quickly drill down from a tabular results page to a single record page."

DynaWeb

Summary:
DynaWeb is a Web management system that includes tools for accessing ODBC databases, SGML document databases, and legacy databases. It works as a server extension program using NSAPI and ISAPI.

Details:

URL	http://www.ebt.com
Platforms	Windows NT, Unix
Web browsers	All
Web servers	Netscape, Microsoft IIS
Data sources	ODBC, DynaText SGML files
Server side interface	CGI, NSAPI, ISAPI, SSI

Client side interface   HTML, Java applets, plug-ins

Demo copy?   No

Contact:

Electronic Book Technologies, Inc. (EBT)

One Richmond Square

Providence, RI 02906

Tel   (401) 421-9550

Fax   (401) 421-9551

Email   info@ebt.com

They say:

About DynaWeb:

"The DynaBase Web Management System is a complete, easy-to-use Web management system combining sophisticated content management capabilities with a powerful development environment. Designed for use by distributed work groups in both Internet or corporate Intranet publishing environments, DynaBase helps bring control to complex Web sites. DynaBase enables Web site publishing teams to create, develop, manage, and publish large volumes of Web content more easily. It is easy to get started and scales up to handle very large Web sites with thousands of HTML pages, images, scripts and multimedia files."

About features:

"...Familiar drag-and-drop interface that works over Internet connections... Powerful link management (URL independence)...Design-centered for distributed Web publishing to enable collaborative authoring, scripting, design, editing, and publishing...Enables 'User extensible HTML' through tag extensions and scripting...Supports 'Multiple Web Editions' for targeting versions of content to specific users...Powerful, built-in full text-, property- and tag-aware search engine...Cross-platform...Visual Basic-compatible scripting language for Web developers...."

About version control:

"Items within the DynaBase WebManager are version controlled, allowing authors and developers to update items within the Web site while end users view past versions. This eliminates the need to maintain duplicate offline Web sites, dramatically simplifying the task of Web updates. Multiple

Editions Web editions provide authors with the ability to bind and publish the current state of their Web, preserving all items and their interrelationships. Once bound, unique endures access rights may be assigned, providing controlled release of information to separate audiences. Subsequent updates may be published with minimal effort."

About EBT's product line:

"Electronic Book Technologies, Inc. (EBT) is the premier supplier of integrated CD/Web publishing solutions for the professional information publisher. EBT's cross-platform software tools enable customers to manage and publish information to CD-ROM, World Wide Web, LAN, and print from a single, standards-based source."

About SGML document searching:

"DynaWeb serves out HTML on the fly directly from large DynaText electronic books stored in SGML. All powerful DynaText searching capabilities (e.g., full-text, Boolean, proximity, structure-aware, wildcards, etc.) are fully enabled."

About extended HTML:

"The WebManager is built on a flexible document database that natively supports HTML as well as extended tag-based documents. This flexibility insulates HTML content from changes in the standards as well as providing extensibility for site-specific requirements."

About Web site management:

"Link Management Location Irrelevance catalog prevents links from breaking by providing a flexible and automatic mapping between the external URL, as seen by the end user, and the item's internal unique name within WebManager Server. The WebManager Server application 'plugs in' to Netscape and Microsoft environments and provides those servers with access control, version management, and indexing for any type of Web content, including HTML pages, images, and Java applets. WebManager Server runs on both Windows NT and Unix servers and acts as both a development and publishing repository for Web site content. Anyone with permissions can add, modify, or delete content across the Internet using standard HTTP protocols and authentication. Using a sophisticated version control technique, each update to items within DynaBase WebManager Server is tracked so that multiple editions of a Web site may exist in parallel."

Edify Electronic Workforce

Summary:

Edify Electronic Workforce is a development system for creating and deploying Web database applications that use software agents to retrieve data. It reads and transmits information from the screens of PC and legacy applications, and can query and update relational databases. It consists of Edify Software Agents, the Agent Trainer development environment, and the Agent Supervisor.

Details:

URL	http://www.edify.com
Platforms	Windows, Windows NT, Unix
Web browsers	HTML 2.0
Data sources	Oracle, Sybase, Informix, CA-Ingres, DB2, SQL Server, GUPTA, BTRIEVE
Client side interface	HTML 2.0
Demo copy?	No

Contact:

Edify Corp.
2840 San Tomas Expressway
Santa Clara, CA 95051
Tel   (408) 982-2000, (800) 944-0056 (US & Canada)
Fax   (408) 982-0777
Email   info@edify.com

They say:

About Electronic Workforce:

"The Electronic Workforce software bridges the gap between customers and traditional information systems. Now you can create and deliver complete interactive service applications through whatever medium is best: phone, fax, email, PC clients or the World Wide Web. All of your back-office systems, whether host, client/server or PC-based, are easily accessed from a single delivery platform—one that schedules and manages interactive applications and coordinates phone, host and network resources. With our award-winning Agent Trainer visual development environment, there's no need to write code. Now you can focus on developing new applications faster and more cost-effectively...Using the Electronic Workforce, you can deliver services through more media—telephones, online PCs, fax, pagers, interactive kiosks, and others—than any other single solution. It has everything you need to quickly and cost-effectively integrate with back-office systems. And we've created a flexible, robust way to deliver and manage interactive services that securely handle thousands of transactions per hour."

What the package consists of:

"The Edify Electronic Workforce has three main components: Edify software agents, the Agent Trainer development environment, and the Agent Supervisor run-time environment."

About agents:

"At the heart of the Electronic Workforce are the 'agents,' advanced software that provides interactive services on behalf of an organization. We've given Edify software agents the widest range of skills possible so they can perform tasks such as answering a phone, operating a host application or exchanging information through online PCs. By defining the sequence of tasks agents will perform, you can quickly create robust interactive service applications that span across various media and back-office systems. Because our software agents are so flexible and multi-skilled, you can concentrate on creative valuable services, without the hassles of hard-coded system integration."

About Agent Trainer:

"Edify's Agent Trainer is a powerful, object-oriented visual development environment where you define and customize interactive service applications. Agent Trainer's unique point and click interface lets you quickly build interactive services that agents will provide. Because all of the agent skills are represented in Agent Trainer as visual objects, you can create sophisticated applications without writing a single line of code. And to make development even easier, we've integrated a set of graphical tools, giving you everything you need to create services unique to your organization."

About Agent Supervisor:

"Agent Supervisor is a robust runtime environment that schedules software agents and assigns them to service applications built with Agent Trainer. Once agents and service applications are paired, Agent Supervisor manages all of the phone, fax, PC, host and network resources necessary for interactive service delivery. All of these resources are managed through an architecture that ensures reliability and security. With Agent Supervisor, you can deploy multiple interactive services, confident that they will be delivered through a secure runtime environment whose capacity scales to meet your needs."

About what agents can do:

"Agents can answer, place, and transfer phone calls, interpret touch-tone and voice commands, assemble and speak recorded phrases, convert text to speech, and record voice messages. Dynamically create and send Web pages (including text, graphics, input fields, radio buttons, checkboxes, list boxes, and submit buttons) and interpret data and commands from Web-based forms. Receive, forward, reply, or create and send messages from all popular electronic mail packages. Receive, create, and send faxes that include variable information, static text, data, and images. Compose and send messages that contain variable information through numeric or alphanumeric pagers...Recognize and navigate PC and legacy host applications screens, identify input and output fields, and enter or retrieve information, including repeating records. Access local or remote relational databases in order to query, retrieve, or update information. Use dynamic link libraries to integrate with existing desktop applications or PBX computer telephony integration (CTI) links. Acquire new skills through your custom-built DLLs...Tell time in order to perform proactive services hourly, daily, weekly, or monthly. Respond to time-triggered events as part of a workflow process. List and track information for action. Use an advanced function calculator to manipulate integer, floating point, text, date, time, phone number, and currency information."

About Fax Builder:

"Fax Builder is a WYSIWYG design tool for laying out the fax pages an agent dynamically builds and sends. Supports image, text and data overlays, drag and drop placement of variable objects, and dynamic formatting of repeating data fields. Automatically paginates across multiple fax pages."

About Page Builder:

"Page Builder is a WYSIWYG Web page composition tool for laying out the Web pages an agent dynamically builds and sends. Provides a full-function text editor; the ability to import GIF and JPEG images; support for text input fields, radio buttons, checkboxes and list boxes; point and click placement of variable objects; hot links and dynamic formatting of repeating data fields."

About Database Access Trainer:

"Database Access Trainer is a graphical database access tool that defines how an agent performs information queries and updates on local or remote databases. Automatically retrieves database schema, performs complex queries with a full range of Boolean functions. Also supports stored procedures via direct SQL commands."

About Host Screen Navigator:

"Host Screen Navigator is a graphical tool that defines how an agent runs legacy host or character-based PC applications. Specifies logon, screen to screen navigation, screen recognition and how an agent enters or retrieves information from various fields. Handles fixed and relative field locations. Supports repeating records. Works with fixed and scrolling screen types."

Esplanade

Summary:

Esplanade is a Web server with built-in ODBC connectivity. Applications are built using a visual GUI tool that lets the user generate SQL statements and Web pages. It also has document processing capabilities that automate the process of making word-processing and graphic files viewable as Web pages.

Details:

URL	http://www.ftp.com/esplanade/
Platforms	Windows NT
Web browsers	All
Web servers	Mosaic, other
Data sources	ODBC, Oracle, Sybase, Informix, SQL Server, Access, DB2, Excel
Server side interface	CGI, SSI
Client side interface	HTML
Demo copy?	No

Contact:

FTP Software, Inc.
100 Brickstone Square
Andover, MA 01810
Tel   (508) 685-4000, (800) 282-4387 (US & Canada)
Fax   (508) 794-4488, (508) 794-4477

Email   info@ftp.com
FTP   support@ftp.com, explore-help@ftp.com

They say:

About document conversion:

"With Esplanade, everything from Word to Wang documents are automatically converted to a format that can be viewed by anyone on the Web...Provides high-quality conversion to many different document formats including HTML, the most widely used format on the Web...Converts more than 30 legacy and PC word-processing formats...Converts 17 graphics formats...Object-oriented converters support complex documents containing headers, footers, frames, styles, tables, embedded graphics, and fonts...Eliminates need to manually convert existing documents to HTML, saving time and money...Documents are viewable with any Web browser—no need to purchase file viewers or additional client applications...Eliminates time and frustration in dealing with incompatible file formats and platforms...Maintains integrity of existing document repositories...Transparent to user—no additional training required...."

About ODBC connectivity:

"Esplanade contains a comprehensive, graphical, database connectivity tool based on industry-standard ODBC. With the Esplanade Database Connector, administrators can construct HTML-based queries, including the automatic creation of Structured Query Language (SQL) statements. Users can then easily gain access to appropriate information from virtually any database quickly and without special training...The Esplanade Database Connector allows users to define SQL statements and create application Web pages through a simple point-and-click query interface. Browser-based end users will then be able to read, update, or delete data in a formatted, easy-to-read manner through any Web browser. You can query and edit multiple databases from this same interface."

About security:

"Security is implemented within the Database Connector via a login query form. SQL statements are never placed on the Web. As a result, users are unable to modify queries, thereby restricting data access."

About site logging and reporting:

"The Web Reporter is a powerful tool for analyzing Web server access activity and generating customized reports, helping you to justify your return on investment. The Web Reporter accepts both extended and common log formats and converts between these two formats. Although you can perform a variety of tasks with the Web Reporter, you will typically use this tool to compose and run reports...You can customize your report by using this graphical user interface to define what information you would like on your report. This enables you to organize useful information about the server log files. In this script, you define which log fields are used, the type of data you want to extract, and the report format...Esplanade's Web Reporter allows you to create detailed reports of NT server log file information...."

About execution priorities:

"...allows you to specify an execution priority for CGI programs. For example, you may wish to specify a low priority for long-running search routines."

About server side includes:

"...allows the server to provide dynamic information within an HTML document dynamically. This can include file information as well as execution of CGI programs."

FoxWeb

Summary:

FoxWeb is a development tool for integrating Web pages with FoxPro databases and programs. Developers use the FoxPro language to develop applications. Several security methods are supported, and CGI is used.

Details:

URL	http://www.foxWeb/com/
Platforms	Windows NT, Windows 95
Web servers	All
Data sources	FoxPro, other sources accessible by Visual FoxPro
Memory required	16 MB
Disk space required	200 K
Server side interface	CGI, ISAPI
Client side interface	HTML
FAQ	Yes, at Web site

Mailing lists   foxWeb-l@dsw.com

Demo copy?   Yes, at Web site

Contact:

EON Technologies (Aegis Group)

3211 Encinal Ave., Suite D

Alameda, CA 94501

Tel   (510) 523-3832

Fax   (510) 523-6794

Email   tiritas@intermedia.net

They say:

About performance:

"FoxWeb is fast because it does not need to start FoxPro with every hit. It installs several FoxPro channels that quietly wait in the background for CGI calls. As requests come in, FoxWeb distributes them to the open channels for parallel processing. No ODBC or temporary files are needed."

About learnability:

"The user does not need to learn a new language to publish FoxPro data on the Internet. The FoxWeb function set takes less than half an hour to learn and the rest is pure FoxPro."

About multithreading:

"Multiple .PRG files can be run at the same time by opening multiple FoxWeb channels. The optimum number of channels depends on the number of processors and available memory."

About HTML code management:

"HTML can be placed in FoxPro tables with description fields for easy management. The code can contain mergeable fields that are evaluated during execution."

About error logging:

"All errors caused by user-created .PRG files are logged in a table for debugging purposes. They can be viewed using the Error Log Viewer."

About Web server compatibility:

"FoxWeb is not dependent on proprietary protocols and can work with any Win32 CGI 1.1 compliant server. This means that if in the future you wish to switch to a different server, then your programs will run without modification."

About input validation:

"Since FoxWeb scripts are real programs, the number and type of validations is unlimited."

About parsing of CGI Data:

"You do not need to search in text files for the CGI parameters and form fields. FoxWeb places all the data in objects and arrays for easy access. You can even ask for specific fields by calling a FoxWeb function."

GemStone WWW Gateway

Summary:

GemStone WWW Gateway is a Web server that connects to the GemStone OODBMS. It is implemented in GemStone SmallTalk.

Details:

URL	http://ftp.tuwien.ac.at/~go/Implementation.html
Platforms	Windows NT, Unix
Data sources	GemStone OODBMS
Demo copy?	Yes, at Web site

Contact:

GemStone Systems, Inc.

15400 NW Greenbrier Parkway, Suite 280

Beaverton, OR 97006

Tel	(503) 629-8383, (800) 243-9396
Fax	(503) 629-8556
Email	info@gemstone.com

They say:

About the GemStone gateway:

"This is a gateway between the GemStone OODBMS and the World Wide Web. It is implemented entirely in GemStone SmallTalk and supports forms and user authentication. While the (slightly edited) code presented here is written for GemStone 4.1.3 it might serve as a starting point for implementations on other platforms."

About GemStone SmallTalk:

"GemStone SmallTalk is an extensible, computationally complete language that supports encapsulation, classes, inheritance, and late, or dynamic, binding...GemStone SmallTalk runs in the GemStone repository's object (or address) space. It runs on GemStone's proprietary multi-user virtual machine (the Gem process, which is written in C)."

About the GemStone SmallTalk Class Hierarchy:

"The GemStone SmallTalk class hierarchy is similar to the class hierarchy of other SmallTalk languages. It is different, however, in the following ways: It does not contain classes for file access, communication, screen manipulation, and the programming environment. It includes classes for transaction control, accounting, ownership, authorization, replication, user profiles, and index control. The class hierarchy is extensible, and new classes may be added as required to model an application."

Genera

Summary:

Genera is a free Web database toolkit for integrating Sybase databases with Web pages. Developers write a schema specification and the program translates the specification into SQL statements and HTML.

Details:

URL	http://gdbdoc.gdb.org/letovsky/genera/genera.html
Platforms	Unix
Data sources	Sybase
Demo copy?	Yes, at Web site

Contact:

Tel	(410) 614-0434
Fax	(410) 614-1061
Email	letovsky@gdb.org

They say:

About Web/Genera:

"Web/Genera is a software toolset that tremendously simplifies the integration of Sybase databases into the World Wide Web. It can be used to retrofit a Web front-end to an existing Sybase database, or to create a new one. To use Web/Genera one writes a specification of the Sybase database, and of the desired appearance of its contents on the Web, using a simple, high-level schema notation. Web/Genera programs process this description to generate SQL commands and formatting instructions that together extract objects from your database and format them into HTML. Web/Genera also supports form-based relational querying and whole-database formatting into text and HTML formats...Once your database schema has been compiled, Web users can retrieve individual objects from your database using URLs. Depending on how you configure the gateway, this retrieval can be done dynamically, with the object retrieved from Sybase when the URL request is handled, or statically, where the object is formatted in advance and retrieved from a file. The gateway can also perform powerful relational queries using simple URLs that do not contain SQL...You can also use Genera to create flat-file versions of your database for use with full-text search. You can create Web/WAIS gateways and Gopher/WAIS gateways. The latter make use of sybfmt's text output format."

GSQL

Summary:
GSQL is a freeware gateway that works with Mosaic browsers. It processes input forms and performs SQL database queries.

Details:

URL	http://www.santel.lu/SANTEL/SOFT/gsql_new.html
Platforms	Unix
Web browsers	All
Web servers	NCSA Mosaic
Data sources	Oracle
FAQ	Yes, at Web site
Demo copy?	Yes, at Web site

Contact:

Email	patrick.harpes@crpht.lu
FTP	ftp.santel.lu/database_related/gsql

They say:

About GSQL:

"GSQL is a C program that is invoked through a shell script by the HTTP server...GSQL is a simple Mosaic gateway to SQL databases. It parses a SQL-specification file (called a PROC file) to create a form, and then with the user-inputs, calls a database back-end program to process the SQL query. The PROC file maps components of the SQL string to widgets (fields, buttons, pulldown menus, etc.) for user input or selection...The Back-end is your database program that processes the SQL query. It is invoked by GSQL through a system() call—after the user has filled in the form. It can be written in C, PERL, tcl, etc."

HAHTSITE

Summary:

HAHTSITE is a Web database development environment. It uses a server extension program that is called from the Web server with API calls and OLE. It can maintain state information across Web pages and on the database side it uses ODBC and native database interfaces. It uses a Visual Basic-like language and comes with an interactive debugger.

Details:

URL	http://www.haht.com/
Platforms	Solaris, Windows NT, Windows 95
Web browsers	HTML 2.0
Data sources	ODBC
Server side interface	NSAPI, ISAPI, DLL, OLE/OCX
Client side interface	HTML, Java, Visual Script
Demo copy?	No

Contact:

HAHT Software, Inc.
4200 Six Forks Road
Raleigh, NC 27609
Tel   (919) 821-1280, (800) 996-3222 (US & Canada)
Fax   (919) 821-1337
Email   info@haht.com

They say:

About HAHTSITE:

"At execution, the HAHTSITE Engine provides complete access to multiple data sources, maintains 'state' or session information, and provides dynamically generated HTML...Visual Basic syntax-compatible language enhances productivity...Includes full-function, interactive debugger with remote debugging for distributed applications...Maintains 'state'—carry user-defined global variables, database connections across pages...."

About development:

"Easy placement and sizing of text, images...Full HTML 2.0 support, plus popular extensions...Integrated list and table support...Intelligent templates—page, project, and site...Form objects—text fields, list and combo boxes, radio buttons, checkboxes, and import filters for existing HTML or RTF files...Graphics processing—palette reduction, scaling, transparency, interlacing...Integrated image map editor...Dynamic URL generation and fix-up...Server-based applications minimize client requirements... Visual Basic syntax-compatible language enhances productivity...Easy drop-in of Java, Visual Script, and other client-side objects...Supports encapsulated, drag-and-drop code objects...Includes full-function, interactive debugger with remote debugging for distributed applications...Accesses any data source—native API or ODBC...Supports any server-based third-party API or DLL, OLE/OCX...Maintains 'state'—carry user-defined global variables, database connections across pages...Utilizes conditional assembly and browser-sensing...."

About system flexibility:

"Independent source/target model—create in one environment, run in another...Partition applications and users to multiple servers for optimal performance...Flexible, low-overhead HAHTSITE Engine scales to accommodate user load...Multiprocess, multithreaded engine runs only compiled, executable code...Built-in security mechanisms ensure data and application integrity...."

About maintenance:

"Uses familiar nomenclature and methodology of project management for all site components...Check-in/check-out of shared objects and project definitions...Incremental site/project update with automatic URL resolution...Contains a built-in interface for version and source...control—Microsoft Source Safe, Intersolv PVCS, and Atria ClearCase...."

Infobase Web Server

Summary:

Infobase is a development system for creating full-text Web database applications. It consists of the Folio Web Server, which is integrated with the Folio Infobase full-text database product. The Web server converts information stored in the document database to dynamic Web pages.

Details:

URL	http://www.folio.com/
Platforms	Windows NT (Alpha, MIPS, Intel)
Web browsers	All
Web servers	Folio Infobase Web Server
Data sources	Folio Infobases
Server side interface	CGI, SSI
Client side interface	HTML
Demo copy?	Yes, at Web site

Contact:

Folio Corp.
5072 North 300 West
Provo, UT 84604-5652

Tel	(801) 229-6700, (800) 543-6546 (US & Canada)
Fax	(801) 229-6787
Email	Sales@Folio.com, TechSup@Folio.com

They say:

About infobases:

"At the heart of FIT is the infobase—a dynamic, single file repository of text, graphics, and multimedia objects. Infobases are perfectly suited for many diverse applications such as customer support, electronic manuals and documentation, online help applications, and commercial publishing...Keeping infobases in their native format reduces costly maintenance of multiple file formats. Also, infobases may be concurrently accessed by a user on the Web and by a local user with Folio VIEWS 3.1

software. This parallel access does not limit the functionality of Folio VIEWS—all editing capabilities are preserved...The dynamic capabilities of infobases are passed on to the Folio Infobase Web Server. Information in infobases on the server may be updated by the infobase owners via Folio VIEWS while other users are accessing the infobase from a Web browser. Remote users have immediate access to the new or changed information."

About authorization:

"Access control by username to individual files, virtual paths, and the entire server."

About SGML document conversion:

"The Folio SGML Toolkit provides a method for end users to seamlessly convert SGML-compliant documents into Folio infobases...Working in conjunction with Exoterica's OmniMark program, the Folio SGML Toolkit provides a driver that integrates an OmniMark program file (an XOM file), the OmniMark compiler and SGML parser, and the Folio VIEWS software (both the Infobase Manager and CREATE). Once the driver is correctly installed on a user's system, it appears like (and may be used as) any other import filter."

Informix-ESQL/C CGI Interface Kit

Summary:

The Informix-ESQL/C CGI Interface Kit is a free library of CGI routines that handle data from HTML input forms. Uses include generating SQL statements, accessing the Informix database, and formatting result sets as HTML.

Details:

URL	http://www.informix.com
Platforms	Unix
Web browsers	All
Web servers	All
Data sources	Informix
Server side interface	CGI
Client side interface	HTML
Demo copy?	Yes, at Web site

Contact:

Informix Software, Inc.
Bohannon Drive
Menlo Park, CA 94025
Tel   (415) 926-6300, (800) 331-1763 (US & Canada)
Email   moreinfo@informix.com

They say:

About INFORMIX-ESQL/C CGI Interface:

"The INFORMIX-ESQL/C CGI Interface Kit is a ready-to-compile library for simple Web access from applications developed in ESQL/C. The library reads and decodes HTML forms, and displays both text and binary large objects (BLOBs) to Web browsers via the common gateway interface (CGI). Included with the kit are three examples that illustrate ways to use ESQL/C to generate SQL code, access the database, and print the results back to CGI."

About INFORMIX-4GL CGI Interface:

"The INFORMIX-4GL CGI Interface Kit is a ready-to-compile library to connect databases to the Web from INFORMIX-4GL applications. A small set of functions simplifies the tasks of reading the CGI environment, reading the values from HTML forms, managing Web files, and displaying both text and BLOBs to Web Browsers. The three examples included with the kit show the 4GL developer how to construct SQL from the HTML form values and how to print back to the Web browser."

InterNotes Web Publisher

Summary:

InterNotes Web Publisher works with a Notes Server and converts data from Notes databases into static HTML pages at specified time intervals. Notes doclinks are converted into HTML hypertext links.

Details:

URL	http://www.internotes.lotus.com/
Platforms	Windows NT
Web browsers	All
Web servers	All
Data sources	Lotus Notes
Server side interface	CGI

Client side interface   HTML

Demo copy?   No

Contact:

Lotus Development Corp.

55 Cambridge Parkway

Cambridge, MA 02142

Email   hostmaster@notes.net

They say:

About InterNotes:

"Lotus InterNotes Web Publisher is a Notes server program that lets users publish information entered in Notes to the Web. By converting Notes forms, documents, views, and databases into HyperText Markup Language (HTML), the format used by standard Web browsers such as NCSA Mosaic and Netscape Navigator, InterNotes Web Publisher provides a simple, automated process for creating and managing both internal Intranet and public Web sites. InterNotes Web Publisher lets you easily build interactive Web applications using Notes. Simply design a Notes form and use InterNotes Web Publisher to publish it in HTML format. Web users can then update the Notes databases in real time using standard Web browsers. When users submit data in this way, any Notes workflow process can be triggered. Web users can also search the published Notes databases from the Web."

"With InterNotes Web Publisher, you can take advantage of Notes' collaborative authoring environment and workflow capabilities to automate the process of creating, approving, and consolidating Web content from multiple departments and locations, ensuring a constant flow of current information to the Web site. InterNotes Web Publisher automatically converts items in Notes views and links in Notes documents to HTML hypertext links, automating the process of managing and updating documents published on the Web. In this way, InterNotes Web Publisher lets you centralize and simplify the management of your Web site."

InterServ

Summary:

InterServ is an integrated Web server and database. The database—the UniSQL ORDBMS (Object-Relational Database)—handles large text files and does searching. It comes with tools for planning searches and creating input screens. The Web server is compatible with standard Web browsers.

Details:

URL	http://www.nttdata.jp/products_services/ network/interserv_e.html
Platforms	Unix
Data sources	UniSQL
Server side interface	HTML
Demo copy?	No

Contact:

NTT Data Communications Systems Corp.
Email   unisql-info@nwc.nttdata.jp

They say:

About InterServ:

"InterServ provides an environment that enables existing information to be viewed on the WWW in its present form. In addition, the advanced functions of InterServ Web server, which was independently developed by NTT Data, can also be put to a wide variety of uses with Web clients...By employing the object-relational database management service (ORDBMS) UniSQL, which provides central support for InterServ, it has become possible to manage rapidly expanding volumes of information. UniSQL's capacity to handle data from different types of databases enables users to integrate information from the databases of other businesses on a network."

Jade

Summary:

Jade lets you use a Java applet on the client side to access ODBC databases on the server side. It uses full ODBC SQL function calls to manipulate data. It does not use HTTP but instead uses a session-based socket connection. Low-cost source code is available.

Details:

URL	http://www.hktrade.com/clients/kwan
Platforms	Windows NT
Web browsers	Java compatible

Web servers	Java compatible
Data sources	ODBC
Server side interface	Jade API
Client side interface	HTML, Java
Demo copy?	No

Contact:

Thomas Kwan
7479, 18th Ave.,
Burnaby, Canada
V3N 1H8
Email   nkkwan@lynx.bc.ca

They say:

About Jade:

"Jade is a client/server solution for the Java programming language to talk to the Microsoft ODBC server. If you want to use Java to access your ODBC data, Jade is the solution for you...If you know ODBC 2.0 APIs call, you know how to program the Jade API. Jade is a direct translation of ODBC APIs. Since the APIs are the same, you will not need to spend a lot of time to learn how to use the program...We give you the source code and you can change it for your own use...Jade consists of two parts: Jade client Java classes library and Jade Microsoft Windows server exe program. The installation of Jade is very easy. You just need to run: Jade.exe in your Microsoft Windows NT WWW server. Then the Jade socket server will listen to the TCP/IP port 4201 for an ODBC request. Once the Jade socket server is running, you can use your Java program to do an ODBC request."

Jagg & JDesignerPro

Summary:

Jagg uses a Java applet on the client side and a CGI program with an extension program on the server side to access ODBC databases. It accepts SQL strings but masks the complexity of the additional ODBC function calls. It uses HTTP and CGI. JDesignerPro is a development tool for building Java front ends to ODBC databases. (See also Chapter 7.)

Details:

URL	http://www.bulletproof.com
Platforms	Windows NT
Web browsers	Java enabled
Web servers	All
Data sources	SQL Server, ODBC level 2
Server side interface	CGI
Client side interface	Java applet
FAQ	Yes, at Web site
Newsgroups	comp.lang.java
Demo copy?	Yes, at Web site

Contact:

BulletProof.com
15732 Los Gatos Blvd., #525
Los Gatos, CA 95032

Tel	(408) 395-5524, (800) 505-0105
Fax	(408) 395-6026
Email	scottm@bulletproof.com

They say:

About the tools:

"JDesignerPro is a system for building simple, intuitive, yet powerful Java database front-ends. JDP is not meant to be a general-purpose Java development environment. JDP gives you a way to quickly create active database applications in Java...JDP includes a built-in version of JAGG, BulletProof's Java ODBC engine. JAGG is what JDP uses to talk with your ODBC data sources. Using JAGG is transparent to the user and largely to the developer."

About database access:

"SQL statements for inserts, updates, and selects are created as the fields are generated. You don't even type in field names. Simply browse your database tables using the JDP ODBC table navigator, then click on the fields you want...Handling of data lists is simple. The included classes for manipulating rows give you immediate power over your data browsing...JDP scans your servers for ODBC compliant databases to bring back a list of the tables and their fields. You can browse through these data sources and add any fields you want to a screen with only mouse clicks."

About JDP code:

"JDP builds all the code necessary for the interface to function, but you may modify the code to add your own logic, validation, or other database manipulation features."

About screens:

"Java interface screens built using JDesignerPro are based around the same look and feel. All JDP screens include our unique tab menuing system. The tab system included with JDP allows you to make navigation between forms a breeze for users. More importantly, you do not need to write the tabbing code, it is automatically built into the interface...You'll also find that most of the screens use the same layout. You'll find search, sort, and result lists on the left side of the screen and the database forms on the right. This is done on purpose to make the system intuitive. This way, when a user learns how to use one JDP interface screen, he or she will know how to use them all. This minimizes the time required for both development and training... Automatic Java screen layouts. JDesignerPro creates field layouts with double clicks of the mouse, like a wizard for Java. Since JDP lays screens out for you, it overcomes many of the screen layout problems with the Java AWT."

About security:

"...JDP allows you to define detailed access control. Many levels of user access can be set. A database interface built with JDesignerPro will modify itself, according to the access level of the user logging in, allowing only authorized persons and groups into sensitive areas."

JDBC

Summary:

JDBC is a database API that allows programs written in Java to access relational databases in a common way. Its functionality is modeled after ODBC, but it was designed from the start to work in the cross-platform environment, rather than in a particular OS.

Details:

URL	http://www.javasoft.com
Platforms	All

Contact:

Sun Microsystems, Inc.
2550 Garcia Avenue
Mountain View, CA 94043-1100
Tel   (415) 960-1300, (800) 821-4643 (US & Canada)

KE Texhtml Web Server and KE Texpress

Summary:

KE Texpress is an object-oriented database that can handle formatted text and multimedia objects. KE Texhtml is a Web database gateway that accesses the contents of KE Texpress databases from Web pages.

Details:

URL	http://www.ke.com.au
Platforms	Unix
Web servers	All
Data sources	ODBC level 2, its own object-oriented structures
Disk space required	40 to 50 MB
Server side interface	CGI
Client side interface	HTML, JavaScript
Mailing lists	texpress-l@ke.com.au
Demo copy?	Yes, at Web site

Contact:

Knowledge Engineering Pty., Ltd.
57 University Street
Carlton, Victoria 3053
Australia
Tel   +61 3-9347-8844
Fax   +61 3-9347-3764
Email   info@ke.com.au
FTP   ftp.ke.com.au

They say:

About KE Texpress:

"KE Texpress is a multi-user, object-oriented database management system that provides the tools and utilities for flexible and cost-effective data management...supports all aspects of data management from design and implementation of models, storage and retrieval of information, through to system evolution and maintenance...The KE Texpress database engine or kernel incorporates features that allow for easy creation and use of applications, logical representation of data, and high-speed retrieval of information. It is an object-oriented database engine that is accessed via a range of interfaces...KE Texpress can support any combination of structured data and unstructured free text."

About performance:

"...the sheer speed of retrieval and the fact that the more complex the query, the faster KE Texpress can determine the results."

About reporting:

"Very extensive reporting facilities with complete layout control. Also supports online restructuring of data, including nesting and unnesting relations, arithmetic operations, etc."

About input validation:

"Extensive data validation including table look-up, dates, ranges, mandatory items, and a completely extensible C-like validation language."

About transaction control:

"Transaction boundaries are defined as object operations. Therefore, the object itself defines the boundaries. (However, the object can 'contain' other objects.) Server treats object operations as 'atomic,' completing the operation successfully or automatically rolling back."

About network communications:

"The network communication layer provides high speed and efficient communications with all KE Texpress applications and supports direct communications (function call access), TCP/IP-based network communications and serial line connections...The KE Texpress communication protocol utilizes a high-level, structured language that provides a sophisticated range of commands while minimizing data transfers between connecting interfaces."

About OO database objects:

"KE Texpress supports object-oriented database structures utilizing text attributes, multi-valued fields, nested tables, and object references. Designers can easily build a KE Texpress system that provides an intuitive or natural representation of the way users visualize their data. Databases can contain any combination of structured (field-based) or unstructured (free-text) information. Forms are designed to describe the information to be stored and indexed. These forms serve as an interface for data entry, query specification, and the display and reporting of results...Object definitions in KE Texpress include support for inheritance via static and dynamic references. These references can be set up between database forms so that new forms can be based on, or utilize, existing forms. KE Texpress also offers encapsulation facilities through assignment, validation, branch, and display expressions, which enable users to define and associate procedures with database forms and individual fields."

About data structures:

"KE Texpress provides strong support for structured data. Designers can use Look-up tables (authority lists) during object insertions and edits, establish hierarchies among various fields, and develop data validation routines for object insertion and edit...KE Texpress retrieves entire object structures. So, in this case, all of the information about matching books is made available to the user. Thus, KE Texpress provides very efficient operations on complex objects. This, combined with the superior retrieval mechanism, makes KE Texpress a very powerful tool for information management...KE Texpress provides a more natural mapping of data than that which could be provided by a purely relational system. It uses a nested, relational database model. This enables it to support complex objects definitions without forcing a de-composition of those objects...By contrast, for a pure relational database, the design process of normalization results in the creation of many tables that require unnatural join keys to associate information. Also, multi-valued fields must become separate rows in separate relational tables. This approach further distances the logical data view from the physical data view and introduces more complicated design and maintenance issues. Pure relational systems cannot support text as an atomic type. Hence word-based retrieval is not possible. For example, performing a library query in a pure relational system would require a complicated SQL query involving resource-intensive joins of numerous tables...The nested relational approach used by KE Texpress circumvents the inherent design and runtime difficulties of pure relational databases."

About high-speed searching and indexing:

"KE Texpress is designed for extremely fast retrieval from data collections of all sizes. In fact, the more complicated the query, the faster KE Texpress can determine the results...KE Texpress delivers this retrieval speed with a simplicity of use rarely found in information management programs. The speed is derived from its indexing method. Each indexed term in an object is encoded into a series of descriptors that form a signature for that object. The object can be retrieved by providing all or part of the signature. The more of the signature provided (the more query terms the user supplies), the fewer the objects that must be accessed, and the faster the query can be performed. This is in marked contrast to traditional inverted file retrieval methods...KE Texpress supports many text operators and provides performance far superior to existing free-text retrieval systems. Indexing is supported on individual words, numbers, field values and complex data types such as dates, times, latitudes, and longitudes. There is also indexing support for word phrases, word stems, and phonetics as well as numeric ranges. Pattern retrieval (use of wild card characters) is also provided."

About internationalization capability:

"KE Texpress has fully integrated support for European languages (8-bit extended ASCII characters) and Asian languages (multi-byte character sets such as Chinese and Japanese)...The KE Texpress user interface can be completely translated to cater to different languages, locales, or even the expertise levels of different users. Indeed, users can simultaneously access a KE Texpress database using completely different interfaces and in different languages."

About open systems and portability:

"The KE Texpress engine is implemented under the Unix operating system and is available on a wide range of hardware. KE Texpress installations exist on PCs, Workstation LANs, and mid-range computers, including 64-bit architecture machines, through to mainframe machines...Despite the broad range of supported platforms and architectures, KE Texpress databases are completely portable between machines running KE Texpress."

About object-oriented features:

"The object-oriented nature of KE Texpress enables users to create database designs that reflect the structure of their existing data. All of the information recorded about a particular physical (or logical) object is stored in a single KE Texpress object. This means that the internal representation of the object, the KE Texpress object, is identical to the external representation (with which the user is already familiar). Hence database design is a very intuitive operation. KE Texpress designs can be readily modified without affecting existing data. This allows database design to evolve over time as user requirements become better defined or an organization's needs change."

About security:

"Built-in protection mechanisms control access to information in a KE Texpress database at several levels...Users must be allocated an account in order to access the database. This account sets the user's data display and entry/edit privilege levels and determines which fields of each object the user can see and edit. Each object in the database also has its own privilege level that determines whether a user can retrieve (or know of the existence of) that object...The user's account also controls the operations that can be performed by the user (e.g., entry, edit, and delete). Users who cannot perform certain operations are generally unaware of the existence of those operations."

About database size:

"KE Texpress imposes no practical database limits other than those imposed by the hardware and operating system. Therefore, the system is applicable to databases of all sizes, from a few objects to hundreds of millions of objects."

About selective dissemination of information:

"KE Texpress applications can be designed to provide Selective Dissemination of Information (SDI) services. Users can enter query profiles indicating items of interest. As new material is loaded, it is compared to all user profiles and users are automatically notified (for example, via email) of information matching their profiles...Automatic data feeds from various sources, such as Reuters and Associated Press, can be configured into KE Texpress database applications."

About industry-specific applications:

"KE Collections-Collections Management—Collections management modules suitable for use by museums, herbaria, botanical gardens, art galleries, and registries. Can be tailored for site-specific requirements...KE Gallery-Art Gallery—A comprehensive collections management system for art galleries...KE Legis-Litigation Support—A package providing flexible litigation support services for legal firms...KE Libris-Reference Library Management—An information management system for reference libraries...KE Media-News Archiving and Dissemination—A package providing data archival and selective dissemination of information for use at sites with online news feed services...KE RMS-Records Management System—A multi-user records management system that provides complete control and management of files and documents...KE SMI-Sales and Market Information—A sales and marketing system for managing client accounts, products, purchases, and initiation and tracking of marketing campaigns...KE WinTunix—A comprehensive terminal emulation package for Microsoft Windows (version 3.1 or later) that provides flexible connectivity facilities to Unix hosts...KE DOS/Tunix—A comprehensive terminal emulation package for DOS (version 3.0 or later) that provides flexible connectivity facilities to Unix hosts."

Krakatoa

Summary:

Krakatoa is a Web database development system for building product catalogs that uses a Java applet on the client side and the Krakatoa database on the server side. It consists of the Krakatoa Knowledge Base Management System, Schema Authoring Tool, and an API (C++ or PERL).

Details:

URL	http://www.cadis.com/
Platforms	Windows 95, Mac, Unix
Data sources	Oracle, Sybase, Informix, DB2, CADIS
Server side interface	CGI
Client side interface	HTML
Demo copy?	No

Contact:

CADIS, Inc.
1909 26th Street
Boulder, CO 80302

Tel	(303) 440-4363
Fax	(303) 440-5309
Email	info@cadis.com

They say:

About Krakatoa:

"Delivered in either Sun's Java programming language or HTML, Krakatoa allows Web users to search through structured content by interactively refining their search criteria with attributes of interest. At each mouse-click selection, the count of qualifying items is instantly updated, allowing the user to quickly locate the products or documents of interest. Once a desired product is identified, Krakatoa enables the user to request additional product or ordering information, or request a sales contact...National Semiconductor Corp. is using Krakatoa to publish its extensive product line of more than 30,000 component parts over the Web. National's Home Page implementation will be the first site of its kind that will enable online interactive access to a manufacturer's product information based on attributes of interest to the user...Krakatoa is an object-oriented client/server system implemented for the Web. The server software consists of the Krakatoa knowledge base management system, schema authoring tool, and an API (C++ and PERL). The Java-based client is a Java applet that is downloaded from the Web browser and will run natively on PCs using MS Windows 95, Macs, and Motif...A set of software development tools including a fully documented API that are used to build a classification schema for the products being published. Schemas can be modified online, with data fully populated, using simple drag and drop commands...CADIS Krakatoa is built using a three-tiered client server architecture. CADIS Krakatoa client software runs natively on all platforms supported by Java, with Web server software supported...."

About searching product catalogs:

"CADIS Krakatoa provides instant feedback to customers as they navigate the classification structure. The Krakatoa Interactive Search Form displays the number of products that qualify at each step, guiding the search process and allowing customers to quickly identify close substitutes if the desired product is not found. This form of Guided Iterative Query enables searches to be done in seconds, even over very large product databases... CADIS Krakatoa is the fast-emerging standard for parametric classification and retrieval of content on the World Wide Web...Customers expect to gain access to product information almost instantly, but are inevitably frustrated that they can't. Searching through catalogs is cumbersome. Calling a sales rep is time-consuming. Searching for and finding the product they need should take as little time as possible, so they can get on with the useful work they want to do with that product...Customers should be able to successively narrow their search for the product, being able to quickly look for substitutes if they don't find what they originally requested. They expect to have access to any information unique to them as customers, such as special pricing, delivery times, or even pre-announced products available only to strategic customers."

Latté

Summary:

Latté is a complete application development toolbox for building Web database applications for deployment on the Internet and Intranets. It includes a visual programming environment, a debugger, and interfaces to databases.

Details:

URL	http://www/borland.com
Platforms	Windows NT, Solaris, NetWare
Web browsers	Java applet compatible
Web servers	All
Data sources	ODBC, JDBC, InterBase
Server side interface	Java
Client side interface	HTML, Java

Contact:

Borland International, Inc.
100 Borland Way
Scotts Valley, CA 95066-3249
Tel   (408) 431-1000

They say:

About their development environment:

"The Latté RAD process has been modeled after Borland's proven and award-winning Delphi visual design environment. Build production Java applications visually by dropping software components onto a form and then 'wiring' them together with minimal Java code."

About objects:

"The object-oriented component model in Latté focuses on maximizing code reuse. This open, extensible architecture allows you to: use existing Java components, create your own components, use components built by third parties, and test components as self-contained objects. The Latté environment does not place any restrictions or limitations on the types of objects that you can create and add."

About database connectivity:

"Latté data connectivity provides high performance access to your databases with full support for Java standards. Latté supports JDBC and data-aware components that help you: create client/server database applications with minimal coding, seamlessly connect to commercial SQL databases, quickly build applications that must access legacy data, and develop applications with distributed data access. Latté delivers robust, cross-platform, Web-delivered Java database solutions."

About InterClient:

"Written entirely in Java, Borland's new InterClient provides a cost-effective means to easily deploy client/server Internet and Intranet solutions. By supporting Sun's JDBC standard, InterClient ensures that all new tools developed to JDBC will automatically be compatible with InterBase, Borland's high-performance RDBMS server. When integrated into Latté, InterClient extends your data access options by enabling Java applets and applications to: open a high-performance direct connection to Web-based data, maintain a direct connection to the server, bypass resource-intensive stateless Web server access methods, and allow higher throughput speeds and reduced Web-server traffic."

About InterBase:

"InterBase is Borland's highly efficient ANSI SQL 92 relational database that provides a scaleable solution for Internet- and Intranet-delivered applications. InterBase provides: a Multi-Generational Architecture for unmatched concurrency, outstanding performance for NT, NetWare, and Unix servers, JDBC/ODBC driver sets for flexible database access, and automatic self-tuning and configuration for reduced maintenance costs. Integrated with Latté, InterBase provides the ideal database solution for a heterogeneous environment characterized by multiple clients querying large sets of data."

LivePAGE WebMaster

Summary:

LivePAGE WebMaster is a set of tools that use a database to help you manage Web sites. It stores HTML and graphics in a SQL relational database. You use WebMaster Publisher to convert the database contents into static HTML documents with headers and footers.

Details:

URL	http://www.inforium.com/inforium.htm
Platforms	Windows 3.1, Windows 95, Windows NT
Web browsers	HTML 2.0, some Netscape extensions
Web servers	All
Data sources	Sybase, Watcom, SQL Server, Oracle
Memory required	8 MB
Disk space required	20 MB
Server side interface	CGI
Client side interface	HTML
FAQ	Yes, at Web site
Demo copy?	No

Contact:

The Information Atrium, Inc.
158 University Avenue West
Waterloo, Ontario
Canada N2L 3E9

Tel	(519) 885-2181
Fax	(519) 746-7362
Email	info@inforium.com
FTP	ftp.livepage.com

They say:

About LivePAGE:

"Our product family, known as LivePAGE, is a system of open, non-proprietary text and information management software products that takes full advantage of SGML and SQL relational database technology. LivePAGE was developed based on commonly used and generally accepted standards. It stores SGML documents in an SQL relational database, on the Microsoft Windows platform, using client/server architecture. The suite of products has been designed using component architecture so that there is seamless integration with other commonly used software products."

"The LivePAGE family of products provides all of the tools needed to manage text, graphics, and multimedia objects in a relational database. LivePAGE also incorporates many of the latest developments in information retrieval, providing a unique combination of the most powerful query capability and the ease of use demanded by today's organizations. Users can search, view, and update text from a central database, providing maximum flexibility and ease of maintenance.

"HTML editors are ideal for creating individual Web pages, but you need an additional tool to manage a full Web site. The LivePAGE WebMaster can be used to create a new Web site or easily upgrade an existing Web site."

About the format of a LivePAGE document:
"When a LivePAGE document is published, all of the generated HTML files and extracted graphics are saved in one directory. You can save your non-HTML files, such as sound and video, in another directory. It is unlikely that you would store these files in your LivePAGE database. The URL reference in your document would be similar to: <img src='video/ vidfile.avi'> In this example, the 'video' subdirectory must exist and contain the file 'vidfile.avi'."

About features:
"Manage your Web site as a single document, publish it for the Web at the press of a button, resolve links, automatically generate navigation buttons and dynamic Tables of Contents, ensure valid HTML...supports HTML 2.0 with some Netscape extensions, works with existing HTML editors, does not require special Web server software."

About Java support:
"Java requires an additional tag. Since LivePAGE is SGML-based, adding a tag is as easy as adding it to the DTD and modifying the LivePAGE DTR and STY files. This is true for most HTML extensions. INFORIUM will likely provide this new DTD (and other related files) at a later date."

About HTML 3.0 support:
"Because LivePAGE is SGML-based, you can support the additional tags for HTML 3.0 by adding them to the DTD and modifying the associated LivePAGE DTR and STY files."

About creating a CD-ROM and a Web site from the same data:
"The LivePAGE CD-Publishing Kit allows you to distribute a LivePAGE document, stored in a Watcom SQL database, on CD-ROM. The Kit includes a special version of the LivePAGE Browser. The only difference between the standard LivePAGE Browser and the CD Browser is that the CD Browser is restricted in such a way that it can only open the documents that you distribute. This restriction reduces the cost per CD-Browser, allowing you to economically distribute your documents."

About the problem it helps to solve:
"Currently, managing a Web site can be a difficult task. Managing any-thing more than a dozen pages requires a special tool or the knowledge of a scripting language. Just the management of the links alone can be a major headache, and the process of inserting and deleting pages makes it even worse. You may also find that some of your pages contain HTML good enough to display in your current Web Browser, but as the rules change, your code may need to be fixed up...What is missing from existing Web sites is a simple way to define the structure and relationship of the various pages. This is exactly what the WebMaster Builder does. It provides a simple-to-use interface to define the structure of a Web site. It will even 'walk' an existing Web site and guess the current structure."

About how it works:
"The WebMaster Builder walks an existing Web site and combines the pages adding hierarchical structure. The Builder combines any number of HTML files and can also handle ASCII text files. If you are starting from scratch, then you can use the Builder to create an outline for a new Web site...The LivePAGE Updater allows you to manage text in a central database reposi-tory where it can be viewed, searched, and maintained. Because the infor-mation is stored in a standard format in a non-proprietary database, you can reuse the information in a variety of ways. For example, you can dis-tribute your information on CD or create custom applications that com-bine traditional table-organized data with your textual information...When you are ready to create or update your Web site, the WebMaster Publisher extracts the pages from the database document creating a file for each Web page and resolving links. For each page, the Publisher adds consistent headers and footers that include navigation buttons and it also generates

corresponding dynamic Table of Contents pages. Once published, you can preview your Web files and then send them to your Web server...The WebMaster Builder includes a drag and drop outlining tool that can be used to easily manage the structure. You can easily add additional HTML pages, merge additional Web sites, and even add ASCII text pages...Once the structure has been defined, it is easy to load the entire Web site into a LivePAGE database. This process uses the LivePAGE Administrator program and is entirely automated. You specify the file you created in the Builder, and tell it what database name you wish to build, and it will load the HTML into the relational database. The database is then ready to be used by the LivePAGE Browser or LivePAGE Updater. You now have the entire Web site, including all of its structure, at your fingertips."

LiveWire and LiveWire Pro

Summary:

LiveWire is a set of tools for authoring and managing Web sites and building Web database applications. LiveWire Pro integrates the Informix database with LiveWire. LiveWire uses JavaScript on the server side to program database applications. (See also Chapter 9.)

Details:

Platforms	Windows NT, Windows 3.1, Windows 95, NT Alpha, Solaris, Macintosh
Web browsers	Netscape
Web servers	Netscape, Microsoft
Data sources	ODBC, Sybase, Oracle, SQL Server, Informix, DB2
Memory required	12 MB
Disk space required	19 MB
Server side interface	CGI, NSAPI, ISAPI
Client side interface	plug-ins, ActiveX
Demo copy?	No

Contact:

Netscape Communications Corp.
501 Middlefield Road
Mountain View, CA 94043

Tel	(415) 254-1900, (800) 528-2285 (US & Canada)
Fax	(415) 528-4124
Email	info@netscape.com
FTP	ftp.netscape.com

They say:

About LiveWire:

"Netscape LiveWire and LiveWire Pro are visual tool suites designed for managing Web sites and creating live, online applications. With LiveWire and LiveWire Pro, developers can create and manage Web content, sites, and applications. LiveWire (available for Windows 95, Windows NT, and Unix) includes Netscape Navigator Gold; LiveWire Site Manager; LiveWire JavaScript Compiler; and LiveWire Database Connectivity Library for direct SQL connectivity to relational databases from Informix, Sybase, Oracle, and Illustra; and ODBC connectivity for dozens of additional databases, from desktops to mainframes. In addition, Netscape LiveWire Pro (available for Windows 95 and Windows NT) includes a developer version of Informix's OnLine-Workgroup high-performance SQL database. The Windows NT version of LiveWire Pro also includes a copy of Crystal Software's Crystal Reports Professional Version 4.5...Netscape LiveWire and LiveWire Pro provide an integrated environment that enables novice users to create and manage Web content, Web sites, and live, online Web applications for Intranets and the Internet, while offering experienced application developers the power to manage highly complex Web sites and applications."

About what the package contains:

"Netscape LiveWire consists of: Netscape Navigator Gold, LiveWire Site Manager, LiveWire JavaScript Compiler, LiveWire Database Connectivity Library...Netscape LiveWire Pro includes the above, plus: Informix OnLine-Workgroup high-performance SQL database, Crystal Software's Crystal Reports Professional Version 4.5 (Windows NT version only)."

About Site Manager:

"...LiveWire Site Manager, a visual site-management tool for creating and managing Web sites with drag-and-drop ease...Visual site management provides a graphical view of the organization of an entire Web site, and uses drag-and-drop technology for restructuring...Automatic link reorganization automatically changes all references to a page, link, or file when changes are made within the site...External link checker determines activity and status of external links...Wizards and templates take novice users step-by-step through the process of creating well-organized Web sites with professionally designed graphics...Automatic site importer downloads entire Web sites from servers across Intranets and on the Internet for local editing and updating...One-button site publishing deploys entire Web sites from the local file system to a designated Web server on an Intranet or the Internet, under secure access control...Document conversion supports popular text formats including Microsoft Word, Corel, WordPerfect, Adobe FrameMaker, and RTF...Image conversion supports popular image formats including BMP, WMF, TIFF, PICT, and PCX...One-button JavaScript Compiler turns server-side JavaScript source code into byte codes ready to run on any Navigator 2.0 Windows NT or Unix Web server...."

About LiveWire JavaScript compiler:

"Supports a variety of linking and execution switches for better runtime performance...For rapid development of client- and server-side applications without requiring extensive programming experience, Netscape and Sun Microsystems developed JavaScript. Today, JavaScript has been widely adopted as the standard scripting language for adding 'intelligence' to Web pages. With LiveWire, Netscape brings JavaScript to Web servers. Netscape's FastTrack 2.0 and Enterprise 2.0 Web Servers both are capable of running compiled JavaScript applications. The LiveWire JavaScript Compiler enables application developers to quickly and easily convert JavaScript applications and HTML pages incorporating JavaScript code into platform-independent byte codes ready to run on any Netscape 2.0 Server. A simplified version of the JavaScript Compiler is also built into the LiveWire Site Manager for one-button compiling...."

About database connectivity library:

"...Supports native SQL client/server connectivity to Informix, Sybase, Oracle, and Illustra databases...Supports ODBC connectivity to databases with ODBC drivers, from the desktop (Microsoft Access, Borland Paradox) to mainframes (IBM DB2)...Uses conventional database cursor model for connecting to a database, putting a cursor into a table, and reading, writing, and updating records in a table...Supports passthrough SQL for database-specific SQL statements and commands...Completely platform- and database-independent when using cursor access methods without SQL

Passthrough...Supports triggers and stored procedures...Includes transaction processing features (commit, rollback, etc.)"

About Informix Online Workgroup database:

"Upward-compatible with Informix OnLine Dynamic Server SQL database...Simplified system configuration and maintenance (compared to OnLine Dynamic Server)...Single-developer, single-server license with unlimited users for economical application development and deployment...."

MiniSQL

Summary:

MiniSQL and W3-mSQL are shareware Web database tools that work in Unix. MiniSQL is a lightweight relational DBMS that comes with source code. W3-mSQL is a server extension program that integrates MiniSQL with Web pages.

Details:

URL	http://www.hughes.com.au
Platforms	Unix
Data sources	MiniSQL
Server side interface	CGI
Client side interface	HTML
Demo copy?	Yes, at Web site

Contact:

Tel	+ 61 75 95 1450
Fax	+ 61 75 95 1456
Email	Bambi@Hughes.com.au

They say:

About MiniSQL:

"MiniSQL is a lightweight, relational database engine that supports a subset of the ANSI SQL specification. It has been designed to perform the operations that it supports quickly and with very little resource overhead. MiniSQL is in use all over the world as a back-end database for WWW servers. MiniSQL is available for several Unix platforms."

About W3-mSQL:

"W3-mSQL is a package that provides an interface between the World Wide Web and MiniSQL. With W3-mSQL you'll never have to write another custom

CGI program again. It extends standard HTML and provides a complete scripting language with mSQL access and enhanced security. Because it is implemented as a set of CGI programs, it can be used with any standard Web server."

Muskrat

Summary:

Muskrat is a development tool for connecting relational databases to Web pages. It comes with a WYSIWYG graphical editor.

Details:

URL	www.glink.com
Platforms	Solaris, SUN/OS, IRIX, HP/UX, Windows NT
Web servers	All
Data sources	ODBC, Oracle, Sybase, Informix, CA-Ingres, SQL Server
Memory required	8 MB
Disk space required	10 MB
Server side interface	CGI
Client side interface	HTML
FAQ	Yes, at Web site
Demo copy?	Yes, at Web site

Contact:

Globalink Technologies, Inc.
2290 North First Street, Suite 210
San Jose, CA 95131
Tel   (408) 526-9200
Fax   (408) 526-1722
Email   info@glink.com

They say:

About development tools:

"WYSIWYG editor allows the Web page developer to visually work with the screen, forms and pages, and database linkage he/she is developing in HTML/DB, and permits on-demand access to the desired database. It can also create and edit standard HTML files. The WYSIWYG Editor supports local database procedures, and provides preview functions against real database and test facilities through popular browsers. Online help is also part of the editor."

NetAnswer

Summary:

NetAnswer is a CGI server extension program that provides full text search and retrieval capabilities. It supports Boolean and comparative operators, positional searches, and fielded searches. It works with a variety of document formats including word processing, desktop publishing, and Adobe PDF. It supports HTML 3.0 and extensions.

Details:

URL	http://www.dataware.com
Platforms	Windows 3.x, Windows NT, Unix, Novell, MS-DOS, VAX/VMS, MVS/CICS
Web browsers	Netscape, Spyglass, Mosaic
Web servers	CERN, NCSA, Netscape, Open Market
Data sources	Dataware full-text databases
Client side interface	HTML 2.0, 3.0
Demo copy?	No

Contact:

Dataware Technologies, Inc.
222 Third Street, Suite 3300
Cambridge, MA 02142
Tel   (617) 621-0820
Fax   (617) 621-0307
Email   info@dataware.com

They say:

About NetAnswer:

"...NetAnswer is a fast, turn-key solution for information publishers who want to publish large volumes of data on the Internet. Scaleable, proven technology; sophisticated searching; flexible data display, and security, metering, and accounting capabilities provide a powerful solution for information publishers. NetAnswer works with the standard browsers operating on the World Wide Web, including Netscape, Spyglass, and Mosaic, and the standard servers, including CERN, NCSA, Netscape, and Open Market."

About support for multiple languages:

"...20 languages, including 13 European languages, Kanji (Japanese), and Chinese (simplified and traditional)."

About their product family:

"The Dataware family of electronic document management, retrieval, and publishing products serves organizations that create, manage, and distribute both structured data, text, and images...Dataware, BRS/Search, Total Recall, CD Author, and CD Answer are registered trademarks owned or licensed by Dataware Technologies, Inc. NetAnswer, ReferenceSet, CD Record, Ledge Multimedia, and GutenbergII."

About searching:

"NetAnswer's core search and retrieval capabilities, extensive data security, and activity monitoring can support hundreds of simultaneous users and databases of 100 or more gigabytes. NetAnswer protects your document design, automatically translating information you have published in other formats into HTML to let you deliver it easily on the Internet without reformatting. NetAnswer's publishing options let you tailor the display and presentation of your information to the needs of individuals or groups of users. With its wide range of query options and searching strategies, NetAnswer meets the needs of less experienced users, yet can be configured easily for sophisticated users. NetAnswer's unique security and logging features protect your organization's most valuable asset, its information, allowing you to protect information access by database, by document, and even by paragraph. Broad accounting functionality allows you to offer a variety of subscription and fee-based services."

About three-tiered architecture:

"A three-tiered architecture enables NetAnswer to work seamlessly with other Internet technologies to make searching large document collections easy, while ensuring the scaleability and throughput needed to handle hundreds of simultaneous requests. NetAnswer is available across a wide range of Unix and Windows NT platforms."

About document retrieval:

"NetAnswer protects the investment you've made in document design. With NetAnswer, you can easily publish your existing word-processing, or desktop-published information on the Internet without reformatting it.

NetAnswer streamlines publication by automatically translating your text content information into HTML, while maintaining links to the original documents. If you've already converted your information into HTML, NetAnswer indexes your Internet-ready documents, and passes the fully formatted information directly to users. NetAnswer lets you publish documents from a variety of formats, including most desktop publishing and word-processing packages and Adobe PDF. Users can search the full-text contents and receive the original fully formatted document. Publishers and Corp.s can prepare their information for internal network or CD-ROM distribution, then deliver the same information on the Internet. The information can be fine-tuned to make use of Internet capabilities without affecting its accessibility from non-Internet environments."

About security, metering, and accounting:

"NetAnswer includes a range of functionality that supports subscription and fee-based services. Specifically, you can use NetAnswer to build basic subscription, premium-level, or pay-per-access services. Tools that simplify the task of managing your database content and user profiles are also provided. Access to your information can be controlled at several levels. For example, you can protect entire databases, selected sets of documents, or specific paragraphs within documents. You also can control which users can use different search commands. To help prospective customers sample your service and content, you can designate some data as freely accessible. All database accesses are logged to create usage analysis reports and transaction logs. NetAnswer lets you quickly generate reports containing statistics on usage patterns, connection time, searches performed, and documents accessed. You also have the option of outputting this information directly to your organization's accounting system for billing purposes."

NetLink/4D

Summary:

NetLink/4D is a CGI server extension program. On the Mac, it connects 4D databases to the Web. The Windows version uses ISAPI or CGI and works with 4D and other SQL databases such as SQL Server.

Details:

URL	http://www.fsti.com/productinfo/netlink.html
Platforms	Windows NT, Windows 95, Macintosh 7.x

Web servers	MacHTTP, WebSTAR, on Windows any CGI-capable Web server
Data sources	4th Dimension for Macintosh v3.2, 4th Dimension for Windows v3.5
Memory required	4001 to 500 K
Disk space required	48 K
Server side interface	CGI, ISAPI
FAQ	Yes, at Web site
Mailing lists	NetLink-talk@liststar.fsti.com, NetLink-beta@liststar.fsti.com
Demo copy?	Yes, at Web site

Contact:

Foresight Technology, Inc.
4100 International Plaza, Suite 538
Fort Worth, TX 76109

Tel	(817) 731-4444, (800) 701-9393
Fax	(817) 731-9304
Email	dennis_vogel@fsti.com
FTP	ftp.fsti.com

They say:

About NetLink/4D:

"NetLink/4D is an external package for 4th Dimension that lets you use 4D as a CGI application with Web servers such as WebSTAR, Netscape, and Microsoft's Internet Information Server. With NetLink/4D, you can let users of World Wide Web browsers such as Netscape, Microsoft's Internet Explorer, or Mosaic access your 4D and SQL databases...handles receiving and sending of all connection events between the Web server and a 4D database...handles parsing all CGI and HTML Form parameters, including all HTML special characters...handles multiple incoming connections from the Web server, and manages multiple 4D processes with no additional 4D programming effort required...supports advanced Web server features such as partial replies, server push, and more...provides commands to convert database images to GIF or JPEG, and manage requests for these images from the Web server...Capability to send email to an SMTP mail server...Full compatibility with Macintosh and Windows Web servers."

About email:

"...allows you to send email from 4th Dimension using SMTP."

About input validation:

"...table-lookups, dates, ranges, and character validation."

About its language:

"4D's Basic-like scripting language eliminates the need to write queries in SQL or C. SQL doesn't have a front-end or programming language (SQL commands are for updating data, but lack other types of programming commands such as loops, conditionals, etc.), which limits what you can do on the Web."

O2Web

Summary:

O2Web is a set of tools for connecting the O2 database to Web pages. O2 is an OODBMS that can store multimedia data and uses the OQL query language.

Details:

URL	http://www.o2tech.com
Platforms	SunOS 4.1.3, Solaris 2.4, HP9.0 and 10, IBM AIX 3.25 and 4., SGI IRIX 5.3, SCO Openserver 5.0, Windows NT 3.5, DEC Alpha AXP OSF1 3.2, NextStep 3.2
Data sources	O2
Memory required	16 MB
Disk space required	40 MB
Server side interface	CGI
Client side interface	HTML
FAQ	No
Demo copy?	No

Contact:

O2 Technology
3600 West Bayshore Road, Suite 106
Palo Alto, CA 94303

Tel	(415) 842-7000, (800) 798-5454 (US & Canada)
Fax	(415) 842-7001
Email	o2info@o2tech.com

They say:

About O2Web:

"O2Web provides a complete set of tools to rapidly develop and deploy a WWW server based on the O2 Database System. O2Web is targeted at users who need to access and manage complex data on the WWW, and at users who want to make an ODMG database available on the Web. O2Web is an add-on component to the O2 system that can exploit the full potential of integrating Internet communication and Object Technology. O2Web turns any O2 database into a Web server by establishing a connection to the Web and translating every object into an HTML format. It provides WWW clients with the ability to browse through hypermedia information stored in any O2 database."

About its language:

"...the OQL language gives users and developers associative access and navigation capability on the Net."

About page generation:

"...automatic generation of HTML: each O2 object is translated into HTML. The standard presentation depends on the structure of the objects. It can be customized for the application, for the class, and/or for the object."

About OO benefits:

"...all benefits of the object-oriented technology: reusability, maintainability, plus the benefits of using a standard tool. O2 is the first ODMG-compliant object database, and the O2Web tool is mainly based on the use of the ODMG query language OQL."

About reporting:

"All capability of OQL, which includes sort, grouping, tables, etc."

About queries, inserts, updates, and deletes:

"Through OQL and C++ or O2C methods."

About input validation:

"Any validations that can be programmed in C++."

About transaction control:

"Transactions are defined by the programmer. State information between client and server is maintained by the system as well as database connection."

About security:

"Security is handled mainly by the Web server, and a method 'connect' is called automatically at each connection. It can be used by the programmer for authentication and security."

OpenScape
Summary:

OpenScape connects legacy and relational databases to the Web. It uses a Visual Basic-like language. OpenScape Enterprise is designed for secure, high-transaction volume applications, and OpenScape Workgroup is for smaller systems.

Details:

URL	http://www.busWeb.com/
Platforms	Windows 3.1, Windows NT, Windows 95
Web browsers	Netscape, Microsoft
Web servers	Netscape, Microsoft
Data sources	ODBC, Oracle, Sybase, Informix, IMS, VSAM, SAP R/3, Baan IV, PeopleSoft, Entera
Client side interface	HTML, ActiveX, plug-in
FAQ	Yes, at Web site
Demo copy?	Yes, at Web site

Contact:

Business@Web
One Arsenal Marketplace, 2nd Floor
Watertown, MA 02172
Tel   (617) 923-6500, (800) 700-8598
Email   Webmaster@busWeb.com

They say:

About OpenScape's architecture:

"OpenScape's component approach to application development provides for integration of disparate systems and for Internet-enabling of mission-critical applications. Since application functionality and data access rules are kept separate from the user interface in OpenScape's component architecture, the presentation aspect of the application, either desktop or

Web-based, can remain independent of existing back-end processes. In addition, with OpenScape, a single graphical user interface (GUI) can be developed that runs in both client/server systems and Web browsers."

"OpenScape wraps application programming interfaces (APIs) for legacy systems, existing applications, and databases, so that they are accessible via common communication protocols such as remote procedure calls (RPC), OLE, and ODBC, eliminating much of the complexity associated with integrating disparate systems...A three-tiered client/server architecture separates an application into the following three parts: presentation layer—the graphical interface between the user and application; functionality layer—the non-visual, server side of an application where business rule functionality resides; data access layer—where communication protocols between servers and databases are translated."

"OpenScape's thin runtime is downloaded to the client computer. This free runtime code must be on the client machine to use OpenScape components."

"When visual or nonvisual components are created with OpenScape, they may be accessed as ActiveX controls and simply embedded in any ActiveX container application such as Microsoft Visual Basic or Internet Explorer."

About security:

"Business@Web recognizes security as one of the most critical areas in Internet application development. The current version of OpenScape (v1.42) allows users to restrict activities that downloaded Web applications can perform. Web applications may be prevented from: performing dynamic data exchange (DDE) calls, accessing local files, modifying local files, accessing local directories, activating other desktop applications, changing/reading environment settings, executing local programs, calling external DLLs, registering OCXs (ActiveX controls)...In addition, logic components that access middleware services do so under a specific identity, which the application programmer can specify."

"Ensures a secure transaction between the user and back-end systems. Communications must pass from the OpenScape Web Engine Client, which utilizes 40-bit key RSA encryption, to the OpenScape Distributed Web Engine, which only accepts encrypted messages through the firewall from qualified users."

About component technology:

"Component technology builds on and refines object technology, adding a universal interface to objects. Components, unlike objects, can interoperate regardless of the programming language with which they were developed. OpenScape builds true components that may be used and reused from one application to the next, across traditional programming language and platform barriers, and in both desktop and Web browser environments...increases developer productivity...simplifies application customization...reduces time to market for strategic applications...runs in desktop applications as ActiveX controls or OLE objects...runs in Internet browsers such as Netscape Navigator and Microsoft Internet Explorer.... interoperates with Java applets...components may be developed independently and later assembled into applications...OpenScape does not require developers to use traditional OO programming languages such as C++ or SmallTalk to build servers. Servers may be coded in PERL, C, or COBOL, as well as C++. Visual components may be quickly built with a point-and-click, Visual Basic-like tool instead of with character-based development languages."

About integration with Microsoft's Internet offerings:

"Business@Web interoperates with, and leverages, Microsoft's Internet offerings and desktop standards. OpenScape components may be embedded in both OLE-enabled desktop applications such as Microsoft Excel, Word, and Visual Basic and Microsoft's browser, Internet Explorer. OpenScape components also interoperate with hundreds of other OLE-enabled environments such as Powerbuilder and Lotus Notes...ActiveX technology (formerly known as OCX) also fits well with OpenScape because OpenScape enables ActiveX controls to be embedded in non-Microsoft Internet browsers such as Netscape Navigator."

About OpenScape's development environment:

"OpenScape allows the creation of reusable components through a point-and-click tool familiar to all of the more than three million Visual Basic programmers. In addition, OpenScape's development environment employs a full Visual Basic for Applications (VBA) scripting language. For developers not familiar with Visual Basic, it is an intuitive graphical environment that is easily learned as compared to character-based development languages...OpenScape components, unlike those created with Visual Basic, may be embedded in any Internet browser or OLE-enabled application without repetitive and time-consuming recoding."

"The OpenScape Workbench is an integrated development environment for visual and logical component creation, storage, browsing, and reuse. Components may be run within the Workbench to allow immediate testing and iterative development. Within the Workbench, both visual and logical components may be indexed and viewed graphically to facilitate reuse...The Visual Component Builder is a point-and-click development tool similar to Microsoft Visual Basic that supports a Visual Basic for Applications (VBA) scripting language. It can be used to quickly create reusable presentation components. Visual components built with OpenScape can also contain other simpler visual components, which have been built with OpenScape or purchased from a third-party vendor...Logical components, which consist of business rule components and integration components, are created with Business@Web's OpenExtensions. These point-and-click tools, sold separately from OpenScape Enterprise, provide a simple, graphical means for "mapping" logical components with back-end legacy and client/server systems. Logical components provide a consistent programming interface to multiple platforms and back-end systems, greatly simplifying development of Internet applications that rely on existing functionality and data. (OpenScape Enterprise includes the OpenExtension for OLE Automation and the OpenExtension for ODBC.)"

About version control:

"OpenScape components remain linked to their source on the Web server and therefore receive any updates or edits automatically via HTTP, the communication protocol between the Web server and Internet browser. In addition, OpenScape components may use the OLE mechanisms of linking and embedding to access their source."

About application installation:

"OpenScape visual components are deployed to a Web server from which they may be downloaded to the user's desktop. Logical components are deployed on a separate application server designed to meet the demands of high-volume transaction processing. OpenScape includes software that ensures flexible and robust visual and logical component execution at runtime...The Web Engine Client resides on the user's desktop. Its purpose is to dynamically provide the appropriate interface for visual components, depending on the environment in which they are to run. The Web Engine Client automatically exposes OpenScape components as 'plug-ins' in Netscape Navigator, ActiveX controls in Microsoft Internet Explorer, or OLE objects in any OLE-enabled desktop environment. The Web Engine Client will also spawn an external viewer to allow OpenScape visual components to run from all other Web browsers. In addition, the Web Engine Client utilizes 40-bit RSA cryptography to ensure a secure connection to the Distributed Web Engine. The Distributed Web Engine resides on an enterprise server. It receives and sends encrypted TCP/IP socket calls from the Web Engine Client. The Distributed Web Engine automatically routes all requests from the Web Engine Client to the appropriate logical component, which communicates to the target back-end system(s). Thus, no networking or application functionality software is required on the user's desktop. The Distributed Web Engine is also multithreaded, and may be distributed to multiple machines to provide for high performance and application scaleability."

Oracle WebServer

Summary:

Oracle WebServer is a Web server that connects to Oracle databases. It uses the native Oracle interfaces and provides security features. It has integrated the Java interpreter into the Web server and has added special extensions for Oracle 7.

Details:

URL	http://www.oracle.com/mainEvent/ WebServer/ois1.html
Platforms	Windows NT, Solaris, HP-UX
Web browsers	All
Web servers	Oracle WebServer
Data sources	Oracle
Server side interface	CGI
Client side interface	HTML, Java
Demo copy?	No

Contact:

Oracle Corp.
500 Oracle Parkway
Redwood Shores, CA 94065
Tel   (415) 506-7000
Email   Websupp@us.oracle.com

They say:

About Oracle WebServer:

"Oracle WebServer 2.0 is built around Oracle Web Request Broker, a high-performance system for linking Oracle's WebServer to applications, databases, and ultimately even other HTTP listeners. Web Request Broker bypasses the high-overhead Common Gateway Interface (CGI) used by most Internet servers today for linking to back-end services. Web Request Broker also enables a high-performance native connection to the Oracle7 Server, which allows WebServer 2.0 to deliver relational, text, audio, video, and spatial data through standard Web browsers."

"While including a robust HTTP server, the core of the Oracle WebServer is the Web Request Broker, a high-speed mechanism for dispatching, load-balancing, and adding third-party server extensions. Built on a true multithreaded, multiprocess architecture, the Web Request Broker offers a superior application environment over low-level, first-generation HTTP APIs. Through the WRB, the Oracle WebServer delivers vastly superior performance, dispatching, and access times, even in extremely high network traffic environments. Running all server extensions as individual processes, the Web Request Broker provides true asynchronous independent processing. Through the unique, independent processing architecture, the WRB guarantees that third-party server extensions will not affect other parts of the system, thus delivering unparalleled reliability for all your users."

About open architecture:

"Oracle WebServer 2.0 offers an open, extensible architecture. Web Request Broker ensures interoperability of applications written in different languages and residing on different Web servers. As a result, users are able to write their own back-end services and plug them into the system...Web Request Broker facilitates exchange of components implemented in all relevant industry standards, providing Oracle WebServer 2.0 with the highest level of openness in the industry. Web Request Broker supports any development language including Java, PL/SQL, and C/C++, and provides an open API (application programming interface) for building server objects to extend WebServer's capabilities. Unlike simple protocol programming interfaces at the HTTP level, the Web Request Broker API is a true application programming interface for building robust, secure and manageable applications."

About Java extensions:

"Oracle WebServer 2.0 offers an integrated Java runtime environment with extensions for Oracle7, effectively enabling developers to implement dynamic Web applications using native Java classes on the server."

About database access:

"Oracle WebServer 2.0 performs native Oracle7 processing through the PL/SQL Agent, which translates and dispatches client requests directly to the Oracle7 Server. This enables data-driven Web applications to be implemented using PL/SQL, Oracle's procedural development environment for Oracle7."

About SSI:

"Oracle WebServer 2.0 allows developers to use Server-Side-Includes, a mechanism for extending the capability of HTML pages by making callouts to applications and back-end servers."

About site administration:

"All components of the Oracle WebServer are fully configurable and manageable through the Oracle WebServer System Manager: a collection of HTML forms and online, context-sensitive help. These administration pages allow an administrator to quickly configure the Oracle WebServer with the click of a button."

About data types supported:

"...by supporting native connectivity to the Oracle7 database, you get full access to all supported data types including text, relational, and spatial, so you can deliver media-rich applications over the Internet."

About development tools:

"The WebServer SDK fully encapsulates the Web Request Broker API enabling you to harness its power with your favorite Web development tool. With full support for JAVA, PL/SQL, LiveHTML, and C++, Oracle WebServer 2.0 is the only language-independent Web server available today! The

WebServer SDK includes a full set of sample applications, procedure libraries, and comprehensive documentation, delivering everything you need to build robust Internet and Intranet applications out of the box. To make development easier and deployment faster, Oracle WebServer applications can utilize the same procedure libraries in their native languages."

About security:

"...Oracle WebServer is the first Web server to support full end-to-end security—at the client, at the WebServer, and through the firewall to an Oracle7 database. Oracle WebServer contains an integrated Proxy extension, which enables it to cache frequently accessed Web pages in high-traffic network environments, thereby improving page access times through the corporate firewall to the Internet...Oracle WebServer also supports two common authentication and restriction mechanisms: Basic and Digest Authentication and both IP-based & Domain-based restriction. These mechanisms allow resources to be protected by username/password combinations and ensure that only authorized users visit your site...supports Oracle Secure Network Services (SNS). SNS ensures secure communication between Oracle WebServer 2.0 and Oracle7, even through a firewall, enabling Web applications to incorporate and use valuable information and applications. SNS is fully compatible with the majority of popular firewalls available, including TIS, Raptor, SMTI, Sun, and Digital...IP Address Restriction... Domain Name Restriction...Basic Authentication...Digest Authentication... SSL 2.0 (International version uses 40-bit key.)."

About portability:

"...Oracle WebServer is open and supports all existing Web standards. Oracle WebServer applications are fully portable across 14 different platforms including Sun Solaris, HP-UX, SGI-IRX, and Windows NT. In addition, it is fully compliant with all recognized and published Internet standards including HTTP 1.0, HTML 2.0 with extensions, CGI 1.1, Java, and C/C++."

Personal Web Site (PWS) Toolbox 1.1

Summary:

W3 Toolbox creates HTML documents from simple flat files. It has a search engine, can generate custom responses to input from forms, and does search and replace functions on HTML documents.

Details:

URL	http://www.w3.com/
Platforms	Sun OS, Solaris, IRIX, Linux, BSDI
Web browsers	All
Web servers	All
Data sources	Oracle7, flat file
Memory required	16 MB
Disk space required	15 MB
Server side interface	CGI
Client side interface	HTML
FAQ	Yes, at Web site
Demo copy?	Yes, at Web site

Contact:

w3.com
459 Hamilton Avenue, Suite 202
Palo Alto, CA 94301
Tel   (415) 323-3378
Fax   (415) 323-2420
Email   info@W3.COM

They say:

About the W3 Toolbox:

"...The W3 Toolbox is a set of applications designed for Unix platforms that significantly improves the Web site development process and adds powerful new features to Web sites...The W3 Toolbox consists of four integrated applications...."

About WebSpin:

"WebSpin TM: automates the process of creating HTML Web pages by generating them directly from database output files and applying them to intuitive templates...WebSpin TM is ideal for presenting large collections of documents that have a similar format, or documents that need to be listed in a hierarchical, alphabetical, or numerical order. The process of constructing a Web site involves: creating a single database text file, writing several template files that specify the layout of the Web pages, and writing a script to pass the content from the database text file to the templates."

About WebScan:

"WebScan TM: provides easy access to database output files through specialized search functions such as 'and/or' keyword searches, multiple value searches and record matches...With WebScan you can quickly create online search forms and let your users type queries to perform complex searches on your Web site. WebScan will allow you to: perform 'and/or' keyword searches, have multiple values for any searched field, search more than one field at a time, return a customized HTML page of matched records...WebScan automatically recognizes and supports three separate types of datafile formats: carriage-return delimited (default), comma delimited, and tab delimited."

About WebForm:

"WebForm TM: promotes user interaction by directly processing data entered into HTML forms over to text files or email addresses and returning custom responses...For any given form, WebForm TM will allow you to: save the results of the form to a file, send a customized email message to any address based on the form input, return a customized HTML response to the user once the form has been selected, return a customized error message to the user if the form is not filled out properly...."

About WebSweep:

"WebSweep TM: allows the quick updating of bodies of text, which are common to multiple HTML Web pages, by simply replacing common data with macros...WebSweep TM is a software tool for quickly updating specific bodies of text on any Web Page on your site. For any given form, WebSweep TM will allow you to: change the specific text on all given HTML files, such as headers, footers, background graphics, and menubars, and change the content of graphic files, advertisements, or hypertext links."

PowerBuilder 5.0

Summary:

PowerBuilder 5.0 is a Web-enabled version of PowerBuilder, which is a development tool for building full-strength database client applications. It works both visually and by writing code. The Web-enabled version can be called from a Web browser and works as a window in the browser, but uses a session-oriented protocol rather than HTTP. (See also Chapter 10.)

Details:

URL	http://www.powersoft.com
Platforms	Windows 95, Windows NT, Windows 3.x
Web browsers	Netscape, Microsoft
Web servers	na
Data sources	ODBC, Sybase, SQL Server, Informix, Oracle, dBASE2, Fulcrum, Verity
Memory required	12 MB
Disk space required	19 MB
Server side interface	na
Client side interface	plug-in, ActiveX
Demo copy?	No

Contact:

PowerSoft Division of Sybase, Inc.
561 Virginia Road
Concord, MA 01742

Tel	(508) 287-1500 (switchboard), (508) 369-4695 (sales)
Fax	(508) 287-1600 (fax back)
FTP	ftp.powersoft.com

They say:

About PowerBuilder:

"...PowerBuilder Enterprise 5.0 will let you extend your WWW Browser with a DataWindow Viewer available as Plug-In or an ActiveX Control. PowerBuilder 5.0 will also enable the creation of PowerBuilder Window Plug-ins to client/server-enable your browser applications. You can also use distributed PowerBuilder to build customizable Web servers that generate dynamic content for any Web browser."

About the PowerBuilder DataWindow:

"PowerSoft's patented DataWindow gives you a powerful, graphical view of the database via a presentation style you select. Save your DataWindows as objects, and reuse them in other applications—soon including Internet or Intranet applications. The Data Pipeline gives you a highly efficient method for transferring vast quantities of data between different DBMSs."

About objects:

"PowerBuilder's new distributed architecture gives you the flexibility of distributed objects throughout your development environment. You can easily create distributed, compiled objects and partition them across your network...PowerBuilder 5.0 also offers plug and play support for ActiveX controls and OLE automation servers. The new 'PowerBuilder Foundation Class' (PFC) will greatly accelerate your development efforts with a set of reusable objects and services, including a sample framework. And the new server-based object manager, ObjectCycle, provides secure version control and reporting."

About distributed applications:

"PowerBuilder 5.0 meets the heterogeneous computing demands head-on with its ability to create applications that can be run anywhere. Not only is PowerBuilder 5.0 a 32-bit, 'Designed for Windows 95' logo-compliant product that includes many of the new Windows 95 controls, but it's also available on multiple platforms. This gives you the ability to develop on any platform, then deploy on any platform without having to rewrite your application. We've also structured PowerBuilder 5.0 controls as a superset of Windows 95 controls. That means you can build your application on Windows 95 using these new controls, then deploy your application on Windows 3.1, NT, Macintosh, or Unix and maintain the same user interface on all platforms."

About compiled code:

"With native, compiled code generation based on superior Watcom C technology, PowerBuilder 5.0 will improve your application performance, including faster script executions, mathematical expressions, integer and floating point arithmetic, and array processing. Plus, PowerBuilder features highly optimized native database drivers for connecting your applications immediately to a broad range of data sources."

About database drivers:

"...In keeping with the PowerBuilder tradition, PowerBuilder 5.0 continues to provide the industry's most comprehensive set of native database drivers, providing connectivity options to multiple SQL databases. In addition to native driver support, PowerBuilder 5.0 offers full ODBC support, along with a broad range of ODBC drivers. Sybase SQL Anywhere 5.0 is bundled with PowerBuilder 5.0 as a standalone engine to provide full relational database capabilities for PowerBuilder developers."

PROCGI Toolkit

Summary:

PROCGI is a library of PERL scripts that integrates Web pages with the Progress database.

Details:

URL	http://www.progress.com/Webtools/procgi.htm
Platforms	Unix
Data sources	Progress
Server side interface	CGI
Client side interface	HTML
Demo copy?	Yes, at Web site

Contact:

Progress Software Corp.
14 Oak Park
Bedford, MA 01730

Tel	(617) 280-4000
Fax	(617) 280-4895
Email	sales-info@progress.com

They say:

About PROCGI:

"PROCGI version 1.0 is a free toolkit for writing Web front-ends to Progress databases. We have attempted to write a simple and straightforward tool so individuals and companies can get started on the Web, learn from our work, and then develop more sophisticated tools and applications...PERL scripts that can: receive Common Gateway Interface (CGI) input from a Web server...search your Web server's CGI directory structure for a PROCGI application sub-directory...run Progress p-code or other scripts from the PROCGI application directory...return the Progress output back to your Web server...you can easily use existing text-based reports and output them to the Web."

Quest Server

Summary:

Quest Server is a concept-based search engine that uses fuzzy logic. The results of database searches are automatically converted to HTML. It uses CGI and ODBC and comes with a Windows-based authoring tool for developing applications.

Details:

URL	http://www.l5r.com/
Platforms	Windows NT, Windows 95, Windows 3.1, Unix
Web browsers	All
Web servers	Netscape, CERN, EMWAC, Website, NCSA, Alibaba, Purveyor
Data sources	ODBC
Server side interface	CGI
Client side interface	HTML
Demo copy?	Yes, at Web site

Contact:

Level Five Research
1335 Gateway Drive, Suite 2005
Melbourne, Florida 32901

Tel	(407) 729-6004, (800) 444-4303 (US & Canada)
Fax	(407) 727-7615
Email	sales@l5r.com

They say:

About Quest:

"Quest employs a powerful, unique fuzzy logic and concept-based search engine that is unavailable in any other Web-based database publishing scheme. First, Quest always returns the best answer—you never get a 'No records found' message. Using proprietary search technology, Quest is able to give you answers that best fit the criteria you are using in your search. If there isn't an exact match in your database, Quest gives you answers that are close enough. Moreover, Quest returns results visually ranked by how closely they match your personal preferences...Using Quest, the process of publishing databases on the Web is simple, straightforward and cost-effective.

No HTML, no CGI—just set up the views you want to publish using Quest's powerful Windows-based authoring tool, and you're done. Users with the most popular Web browsers can now search and explore your databases."

About collecting user data:

"With Quest, your market research is done for you. Quest enables your users to set personal preferences and specify how important each aspect of your data is to them. This invaluable, user preference information is collected by the Quest Server and made available to you, the database publisher. So you know what's important to your users and who they are."

About the development process:

"All database connectivity, fuzzy search engine settings, and search results format settings are controlled using the Quest Server Authoring Tool; an interactive Windows application. Putting a database online can take place in as little as a few minutes...Quest Server requires no HTML or CGI script coding. All input forms and search results are automatically generated in HTML format. 'Wrapper' HTML can be easily integrated so you can customize the images and layout for each database view."

About "fuzziness":

"You control what 'near' means. The fuzziness button controls how tight or loose the Search Engine will score a column value's nearness to a target."

QuickServer

Summary:

QuickServer is a Web server that is optimized to run at high speeds on LANs and uses ActiveX controls or Netscape plug-ins on the client side. It also provides tools for moving standard client/server applications to the Internet.

Details:

URL	http://www.wayfarer.com/
Platforms	Windows 95, Windows NT
Web browsers	Netscape, Microsoft
Web servers	QuickServer
Data sources	All
Server side interface	QuickServer API

Client side interface HTML, plug-ins, ActiveX
Demo copy? Yes, at Web site

Contact:

Wayfarer Communications, Inc.
1947 Landings Drive
Mountain View, CA 94043
Tel (415) 903-1720
Fax (415) 903-1730
Email info@wayfarer.com

They say:

About QuickServer:

"Wayfarer's QuickServer is an Internet application server for developing, deploying, and managing high-performance, business-critical applications for private Intranets and the Internet. QuickServer is for corporate users, system integrators, value-added resellers, and commercial software application developers who want to build new, or port existing, client/server applications to the Internet. QuickServer reduces development time by leveraging the leading client/server development tools, such as Visual Basic, PowerBuilder, Visual C++, Delphi and Java, and by eliminating the complexity of communications programming. See for yourself by downloading the 30-day evaluation version of the QuickServer SDK."

About support for Microsoft Web tools:

"...QuickServer now supports Microsoft's ActiveX controls for Internet browser applications. Application developers can build ActiveX (formerly OLE controls) using Visual Basic and other leading client/server tools and run them inside Internet Explorer 3.0 for high-performance, two-way client/server applications using QuickServer."

About support for Netscape Web tools:

"Wayfarer's plug-in for Netscape Navigator 2.0 enables application developers to build the client component of Internet applications using the leading development tools and run them inside Netscape Navigator."

About two-tiered and three-tiered architectures:

"With QuickServer, existing client/server applications can be ported to run at LAN-level performance over the Internet or an Intranet using the same client/server tools they were built with, whether Visual Basic, PowerBuilder, C++, or Java. In addition, QuickServer's integration with the leading Web browsers lets users download, launch and run mission-critical, high-performance applications from within their browser. The Wayfarer QuickServer thus fills a major gap in delivering application services to end-users over the Internet or an Intranet."

"Applications based on a two-tiered client/server architecture perform unacceptably or don't work at all on the Internet or an Intranet. With much of the application's logic residing at the client, there is extensive communications overhead between the client and server. This sharply degrades the application's performance over Internet links that are much slower than corporate LANs. Typical modem, ISDN and T1 connections (10-1,000Kbps) have 10X to 1,000X less bandwidth than Ethernet LANs (10-100Mbps). Latency, the time required to access the bandwidth, is 10X to 100X slower over the Internet or an Intranet (100ms-450ms) than on LANs (3ms-10ms), even with high-bandwidth connections."

"Although development tools do exist for building complex multitiered client/server applications, they do not leverage the substantial investments that enterprises, integrators, and VARs have already made—and wish to preserve—in the leading tools such as Microsoft's Visual Basic or PowerSoft's PowerBuilder. Moreover, they require a much higher level of programming expertise and are not geared for Internet application development."

"Not only do traditional client/server tools not support Internet applications, but the converse is also true: 'traditional' Internet tools do not support client/server applications. HTML Web servers are excellent document publishing tools, and newer environments such as active HTML will support electronic commerce, such as ordering from electronic catalogs. When these environments are used with CGI, NSAPI or ISAPI tools, they provide data access support, including the ability to create live applications. But these environments don't provide crucial data delivery components for live applications supporting two-way transactions for multiple users, and they are exceptionally difficult to program for applications any more complex than simple database queries. Furthermore, they do not leverage the enormous enterprise investment in code and expertise in the leading development tools."

"The Wayfarer QuickServer gives MIS departments, system integrators, value-added resellers (VARs), and independent software vendors (ISVs) the development, deployment, and management components they need to easily move client/server applications across the Internet or an Intranet."

"Wayfarer's multitiered architecture provides an easy-to-use platform to develop and manage high-performance client/server applications over private Intranets and the Internet. The QuickServer application server provides the data-delivery component required for high-performance Internet applications. The data-delivery component simplifies network programming, supports application partitioning and manages all data routing and delivery between client applications and data sources. By offloading network traffic from the Internet, QuickServer reduces network usage by 10X or more, delivering desktop LAN performance even on dial-up modems over the Internet, and reducing telecom costs. Using simple programming extensions to the leading development tools such as Visual Basic, developers can rapidly prototype and deploy departmental, enterprise or inter-enterprise applications. Alternatively, they can port existing client/server applications to take advantage of QuickServer's performance and security. QuickServer helps developers leverage the leading development tools. Wayfarer's flexible message formatting simplifies communications programming. Developers can deploy Wayfarer applications as Web browser plug-ins or as standalone applications. Wayfarer's security architecture guarantees the control, confidentiality, and integrity of data, transactions, systems, and users."

About Web limitations:

"...enabling client/server applications created using the leading client/server development tools to run on the Internet and Intranets at LAN-level speeds for the first time. By overcoming critical performance and security issues associated with Intranets and the Internet, the Wayfarer QuickServer is geared to make client/server computing a mainstream technology for these networks...The QuickServer Internet application server addresses fundamental shortcomings of the increasingly popular HTML/HTTP Web server and the newer Internet commerce server, which have been the tools of choice for the first wave of Web/Internet applications. While these servers are outstanding for document publishing and capable of supporting very simple database transactions, they are entirely inadequate—with respect to both performance and functionality—for supporting complex, business-critical applications. Furthermore, these traditional Internet server technologies are exceptionally difficult to program for applications any more complex than basic database queries and updates...."

"HTML and the HTTP protocol it uses to transport data are based on strings of text. HTML/HTTP is a heavyweight synchronous bandwidth user (8X and above a comparable QuickServer application), resulting in slow performance and expensive telecommunications costs. It offers no means to economically and simply format and transfer data, resulting in significant programming complexity with tools already unfamiliar to client/server developers. Finally, HTML is not connection-based, i.e., it severs contact with the server each time the user moves to a different page, introducing delays, forcing new logins and preventing the user from receiving timely application response."

About QuickServer modules:

"The Wayfarer QuickServer consists of three software core components that address the development, deployment and management of Internet-based client/server applications:...QuickServer API: programming extensions to standard tools such as Visual Basic, Visual C++, Java, and PowerBuilder. The API also lets developers run client applications as live Web browser plug-ins...QuickServer Message Router: a high-speed software message router using asynchronous messaging for data delivery and communications between client/server application partitions over the Internet or an Intranet...QuickServer Manager: systems and application management tools including critical security features."

"The QuickServer partitioning model offloads processing and storage from clients and network traffic from slow Intranets (or the Internet), pushing them onto a high-power server and high-bandwidth LAN, respectively. QuickServer developers partition applications by creating client-user presentation and server-agent components using their preferred client/server tool. The client application component provides user presentation and includes all user interface elements, information input, and display. Server agents, running on a LAN-based server machine, access one or more enterprise data sources and embody business rules and application logic."

"Between the client and server agents lies the centerpiece of QuickServer partitioning: the Windows NT-based QuickServer Message Router, a powerful software-based routing engine that transparently manages all traffic between server agents and clients—quickly and reliably. The essential and unique role of the Message Router is Internet-optimized data delivery. Data delivery comprises several functions including data formatting, data routing and delivery between data sources and clients, bandwidth optimization, store and forward, and server agent processing. The router's operations are completely transparent to application developers."

"The QuickServer Message Router uses a highly efficient messaging architecture optimized for client/server applications over Intranets or the Internet. The router's asynchronous, or event-based model overcomes the Intranet's or Internet's particularly low-bandwidth and high latency, both of which significantly degrade client/server performance."

"When used with partitioned applications, the Message Router's asynchronous messaging increases performance by a factor of 10 or more for Internet/Intranet applications, eliminating most network delays, increasing response time and reducing network traffic and telecommunications costs. The Message Router also uses a bi-directional server-push approach, rather than polling, which further reduces both traffic and usage costs."

"The combination of QuickServer's messaging and multitiered architectures yields performance breakthroughs for client/server applications running on the Internet or Intranets. Total network traffic and the number of end-to-end 'round trips' are reduced by a factor of 10 or more, yielding LAN-level response times—often tantamount to a reduction of many seconds for every transaction. Users enjoy rapid response even over dial-up modem connections, typically the slowest type of Internet/Intranet connection. The high-performance QuickServer Message Router is also highly scaleable, supporting 1,000 users at once with sustained two-way data delivery."

"Simple set of calls extends the leading client/server tools. QuickServer provides a simple set of calls for programmers to communicate between client and server agent via the Message Router. The programming extensions are integrated into the leading development tools, providing an interface to the QuickServer Message Router. By using these calls, developers are shielded from the complexities of data delivery for Internet/Intranet programming; the QuickServer Message Router manages all message dispatch and delivery transparently to the programmer."

"The QuickServer extensions, called the QuickServer API, are identical for the client and server agent and are the same in each supported language: Visual Basic, PowerBuilder, C++, Java...Thus, developers are free to use their choice of leading client/server tool, enabling rapid adoption and deployment of Internet/Intranet-based client/server applications for competitive advantage. In addition, developers can efficiently create a single version of an application that is deployable for all users on all networks—LANs and Intranets/the Internet alike—over any standard network transport. Developers can also use QuickServer to extend existing client/server applications to run over Intranets/the Internet with high-performance, management, and security, which typically amounts to only 20 percent revised code."

"Furthermore, QuickServer clients (presentation component) and server agents (data access, business rules) can be authored in different languages. For example, a server agent with intensive computational requirements might be developed in C++, while the client presentation might use Visual Basic to take advantage of rapid, user interface development."

"To further ease integration of QuickServer-extended applications within existing environments (and skill sets), QuickServer leverages the same standards built into Windows and used on the Internet. All QuickServer components reside on clients, server, and server agents as OLE custom controls (OCXs). QuickServer applications communicate directly with Winsock and TCP/IP on Windows-based computers."

"A key QuickServer feature for easing the communications programming burden is data-type independence. QuickServer's MessageValues are flexible and 'self-identifying,' eliminating the need for programmers to track data types. Used to format and exchange data between client and server agent applications, MessageValues enable programmers to format and present different data types from multiple sources such as SQL databases, custom databases, legacy systems, and live data feeds. Data types can be in any order in a message and can even be nested in other data types. This highly flexible messaging format greatly simplifies communications programming since programmers only need to format messages once and Quick Server manages all message delivery and routing."

"QuickServer enables developers to run the client component of their client/server applications inside Web browsers, including Netscape Navigator 2.0 (as plug-ins). The user's view of QuickServer applications is entirely in the context of the Web browser, but the applications are developed using standard tools and techniques. The same application code can be run within a browser (as a live Web application) or as a standalone application, or migrated from one to the other with no code change, increasing flexibility and reducing duplication of effort."

"By allowing transaction-oriented, client/server applications to run inside Web browsers, QuickServer dramatically increases the power of Web browsers for organizations that want to use browsers for business-critical applications. Unlike HTML-based applications, when QuickServer client applications run within Web browsers they continue to maintain their connection with the server (including user login and authentication) and receive and process information in the background, providing up-to-the-minute information for critical applications. Users do not need to reconnect, log in, or refresh to receive or send the latest information."

About security:

"In the extended enterprise, applications reaching users beyond corporate firewalls are more vulnerable to outside intrusion. Thus, the Wayfarer QuickServer Manager, based on Windows 95 or Windows NT, provides centralized control, management, and monitoring of system access and usage. Administrators can use the QuickServer Manager 'out of the box'; it requires no programming; only configuration of clients, QuickServer Message Routers, and server agents using a graphical Windows interface. QuickServer Manager also provides programming extensions for developers to customize management features for their specific applications."

"QuickServer Manager implements session-based authentication for clients and server agents. Each user and server agent is authenticated to the QuickServer at connect time for each session. QuickServer's authentication uses challenge/handshake exchange with a randomized key, eliminating the chance of intruders masquerading as authentic clients or server agents. Built-in user-level firewalls complement network and packet-based firewalls by providing user access on a 'need-to-know' basis. The QuickServer Manager extensible security framework provides several datastream encryption options including DES datastream encryption (for use in the U.S.) implemented for end-to-end communications between clients and server agents. RSA's RC-4 datastream encryption is also available as an optional add-in."

R:WEB

Summary:

R:WEB is a runtime version of the R:BASE database that can be integrated with a Web server. When R:WEB is installed, forms created using the R:BASE Form Designer will be converted to HTML and used over the Web. The R:BASE data integrity rules can limit what will be visible via the Web browser.

Details:

URL	http://www.microrim.com
Platforms	Windows 3.1, Windows NT, Windows 95, DOS, OS/2
Web browsers	Netscape, Microsoft, Mosaic
Web servers	All
Data sources	R:BASE, ODBC level 2
Memory required	8 MB
Disk space required	6 MB
Client side interface	HTML
FAQ	Yes, at Web site
Mailing lists	CompuServe forum at GO MICRORIM or GO R:BASE
Demo copy?	Yes, at Web site

Contact:

Microrim, Inc., a subsidiary of Abacus Software Group
15395 SE 30th Place
Bellevue, WA 98007-9918

URL	http://www.microrim.com
Tel	(206) 649-9500, (800) 628-6990 (US & Canada)
Fax	(206) 649-2785
Email	sales@microrim.com

They say:

About R:WEB:

"In brief, R:WEB directly connects your World Wide Web site to your database management system. With R:WEB, you can collect, process, and provide live data globally to Internet browsers using a single database solution. R:WEB provides 32-bit database connectivity for World Wide Web browsers such as Netscape Navigator, NCSA Mosaic, and Microsoft Internet Explorer—without requiring HTML (HyperText Markup Language) or CGI (Common Gateway Interface) programming skills."

About the development process:

"R:BASE offers Application Express, a straightforward approach to application development, Query-By-Example, R Prompt Command Line interface, Automatic Multi-User Performance, many security features, and an Interactive Debugger."

"To use R:WEB, you simply create R:WEB-compatible databases and forms using R:BASE, which is included for free in the R:WEB package as a point-and-click, database and forms design tool. You simply install R:WEB, the R:BASE forms, and the associated database on the Web server."

"...R:BASE uses the fourth-generation language (4GL) with embedded SQL for data management and manipulation and all the graphical interface design tools needed to design a truly powerful Internet database solution...R:WEB-compatible form can include objects such as: column fields, variable fields, text objects, page titles, custom push buttons, images, horizontal lines, non-editable combo boxes, checkboxes, radio buttons, field passwords, hyperlinks to other HTML documents, and background wallpaper...After saving the forms, run them on the Windows NT Web Server using R:WEB and the associated database. R:WEB-compatible forms can be associated with any R:BASE database or ODBC-compliant database without the need to make any changes to the data structure...R:WEB converts the R:BASE 5.5 form into an R:WEB form and displays it as a Web page on the WWW. R:WEB dynamically interprets and supports real-time information between the database and the Internet HTML form displayed on the end user's Web browser."

About security:

"With R:WEB using R:BASE's data integrity rules, constraints and password security, you have complete control of what information an Internet browser can or cannot access...by using R:BASE's powerful SQL GRANT/REVOKE security system, you can assign usernames and passwords to protect sensitive parts of your database system."

ROFM CGI

Summary:

ROFM CGI is a server extension program that lets you connect FileMaker Pro databases to the Web. It runs only on Macintosh computers and requires a Web server that is compatible with WebSTAR.

Details:

URL	http://rowen.astro.washington.edu/
Platforms	Mac
Web servers	WebSTAR, MacHTTP, InterServer
Data sources	FileMaker Pro
Client side interface	HTML
Server side interface	CGI

Contact:

Russell E. Owen
University of Washington Astronomy Dept.
Box 351580
Seattle, WA 98195-1580
Email   owen@astro.washington.edu

They say:

About ROFM:

"ROFM CGI allows searching, adding, modifying, and deleting records in FileMaker Pro databases via the World Wide Web. It supports multiple databases and is easy use. Features include an easy-to-use security system, return of large 'hit-lists' on multiple pages, and support for ISO-Latin1 character translation. ROFMfr, a French adaptation by François, is also available from this site...ROFM CGI allows you to serve FileMaker Pro databases to the World Wide Web (WWW). It supports searching, adding, modifying, and deleting records. Any of these operations may be separately enabled or disabled using the built-in security, and modification and deletion also have password protection. Records may be emailed, and ISO-Latin support handles some special characters."

Salvo

Summary:

Salvo is a program that allows IBM mainframe databases to be accessed via Web pages. It works with a Web browser and acts as a protocol converter that translates 3270 data streams to HTML and vice versa.

Details:

URL	http://www.simware.com/welcome.html
Platforms	Windows 3.1, Windows for Workgroups, Windows 95, Windows NT
Web browsers	HTML 2.0
Web servers	CGI capable, NT, Unix
Data sources	IBM 3270
Memory required	8 MB
Disk space required	5 MB
Client side interface	HTML
FAQ	Yes, at Web site
Demo copy?	No

Contact:

Simware, Inc.
2 Gurdwara Road
Ottawa, Ontario
Canada K2E 1A2
Tel   (613) 727-1779, (800) 267-9991 (US & Canada)
Fax   (613) 727-3533

They say:

About Salvo:

"The Salvo Personal Edition is the first PC solution to allow access to enterprise applications through a Web browser, by translating 3270 datastreams into HTML and vice versa. It is a plug-and-play application that installs on the user's PC. It requires no changes to host applications and no programming by the user. The upcoming Server Edition of Salvo will provide even greater flexibility and functionality, and is easy to install. The Salvo Server Edition will be especially useful in the construction of corporate Intranets."

About access to legacy databases:

"For many organizations, the key to making their Intranets effective will be the ability to give Web users access to the vast amounts of information provided by 10 to 20 years worth of mainframe 3270 applications. A 3270-to-HTML conversion service that allows a user with a standard Web browser to execute and interact with unmodified 3270 applications is an essential Intranet component for any enterprise with mainframe-based applications... Simware's Salvo product family uses a server-based architecture to provide 3270 access for users with Web browsers. It has many benefits that sharply lower the cost of ownership compared to traditional 3270 terminal emulators...Supports IBM mainframe or compatible applications that support terminal type 3278 Models 2 through 5...Supports National Language (NLS) for single-byte character sets...Salvo does not require any special software, other than TCP/IP, to run on a mainframe...Salvo will run with any 3270 screen-based application running on CICS, VM, MVS, or TSO...There is no need to change your 3270 application to use Salvo."

About connectivity:

"Supports locally attached PCs to a TCP/IP network, or remotely attached PCs via dial-up SLIP, or PPP (for example, with A2B for remote LAN access). Supports any TCP/IP kernel that is WSA 1.1 compliant. The following TCP/IP kernels have been tested to ensure compatibility: A2B TCP/IP Kernel, Wollongong Pathway Runtime TCP/IP Kernel 4.0, FTP OnNet 2.0, and Microsoft TCP/IP."

About security:

"Salvo Personal Edition will work with existing host security systems such as RACF or ACF2. Since Web communications are transaction-based and not session-based, Salvo also provides session security on a transaction-by-transaction basis...If you use Salvo over the Internet, you can achieve security with secure connections, such as S-HTTP and SSL...Salvo Personal Edition does not require any Web server software. It uses TN3270 for connections to a mainframe."

About firewalls:

"Salvo Personal Edition will only work to a host site that can be accessed via TN3270. If a corporate firewall restricts TN3270 access to a mainframe from the Internet, Salvo Personal Edition will not work...if the Web server is placed outside the firewall and the Salvo Server is placed inside the firewall, then Internet users can be allowed access to the host applications."

About differences between Salvo and other 3270 emulation software:

"Since the user is interacting with Web Browser software and not a 3270-like device (or emulation software), there are certain usability issues that are different: User cannot use keyboard function keys (F1-F12) to submit 3270 aid keys. Instead, users click the appropriate button on the HTML generated form. Salvo displays the mainframe applications PF key descriptions as buttons on the HTML-generated pages (for example, 'PF1=Help' would show an HTML button labeled 'Help'). Salvo can present a static keypad on the bottom of each HTML page with configurable PF key combinations. As HTML does not transmit cursor position, for mainframe applications that require field-specific input (i.e., the cursor must be in a specific location prior to submission) Salvo uses a secondary HTML form that allows the user to select the specific field prior to submission. Using the buttons on your Web browser, you can view previous 3270 application screens, but you cannot resubmit them."

Sapphire/Web

Summary:

Sapphire/Web is a Web database development system. It comes with a visual development environment and generates CGI programs in C or C++ source code from specifications. It also comes with its own database API.

Details:

URL	http://www.bluestone.com
Platforms	SGI, SUN, HP, IBM, DECAlpha, Windows NT
Web browsers	Netscape, Internet Explorer, Spyglass, Mosaic, Lynx
Web servers	Netscape, IIS, OpenMarket, NCSA, CERN
Data sources	Informix, Oracle, Sybase, SQL Server, ODBC
Server side interface	CGI
Client side interface	HTML, Java, JavaScript, VRML
FAQ	Yes, at Web site
Demo copy?	Yes, at Web site

Contact:

Bluestone, Inc.
1000 Briggs Road
Mt. Laurel, NJ 08054
Tel   (609) 727-4600, (408) 451-8444
Fax   (609) 778-8125, (408) 437-4945
Email   info@bluestone.com

They say:

About Sapphire/Web:

"Sapphire/Web is a powerful client/server, application development tool designed specifically for creating inter- and intra-enterprise applications running on the World Wide Web. Sapphire/Web creates applications that use HTML as the cross-platform user interface language, running with Oracle, Sybase, Informix, Microsoft SQL, and ODBC databases, as well as application objects and legacy applications. Sapphire/Web has a powerful visual programming paradigm that drastically reduces the coding effort normally associated with developing Web applications."

About visual development environment:

"...an easy-to-use environment to reduce training and speed development... Point and click interface...Automatic CGI generation (no hand coding)...Toolbars with HoverHelp (unique in Unix products)...Context-sensitive help documentation in HTML (>700 pages)...Database browser...HTML previewer with hook to user's favorite browser...."

About open architecture:

"...take advantage of the full features of other tools, platforms and databases...Sapphire/Web tool can be extended with custom APIs and objects. For example, the database table components...Generates C or C++ code for performance and security....Integrates with code management and debugging tools for large project teams and complex applications.. .Allows for custom coding in C, C++, callable objects beyond the visual programming level....Supports full SQL and stored procedures for power applications....Supports application objects—beyond databases to any function, files, or executable for legacy application support...."

About the development process:

"Sapphire/Web is designed to work in a manner similar to other application builders for Windows and Motif...Create your HTML forms (for data input and request) and HTML templates (which will hold data returned to the end user from your application). These can be created in your favorite HTML authoring tool such as Microsoft FrontPage or Word, HoTMetaL, SGI's WebAuthor, or any of the emerging sets of tools for creating these documents. Any tool may be fully integrated into Sapphire/Web...Create application logic. Browse and create your application objects from Sapphire/Web. These can be: stored procedures in your database, dynamic SQL, functions, executables, file (for read and write)...Bind user interface objects to application objects. Select the appropriate object, and Sapphire/Web will bring up a 'bind editor' with appropriate arguments, results and special editors. Select via context-sensitive option menus or drag and drop from your HTML documents onto the bind editor. This 'binds' HTML elements such as a text input field or an option menu to arguments; and results, returning from your object to other HTML elements such as an ordered list or table. Sapphire/Web automatically populates the returned data into your HTML templates...Add conditional processing code, or modify the default methods of populating data...Generate code in pure C or C++. This generates a CGI program for immediate use. It is that simple—without writing a single line of code. Sapphire/Web also provides for testing and loading of the CGI program in the specified, HTTP server CGI directory."

About supported object types:

"...Dynamic SQL, stored procedures, functions, executables, files, OLE on Windows 95 and NT...Sapphire/Web's open architecture allows reuse of existing code. For example, stored procedures may already exist for implementing current client/server applications. Sapphire/Web can fully reuse these stored procedures without any changes. Sapphire/Web also supports the ability to register pre-existing functions in the tool. This makes it simple to put an HTML interface on existing applications since most applications are already modularized in functions, or can be wrapped as function calls."

About compatibility with other tools:

"Sapphire/Web's open architecture allows for integration with leading tools—providing a professional development environment. This includes leading software development environments such as Visual C++, Borland C++, SoftBench, SPARCWorks, CodeCenter, ObjectCenter, and SGI's development kit. In addition, it can be used on larger projects in conjunction with products such as PVCS, Visual SourceSafe, RCS, SCCS, or ClearCase...When used in C++ mode, it can be integrated with various class libraries, such as Rogue Wave's Tools.h++, and advanced C++ tools such as Look!...One of the most important features of Sapphire/Web is that it allows you to use the database vendor's native SQL. This means you can stay within the standard SQL and get portability, or you can take full advantage of the features of the specific database vendor of your choice—such as PL/SQL for Oracle, and TransactSQL for Sybase."

About comparison to other client/server development tools:

"Sapphire/Web is similar to leading client/server development tools such as PowerBuilder, SQL/Windows and Bluestone's own db-UIM/X in many ways. For example, it allows you to develop a complete client/server application without having to worry about the underlying network infrastructure, and the visual programming environment improves productivity. It is similar to db-UIM/X in that it uses standard C and C++, and supports the native SQL implementations of the database vendors (a different strategy than PowerBuilder)."

About the Sapphire/Web Gateway:

"Bluestone developed the Sapphire/Web Gateway based on the CORBA standards to facilitate a transparent network architecture to our tools. This is not meant to be a complete implementation (for example, it does not include IDL)—and implements only specific functions needed for communicating to databases. The Sapphire/Web Gateway can run in conjunction with a general-purpose gateway, such as Orbix, or DSOM...Specifically, the gateway implements only two types of functions—first to get the metadata about a database, and second to execute something—whether it is raw SQL being passed by the client, or a stored procedure, or a remote function, file, or executable...There can be multiple gateways running on the network, and they can run anywhere on the network. Clients talk to gateways based on a 'seed' number that can be set through a convenient resource setting. The NT version implements the gateway as standard NT services and includes a graphical interface for managing distributed gateways."

About the Sapphire/Web API:

"Bluestone has publicly documented its API layer. This can be used for hand coding Web applications in a much easier manner than can be done using native database calls, or scripting languages. It also ensures portability and openness for developers using Sapphire/Web's advanced features for increased productivity and functionality. Source code is also available to ensure portability."

Sibylla

Summary:

Sibylla is a software development kit for creating server extension programs for several databases, including those that support the Visigenic ODBC driver on Unix. It uses the TCL language with special Sibylla extensions.

Details:

URL	http://www.cib.unibo.it/guests/ariadne/ sibylla/sibyllaeng.html
Platforms	SunOS 4.1.3, HP-UX 9.0, OSF1 1.3, Linux, VMS
Data sources	BasisPlus, Informix, Ingres, SQL Server, mSQL, Oracle, Sybase, ODBC
Demo copy?	No

Contact:

Via Campeggi 13
27020 Torre d'Isola (PV)
Italy

Tel	+39 382 407538
Fax	+39 382 407538
Email	ricotti@ariadne.it

They say:

About Sibylla:

"Sibylla is an application development framework for World Wide Web-based application...Sibylla allows the access, through Internet or TCP/IP LAN, to data stored in a database, to indexed HTML files or, in general, to data managed by a server-side application...Sibylla lies between the information sources (e.g., a database), the user application, and the WWW server.

The user application is a custom application and defines, for each application, how the user can interact with the information sources...."

About the development process:

"Software developed with Sibylla is organized in simple modules that allow rapid application definition and prototyping together with simplicity in integrating external applications. Sibylla modules are written with the innovative, non-proprietary, shell-like Tool Command Language (Tcl), which makes it easy to develop tests programmatically. Tcl is respected in the industry as robust and easy to learn...According to our experience, the single Tcl/Sibylla average program does not require more than 80 lines of code; this results in a user application with a plain structure and consequently in rapid prototyping and short development time...Sibylla allows fast development and prototyping. With Sibylla you just write the Tcl/Sibylla script, save it, and run it. You do not have to load procedures into the database or compile anything. And if something goes wrong, the Sibylla script returns the detailed Tcl interpreter stack trace in HTML format. This powerful debugging system allows you to trap database error messages, Tcl code errors, and server errors, thus locating in a few seconds where the system has failed. The dynamic HTML document can be written using your favorite HTML editor and then pasted into the Sibylla script. You are not bored in learning new pseudo-HTML functions, nor are you limited to the HTML tags of the Web tools you are using. In addition, using a SGML-compliant HTML editor, you are sure that your dynamic documents are HTML compliant."

About portability across platforms:

"Sibylla architecture has been designed to guarantee complete portability of user application among different hardware and OSs where Sibylla is available."

SiteBase (formerly Hype-It)

Summary:

SiteBase is a Web server with a built-in relational database. It includes a dBase-like development language and text searching capabilities.

Details:

URL	http://www.cykic.com
Platforms	Windows NT

Web browsers	All
Web servers	Hype-It
Data sources	FoxPro, dBASE, Clipper
Memory required	8 MB
Disk space required	80 MB
Server side interface	CGI
Client side interface	HTML
FAQ	Yes, at Web site
Demo copy?	Yes, at Web site

Contact:

Cykic Software, Inc.
123 Camino De La Reina, Suite N200
San Diego, CA 92108
Tel   (619) 220-7970, (800) 295-4295 (US & Canada)
Email   Cykic@cykic.com

They say:

About SiteBase:

"...built-in HTML editor, link trees, graphical user interface throughout, support for TrueSpeech, Java Script, point and click ISMAP creation (clickable regions within images), automatic linking of forms into databases with report writer, point and click creation of databases and reports, SMTP mail server, FTP server, Telnet server with built-in HTML converter, automatic server reports and graphs, powerful text search engine, and models with easy-to-use built-in CGI scripting and full relational database programmability, to the easy installation with GUI setup and full on-screen help both context-sensitive and searchable...Supports a multi-user, multitasking program development (dBase-like dot prompt) environment... Allows the programmer to create CGI programs to function with HTML documents...Supports native xBase language—a composite of FoxPro, dBase, Clipper, and more than 150 function extensions...Supports a relational database for Web applications...Supports powerful search functions for text or data search requirements...Includes graphics library for image manipulation and graphic image database types...Includes fax functions to tie into the Web application (fax-back abilities)...Supports programmers tools for debugging; cross-referencing; text editing...Supports multiple workstations for program development across a LAN...Gives programmers TCP/IP functions for direct access to the Internet: ping a site, send email, reverse name look-up, etc...."

About searching:

"...comes with a built-in search engine. Just enter key words or phrases in this field to find a list of documents where these words occur. A space or + sign between words means 'and,' the vertical bar | means 'or.' 'HTML+server+PC | CGI' is a proper search request."

Software Engine

Summary:

Software Engine is a development system for creating Web database applications. It requires a Sybase database and generates an application from a database schema. HTML forms and tables are generated automatically, and it also creates Java applications without programming.

Details:

URL	http://www.engine.com
Platforms	SunOS 4.1.3 and up, Solaris 2.3 and up
Web servers	All that run on Sun
Data sources	Sybase
Memory required	16 MB
Disk space required	55 MB
Server side interface	CGI, Java Application Server
Client side interface	HTML, Java applet
FAQ	Yes, at Web site
Demo copy?	Yes, at Web site

Contact:

Software Engines, Inc.
129 Washington Street, Suite 400
Hoboken, NJ 07030
Tel   (201) 963-7731
Fax   (201) 963-0768
Email   eric@engine.com

They say:

About the development process:

"Generates all input and output HTML pages automatically...No need to learn, program or implement complicated third-party software interfaces such as Java and Sybase. The Software Engine interface is GUI-oriented, yet keeps an open Unix-style philosophy. The application is driven by metadata, and no code is generated. Maintenance is therefore a trivial task."

About reporting:

"Tables are visually displayed on the Netscape screen in Netscape table format, based on search queries. The Java interface presents a similar table that can interactively be updated directly to the database. A full-featured report generator is also included in the product."

About queries, inserts, updates, and deletes:

"All SQL code to access the database is generated automatically (on the fly) based on the user interaction. A query form is created for each object in the application. Inserts occur by filling data in the form and clicking the Insert button. Updates occur by point and click in the Java interface and with an extra button click in the HTML interface. A delete occurs after a search was executed. The user selects the row to be deleted from the collection of rows obtained by the search and clicks the delete button."

About input validations:

"Table-lookup, dates, and ranges are all supported and occur automatically. Table-lookups can incorporate complex data relationships without programming. An open server-side API supports the rarely needed addition of proprietary code for complex validation."

About transaction control:

"All connections are short-lived. The application preserves state logically, but is physically stateless as far as the server is concerned. This much is also true for the Java applet interface. Single statement transactions are executed automatically and protected by the Sybase automatic transaction facilities. Multi-statement transactions are created by defining objects that hold the transaction information. Then a single server call executes the transaction as a single unit of operation."

About security:

"User authentication, secure transmission, and firewalls are all supported. Depending on the security level of the Web server, the Web browser and the firewall in place, any security level can be accomplished. The Sybase security mechanisms are typically also leveraged for this purpose in combination with client/server authentication."

Abut programming languages:

"Being able to design a database schema is required. Software Engine generates full features applications without any programming...while it is rarely needed, knowledge of SQL, HTML, C, C++, Java, Unix Shells (csh, ksh, sh), or scripting facilities like awk, perl, sed, etc., can all be leveraged to create more refined applications."

Spider

Summary:

Spider is a Web database development system that consists of Spider Development—a visual development tool—and Spider Deployment, which runs applications.

Details:

URL	http://www.w3spider.com
Platforms	Sun Solaris 2.3 and up, HP-UX 9.05 and up, IRIX 5.3, Windows NT, Windows 95
Web servers	All
Data sources	Informix, Sybase, Oracle7, ODBC
Server side interface	CGI, NSAPI, ISAPI
Client side interface	HTML, JAVA, JavaScript
FAQ	Yes, at Web site
Demo copy?	Yes, at Web site

Contact:

Spider Technologies, Inc.
1054 Elwell Court
Palo Alto, CA 94303
Tel   (415) 969-6665
Fax   (415) 969-6883
Email   info@w3spider.com

They say:

About Spider:

"Spider 1.5 is a robust Web database application solution that integrates visual development with a high-performance deployment engine. Developers can quickly and easily develop and maintain Web database applications using the visual development environment. These applications are executed by the Spider 1.5 deployment engine. This engine delivers unrivaled performance, scaleability, and reliability...Spider is an open solution that integrates easily with existing hardware and software environments. Additionally, Spider's architecture is designed to adapt easily to new technologies as they emerge. This protects a company's current and long-term investment."

About security:

"Interoperable with Web server, firewall, and database security mechanisms and provides interface for custom security features."

About programming languages:

"No programming languages are required in the visual interface...Supports SQL, stored procedures, JAVA, Javascripts."

About the development process:

"...Open an HTML file in the HTML viewer. This file can be created ahead of time in an HTML editor, or can be a file that is dynamically generated from the database by another application file...Select the action on the database: query, insert, update, delete, stored procedure. Define the SQL statement in the SQL editor. The SQL editor supports multiple clauses and table joins. Define output, by dragging columns or tables from the output fields list...Customize output, error handling, and security restrictions. Save the file...In deployment, the Spider deployment module will dynamically generate the SQL as input to the database and HTML as output to the browser."

About architecture and technology:

"...Spider is an open solution. Developers are free to choose the Web server, HTML editor, Unix platform, and relational database that best suit their needs. In addition, developers are able to standardize on one technology for developing and deploying Web database applications from different types of relational databases...Spider is based on an object-oriented architecture and patented technology, PowerConnect, which makes it extremely easy to support new technologies in user interfaces, such as JAVA and PDF, and databases. This guarantees developers that the efforts expended today can be incorporated into solutions that take advantage of tomorrow's technology...."

About database connections:

"Web database applications are currently deployed via the Common Gateway Interface (CGI). CGI is the current standard method for interfacing external applications with HTTP servers. CGI programs are executed in real-time and output dynamic information. Web servers typically specify one directory as a CGI directory, in which users store executable programs. CGI, however, has certain limitations, among them speed and scaleability. Spider's deployment engine addresses these issues, providing developers with an alternative standard that is robust and suitable for the workgroup and enterprise...Spider 1.5 deployment is a resident program that maintains multiple open connections to the database. This dramatically reduces the time involved in executing Web database applications, because it eliminates the time involved in forking a new process, opening the database, and closing the database. Current benchmarking places the speed of Spider 1.5 at ten times faster than standard CGI...."

SQL~Surfer

Summary:

SQL~Surfer is a CGI server extension program that connects relational databases to the Web. It comes with a macro language (statements are embedded in HTML documents) and has capabilities for generating reports as Web pages.

Details:

URL	http://www.netaway.com/
Platforms	Solaris, HP-UX, AIX, IRIX, Windows NT
Web browsers	All
Web servers	All
Data sources	ODBC, SQL Server, Informix, Oracle, Sybase
Memory required	2 MB
Disk space required	10 MB
Server side interface	CGI, NSAPI, ISAPI
Client side interface	HTML 2 & 3, VRML, Java, JavaScript
Demo copy?	Yes, at Web site

Contact:

NETAWAY (SA)
105, rue des Moines
Paris, France 75017
Tel   (+33 1) 40 25 47 11
Fax   (+33 1) 40 25 47 14
Email   infocust@netaway.com

They say:

About SQL~Surfer:

"SQL~Surfer...generic Web/SQL gateway gives you a simple and efficient way to publish relational data on the Web and to easily create full-scale client/server applications on Wide (like Internet) and/or Local (Intranet) Area Networks...SQL~Surfer lets you access databases from your Web browser by dynamically handling SQL statements in HTML pages. You see up-to-date information that can be used immediately as input for Java Classes in your HTML pages. So, without developing or generating any CGI scripts, you quickly build top-level GUI client/server applications."

"SQL~Surfer has been conceived to be both a natural extension of HTML and a natural tool to query relational databases. The product consists of two components:...The SQL~Surfer engine, a cooperative group of processes, split over coordinated CGI executables and persistent database gateways...SQL@Way, a set of macro commands that can be directly embedded in HTML pages to give them a SQL-like flavor. Embedded SQL@Way macros are read and dynamically interpreted by the SQL~Surfer engine...SQL~Surfer presents itself as a CGI executable 'cgi-proc' that is called in the standard HTML way by appending arguments to its URL...."

About performance:

"The functional split between a minimum CGI stub executable and persistent gateways maintaining database connections offers a significant increase in performance over simpler architectures where large CGI executables have to be forked and a database connection re-established for each call. If appropriate for the platform, several instances of the same database gateway can be started in parallel. SQL~Surfer automatically balances loads between the gateways obtaining maximum performance from SMP systems."

About SQL@Way macros:

"SQL~Surfer, a fully HTML- and CGI-compliant engine, lets you write SQL@Way macros into HTML pages using your HTML editor. With SQL@Way, you can quickly create without development efforts a relational database-based Web server from scratch or easily integrate database access into existing HTML pages. SQL@Way, an SQL extension of HTML, can be thought of as SQML (System Query Markup Language)."

About reports:

"Master/Detail relationships between database tables can easily be captured through SQL@Way and output either in a nested report or break into Master/Detail HTML pages coordinated by means of dynamically generated embedded URLs...End user can interactively and dynamically sort a report on different columns with a simple click on column header."

About database connectivity:

"The SQL~Surfer engine knows how to connect to the most popular RDBMS engines today on the market. This makes your HTML pages with embedded SQL@Way RDBMS independent...Cursor navigation or n by n fetch. If a query returns many rows at once, they can be retrieved in several fetches rather in a single prohibitively large set. If supported by the underlying RDBMS, SQL~Surfer supports cursor navigation in both forward or backward mode...Persistent database gateways with automatic load balancing enable SQL~Surfer to deliver high performance."

About transaction and state management:

"One way to consider HTML documents with embedded RDBMS queries is to think about them as classical client/server database applications over a Wide Area Network (WAN). Such applications most of the time need to have connections to the database maintained throughout the end user's working sessions. This is necessary for elaborate application logic as well as for delivering reasonable performance...On the other hand, the HTTP server 'httpd' is stateless, meaning that it does not remember anything from one call to the next. This is all very well for a server specialized in fetching plain-text files, but is lacking when trying to build complex database applications...To get out of this quandary, SQL~Surfer gateways maintain user contexts. A context is a memory structure where the characteristics of a user session are stored. This information is enough to enable the engine to act as a proxy to keep connections opened to the database. Moreover this allows an application to memorize its state(s) between user interactions. The session identifier is generated by the gateway when the session is initiated and transferred between client and gateway for each call and answer."

"...SQL~Surfer maintains one or several connections to the database and maintains client contexts. Client contexts are multiplexed on database connections resulting in less resource allocation. Client contexts are used to: keep state between client and server (so reducing network traffic), handle database cursor, so client has control on array fetch, a sequence/key is used so a context cannot be captured by another client...When a client performs a query, it has choice (default or defined in templates with SQL@way) to use: a common database connection (when selecting only or in autocommit mode), selecting is most of what a client does, no extra resources are allocated in this case...a specific database connection (when beginning transaction). Beginning transaction is implicit when entering a non-select request and not in autocommit mode...Ending transaction is explicit when commit or rollback is done using HTML arguments...."

About pooled database connections:
"...a pool of database connections is available, avoiding many database connection/disconnection sequences, more connections may be done if required."

About security:
"System level security is achieved using a Web server that implements good security features and using firewalls...Applicative security is achieved using user authentication (login/password) for a whole application and/or using request against applicative SQL tables that contain the authentication information."

About SQL~Surfer Directory:
"...is an SQL~Surfer application that offers your company a complete multimedia corporate directory you can configure to match your needs. As it is based on X.500 directory concepts, it has powerful searching capabilities and information fields can be easily added."

SQLGate

Summary:

SQLGate is a server extension program that uses CGI to connect MiniSQL databases to the Web. It works by embedding SQL statements in HTML documents.

Details:

URL	http://think.ucdavis.edu/~cgi/SQLGate/index.html
Platforms	Linux
Server side interface	CGI
Client side interface	HTML
Demo copy?	Yes, at Web site

Contact:

J. Fritz Barnes
Graduate Group in Computer Science
1943 Gauguin Place
Davis, CA 95616
Tel   (916) 754-9470
Email   jfbarnes@ucdavis.edu

They say:

About SQLGate:

"The SQLGate package is a CGI-bin program that provides the capability to access a database from World Wide Web browsers. Information in the database is available for anyone surfing the Web. To provide information that ties in information from the database, the information provider embeds SQL commands in the regular HyperText Markup Language (HTML), World Wide Web documents...The SQLGate package is designed to simplify access to databases from the WWW. Use of the SQLGate program should drastically reduce the time it takes to create interfaces from your World Wide Web documents to your database. The SQLGate package is intended to be used by someone with a strong understanding of HTML, a minimum of knowledge of SQL, and some basic programming experience, since the embedded SQL commands are similar to a script language."

About SQLGate features:

"Provides access from the WWW to information in databases...Provides flexibility, and easy maintenance of WWW gateways to databases. Information providers do not have to write a new program for every information access application...Allows use of conditions to tailor a WWW page to the current situation...Utilizes access to the mSQL or MiniSQL database...."

SQLWeb

Summary:

SQLWeb is a CGI server extension program that connects a large variety of DBMS products to the Web, including legacy and ODBC systems. It uses special tags that are embedded in HTML documents.

Details:

URL	http://www.sqlWeb.com/
Platforms	Windows NT, Sun OS, Solaris, HP-UX, PTX, SCO
Web browsers	Netscape, Microsoft
Web servers	Open Market, Netscape, CERN
Data sources	ODBC, Oracle, Sybase, Informix
Server side interface	CGI
Client side interface	HTML

Contact:

Don Schindhelm
SQLWeb Technologies, Inc.
Tel   (410) 203-1999
Email   dschindh@cst.com

They say:

About SQLWeb:

"The SQLWeb Interactive Server provides fully dynamic database interactivity. It activates events based on your rules and criteria, stored in the database, which you can easily catalog and update. In technical terms, it inserts, updates, deletes, queries and executes triggers and stored procedures. It changes its appearance based on the data available to it. It takes orders, places orders, sends messages and interacts with legacy systems on your internal network or through Internet connections."

About database interfaces:

"The SQLWeb Interactive Server contains an uncomplicated open database layer that is entirely open. It allows the entry of new HTML tags. It enables configuring the server to use any database or network for which there is an adequate 'C' code API. The open layer provides 'User Exits' that easily interface the SQLWeb Interactive Server with existing applications. It also accommodates specialized drivers, if desired. For those who do not want to do it themselves, SQLWeb provides the source code needed to interface with Oracle, Sybase, or Informix. The SQLWeb Interactive Server includes the libraries, the database-interface source code of choice, and the 'make file' for easy compilation and installation. SQLWeb Technologies, Inc. will gladly compile and install the SQLWeb Interactive Server."

About special tags:

"The SQLWeb author achieves all of this interactivity and the resulting dynamic scenario using three new tags (cursor, if, include). The author builds SQLWeb pages applying the same declarative authoring paradigm and tools used for static pages (i.e., markup tags with attributes, text, etc.). Then SQLWeb easily creates the database interactions without any complicated programming. There is no PERL or C programming required."

About reverse-engineering existing Web pages:

"Included with the server is The SQLWeb Tool Kit that enables the reverse-engineering of existing or newly authored Web pages. It also provides tools for the maintenance of the Web-pages database."

Tango

Summary:

Tango is a development tool for integrating SQL databases with Macintosh Web servers via CGI. It uses a visual development interface so it can be used by people with no knowledge of SQL or HTML.

Details:

URL	http://www.everyware.com/
Platforms	Mac, Unix, Windows NT, Windows 95
Web servers	All CGI Mac-based Web servers
Data sources	ODBC level 1
Memory required	5 MB

Disk space required	2.5 MB
Server side interface	CGI
Client side interface	HTML
FAQ	Yes, at Web site
Mailing lists	Tango-Talk, Butler SQL-Talk, Bolero-Talk
Demo copy?	Yes, at Web site

Contact:

EveryWare Development Corp.

7145 West Credit Avenue, Bldg. 1

Mississauga, Ontario

Canada L5N 6J7

Tel	(905) 819-1173 ext 262, (888) 819-2500 (US & Canada)
Fax	(905) 819-1172
Email	info@everyware.com
FTP	205.189.228.11

They say:

About the development process:

"Tango provides Webmasters the ability to rapidly create online solutions that interact with databases without writing any code."

About reporting:

"...summary, tables, group-by's...."

About input validation:

"...database server validation or JavaScript...."

TEC Webserver

Summary:

TEC Webserver is an HTTP Web server that connects directly to Area Code: Oracle and Sybase databases. It uses its own proprietary connection between the Web server and the database (i.e., not CGI). Application development is done using HTML and SQL. An administrator tool called TECAdmin comes with TECWeb and can be used for administering both the Web pages and the database.

Details:

URL	http://www.tecs.com/
Platforms	Solaris, HP-UX
Web servers	comes with its own server
Data sources	Oracle 7, Sybase
Memory required	10 MB
Disk space required	3 MB
Server side interface	Direct
Client side interface	HTML
FAQ	Yes, at Web site
Demo copy?	No

Contact:

TEC Solutions, Inc.
19672 Stevens Creek Blvd., Suite 169
Cupertino, CA 95014

Tel	(408) 973-8855
Fax	(408) 973-8979
Email	sales@tecs.com
FTP	ftp://ftp.tecs.com/

They say:

About TECWeb Server:

"The TECWeb Server is a superset of standard Web servers and can maintain multiple, concurrent client logons to multiple RDBMSs from multiple vendors. HTML-like tags in Web page definitions allow the user to specify what information is to be obtained from the RDBMS and where in the Web page the information is to be inserted. This provides for very flexible, dynamic HTML generation based on the amount of information obtained from the RDBMS as well as the content itself. Web content changes automatically with changes in RDBMS content...TECWeb Servers leverage the skills and tools of existing database staffs, shorten development and publishing times, and have superior cost of ownership advantages for WWW publishing on large, commercial WWW sites."

About features:

"Session variables for communications between pages...System variables for date, browser type, user and server IP addresses, etc....Customized responses tailored to the user and browser based on system variable values...TECWeb Server and RDBMS server can be on same or different machines...Support for multiple domains on the same machine...Support for secure client/server communications using separate daemons for PCT, S-HTTP, or Netscape's SSL...Use standard reporting tools to generate site usage reports...."

About reporting:

"All reporting data is stored in standard SQL tables. Any reporting tool can be used."

About data manipulation:

"...done by direct commands to the SQL engine. Can use stored procedure calls or direct SQL commands."

About input validations:

"...all that are available through SQL."

About transaction control:

"The DBMS, as specified by the designers or the site manager, determines how to respond to a user's request and directly manages any context for the user."

TILE & TGate

Summary:

TILE converts information stored in Lotus Notes databases to Web pages. It manages links and automatically builds tables of contents. TGate works the other way and is a tool for updating Lotus Notes databases from a form on a Web page. It is written in PERL and comes with source code.

Details:

URL	http://www.shelby.com/
Platforms	Windows 3.1, Windows 95, Windows NT, Mac, OS/2, Solaris
Web servers	All
Data sources	Lotus Notes
Memory required	16 MB
Disk space required	10 MB
Server side interface	CGI
Client side interface	HTML
Demo copy?	Yes, at Web site

Contact:

Shelby Group Ltd.
4618 Maple Avenue
Bethesda, MD 20814
Tel   (301) 718-7840
Fax   (301) 654-3713
Email   info@shelby.com
FTP   ftp://ftp.shelby.com/pub/wsg/

They say:

About TILE:

"Word-processing, WYSIWYG ease in writing documents...Automatic building of table of contents, indexes, and multiple pathways to all your documents...Managed hypertext links: you'll never get a dead link with TILE. No more 'the requested document could not be found'...Consistent look and feel, which you can customize to your organizational standards...TILE can read databases residing locally or on any Lotus Notes server, regardless of platform. TILE can run interactively and as a standalone conversion server on all these platforms...Can be run manually or automatically, keeping a database and Web site in perfect synchronization...The HTML documents that TILE creates can be automatically made accessible on a Web server running on the same machine, on a networked machine, or copied to a Web server running on any computer platform."

About TGate:

"...if you maintain a World Wide Web site, and want Internet users of your site to be able to sign a guest book, make a purchase, or request more information: TGate will accept these submissions and put the data in the Lotus Notes database of your choosing. Lotus Notes users in your organization can then act upon this information."

TGate features:

"Support for all HTML form features, including text boxes, checkboxes, radio buttons, drop-down listboxes and multi-select list boxes...Does not require a Lotus Notes server running on the same machine as TGate. A Lotus Notes client and WWW server is all that is needed...Can add the data to a local Lotus Notes database, or any remote Lotus Notes database your Lotus Notes client has access to...Ability to require fields to be filled in. If the required pieces of information are missing, the person submitting the information is told what these are, and is given the opportunity to add the information and resubmit...Support for Lotus Notes data types. Fields can be created in Notes as text, rich text, number, number list and text list. Support for multi-selection boxes. TGate does automatic type checking and conversion on number, number list and text list field types...All the environment variables your Web browser passes can be automatically saved in your Lotus Notes document along with the user submission. The environment variables specify things such as the user's Internet address and domain, the user's Web browser software, and many other things...Full source code to TGate is included—you can extend the program to suit your particular needs. TGate is written in PERL, and a PERL language interpreter is included with TGate...."

Toolkit Internet

Summary:

Toolkit Internet is a royalty-free library of Visual Basic procedures that work with the O'Reilly WebSite Web server to connect databases to Web pages. It includes Survey Internet, which is a tool for developing surveys for the Internet, and several other application-specific Web database programs.

Details:

URL	http://highsierra.com/highsierra/products.htm
Platforms	Windows NT
Web browsers	All forms-capable
Web servers	Netscape, Microsoft IIS, WebSite
Data sources	Access, FoxPro, dBase, Paradox
Server side interface	CGI
Client side interface	HTML
Demo copy?	No

Contact:

Aufrance Associates
PO Box 19338
South Lake Tahoe, CA 96151
Tel   (916) 577-5709
Fax   (916) 577-9017
Email   tmaufr@highsierra.com

They say:

About Toolkit Internet:

"...what Visual Basic developers need to write database Web systems...Toolkit Internet is a tool for the serious programmer who needs the versatility and capability of a 'computationally complete' language such as Visual Basic to create database-to-Internet systems. Instead of being limited by SQL-only or other 'programming free' or 'GUI' tools, Toolkit Internet provides a set of Visual Basic classes and functions to help you get the job done...Toolkit Internet provides direct access to Access databases or any file attached to an Access database (FoxPro, Paradox or whatever else can be attached to Access)...In a nutshell, the Toolkit lets your Visual Basic program take database information and 'plug it into' special HTML template field tags, or retrieves information from the special HTML template field tags to be edited, processed or 'plugged back into your database'...."

About Survey Internet:

"...Internet-to-database for marketing lead collection or any information gathering...A great tool for generating leads, customer responses or gathering just about any information you want! Survey Internet lets you set up your own questionnaire without programming. Then, Survey Internet collects user responses into a Microsoft Access database, which you can view and print either with your Web browser or by using Microsoft Access. Survey Internet also provides a business system to keep track of your survey customers, their surveys and database tables, and also their billing!... Customizable survey form and database record layout allows you to collect any information you desire, using any Web browser, such as Netscape. You can define more than one survey form per customer. Each survey form collects data into its own corresponding table in the database. Collect data into a Microsoft Office compatible database, which can be used with other office functions and marketing processes, such as to create mailings or to analyze the data each survey collects. The information in the database can be retrieved using any Web browser. Survey Internet keeps track of what records your customers have retrieved using your Web browser...."

About Real Estate Internet:

"...a full business solution for real estate advertising and billing...Real Estate Internet lets real estate agents enter their own information about their listings and their professional profiles into a database, using their own Web browser! Then, REI automatically generates Web pages from the information in the database, giving each agent control over the content of his or her Agency Page, Agent Page, and Property Pages. Also, Real Estate Internet automatically bills each realtor for the Web pages they create. Billing can be accomplished via secure credit card transactions...."

About Calendar Internet:

"...interactive data entry of events via any Web browser...automatic and customizable transaction-based fee per event, if desired...search-for-events form can be used by any Web browser...search by event type, date, location and other categories...wall calendar allows finding events for a particular day...list of participating organizations includes links to each organization's events...event descriptions can include HTML code, hot links, text formatting and graphics...password-protected edit form provides security for each organization's events...credit card data entry is password protected and encrypted...database includes organizations, events, charges and back-office processes for customer lists, invoicing, and other important business tasks...."

WDB

Summary:

WDB is a software toolkit for integrating databases with Web pages without writing code. It uses CGI and works with Sybase, Informix, and MiniSQL. The developer writes 'Form Definition Files' that describe views of the database and WDB generates HTML documents from the descriptions.

Details:

URL	http://arch-http.hq.eso.org/bfrasmus/wdb/
Platforms	SunOS, IRIX, Microport SVR4, AIX
Web browsers	All
Web servers	NCSA
Data sources	Sybase, Informix
Server side interface	CGI
Client side interface	HTML
Demo copy?	Yes, at Web site

Contact:

Space Telescope-European Coordinating Facility
Karl-Schwarzschild-Strasse 2
D-85748 Garching bei München, Germany
Tel   +49 89-320 06-365
Fax   +49 89-320 06-480
Email   bfrasmus@eso.org

They say:

About WDB:

"WDB is a software toolset that tremendously simplifies the integration of SQL-based databases into the World Wide Web. WDB lets you provide WWW access to the contents of databases without writing a single line of code. At the moment, WDB supports Sybase, Informix, and mSQL. However it is relatively easy to port it to other SQL-based databases. All there is needed to use WDB is the WDB script (written in PERL) and a set of high-level form definition files, each describing a different view on the database. WDB automatically creates HTML forms, on-the-fly, to allow the users to query the database, and given the user's query constraints, it will query the database and present the result to the user. WDB even comes with a utility to automatically extract information about a table from the database and create a working template form definition file."

Web Base & Web Base Pro

Summary:

Web Base is a Web server that interacts with ODBC databases. It uses SQL statements embedded in HTML documents and comes with a macro language that supports conditionals and loops. Web Base Pro includes modules for email, shopping carts, and Web data collection.

Details:

URL	http://www.Webbase.com
Platforms	Windows 3.1, Windows 95, Windows NT, Windows for Workgroups
Web browsers	All
Web servers	All
Data sources	ODBC, SQL Server, Access, FoxPro, Excel, Btrieve, dBASE III, dBASE IV, Paradox, Oracle6, Oracle7, text files
Client side interface	HTML
Demo copy?	Yes, at Web site

Contact:

ExperTelligence, Inc.
203 Chapala Street
Santa Barbara, CA 93101
Tel   (805) 962-2558
Fax   (805) 962-5188
Email   Webmaster@expertelligence.com

They say:

About WebBase:

"WebBase is a Web database server that allows you to easily and powerfully include existing databases on your Web site. It works standalone or in co-operation with any Web server...WebBase allows any browser to hypersearch a database as easily as hypertext is used in a document. If it's contained in a database, then you can display it on a Web page...WebBase works with more than 50 database formats...Database pages can have pictures, input forms, anchors, and any other feature provided by HTML. The fields in a database record may be placed anywhere in an HTML document...."

About the WebBase macro language:

"SQL statements...can be embedded anywhere in HTML documents...a full-featured macro language including: if, case, forRow, forIndex and more...dozens of functions including math, logic, comparisons, string manipulation, dates...an include facility for easy maintenance...user-defined variables...session variables that hold state between pages...can support multiple domains on the same machine."

About WebBase Pro:

"E-Merge: allows Web pages to search the database and send mail-merge letters that are individualized and customized by criteria. It facilitates normal and timed email. Fields from the database can be merged into emails, and paragraphs may be conditioned on calculations...Agent3W: allows WebBase Pro to conduct Web data interchange ('WDI') with other Web sites. Agent3W uses standard HTTP get and post commands, so it is compatible with all existing Web sites. It can retrieve data from multiple Web sites in parallel and consolidate the results into a single document...Forum: allows users to store and view threaded messages in a database...Shopping Basket: an object-oriented software device that creates a metaphorical place where Web site visitors such as catalog shoppers can store selections and complete their purchases. Shopping Basket can also store information from previous hits on the site. It is integrated in with 'cookies,' automatically making catalog sites easier to build."

About access control:

"You can make available anything in your database to anyone browsing your site or allow access to a specific audience that you control through password protection. You can also make existing databases far more powerful by adding hypertext links into reports. This feature allows users to delve into a report in greater detail, while maintaining the simplicity of a high level view."

Comparison with other Web servers:

"Whereas traditional Web servers are designed to handle HTML and do not interface with databases, WebBase is designed to interface to databases rather than process HTML without the requirement of developing CGI scripts. For this reason, many applications developed to take advantage of the database accessing capabilities of WebBase are, in fact, multiple Web server applications. They are designed to use a traditional Web server to present 'Home Page' screens and top-level introductory information to the user while directing database queries to the WebBase Server...WebBase is capable of handling many of the standard HTML features as done by HTTP servers but was not created to be a total replacement for all the functionality provided by the large number of servers in today's market. For this reason, many WebBase applications will also utilize a traditional HTTP server. You can have a single host machine configured with two servers and two ports, e.g., a traditional server on port 80 and WebBase on port 8001, or you can have an extensive collection of hosts, some running traditional Web servers and others running WebBase—whatever the application and anticipated load might require."

Web DataBlade

Summary:

Web DataBlade is a collection of tools for connecting the Illustra OODBMS to Web pages. Its server extension program uses CGI and most Web server APIs. Developers write page templates that hold SQL statements. Both relational databases and full-text databases are supported, as well as files containing multimedia data.

Details:

URL	http://www.illustra.com
Platforms	Windows NT, IRIX, Solaris
Web browsers	All
Web servers	All
Data sources	Informix, SQL, full text
Server side interface	CGI, NSAPI, ISAPI
Client side interface	HTML
Demo copy?	No

Contact:

Illustra Information Technologies, Inc.
1111 Broadway, 20th Floor
Oakland, CA 94607
Tel   (510) 652-8000
Fax   (510) 869-6388
Email   info@illustra.com

They say:

About Web DataBlade:

"Illustra's Web DataBlade module is a comprehensive toolset for creating Web-enabled database applications that dynamically retrieve and update Illustra database content...consists of two core pieces: the WebExplode function, and Webdriver...WebExplode parses the application page. The application page is stored in the database. When WebExplode finds Web DataBlade tags, it issues SQL statements and formats the results based on your formatting instructions...Webdriver handles all aspects of database interface and enables you to customize Web applications based on information obtained from a configuration file, the CGI environment, URLs, and HTML forms. Webdriver manages the database connection and retrieval of the application page from the database...also provides Webclient, a tool for managing high-load Web sites. Webclient, which can be used as an alternative to Webdriver, is a CGI-based application that can be integrated into any proprietary API that supports CGI. Webclient optimizes connection management between the Web server and the Illustra database. Web site administrators can configure a predefined number of database connections, so that no matter how many CGI processes are invoked, the requests to the database are all managed and processed through these already-established connections. This feature means that administrators can customize their system configuration to optimize the underlying CPU architecture and efficiently handle peak loads."

About click stream analysis:

"Illustra's rules system makes click stream analysis possible so that you can understand exactly who your customers are and how they view your application. Click stream analysis means that you can track where and how often a user clicks on a particular application area. With the feedback gathered through click stream analysis, you can build a business model around the usage of an application. You can, for example, give popular products more prominence in your application, or redesign an infrequently visited portion of your application."

Web FM

Summary:
Web FM 2.0 is a CGI interface that links FileMaker Pro 3.0 databases with the WebSTAR Web server. It runs on Mac OS.

Details:
URL	http://www.macWeb.com/Webfm/
Platforms	Mac
Web servers	WebSTAR

Data sources	FileMaker Pro 3.0 for Mac
Memory required	1 MB
Disk space required	1 MB
Server side interface	CGI
Client side interface	HTML
Mailing lists	FMPRO-CGI, WEBSTAR-TALK

Contact:

Web Broadcasting Co.
555 Bryant Street, #386
Palo Alto, CA 94301
Tel   (415) 329-9676
Email   info@macWeb.com

They say:

About the development process:

"With Web FM, it's easy to build dynamic Web sites. There's absolutely no CGI programming required. Simply create HTML fill-out forms with input fields that have the same names as fields in your FileMaker Pro database. Web FM offloads the complexities of the Web onto FileMaker Pro, where many people feel more comfortable. For example, Web FM relies on FileMaker Pro's powerful calculation fields to format highly customizable, dynamic HTML documents."

Web Publisher

Summary:

Web Publisher is a toolkit for integrating askSam databases with Web pages and for general Web page development. It handles full-text data.

Details:

URL	http://www.asksam.com
Platforms	Windows 95, Windows NT, OS/2
Web browsers	All
Web servers	All
Data sources	askSam databases
Memory required	16 MB
Disk space required	2 MB

Server side interface	CGI
Client side interface	HTML
Demo copy?	No

Contact:

askSam
PO Box 1428
Perry, FL 32347

Tel	(904) 584-6590, (800) 800-1997
Fax	(904) 584-7481
Email	info@askSam.comor, CompuServe:74774,352

They say:

About Web Publisher:

"Create and publish full-text searchable documents and databases on the Internet without HTML codes and without programming. You simply type or import the information into askSam...Set formats like you would in a word processor, and you're ready to go. The Web Publisher automatically lets you do full-text searches for any word or phrase anywhere in the database...You do not need to know a single HTML command to format your documents. You can quickly import word-processing documents (Word, Word Perfect, AmiPro, RTF, etc.), data files (dBase, CSV, etc.), any text, or any HTML document into askSam. Once imported, you can place your database on the Internet and anyone can search and browse your information. Any Internet user with a browser (Netscape, Mosaic, etc.) can search, page through, or execute hypertext links in your database. Absolutely no programming is necessary to create or query an askSam database...It is simple enough that any doctor, lawyer, PR person, professor (i.e., non-techie) can create a full-text, hypertext-linked database for the Internet."

About document conversion:

"With the Web Publisher you can quickly convert existing documents and place them on the Internet. The Web Publisher greatly reduces the time and cost of placing documents on the Internet."

About their integrated WYSIWYG word processor:

"Special mode for entering structured data...Insert graphics and OLE objects...Can use all features of HTML (versions 1, 2, and 3)...Set hypertext links in your askSam files without typing URLs...Drag & drop editing...Spell checker...Network version allows multiple users to work in a database."

About import filters for askSam databases:

"askSam can import: text (ASCII), HTML, Eudora, Word for Windows 6.0–
7.0, WordPerfect 5.0–6.0, CompuServe Information Manager, Lexis/Nexis,
RTF files (Microsoft's Rich Text Format), DBF files (dBase, FoxPro, Clipper, etc.), Comma Delimited Data (CSV files), Tab Delimited Data, Fixed
Position Data...."

About searching:

"Find any word or phrase—anywhere in your documents...Full-text searches
for any word or phrase...Wildcard searches with * and ?...Boolean searches
(and, or, not)...Proximity searches (in paragraph, sentence, line, or within
a specific # of words)...Numeric searches (>, <, >=, <=, <>)...Date searches
(date ranges and date comparison)...Fuzzy searches...Search through multiple askSam databases...."

About their approach:

"Getting information onto the Internet has traditionally been a time-consuming and complex task. To place a document on the Internet you were
forced to convert it to HTML (HyperText Markup Language). With even
single-page documents requiring considerable time, converting a 300-page
manual was often too expensive and time-consuming to consider...The
askSam Web Publisher lets you create full-text searchable documents for
the Internet without knowing a single HTML code. You simply type or
import the information into askSam. Set formats as you would in a word
processor, and you're ready to go. With askSam, even novice computer
users will be able to create documents and databases for the Internet...
Publishing tools for the Internet either assist you in converting your files
to HTML, or they assist you in creating HTML files. Our approach with
askSam is different. We let you import or create content in askSam. The
file you place on your server is a 'live' askSam database (not converted to
HTML). You can add to and update the askSam data file that resides on your
server...Since the information on your Web site is in a 'live' askSam database
(not in separate HTML files), the information can be easily edited and
updated. This cuts the costs associated with maintaining a Web site. askSam
is an ideal solution for corporate Intranets...Rather than creating hundreds
of HTML files from imported documents, askSam holds your documents
in a full-text searchable database. Users can search and page through your
information without forcing you to create hypertext links between all the
documents and without forcing you to index the information."

Web Server 4D

Summary:

Web Server 4D is the 4th Dimension DBMS with a Web server built in. The developer's edition comes with source code. It can be programmed to respond selectively depending on the user's domain or the Web browser being used.

Details:

URL	http://www.mdg.com/
Platforms	Mac
Web browsers	All
Data sources	4th Dimension DBMS
Server side interface	CGI
Client side interface	HTML
Demo copy?	Yes, at Web site

Contact:

MDG Computer Services, Inc.
231 Faircroft Road
Bartlett, IL 60103-1363

Tel	(630) 497-0220, (847) 622-0220
Fax	(630) 497-8893, (847) 622-8893
Email	sales@mdg.com

They say:

About Web Server 4D:

"...a 'wicked fast' Web server for Macintosh for the Internet or Intranet...A database with a built-in, full-feature Web server that offers unbelievable speed and the ability to create Web pages on the fly! Track new vs. repeat users, serves different pages based on domain, IP or browser, every page, every user request is stored in database, supports clickable maps, form to email, inserts page counts, odometer page counts, current date, current time—all without using CGI—although WS4D is compatible with CGI! Developer edition includes open 4D source code that allows complete customization or integration with existing databases."

About Web Server 4D features:

"Web Server 4D can now return real-time Web site statistics...HTML on-the-fly demo...Questionnaire demo will analyze a questionnaire that you fill in...Odometer page counts...Form to email demo will take a posted form and email it to you in seconds...HTML custom tags allow inserting of date, time, page counts...."

Web.sql

Summary:

Web.sql, from Sybase, is a server extension program that connects Sybase databases to Web pages. It works by embedding SQL statements and PERL scripts into HTML documents. CGI and NSAPI are supported.

Details:

URL	http://www.sybase.com/products/internet/Websql
Platforms	Solaris, IRIX, HP-UX, Windows NT
Web browsers	All
Web servers	All
Data sources	Sybase
Server side interface	CGI, NSAPI
Client side interface	HTML
Demo copy?	Yes, at Web site

Contact:

Sybase, Inc.
101 Huntington Avenue, Floor 22
Boston, MA 02199

Tel	(617) 422-7100, (800) 8-SYBASE (US & Canada)
Fax	(617) 422-0894
Email	Websql-list@sybase.com

They say:

About Web.sql:

"...With Web.sql, you can insert database instructions such as SQL statements and PERL scripts into the text of HTML pages. These database queries elicit an electronic response that returns to the Web server in the form of pure HTML text. This enables you to write Web pages that automatically generate personalized content for each individual user, based on the patterns and preferences he or she displays...Web.sql enables you to form active profiles of your online customers, and to structure your programming in such a way that best targets their needs and interests. For example, rather than posting a static product list on the Web, you can easily devise a catalog that is automatically customized for each user, thus highlighting items that the customer is most likely to be interested in."

About database access:

"Sybase Web.sql also represents a major innovation in database performance. Since it is directly linked with the Web server, Web.sql is designed to support in-line scripting and scripting calls rather than the separate scripting that is required for Common Gateway Interface (CGI) scripts. The result is dramatically improved database access and response time."

About integration with other Sybase tools:

"And Web.sql integrates perfectly into the Sybase enterprise architecture, with built-in capabilities to access: Sybase IQ, which delivers highly sophisticated data analysis features; Replication Server, the industry's leading real-time replication engine; SQL Server support on massively parallel systems; and Enterprise CONNECT, which provides access to multiple data sources."

Web2SQL

Summary:

Web2SQL is a tool for connecting Microsoft SQL Server to Netscape's Web server via NSAPI. It uses direct SQL statements and supports state maintenance with cookies.

Details:

URL	http://www.nutech.com/products/
Platforms	Windows NT
Web browsers	Netscape
Web servers	Netscape
Data sources	SQL Server
Memory required	16 MB
Disk space required	500+ MB
Server side interface	NSAPI
Client side interface	HTML

Contact:

Nu Tech Software Solutions, Inc.
12753 SW 68th Avenue, Suite 220
Tigard, OR 97223-8355
Tel   (503) 968-9035
Fax   (503) 968-1877
Email   info@nutech.com

They say:

About Web2SQL:

"...is a solid bridge between Microsoft SQL Server and Netscape Server under Microsoft Windows NT x86, which overcomes the limitations of HTML when it comes to representing your data on the World Wide Web...Web2SQL uses the native Application Program Interfaces (APIs) of both Microsoft SQL Server and Netscape Server to provide a binary bridge between these powerful servers. Using an API interface method versus CGI and ODBC connectivity results in seamless server interaction and maximum speed. The end result is that your SQL Server receives an HTML client interface and your Netscape Server receives a powerful, industry-standard database engine. This combination provides a powerful and secure client/server database system that any World Wide Web client can access both within an office and around the world...By using Microsoft's SQL Server on the Windows NT platform, Web2SQL provides continuous multithreaded, multi-user database connectivity with minimal overhead. Other systems that use Common Gateway Interface (CGI) scripts and Open DataBase Connectivity (ODBC) commands must constantly reload CGI programs from disk and do not permit multithreaded access."

About Web2SQL Features:

"Seamless API-native integration of SQL Server and Netscape Server. Nowhere else will Microsoft and Netscape speak this intimately!...Native SQL execution for full multi-user and multithreaded access...Eliminates the need for external CGIs for unparalleled performance...Takes full advantage of both SQL Server and Netscape Server. Uses standard SQL and HTML. No new languages to learn...Data persistence between HTML pages. No dropped variables as with CGIs...Full support for cookie variables...Allows for all HTML data to reside in database, not directories...Allows for the generation of HTML pages completely from database. Update your tables, not your HTML files...Handles a variety of data types including images and sounds...Secure Socket Layer compatible. Ensures full security with the combined forces of Windows NT, SQL Server and Netscape Server...Fully compatible with Nu Tech's Redirect and NutLog products...Provides fast and consistent performance with SQL Server 6.0's advanced indexing and table caching technologies...Robust data management and updating using triggers, commit transactions, rollback, and other data integrity functions...Full use of the SQL Language including: function calls, database cursors, switch statements, dynamically built string execution, and distributed database support...."

About other related NSAPI products:

"Redirect.dll is an enhancement to Netscape servers that allows for multiple IPs/domains to be run off one copy of a Netscape server. This solution doesn't require the additional overhead of more server processes... NutLog.dll is an enhancement to Netscape servers that allows you to store server transaction log information into the standard dBase IV file format. The use of a database file format in place of the flat ASCII format allows for highly advanced and flexible analysis of activity on your Netscape server."

About security:

"Web2SQL provides complete security by taking advantage of all SQL, Netscape, and Windows NT security measures. This results in a security model with flexible and scaleable options. You can also take advantage of the auditing qualities of Nu Tech's NutLog product to track client access information. Web2SQL system administrators have full control of 'who, what, where, when, and how' regarding access to their server, using industry-standard protocols."

"Web2SQL provides flexible security by using a secure path with the HTTP server. Each HTML link to your SQL server uses an alias representing the user, database, and password login information. At that point the Netscape server can request login authentication from the user (or you might provide your own login authentication using your own custom SQL database). Once the Netscape server processes authentication, Web2SQL translates the alias information and hands it over to the SQL server. At that point, the SQL server can invoke system security measures and request login authentication, as designed by your system. Web2SQL further provides your SQL server access to Netscape's internal pwf file, giving your SQL server additional flexibility for password authentication procedures...End users will not see one line of SQL code on your system by 'viewing HTML source code.' Furthermore, because Web2SQL uses aliases, end users will not gain information about your system databases names, or login names."

About installation:

"...Web2SQL's simple installation does away with the countless CGIs and external DLL files used in other database-to-World Wide Web connectivity products."

About standards:

"Because Web2SQL takes full advantage of the SQL and HTML industry standards, developers will not have to learn any new languages or procedures, resulting in a short and rewarding learning curve and a quick entrance into the world of Nu Tech Enhanced World Wide Web communications."

About HTML interface:

"Although Web2SQL has front-end services for administration purposes, Web2SQL is not a front-end package itself. The GUI to a Web2SQL server is simply anything you can represent in HTML. Unlike other Web-to-database products, Web2SQL really shifts power to your SQL server, giving it the functionality to manage your HTTP requests. You will predominantly use your SQL management tools to author and return HTML-formatted pages."

WebC

Summary:

WebC is a Web database tool for C and C++ programmers. It provides tools for maintaining state across multiple Web pages, and for performing input validations. It includes the CodeBase library, which gives access to x-Base databases.

Details:

URL	http://www.maxinfo.com/
Platforms	32-bit Windows, Unix
Web browsers	All
Web servers	Netscape, Microsoft IIS, WebSite, SPRY, Purveyor, Internet Factory, SAIC-HTTP

Data sources	CodeBase, dBASE, FoxPro
Server side interface	CGI
Client side interface	HTML
Demo copy?	No

Contact:

Maximum Information, Inc.
530 Jackson Street, Suite 202
San Francisco, CA 94133

Tel	(415) 981-5800, (800) 300-6072 (US & Canada)
Fax	(415) 981-5828
Email	info@maxinfo.com

They say:

About transaction and state management:

"The Web's architecture makes it difficult to write applications that maintain program information from page to page. Today, programmers are solving this through complicated and non-standard state-based implementations. WebC's Application Manager solves this problem by giving you an application state-based environment so you can focus on real application programming."

About session and application management:

"Using WebC, you can track a visitor on a temporary and permanent basis. Now you can quickly implement user registration and login sequences to control who has access to your site. Other services include session time-out for users who have been away from your site too long and URL encryption for an additional layer of security. WebC also has automatic support for multiple application and domain names on the same site."

About visitor tracking:

"Finally, you can keep track of what your visitors are looking at, when, how often, and how they navigate through your site. Using WebC's event trapping and logging, you can log information on every action, movement, and error within your application and site. This means you can view application trends and even dynamically respond to visitor behavior, which allows you to deliver truly personalized sites.

About input validation via forms:

"WebC solves the difficult problem of handling forms-based input. WebC encapsulates page output and form validation so you can implement user input and validation on the same page. This is handled through the WebC Forms Validation System, which provides you with a suite of tools to input, validate, and convert any type of information directly into your program variables and structures. The WebC runtime library includes a comprehensive set of validation and conversion routines including credit card validation, address normalization, and more."

About dynamic HTML:

"WebC provides you with a full suite of dynamic HTML generation functions that simplify the creation of tables, lists, and forms. And with header and footer capabilities, you can instantly create a standard look and feel to your Web application. In fact, you can have your WebC application generate different HTML commands based on the visitor's browser type."

About database access:

"Almost all applications need to access external data and information. Since WebC lets you connect with any existing programming libraries, database connectivity is a breeze. WebC includes Sequiter's award-winning CodeBase programming library. With WebC and CodeBase you can instantly generate and access 100 percent x-Base-compatible databases. Best of all, these databases can be modified and edited with any x-Base-compatible software including dBase and FoxPro."

About portability:

"WebC's server-independent Application Programming Interface (API) lets you write complete applications that are scaleable across 32-bit Windows and Unix-based operating systems. Applications created using WebC are enabled through the WebC Application Manager, a non-intrusive server extension that can be freely distributed along with your WebC applications. Furthermore, WebC is compatible with emerging standards including VRML and Java."

About performance:

"WebC applications are fully compiled, robust, and fast. The application manager intelligently manages resources on your Web server to correctly balance server load with application activity. Since the WebC Application Manager takes advantage of your native operating system and Web server's capabilities, your application performs at optimal levels."

About debugging:

"If you've ever tried to debug an interactive Web application, you know how difficult this can be. WebC solves your debugging needs by using your debugger of choice to step through and solve problems as they arise in your WebC application."

Supported compilers:

"Visual C++ 2.x, Visual C++ 4.0"

About features and components:

"C variables can be output directly in HTML statements. HTML-based form input data is assigned directly to C variables...Developers can easily add form validation to ensure data input C variables can automatically maintain state between 'pages'...Data can be made persistent from one user's visit to the next...Full multi-user database tools are included...A rich set of libraries simplify Web development tasks, e.g., creating forms, creating tables, etc....WebC consists of three major components, the IDE/compiler, the runtime library and the application manager. The IDE and compiler are used to create projects and compile them into your site. The runtime libraries consist of routines that are central to the operation of WebC as well as an extensive set of routines that can be called from a WebC application. The application manager is a server extension, in the form of a CGI application, which controls application flow and interaction among the various pages that make up an application. The application manager can be deployed across multiple platforms for true scaleability and portability."

WebDBC

Summary:

WebDBC is a Web database development tool. Its server extension program integrates Web servers with ODBC databases via NSAPI, ISAPI, and BGI. It uses a wizard to create pages that are interfaced with databases. Knowledge of HTML and SQL is not needed. It offers enhanced security features.

Details:

URL	http://www.ndev.com
Platforms	Sparc Solaris, Windows 95, Windows NT, MacOS, Power PC
Web browsers	All

Web servers	All
Data sources	ODBC
Server side interface	CGI, ISAPI, NSAPI, BGI, DLL, NT Service
Client side interface	HTML
Demo copy?	Yes, at Web site

Contact:

Nomad Development Corp.
316 Occidental Avenue South, Suite 406
Seattle, WA 98104
Tel   (206) 812-0177
Fax   (206) 812-0170
Email   info@ndev.com

They say:

About typical applications:

"...shopping carts, classified ads, threaded discussion groups, user registration systems, online questionnaires, customer support systems, workflow applications...."

About hybrid CGI:

"WebDBC can now be invoked as a DLL, an NT Service, or a CGI program. Running WebDBC as a DLL or a service yields performance up to 10 times faster than CGI, especially in multi-user situations. This also gives you the flexibility to choose whichever configuration meets your needs."

About database connection caching:

"WebDBC's Connection Manager caches and reuses database connections, which improves overall performance of your Web-based applications. You control how many database connections you want open for optimal performance."

About user access control:

"You can control access on a per-table and even per-operation basis."

About development aids:

"WebDBC Instant-Page Wizards. These new Web-based wizards take you step-by-step through the Web database application building process, making it easier than ever to use WebDBC to interact with your database or data warehouse."

About reasons for using a Web database toolkit:

"There are many contexts in which there is simply too much information to convert into static Web pages. And often that information is changing regularly, so that maintaining Web pages becomes a nightmare. Good examples of this are catalogs and today's news. Much more effective would be to draw the most current information from a central repository, creating pages that contain a timely and appropriate subset of the information available."

WebHub

Summary:

WebHub is a programmer's toolkit for building CGI Web database applications with Delphi. Tools are included for tracking surfers and saving states. Java and JavaScript are both supported.

Details:

URL	http://www.href.com/
Platforms	Windows 3.1, Windows 95, Windows NT
Web browsers	All
Web servers	Netscape, Microsoft IIS, SPRY, WebSite
Data sources	All Delphi-accessible SQL databases
FAQ	Yes, at Web site
Mailing lists	Webhub-list@sonic.net, majordomo@sonic.net
Demo copy?	Yes, at Web site

Contact:

HREF Tools Corp.
300 B Street, Suite 215
Santa Rosa, CA 95401

Tel	(707) 542-0844
Fax	(707) 542-0896
Email	ann@href.com

They say:

About WebHub:

"WebHub's strength and flexibility come from its platform, which is Borland's Delphi for Windows. The WebHub Components are 100 percent Delphi code—and fully object oriented. So applications built with

WebHub are some of the fastest and most capable Windows .exe's running today. If you build your custom .exe with Delphi Client/Server, then you can connect to virtually any SQL database on the market."

About typical applications:

"...custom graphics, email, ftp, and online electronic commerce to sophisticated database-driven presentations."

About performance:

"WebHub is designed for use in high-traffic environments, with multiple simultaneous surfers. The hub system controls multiple copies of your custom .exe, and will queue page requests across those instances. WebHub also bounces page requests to alternate machines within a cluster for further scaleability...The WebHub System, and applications built with its components, stay loaded in memory between HTTP requests. This means they can respond far faster than regular CGI programs."

About site traffic analysis:

"...Hits by page instead of by file—the data isn't clouded by errors and graphics file requests...Hits by surfer—because WebHub tracks the surfer as an individual, you know how many pages a single surfer looked at...Duration—how much time the surfer spent on each page (except the current one, because you never know when the person leaves)...."

About Java:

"WebHub supports Java...applets (by dynamically passing parameters) and JavaScript (by dynamically generating the code)."

About the development process:

"WebHub makes it easy for teams to work on Web sites. Because the HTML is kept outside the WebApp, it's easy to separate the job of the Delphi specialist from the HTML and graphics tasks. Furthermore, WebHub offers no-recompilation-necessary site maintenance. Page layout, macros, grid layout and much more can be configured via .ini and .html files outside the Delphi project. You can change these, tell your WebApp to refresh, and your site continues to serve pages without interruption."

Webinator

Summary:

Webinator is a development system for creating Web database applications that use relational and full-text databases. It works with the Texis database and the Metamorph retrieval engine as well as other databases via ODBC. Webinator provides detailed verification and logging of document linkages. It allows multiple databases at a site and will index/update documents while a database is in use.

Details:

URL	http://www.thunderstone.com
Platforms	Solaris 2.3, Windows NT 3.51, Windows 95, DOS, VMS, MVS
Web servers	All
Data sources	Texis, Access, ODBC level 2
Server side interface	CGI
Client side interface	HTML
Demo copy?	Yes, at Web site

Contact:

Thunderstone
11115 Edgewater Drive
Cleveland, OH 44102
Tel   (216) 631-8544
Fax   (216) 281-0828
Email   info@thunderstone.com

They say:

About Webinator:

"Provides an SQL query interface to the database for maintenance and report. Allows remote sites to be copied to the local file system. Multiple index engines may run concurrently against a common database...Powerful and easy-to-use queries for: natural language, set logic, special pattern matchers (regular expressions, quantities, fuzzy patterns), relevance ranking, proximity controls, document similarity searches, in-context result listings."

About Texis:

"Texis merges the horsepower of concept-based text retrieval with an SQL relational database server, bridging the gully between traditional databases and document-driven activities by allowing the import, export, management, and retrieval of textual information."

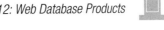

"Texis bridges the gully between traditional databases and document-driven activities by allowing the import, export, management, and retrieval of textual information."

About Metamorph:

"Metamorph is an advanced, concept-based, text retrieval software package. Metamorph uses a natural language interface, has a built-in thesaurus of more than 250,000 associations, filters for certain word-processed formats, audit trails, cut and paste, and automated report generation. No pre-indexing or pre-processing required, locates quantities/numbers in any form, along with typos, misspellings, and 'similar-tos.' Metamorph any form, along with typos, misspellings, and 'similar-tos.' Metamorph is available for DOS, any Unix, Windows, NT and certain MVS environments... Metamorph has search algorithms to locate occurrences of complex intersections of multiple, concept set members, using weighted 'and,' 'or,' and 'not' set logic...Metamorph has a regular expression pattern matcher to locate any fixed or variable length expression, such as part and social security number, dates, chemical formulae, footnotes, or special headers."

WebinTool

Summary:

WebinTool is a generic WWW-to-SQL database interface building tool. WebinTool allows the user to create customized Web interfaces to SQL databases through a series of user-defined WebinTool forms. A WebinTool form is a document written in HTML that includes a set of SQL-based Webin statements. WebinTool is freeware.

Details:

URL	http://www.ri.bbsrc.ac.uk/Webintool.html
Platforms	Unix
Web servers	NCSA 1.4
Data sources	Ingres 6.4/05, Unify 2000
Server side interface	CGI
Client side interface	HTML
Demo copy?	Yes, at Web site

Contact:

Roslin Institute, Edinburgh

Midlothian, UK
EH25 9PS
Tel   1 31 4402726
Fax   1 31 4400434
Email   jianhu@bbsrc.ac.uk

They say:

About its programming language:

"Webin is a script-like language that combines HTML statements and SQL-based statements. Additional programming languages are SQL and C."

About development:

"It provides a framework for rapid building and easy maintenance of WWW interfaces for interface developers."

About reporting:

"Reports can be specified by the user through WebinTool forms."

About queries, inserts, updates, and deletes:

"Data manipulation is done by SQL statements in WebinTool forms."

WebObjects

Summary:

WebObjects is a CGI-based development system for building Web database applications. It uses an object-oriented scripting language. It supports a wide array of databases, including legacy databases. It can do load balancing and is scaleable.

Details:

URL	http://www.next.com/WebObjects/
Platforms	Windows NT, HP-UX, Solaris, DEC Unix, NeXTSTEP
Web browsers	All
Web servers	All
Data sources	Oracle, Sybase, Informix, DB/2
Server side interface	CGI, NSAPI
Client side interface	HTML, HTML 3.0, Java applets
Demo copy?	Yes, at Web site

Contact:

NeXT Software, Inc.
900 Chesapeake Drive
Redwood City, CA 94063
Tel   (415) 366-0900, (800) TRY-NeXT (US & Canada)
Fax   (415) 780-3929
Email   Webmaster@next.com

They say:

About WebObjects:

"WebObjects contains development tools to build components for your application logic, as well as a set of reusable components to manage the rendering of your application. Those components reside on your enterprise server alongside any HTTP server and can be accessed by any Web browser. Scripting language support for handling pre-built graphical components and Java applets helps you rapidly develop complex applications. Scripting applications with WebObjects is simple enough for both programmers and non-programmers—a Webmaster skilled in PERL, or a COBOL programmer in your MIS organization, can use it immediately. What's unique about WebObjects is the ability to share the logic of your Web application and your data with other internal applications. It means that you are not required to maintain a dedicated database or write specific application code for your Web application. If you're already running an application on a mainframe or Unix server, and your data is stored on a Sybase or an Oracle database, WebObjects can easily and safely make your computing resources accessible to anyone with Web access."

About three-tiered architecture:

"WebObjects separates your application into three tiers: the Web graphical presentation layer, the business logic, and the data access. This partitioning allows you to share a piece of application logic or data with your internal Windows-based client/server applications. Your Corp. can take advantage of the power of enterprise-wide, dynamic Web applications while continuing to make use of the existing business infrastructure."

About its scripting language:

"WebObjects comes with WebScript today, and will support JavaScript in the near future. The scripting language helps you manipulate WebObjects components and hides the complexity of programming with CGI and PERL. It makes programming WebObjects quick and easy for any Webmaster or member of your MIS organization."

About OO compatibility:

"WebObjects is object model independent. As a result, WebObjects applications can coexist and cooperate with Windows applications based on OLE. Additionally, WebObjects servers can communicate with CORBA 2.0 objects and DCE services, giving developers the ability to extend this functionality to the Web."

About legacy databases:

"With WebObjects and NeXT's solution partners such as Connextions, developers can integrate existing mainframe applications with Web applications. For example, mainframe applications based on SAP R/3, MVS, and OS/400 can be tied into a WebObjects solution."

About security:

"WebObjects supports security standards such as SSL and SHTTP. WebObjects leverages any security systems included with popular HTTP servers, such as the Commerce Server from Netscape. WebObjects includes built-in mechanisms to handle user authentication in the inherently multiuser environment of the Web. Furthermore, WebObjects can operate in environments that use firewalls to block all unauthorized requests to machines on the network. WebObjects offers you all the necessary safety and reliability to conduct your business over the Web."

About access to Windows applications:

"Through the NeXT Object Model, Web-based applications can communicate with any OLE-based application that supports OLE automation (such as Microsoft Office)—allowing Windows applications to share information with Web applications. For example, WebObjects applications can leverage existing data that is computed and stored in spreadsheets such as MS-Excel."

About access to mainframe databases:

"WebObjects and Connextions' Enterprise Builder Series products allow Corp.s and organizations to build Web applications that directly integrate legacy applications based on environments such as CICS, IMS, TSO, VM/CMS via 3270Builder Workbench; IBM AS/400 systems via

5350Builder Workbench; Tandem-based CableData DDP/SQL systems via QSBuilder Workbench; and a variety of ASCII hosts and operating environments such as Open VMS, Unix, etc., via ASCIIBuilder Workbench."

WebQuest

Summary:

WebQuest is a Web server that directly accesses ODBC databases by using server-side includes. It also provides conditional execution, SMTP email capability, and remote administration.

Details:

URL	http://www.questar.com
Platforms	Windows NT, Windows 95
Data sources	ODBC, SQL Server, Access, Paradox, Excel, Dbase
Server side interface	SSI
Client side interface	HTML
Demo copy?	Yes, at Web site

Contact:

Questar Microsystems, Inc.
19501 144th Avenue N.E., Suite 900A
Woodinville, WA 98072

Tel	(206) 487-2627, (800) 925-2140 (US & Canada)
Fax	(206) 487-9803
Email	qmi.admin@questar.com

They say:

About WebQuest:

"WebQuestNT combines our advanced feature Webserver; WebMeister—our graphical Webspace manager; and WebEdit, an HTML editor...Graphical multi-domain installation, configuration and operation...Graphical administration and validation of directories, local and remote hyperlinks, access control, and more...The only implementation of the SSI+ 1.0 specification. Powerful interactive functions without programming or CGI scripts. 'Server side includes' allows Web Browsers to serve as platform-independent front ends to live databases to provide the user with up-to-the-minute information...ODBC/SQL database updates and queries...SMTP email, conditional execution, insertion of runtime values...ODBC logging, NT event logging, and file logging of: access, events, requests, and operations...User access authentication and control...."

About SSI (server side includes):

"...In its more advanced usage, SSI provides you with a powerful interface to corporate relational databases, OLTP and data warehouses. Very simply, SSI is the ability to automatically insert one file into another. SSI allows broad interactivity to your enterprise relational database with much greater efficiency and flexibility than CGI scripting using C+, PERL or TCL...The usefulness of this capability is further enhanced by another feature, conditional execution based on logical comparisons. WebQuestNT and WebQuest 95 servers allow whole or portioned documents to be served only to certain hosts, or to clients based on WebMeister-defined variables. Using the 'else' construct allows alternate text segments for clients meeting/not meeting the desired criteria, allowing WebMeisters to create specific Webspaces for different audiences...Email (mailback forms) without CGI scripts! No programming required. Includes full SMTP client. Eliminates need to access local email resources. Logs directly to database...Access control. Allows invisible accept/decline access to Webspace or redirection of client...Client-specific file parsing. Allows WebMeister to meter and audit specific client transactions on a per client/group/IP basis...Direct access and querying/updating of relational database via ODBC. WebQuestNT and Webquest95 Webservers include ODBC drivers and driver managers for SQL Server, Access, Paradox, Excel, dBase, and more...Provides single point of Web content management and updates...Integration of online commerce with existing auditing, fulfillment and credit-card processing software packages...Flexible metering of Webspace by page, time, file type, and much more...."

WebRex

Summary:

WebRex is a Web server with object-oriented programming capabilities. WebRex can function as a standalone server or can work with the Netscape server via NSAPI.

Details:

URL	http://www.its.com:8005/its.bundle/
Platforms	Solaris, HP-UX, DEC Unix, NEXTSTEP
Web browsers	Netscape
Web servers	Netscape
Data sources	Sybase, Oracle
Server side interface	NSAPI
Client side interface	HTML
Demo copy?	No

Contact:

IT Solutions
641 W. Lake Street, Suite 402
Chicago, IL 60622
Tel   (312) 474-7700
Fax   (312) 831-1400
Email   info@its.com

They say:

About WebRex:

"WebRex turns HTML requests for URLs—which enter the server from the Internet (or corporate Intranet)—into object messages to specific application objects. These objects then do some work and return a page of HTML, to be returned to the client via the server...Any standard HTML browser sends a standard URL through a network to WebRex. The request is transmitted via standard HTTP over a network...These requests can be sent to a Netscape secure server (for secure applications) and then passed to WebRex via the NSAPI, or they can be sent directly to WebRex, which acts as a standard HTTP server...Each URL can be mapped to an object-oriented program function (called a method), allowing the server to generate a dynamic reply document, based on the method called, any data transmitted, and any other function that the developer may wish...."

About user authorization:

"HERB, or the 'HTML Event Request Broker,' is a Netscape Commerce Server extension that utilizes Netscape's server API. With HERB, you can use a single access server to validate users and encrypt HTML communications, but provide information to users from multiple servers. HERB maps URL document realms to server locations, allowing an HTTP request to be 'brokered' among multiple responding servers...Your company has three HTTP servers for three different departments: sales, human resources, and manufacturing. For security purposes, you want to restrict access to these machines from Internet users...Without HERB, it might be difficult or impossible to allow access to these systems from the Internet. At best, a user might have to log in three times—once when connecting to each of the three servers—to establish a secure connection. Using HERB, a single Netscape secure Commerce Server can be used as the gateway machine, validating outside users and brokering document requests to each of the internal departmental servers. Responses are then routed back through the Netscape server to provide encrypted communications to your users...Using HERB, you can easily make your Intranet applications securely accessible to your employees connecting from other parts of the public Internet."

About WWWStore:

"A complete catalog product for the World Wide Web. Running as a complete database-driven application, with either Sybase or Oracle as the 'back-end' storage server, and with a WebRex application connecting to the World Wide Web through Netscape's Commerce Server, this solution is economical, scaleable, and reliable for real commerce on the Internet. The first catalog using this technology, The Giftsender, is operating today, and more sites are under development. View an explanatory template. This software is available in three configurations:...Resellers—a package for independent ISPs to use, to either develop and host their customer's catalog sites themselves, or transparently host these catalogs through the IT Solutions Service Bureau...Service Bureau—a service from IT Solutions, where we will host a company's catalog at our virtual hosting facility, providing the back-end database and the secure Netscape Commerce Server for online transactions...Catalog Companies—for companies that want to develop and serve their own catalogs, the complete software tool, including WWWStore source code and WebRex."

About network objects:

"Database access is not the only strength of an object-oriented Web server that can efficiently message objects. Any object on any system that supports a standard object communication protocol such as CORBA, can be sent a message directly from the Web server and asked to perform some operation and return some data, which can then be efficiently packaged inside an HTML page and returned to the client Web browser."

WebSite

Summary:

WebSite is a Web server that calls Visual Basic programs that access ODBC databases or other Visual Basic programs.

Details:

URL	http://Website.ora.com
Platforms	Windows NT, Windows 95
Web browsers	All
Data sources	ODBC, Access, all VB-accessible
Memory required	16 MB
Disk space required	10 MB
Server side interface	WSAPI, CGI, SSI, Visual Basic
Client side interface	HTML
FAQ	Yes, at Web site
Mailing lists	WebSite-talk@online.ora.com, listproc@online.ora.com
Demo copy?	Yes, at Web site

Contact:

O'Reilly & Associates, Inc.
101 Morris Street
Sebastopol, CA 95472

Tel	(707) 829-0515, (800) 998-9938 (US & Canada)
Fax	(707) 829-0104
Email	Website@ora.com, order@ora.com

They say:

About security:

"WebSite provides Web-standard security in the form of basic authentication and access control. You can specify user names and passwords for individuals and groups, and then control access to any part of your server based on username, group, or IP address. WebSite Professional, available in Spring 1996, will have full cryptographic security, including S-HTTP and SSL."

About WebSite Professional:

"In addition to all of the features contained in WebSite 1.1, WebSite Professional provides a complete Web server security solution that includes digital signatures and privacy for the exchange of payment information, personal identification and intellectual property. WebSite Professional supports the two major Web cryptographic security systems, Secure Sockets Layer (SSL) and Secure HyperText Transfer Protocol (S-HTTP). WebSite Professional has an easy interface for S-HTTP administration through WebView. WebSite Professional also includes a new WebSite Application Programming Interface (WSAPI) with enhanced logging, post processing, document generation, authentication, and other features. WebSite Professional also comes with Cold Fusion, a powerful database application development tool for easily incorporating database information into your Web documents. Cold Fusion lets you quickly develop applications to add customer feedback, online ordering event registration, interactive training, online technical support, and more to your site. WebSite Professional is a must for sophisticated users who want to offer their audiences the best in Web server technology."

About WebBoard:

"WebBoard is an advanced multithreaded conferencing system that can help attract users to your Web server. WebBoard runs with WebSite or with any Web server that fully supports the Windows Common Gateway Interface (Win-CGI). With WebBoard, people can use their Web browsers to participate in online discussions about any number of topics. Like a newsgroup, each topic is organized and maintained in its own separate area. WebBoard is ideal for use in business environments and in legal or educational organizations—anywhere online discussions can help groups communicate and keep track of ongoing decisions and issues. Users log in with a unique name and password, and each transaction is verified to ensure a secure conferencing environment. WebBoard also includes functions such as private email response, user listings, top-ten lists, caller logs, and bulletins."

About PolyForm:

"PolyForm is a forms tool that can help make your Web pages interactive. PolyForm enables you to create Web pages with forms, so you can gather and manage information supplied by your Web visitors. For example, with a PolyForm form, users can order products, request information, provide customer feedback, or answer surveys. Each form can be configured separately, so you can collect and store response data as well as recipient information. Information submitted on a form can be sent to specified email addresses, and data can be sent back to the user who fills in the form. PolyForm runs with any Windows Web server that fully supports the Windows Common Gateway Interface (Win-CGI), including WebSite and others."

XWorks

Summary:

XWorks is a tool that makes programs written in Visual Basic resident and enables them to communicate with the Web server. It also works with programs written in other programming languages.

Details:

URL	http://ciint1.ciinc.com/Weblink/index.htm
Platforms	Windows NT, Windows 95
Web browsers	All
Web servers	WebSite, Netscape, MSIIS, Purveyor, EMWAC
Data sources	FoxPro, Access, SQL server, any DB accessible via VB or VFP
Memory required	30 K
Disk space required	120 K
Server side interface	CGI 1.1
Client side interface	All
FAQ	Yes, at Web site
Demo copy?	Yes, at Web site

Contact:

PLACE, Inc.
7200 Falls of the Neuse Road
Raleigh, NC 27615

Tel	(919) 676-8855, ext 158
Fax	(919) 676-8484
Email	RogerKo@ciinc.com

They say:

About how it works:

"X-Works uses a DLL for either VFP or VB that enables the VB or VFP programmer to use Visual Basic or VFP code as CGI code. For example, with the VFP version, you could access a VFP database using 100 percent VFP code through an HTML form."

About performance:

"It is very fast and uses the least system resources compared to any other method. It can handle heavy CGI traffic for most demanding commercial customers."

About queries, inserts, updates, and deletes:

"Data is accessed via the language used, i.e., VFP or VB."

About input validations:

"...does whatever input validations can be programmed in VB or VFP."

About transaction control:

"...done through VB, VFP, or whatever database engine is used."

About security:

"Whatever your Web server or your LAN provides."

References

The Web
Books

Serving the Web
Robert Jon Mudry,
Coriolis Group Books

Java in a Nutshell: A Desktop Quick Reference for Java Programmers
David Flanagan,
O'Reilly & Associates, Inc.

URLs

http://cscsun1.larc.nasa.gov/~beowulf/db/existing_products.html
Jeff Rowe's Web site on Web/database tools and techniques.

http://www.webtechniques.com/

Web Techniques magazine.

http://www.javasoft.com/
Sun's official Web site for Java developers.

http://home.netscape.com/eng/mozilla/Gold/handbook/javascript/index.HTML
Netscape's JavaScript authoring guide.

http://www.freqgrafx.com/411/
Source for JavaScript information.

http://www.entmp.org/cgi-bin/lwgate/strong-java/
Forum for full-blown, serious Java application development.

http://www.io.org/~mentor/J___Notes.html
(Yes, folks, they really put three underscores in their URL.) Digital Espresso:
a bi-weekly digest of information summarized and gleaned from newsgroups
focusing on the Java language, the HotJava browser, and other associated
topics.

http://www.javaworld.com/
Java World: electronic zine published by IDG Communications that focuses on the Java programming language.

http://www.gamelan.com/
Directory of Java-related products, objects, and sites.

Newsgroups

comp.infosystems.www.announce
World Wide Web announcements (moderated).

comp.infosystems.www.authoring.cgi
Writing CGI scripts for the Web.

comp.infosystems.www.authoring.html
Writing HTML for the Web.

comp.infosystems.www.authoring.images
Using images and imagemaps on the Web.

comp.infosystems.www.authoring.misc
Miscellaneous Web authoring issues.

comp.infosystems.www.browsers.mac
Web browsers for the Macintosh platform.

comp.infosystems.www.browsers.misc
Web browsers for other platforms.

comp.infosystems.www.browsers.ms-windows
Web browsers for Microsoft Windows.

comp.infosystems.www.browsers.x
Web browsers for the X-Window system.

comp.infosystems.www.misc
Miscellaneous World Wide Web discussion.

comp.infosystems.www.servers.mac
Web servers for the Macintosh platform.

comp.infosystems.www.servers.misc
Miscellaneous Web servers.

comp.infosystems.www.servers.ms-windows
Web servers for Microsoft Windows and NT.

comp.infosystems.www.servers.unix
Web servers for Unix platforms.

comp.lang.java
The main Java newsgroup.

comp.lang.javascript
Netscape's JavaScript language.

alt.www.hotjava
Discussions of HotJava and the Java language.

Mailing lists

java-announce
Announcements of new Java/HotJava releases, ports, etc. To subscribe, send email to *listserv@javasoft.com* with *subscribe java-announce* **your_name** in the body of the message.

javascript-talk
JavaScript programming. To subscribe, send email to *majordomo@bridge.net* with *subscribe javascript-talk* in the body of the message.

Databases
Books

The Relational Model for Database Development: Version 2
E. F. Codd,
Addison-Wesley, 1990.

A Guide to The SQL Standard: Third Edition
C. J. Date and Hugh Darwen,
Addison-Wesley, 1993.

An Introduction to Database Systems
C. J. Date,
Addison-Wesley, 1993.

The Practical SQL Handbook
Judith S. Bowman, Sandra L Emerson, Marcy Darnovsky,
Addison-Wesley, 1993.

Relational Database: Selected Writings
C. J. Date,
Addison-Wesley, 1989.

Transaction Processing Concepts and Techniques
Jim Gray and Andreas Reuter,
Morgan Kaufmann, 1993.

Essential Client/Server Survival Guide
Robert Orfali, Dan Harkey, Jeri Edwards,
Wiley, 1994.

URLs

http://pwp.starnetinc.com/larryg/index.html
A large collection of links and references about data warehousing.

http://www.redbrick.com/rbs/Welcome.html
Detailed discussion of data warehousing.

http://gdbdoc.gdb.org/letovsky/genera/dbgw.html
Page of links about Web/database gateways.

http://cybermart.com/web/webdev/html/webdb.html
Page of links about Web/database.

http://www.lpac.ac.uk/SEL-HPC/Articles/DBArchive.html
Large bibliography of scholarly papers on relational, full text, and multi-media database software.

http://www.microsoft.com/oledev/olerem/3tierwp1.htm
A white paper about the three-tier client/server architecture on Microsoft's developer-support web site.

http://www.cis.ohio-state.edu/hypertext/faq/usenet/client-server-faq/faq.html
A long, detailed FAQ about client/server computing.

http://cybermart.com/web/webdev/html/webdb.html
A white paper discussing the use of networks to "liberate" data stored in legacy systems.

http://tuxedo.novell.com/indepth/api.htm
White paper on developing database applications with transaction processing middleware using Novell's TUXEDO/E.

Newsgroups

comp.databases
Database and data management issues and theory.

comp.databases.adabas
ADABAS database topics in general.

comp.databases.gupta
Gupta SQL Windows client-server development.

comp.databases.ibm-db2
Problem resolution with DB2 database products.

comp.databases.informix
Informix database management software discussions.

comp.databases.ingres
Issues relating to INGRES products.

comp.databases.ms-access
Microsoft Access, relational database system.

comp.databases.ms-sqlserver
Microsoft's SQL Server and related products.

comp.databases.object
Object-oriented paradigms in databases systems.

comp.databases.olap
Analytical processing, multidimensional DBMS, EIS, DSS.

comp.databases.oracle
Topics relating to the Oracle SQL database products.

comp.databases.paradox
Borland's database for DOS & MS Windows.

comp.databases.progress
Progress 4GL & RDBMS.

comp.databases.rdb
DEC's relational database engine RDB.

comp.databases.sybase
Implementations of Sybase SQL Server.

comp.databases.xbase.fox
Fox Software's xBase system and compatibles.

comp.databases.xbase.misc
Discussion of xBase products.

comp.lang.basic.visual.database
Database aspects of Visual Basic.

comp.sys.mac.databases
Database systems for the Apple Macintosh.

comp.lang.pascal.delphi.databases
Discussions of database aspects of Borland Delphi.

comp.client-server
Topics relating to client-server technology.

comp.os.linux.x
Linux X Window System servers, clients, libraries and fonts.

comp.protocols.smb
SMB file sharing protocol and Samba SMB server/client.

comp.soft-sys.app-builder.uniface
Uniface Client-Server App Development.

Mailing lists

oraweb-l
Discussion of Oracle WebSystem. To subscribe, send email to *majordomo @labyrinth.net.au* with *subscribe oraweb-l* **your_name** in the body of the message.

access-l
About Microsoft Access database. To subscribe, send email to *listserv @peach.ease.lsoft.com* with *subscribe access-l* **your_name** in the body of the message.

sqlinfo
About SQL/DS and related topics. To subscribe, send email to *listserv @listserv.uic.edu* with *subscribe sqlinfo* **your_name** in the body of the message.

sybase-l
Discussion of SYBASE products, platforms, and usage. To subscribe, send email to *listserv@ucsbvm.ucsb.edu* with *subscribe sybase-l* **your_name** in the body of the message.

Networks
Newsgroups
bit.listserv.banyan-l
Banyan Vines network software discussions.

bit.listserv.snamgt-l
SNA network management discussion.

comp.dcom.frame-relay
Technology and issues regarding frame relay networks.

comp.dcom.isdn
The Integrated Services Digital Network (ISDN).

comp.dcom.lans.misc
Local area network hardware and software.

comp.dcom.lans.token-ring
Token ring networks.

comp.dcom.net-management
Network management methods and applications.

comp.os.linux.networking
Networking and communications under Linux.

comp.os.ms-windows.networking.misc
Windows and other networks.

comp.os.ms-windows.networking.tcp-ip
Windows and TCP/IP networking.

comp.os.ms-windows.networking.windows
Windows' built-in networking.

comp.os.ms-windows.programmer.networks
Network programming.

comp.os.os2.networking.misc
Miscellaneous networking issues of OS/2.

comp.os.os2.networking.tcp-ip
TCP/IP under OS/2.

comp.os.os2.networking.www
WWW apps/utils under OS/2.

comp.protocols.ibm
Networking with IBM mainframes.

comp.protocols.nfs
Discussion about the Network File System protocol.

comp.protocols.snmp
The Simple Network Management Protocol.

comp.protocols.tcp-ip
TCP and IP network protocols.

comp.security.misc
Security issues of computers and networks.

comp.sys.ibm.pc.hardware.networking
Network hardware & equipment for the PC.

comp.unix.large
Unix on mainframes and in large networks.

info.snmp
Simple Gateway/Network Monitoring Protocol (moderated).

vmsnet.networks.tcp-ip.ucx
DEC VMS/Ultrix Connection, TCP/IP services for VMS.

comp.os.ms-windows.nt.admin.networking
Windows NT network administration.

comp.os.ms-windows.networking.ras
Windows RAS networking.

comp.security.firewalls
Discussions pertaining to network firewall security.

comp.os.ms-windows.networking.win95
Win95 to Novell, TCP/IP, other nets.

Mailing lists

info-nets
About networks, focusing on inter-network connectivity. To subscribe, send email to *listserv@vm.marist.edu* with *subscribe info-nets* **your_name** in the body of the message.

Electronic Document Processing
Books

The SGML Handbook
Charles F. Goldfarb,
edited by Yuri Rubinsky,
Oxford University Press, 1990.

Practical SGML: 2nd Edition
Eric van Herwijnen,
Kluwer Academic Publishers, 1994.

URLs

http://www.sil.org/sgml/sgml.html
Large collection of SGML material: references, links, FAQ, comments.

http://www.sq.com/htmlsgml/htmlsgml.htm
SGML pages maintained by SoftQuad.

http://www.sgmlopen.org/sgml/docs/index.html
The Web site of the SGML Open Consortium.

http://www.optimedia.co.il/epub/epub.htm
A page of links on electronic publishing.

http://www.loc.gov/global/etext/etext.html
Electronic Texts and Publishing Resources, maintained by the U.S. Library of Congress.

Newsgroups

news:comp.text.sgml
Topics relating to SGML.

Miscellaneous

The New York Public Library Writer's Guide to Style and Usage
Edited by Andrea J. Sutcliffe
Stonesong Press — Harper/Collins, 1994

The Chicago Manual of Style: Thirteenth Edition
Catherine Seybold and Bruce Young
Univerity of Chicago Press, 1982

What's on the CD?

Keep in mind that much of the software on this disk is either shareware or freeware. Shareware means that the author or authors of the software are allowing you to try out the software with the expectation that, if you like it, you will pay them for it or upgrade to a commercial version. Freeware means that you can use the software as much as you want with no charge, but there is usually a more advanced version available for a price. Check for a README or LICENSE file with each of the applications you use to see what restrictions the author has placed on the software and its distribution and use.

Now, let's take a look at some of the more useful applications on the CD. Don't be afraid to experiment a little and play with all the different types of software. Most of the software is described below, but for those programs that aren't, just check in the applications directory for more information.

Application: EMWAC Web Server
Where on CD: \PRODUCTS\EMWAC
Where online: http://www.emwac.ed.ac.uk/
Description: EMWAC stands for the European Microsoft Windows NT Academic Centre. These guys are a group of college students and professors who are working on some cool NT-based Internet solutions along with some industry giants. The HTTP Server for Windows NT implements the HTTP/1.0 protocol. It runs as a Windows NT "service," just like the FTP Server that comes with Windows NT. By analogy with the Unix HTTP server daemon, which is called httpd, the Windows NT HTTP server service is called https. The HTTP server service is configured using a Control Panel applet. Very nice software, and it's free!

Application: Cold Fusion
Where on CD: \PRODUCTS\CFUSION
Where online: http://www.allaire.com/
Description: Cold Fusion is a Web Application Development (WAD) platform for Windows NT and Windows 95. Cold Fusion can be used to create a wide variety of applications that integrate relational databases with the

Web on Intranets and the Internet. Applications range from dynamic Web sites to enterprise-wide groupware.

Cold Fusion enables dynamic, data-driven Web sites that use pages generated on the fly from information stored in databases and provided by users. Page content can be instantly customized based on user requests. Dynamic sites allow users to enter and retrieve information and offer unparalleled ease of maintenance and administration.

Application: JAGG Java Classes
Where on CD: \PRODUCTS\JAGG
Where online: http://www.bulletproof.com/jagg/
Description: BulletProof software has created some timely Java classes that allow your Java applications and applets to connect to ODBC databases. JAGG is BulletProof's own Java Language ODBC Engine. JAGG gives developers the ability to access ODBC-compliant databases using Java across the Internet, with speeds comparable to Intranet client/server systems.

Application: PERL for NT
Where on CD: \PRODUCTS\NTPERL
Where online: http://www.rubynet.com/perl5/ntperl5.htm
Description: PERL is a scripting language that is widely used to do CGI programming on Unix boxes. This NT version works very well and can really help in transitioning from a Unix Web server to an NT-based solution. PERL really isn't a commercial product from any one manufacturer, so it is up to you to do a little Web research to get all the info you will need.

Application: WAIS Search Engine
Where on CD: \PRODUCTS\WAIS
Where online: http://www.ucsd.edu/world/tools/wais/index.html
Description: WAIS stands for Wide Area Information System. It is a search engine that catalogs Web sites into databases that can be searched extremely fast. WAIS is a networked information retrieval system. WAIS currently uses TCP/IP to connect client applications to information servers. Client applications are able to retrieve text or multimedia documents stored on the servers. Client applications request documents using keywords. Servers search a full text index for the documents and return a list of docu-

ments containing the keyword. The client may then request the server to send a copy of any of the documents found.

Although the name "Wide Area" implies the use of large networks such as the Internet to connect clients to servers distributed around the network, WAIS can be used between a client and server on the same machine or a client and server on the same LAN.

Application: Adobe Acrobat Reader
Where on CD: \PRODUCTS\ACROBAT
Where online: http://www.adobe.com/Software/Acrobat/
Description: Adobe Acrobat lets you create electronic documents from a wide range of authoring tools for sharing across different computer platforms. Simply "print" files to the Adobe Portable Document Format (PDF). Now you can distribute your documents over the broadest selection of electronic media, including the World Wide Web, e-mail, Lotus Notes, corporate networks, CD-ROMs, and print-on-demand systems. Adobe is pushing the PDF format as a replacement for HTML. Its advantages are unlimited options for layout, and what you design is what others see, which does not always happen with HTML—good software to have on hand.

Index